RAISED TO RULE

Raised to Rule

Educating Royalty at the Court of the
Spanish Habsburgs, 1601-1634

MARTHA K. HOFFMAN

LOUISIANA STATE UNIVERSITY PRESS)|(BATON ROUGE

This publication was made possible in part by a grant from the
Program for Cultural Cooperation between Spain's Ministry of Culture
and United States Universities.

Published by Louisiana State University Press
Copyright © 2011 by Louisiana State University Press
Manufactured in the United States of America
FIRST PRINTING

DESIGNER: *Amanda McDonald Scallan*
TYPEFACE: *Minion Pro*
PRINTER: *McNaughton & Gunn*
BINDER: *Dekker Bookbinding*

Frontispiece: Juan Pantoja de la Cruz, *Prince Philip and Infanta Ana*
(1607). Kunsthistorisches Museum, Vienna. Used by permission

Library of Congress Cataloging-in-Publication Data
Hoffman, Martha K., 1963–
Raised to rule : educating royalty at the court of the Spanish
Habsburgs, 1601–1634 / Martha K. Hoffman.
    p. cm.
Includes bibliographical references and index.
ISBN 978-0-8071-3833-5 (cloth : alk. paper)—ISBN 978-0-8071-3834-2
(pdf)—ISBN 978-0-8071-3951-6 (epub)—ISBN 978-0-8071-3952-3
(mobi)
 1. Spain—Kings and rulers—Education—History—17th century. 2.
Philip III, King of Spain, 1578–1621—Family. 3. Philip IV, King of Spain,
1605–1665. 4. Spain—History—House of Austria, 1516–1700. 5. Habsburg, House of. I. Title.
 DP183.H64 2011
 946'051—dc22

2011000989

Contents

Acknowledgments

This project has been part of my life so long that I can hardly begin to acknowledge everyone who has contributed to its worldly existence. From the beginning, James Boyden provided me with inestimably valuable insight and encouragement in figuring out the contours of the research needed to address the questions I wanted to ask. Geoffrey Parker's breadth of knowledge and his generosity with his time and advice have been a great example: if I had included every fascinating resource he pointed me to, this would be a much longer study. I have also benefited enormously at various important moments from the advice and encouragement of Richard Kagan, Fernando Bouza, Paula Fichtner, Antonio Feros, Magdalena Sánchez, Sara Nalle, and Paul Bushkovitch. Of the many archivists and librarians in Spain and at Yale who assisted me, I would especially like to acknowledge José Manuel Calderón, of the archives of the Alba family, Palacio de Liria, Madrid, and Mr. Torres, of the archives of the Infantado family, Madrid. I am also very grateful for the gift of space and time from John and Carol Merriman several summers ago, which got this version started, and for the advice of Bonnie Frederick, Joe Self, and Bonnie Blackwell in my little writing group at Texas Christian University. Among organizations, the Program for Cultural Cooperation between Spain's Ministry of Culture and United States' Universities at the University of Minnesota and the National Endowment for the Humanities provided funding in support of both research and writing.

On both a personal and a professional level, I cannot thank Alisa Plant enough for making it sound like a perfectly reasonable thing for me to stop fiddling and just send this study to her. On another level, R. M. Noëlla Marcellino and the community of the Abbey of Regina Laudis have been the example of creativity within stability I have needed in the last few years. Betty and Erwin Hoffman and Elaine and Faraday Strock have supported me in ways intangible and material too numerous to mention. And, finally, over the years Bob has learned much more about the seventeenth century and listened to more sound and unsound theories of historical interpretation than he ever thought possible. And he in turn has searched out the early modern music, the cookbooks, the theater, and the Spanish wines that have put it all in context. If there is a dedication here, it is definitely to Bob.

RAISED TO RULE

1

AT THE CENTER OF THEIR WORLD

On September 22, 1601, the first of the eight children of Philip III of Spain and Margarita de Austria was born in the Castilian city of Valladolid. Ten years later, also on September 22, their last child was born. The king and queen thus fulfilled an essential duty of early modern royalty: they provided a generation of individuals who, by their very existence, embodied the structure and stability of society. In the next few decades, Spanish observers described, idealized, and advised these children and watched them grow into adulthood with an avid concern that reflects the position of royal families at the very center of the early modern world.

Five of these children survived to adulthood. Of most interest to historians has been the eldest daughter, Ana, mother of Louis XIV and regent of France during several years of his youth. In addition to numerous evaluations contained in more general histories, recently she has received two scholarly biographies.[1] The infante Fernando, who was made an archbishop at age ten but later became a general and a governor of the Netherlands, has also found a biographer, although the author completed only half of his intended project.[2] A full biography of Philip IV has not emerged, although R. A. Stradling and J. H. Elliott, while not focusing on the person of the king, present considerable detail concerning his life.[3] The infanta María has made cameo appearances in various accounts of the attempt of the Prince of Wales to woo a Spanish bride, while the infante Carlos has garnered even less mention in historical accounts of the court. None of these works provides significant insight into the childhoods of these individuals, the ways in which the court responded and accommodated itself to the presence of children, or the process by which they were prepared for their proper roles in the world.

Literature concerning the education of princes abounded but did not, for the most part, address the needs of children. Early modern concepts of education more generally provided that a child learn skills through imitation of a master and gradually increased participation in the activities of a workshop. Members of the royal family can be seen to have learned their craft in this manner, both through exposure to others, including their parents, who held the types of positions the children would eventually hold, and through learning about the lives and actions of earlier royal persons, both ancestors and other outstanding historical examples. Royal life was, in a sense, made up of the stories they told one another about themselves, their ancestors, the places they visited, and the buildings they built. Royal identity and ideals were conveyed through books and in person, through paintings, monuments, royal foundations, daily activities, and even the palace rulebooks, which occasionally described particular events and choices.

Maturing within contexts of family and court, the royal children interacted with relatives, members of the royal households, teachers, and confessors and other religious, all of whom played a role in shaping these future leaders. As they began to take on adult responsibilities, decisions concerning their households, marriages, military and church appointments, and instruction in government took place within domestic and international political contexts. Their careers were largely chosen for them on the basis of rank and tradition, described in terms of family and duty and illustrated for them with examples drawn both from written history and from the personal experience of their parents and guardians. Despite the general lack of choice in determining their own careers, they did not function as simple figureheads but instead actively used concepts of royalty, family, and precedent to shape their own roles within a seemingly fixed structure.

Royal Childhood

Philip III and Margarita de Austria named their eldest child Ana Mauricia, after her paternal grandmother and the saint on whose day she was born.[4] Prince Philip, named for his grandfather as much as for his father, also carried the impressive secondary name Domingo Victor de la Cruz—Dominic Victor of the Cross—a name R. A. Stradling describes as "a blue-print for a life of leadership."[5] A contemporary considered the name fair game for the joke that the prince might have been named Sabado (*Domingo* meaning "Sunday," and *Sabado*, "Saturday") if he had been baptized a day earlier. That observer did not include *de la Cruz* as part of the name but instead considered *Victor* to have been chosen in honor of the Prince of Piedmont, Vitorio Amadeo, who served as godparent, although he also connected the name to Spain's desire to bring England back to the Catholic Church.[6]

At the birth of their second daughter, in 1603, Philip and Margarita honored her maternal grandmother, and perhaps also the king's aunt and grandmother, who died that same year, by naming the child María. This child lived only a few weeks, however, and the name was again chosen for the daughter born in 1606, with the second name Ana. The infante Carlos, born in the following year, was also conveniently named for both Philip III's grandfather, Emperor Charles V, and the queen's father, Karl of Styria. Fernando, the name given the next infante, was also a name common on both sides of the family, having passed from Fernando (Ferdinand) the Catholic to his grandson, Emperor Ferdinand I, and thus to the Austrian side of the family. More recently, both parents had brothers named Fernando or Ferdinand, although Philip III's brother of that name had died the year Philip was born. If either Carlos or Fernando was given a second name, these names were so rarely used as to be virtually nonexistent.

Philip and Margarita named their youngest daughter Margarita Francisca, after her mother and, it has been speculated, after the favorite of the king, Francisco Gómez de Sandoval y Rojas, the Duke of Lerma, thus capturing in a name the resolution of a central conflict at court. The queen's decision to give birth in the town of Lerma may also have signaled a better understanding between her and the duke.[7] But if Margarita was calling a truce, that was not her only motive: the baptism of the infanta took place in the chapel of a Franciscan convent, and the queen probably thought of herself as paying tribute to Saint Francis, whom she had already honored in her religious patronage and later honored in her request to be buried in the habit of the female Franciscans. Honoring Francis in such a way would have been a fitting parallel to choosing Philip's second name in honor of Saint Dominic. In addition, choosing the name Margarita may have expressed the queen's intention that this daughter would carry out her own dream of becoming a nun, a probability underlined by the mother's penchant for dressing the child in a miniature habit of a Franciscan nun.[8]

In naming their final child, Philip and Margarita reached deeper into Spanish history and their own inclinations in choosing a name. He was named Alfonso (or Alonso), perhaps after the great medieval lawgiver Alfonso the Wise of Castile, and his second name, Mauricio, matched his eldest sister's, since they were born on the same saint's day. Popularly, however, he was known primarily as Alfonso el Caro, or "the Dear," meaning both cherished and costly, for his birth cost his mother her life. Even the most casual mention of the child was thus imbued with an air of melancholy, as if no one could look at him without being reminded of the price his mother had paid.

While their very names tied the royal children to family and Spanish history, they also began to learn their place in the world and within the structure of court through the titles used to address them. The firstborn traditionally held the title of prince or princess, which indicated his or her position as heir to the crown, with subsequent children called infanta or infante, a princess reverting to the title of infanta when a brother was born. Philip III and Margarita's first child was a girl, and it was a sign of optimism on their part that from the beginning they called her not princess but infanta, expressing their hope that a more appropriate heir, a son, would be born.[9] Checking precedents for the treatment of infantes, a report compiled by the Council of State in 1620 noted that until the year 1558 the prince had been styled *ilustrísima alteza,* or "most illustrious highness," but after that year the styling *serenísima alteza,* or "most serene highness," became the standard usage. By the reign of Philip III, all Spanish royalty other than the king bore the honorific *serenísima.* In recognition, therefore, that although they did not call her princess, Ana was more than an infanta, Philip III himself, in "the year[s] 1603 and 1604, since the prince our lord had not been born, styled [her] as heiress, [by calling] her Most Illustrious Infanta."[10]

The titles attached to members of the royal family also signaled the condition of matters of state and their attendant personal status at court. Once Ana was engaged to the young king of France in 1612, official usage styled her "queen of France" and "Her Majesty" rather than "Her Highness"—on rare occasions adding the French honorific "most Christian"—clearly raising her status at court and preparing her for later life. Court chronicles and *relaciones* referred to her rooms as the queen's rooms and her servants as the queen of France's servants. The new title also resulted in amusing (to our ears) descriptions of events, such as that of the king of Spain giving the "most Christian queen of France" permission to put on a play.[11]

Years later, Philip IV's reaction to titles proposed for his sister María during negotiations for her marriage to the king of Hungary, later Ferdinand III, suggests additional significance of granting titles. When the Council of State discussed how María would be treated after her betrothal, the king noted that when she had been engaged to the Prince of Wales "no novelty was done with my sister,"[12] that is, no change had been made in the form of addressing her. Even though a marriage treaty had been signed and she was very briefly called Princess of England, the lack of change in her treatment indicated the still precarious nature of the alliance. In considering the marriage to Ferdinand, Philip looked to the Wales precedent but also apparently considered the question of María's title a negotiating stance and felt that addressing his sister differently early in the process would deprive him of leverage.

The importance of using a proper title also emerges in the Council of State's discussion of how Fernando should be addressed when he became cardinal and archbishop of Toledo. The king himself had asked the council to investigate precedents of usage so that he would know how to address his son properly. Although the council replied that "it would be well [that] Your Majesty not address the lord infante except as a son" and felt it sufficient that "Your Majesty treat your son as infantes of Castile are treated," the king insisted that the council investigate how his cousin Archduke Albert had been addressed when he was cardinal of Toledo.[13] Albert, it turned out, had been called "the most illustrious lord Cardinal of Toledo." The council noted, however, that the superscript "His Highness" accorded infantes should also be used for Fernando, because he could potentially inherit the throne, while Albert could not.[14] Thus it appears that treating Fernando simply as a son endowed him with greater stature than did addressing him with the full titles of cardinal and archbishop, although the honorific *illustrious* taught him the respect due his office in addition to that due his rank.

Titles clearly reflected the prince's rank above his siblings. The infanta Ana may have experienced some difficulty adjusting to the precedence given to her brother in court matters. Having enjoyed the undivided attention of her mother's servants for almost four years, she reportedly questioned her ladies and servants closely concerning where her brother had been before he was born and warned her servants not to associate with those of her brother.[15] This little incident, presented with gentle humor by Luis Cabrera de Córdoba, who had written a history of Philip II and was assembling notes and descriptions of events during the reign of Philip III, provides a nice contrast to the stereotypical presentations of affectionate relationships between members of the royal family.

Recognition of the prince's more exalted rank evidently was not an easy lesson for the infante Carlos to learn. Cabrera de Córdoba gives us a glimpse of unusual interactions between the eight-year-old prince and his six-year-old brother in 1613: "Indeed one begins to see the ill-feeling that the infante Don Carlos bears the prince, since with slight provocation, and when he finds him alone, he hits him, and the aya does not improve the situation nor reprimand him . . . and he cannot suffer that all do greater honor and give more preference to the prince, and other matters that are expected to improve when they increase in age." The chronicler professed himself mystified by these events, noting, as if in explanation, that "they affirm that they have never seen [Carlos] laugh or cry," as if a young boy would have to be abnormal to act in such a manner toward his brother.[16]

While in some countries the practice of educating a child by breaking his will extended to royal children,[17] Philip IV gives us insight into his childhood that suggests a lack of discipline rather than an excess. Among the problems of teaching royalty, the king noted in the epilogue to his translation of Guicciardini's history of Italy, was the impossibility of anyone's properly disciplining a royal child. Children in general, he noted, are given to pleasure and mischief rather than studying:

> These considerations hold true even more in princes and great persons, because although their parents give them learned and virtuous teachers, and order them to study with care and vigilance, if perhaps they are not inclined to the work or do not undertake lessons with pleasure, it is very difficult to instruct them, since the teachers never dare, nor are they even allowed, to use great rigor in the instruction of such persons, which is what alone works at that age to pursue clear ends. I am myself an example of what I mean.[18]

This lenience is reflected both in Philip IV's description of his childhood and in the account of blows exchanged between the prince and Carlos, which their caretaker made no attempt to stop. No available evidence suggests that the Spanish royal children experienced physical punishment, although if the infanta Ana's mothering reflected her own experience, they may have been sent to their rooms for misbehaving.[19] What other households achieved with harsh discipline, the Spanish court tried to accomplish through gentleness and the repetition of example and treatises calling the royal children to duty. Raising a royal child was a delicate task, not to be achieved by violence, noted one writer in discussing the duties of the prince's guardian. This sentiment appears to have been echoed in the practices of the royal family.[20]

Ceremony and Play

A royal child made his or her first public appearance at baptism. In the late summer of 1601 Philip III's cousin Ranuccio Farnese, Prince of Parma, arrived at court for the specific purpose of serving as godfather for the expected royal child, thus demonstrating the international stature of this event; the Duchess of Lerma served as godmother. Although there may have been some disappointment that the child born the following month was not a boy, Ana's identity as firstborn was nonetheless celebrated by having the eldest sons of several great noble houses serve as *meninos* at the ceremony, carrying the regalia and objects necessary for the occasion.[21]

The baptism ceremony and godparentage served as opportunities to bind the royal children even more closely together. In the spring of 1605, shortly after the birth of the prince, the king solicited opinions from various clergymen concerning the propriety of the not yet four-year-old infanta Ana's serving as her brother's godparent.[22] One of the respondents, Fray Francisco de Castroverde felt, and Padre Hieronimo de Acosta concurred, that it was inappropriate for Ana to be a godparent if that meant there would be no others. Although the tone of Dr. Pedro Gonçalez de Castillo's response was both more positive and more flattering, he gave essentially the same opinion: that while, of course, the infanta could be the godmother, there ought to be an older, male godparent as well. Both of these men quoted great authorities and referred to the decrees of the Council of Trent on the matter. A final decision, endorsed by the three aforementioned and five additional clergy, simply cited the need for a second godparent of competent age.

The designation of Ana as godmother for Prince Philip followed the practice of the previous generation and set the precedent that the family would continue to follow. Their cousin Vitorio Amadeo of Savoy served as the other godparent, at eighteen years of age presumably considered old enough to meet the clerical requirements of providing an adult for the role. The precaution of having an adult godparent to balance a royal child as godparent was not, however, consistently followed, since the prince and the eldest infanta served as godparents to most of their younger siblings. At the baptism of the infanta María, the

Duke of Infantado carried the newborn, while the Duke of Lerma carried her one-and-a-half-year-old godfather, Prince Philip. The two nobles exchanged children at the time of the actual baptism, with both the prince and the infanta, the chronicler noted, crying the entire time. The infante Carlos, born quickly after a day of hard travel between Madrid and San Lorenzo, came into the world very pale and with his umbilical cord around his neck. Thought at first to have been premature as well, the child was baptized immediately, after which he nursed and cried normally.[23] A month later, a public christening took place, with the constable of Castile carrying the infante and Lerma again carrying the prince, who was the godfather, while Ana again served as godmother. The two-and-a-half-year-old prince once more drew as much attention as the newborn. Dressed in stockings, jacket, cap, and boots, rather than the dress usually worn by all children, and wearing a sword and dagger, he charmed the assembled court. In addition, he cried and demanded to be taken to his parents, who were seated separately; he had to be calmed by one of the queen's ladies before the ceremony could continue. In 1609, when Ana and Philip served as godparents of the infante Fernando, the Duke of Lerma again carried the baby, although the prince walked by himself; the royal chaplain gives us the detail that the prince reached up and placed his hand on the infant during the baptism itself.[24]

For the youngest daughter, Margarita Francisca, the Duke of Lerma and the infanta Ana served as godparents, although the infanta María accompanied them to the baptismal font as if she were a second godmother.[25] Lerma's role as godparent may have given rise to the argument that the child was partially named for him, although the absence of the prince owing to a serious illness is the more likely explanation for the substitution of the duke in the role that the prince had played for his other younger siblings.[26] For the last child of Philip and Margarita, baptized quietly at twenty days, a week after his mother died, the infanta Ana again stood as godmother, with Prince Philiberto of Savoy as godfather.[27]

The practice of godparentage placed persons in relationships that had great resonance within a system based on both familial and clientage relationships. Conventionally, a godparent pledged to help in the religious education of a child and occasionally undertook the responsibility of raising the child in the case of the loss of parents. Although the precise details of their obligations were not clearly articulated in the case of royal children, the understood central presence of godparents in children's lives helps to explain the royal family's use of relatives in this role whenever possible, since it precluded a situation in which a noble could claim political power through godparentage. Only the lack of nearby relatives led Philip and Margarita to name the Duchess of Lerma to serve as Ana's godmother, while the Prince of Parma served as godfather. Philip III underlined the importance of godparenthood in his letters to Ana by consistently calling the Duke of Lerma her *compadre,* apparently referring to their shared role in the baptism of Margarita Francisca, although it is also possible that he considered the duke, alongside his wife, an additional godparent to Ana, able to be active in a way that her distant true godfather could not be.[28] Echoing the practice by which royalty referred to one another more by relationship than by name, this description carried far greater significance than any other the king could have applied to his favorite, since it indicated a direct relationship to the royal family.

The prince made a second, very important early public appearance at his *juramento,* the ceremony in which all the great nobles and prelates of Castile swore allegiance to him as their future king. This event can be seen as a formative experience both for the prince and for the eldest of his sisters.[29] On the morning of January 13, 1608, the day appointed for the juramento, the king, queen, eldest infanta, and prince emerged from the royal apartments at San Jerónimo of Madrid dressed in radiant white and abundant jewels. With the cardinal of Toledo presiding, the oath was read aloud. While the representatives of Toledo and Burgos argued over who was to swear loyalty first, other issues of precedence were smoothed over by having members of the nobility rise to take the oath not according to rank but according to where they were seated. The numerous ladies of the queen in attendance played no role in the oath taking itself, although they are mentioned in descriptions as an indispensable part of the audience (and indeed one proved necessary in helping to calm the prince).

During the mass that preceded the main ceremony, attendants whisked the prince quietly into the sacristy to be fed, since, the chronicler commented, the ceremony would be long. The prince was then seated on a small chair slightly in front of his parents, while the infanta sat next to her mother. The true immediate impact of the occasion on the prince's understanding is questionable, given that when he saw the ceremonial objects by which the cardinal would confirm the two children, he seemed to think that he was going to be bled and began to cry. In one account, the people close at hand calmed the prince by explaining the ceremony; in another, the children's *aya* (their principal caretaker) had to hold the child and comfort him before the service could continue.[30] After the initial ceremony, the young prince slept quietly in his brocade chair, his little hand resting on the arm of the chair, conveniently placed to accept the kisses of his future subjects.

In some ways the ceremony might be considered more important for the infanta Ana than for the prince, since, being four years older, she actively participated in and observed it, while he slept through the greater part of it. Hers was the first name to be called by the booming voice of the *rey de armas*, placing her above the many assembled prelates, grandees, knights, gentlemen, and *procuradores* of the Cortes. As the representative of all of the royal siblings, Ana was the first to swear the oath of allegiance, bowing first to the uncovered Host and then to her parents and brother and finally taking her brother's hand and kissing it, her eyes full of tears. Although it was perhaps the excitement of the day that brought tears to the infanta's eyes, others saw a greater significance in her display of emotion, conceptualizing her oath not just as swearing her devotion and that of her siblings but as recognizing the relinquishing of her rights as firstborn: "Born the heiress, and [now] her rights cease."[31]

The royal children can also be glimpsed at play. Philip III and Margarita maintained a lively theater at court, in which the royal children participated at an early age.[32] Four-year-old Ana performed in a pantomime allegory of the virtues on the occasion of the prince's baptism. As a nine-year-old, Philip participated in an unfortunate theatrical performance in front of the ladies of court that ended with him vomiting in front of the gathered company. Some questioned the propriety of allowing him to participate in such an event, although Cabrera de Córdoba was inclined to excuse this activity on the basis of the prince's youth and, further, because it served as a distraction at a time when he was distraught over the death of the dwarf Bonami, of whom he had been very fond.[33] Later that same year, the prince directed his siblings and several ladies of the court in an elaborate performance of Lope de Vega's *El premio de la hermosura*, complete with numerous theatrical machines and fantastical set pieces constructed along the banks of the river in Lerma. The spectators marveled at the prince's cleverness both in the organizing the production and in acting. One observer, the poet Antonio Hurtado de Mendoza, drew conclusions about the promise of the future king from the evidence of his abilities on stage. Ana's beauty and her skill in leading the final masque were likewise remarked, suggesting a parallel assessment of qualities appropriate to a queen. The playwright acknowledged the rank of his actors by adjusting the details of the story on which he based his play so that the winner of beauty's prize, played by the infanta Ana, was the empress Aurora, daughter of Jupiter, rather than the humble Angelica.[34]

Dancing was an integral part of such theatrical performances, and the royal

children spent considerable time rehearsing under the direction of their dancing master, Alonso Fernández. In the spring of 1618 they danced a masque in
El Pardo, which they repeated at the convent of the Descalzas Reales for the
entertainment of the king's aunt Margarita de la Cruz.[35]

The royal family also attended bullfights and tournaments as entertainment,
although Queen Margarita tended to excuse herself during pregnancy for fear
of suffering the shock of seeing someone hurt. Such events offered opportunities for the public to see the royal family, including the children, such as an
occasion in March 1609 when the king and queen and their two eldest children
had dinner in the *panadería* on Madrid's plaza mayor and then watched the
entertainments from the windows.[36]

The boys participated in active sports from an early age. In April 1618 Philip
III wrote to his daughter that her brothers were practicing in the great hall of the
palace for a tournament they planned to present as part of Easter celebrations.
Sixteen meninos also participated, all dressed at the prince's expense and "none
of them past the age of eleven years."[37] Philip III ordered child-sized suits of
armor for all three of his sons. He had been given armor by his brother-in-law
Carlo Emanuele of Savoy, when he was seven years old; likewise, years later, the
cardinal-infante Fernando gave Prince Baltasar Carlos such a gift, suggesting a
continuing practice of male relatives participating in introducing the prince to
masculine activities.[38] The prince, or perhaps the boys in general, also received
a collection of toy soldiers, carefully sculpted in wood, comprising all ranks,
on foot and horse, with detailed dress, weapons, and a few other accessories of
artillery and fortifications. Built at the court of the archdukes in the Low Countries, it was brought to Madrid by its designer, Alberto Struzzi, a gentleman
of Archduke Albert, along with the dwarf Soplillo, who later became a close
companion of Philip IV. The designer expressed the educational nature of his
creation, asserting that the toy army would be "no less useful than entertaining,"
although it is somewhat difficult to imagine, as Struzzi apparently did, that the
prince would use the soldiers to learn about the finances of war.[39]

The boys also learned at an early age to hunt, an activity that required skills
in riding, shooting, and occasionally living under relatively rough conditions.
Although exact descriptions of their acquisition of these skills are not available, Philip IV later described learning to ride as something in which he had
taken great pleasure. Hunting was not a risk-free undertaking. In 1618, when the
prince and his cousin Philiberto of Savoy were hunting near Velada, a misfiring

gun exploded, costing the unfortunate Philiberto half his beard and mustache and one of his eyebrows.[40]

Although Spanish royal women had been accomplished hunters in earlier generations, there is little evidence to suggest that the daughters of Philip and Margarita spent significant time hunting. Queen Margarita apparently learned to shoot both gun and bow and arrow after her arrival in Spain and sometimes accompanied the king when he hunted, although he often went without her. In addition, the royal chaplain occasionally recorded that while the king hunted, the queen fished, which may have been her primary activity during hunting trips. When the children were very young, Diego de Guzmán described the queen as taking them "to hunt" in the gardens, an activity that neither the location nor the ages of the children suggest was actually hunting. Hunting in the gardens may have meant pursuing small game; years later, the king's confessor described Prince Baltasar Carlos as declaring "war on the rabbits" in the gardens of the Casa de Campo when left to his own devices.[41]

The daily activities of the royal children were also shaped by illness and by concerns about their health. When the king and queen considered sending for their children to join them in Segovia in 1608, the royal physicians ruled conditions in the city unhealthy for children and vetoed the plan. When the prince fell ill in 1609, the infanta Ana lived in the convent of the Descalzas Reales for nearly two months to avoid exposure to his illness. The following year, she and María also spent a significant amount of time there when their brothers suffered fevers at the royal palace.[42] In 1610 the royal physicians disagreed concerning whether the prince, who had a fever, should travel to join his family in the town of Lerma. In this instance the king resolved the argument and sent his own physician to accompany the prince on the journey. The king surely regretted his decision, for the prince became more seriously ill on the way, experiencing a lengthy illness that deeply affected both his parents, especially his mother, who did not leave his bedside for several days. The infanta María's illness in the same year caused less immediate concern, although it too was carefully documented by the courtier who maintained a household for her in Lerma while she convalesced.[43] After her marriage was arranged, Ana's health also became a concern for French residents at the court of Spain, who monitored the course of her smallpox and reported with relief her lack of facial scars.[44] Court and community responded to the prince's illnesses in 1609 and 1610 with processions of images and relics, as well as orders to various monasteries and convents to pray for his health. Illness continued to inform activities after recovery, as in 1613, when the king, prince, and eldest infanta traveled to Burgos to fulfill a vow the king had made during one of the prince's illnesses.[45]

Representation

Paintings were another method by which the royal family taught itself its place in the world and presented itself to a larger audience. Particular paintings reflect the mood of the court: Titian's depiction of Philip II offering his son Prince Diego to the heavens in an energetic swirl of images suggests the sweeping ambition and confidence of the Spanish monarch in the years between Lepanto and the Great Armada, while the more subdued painting by Justus Tiel presenting an allegory of the education of Philip III surrounds the somber prince with a variety of metaphorical and mythological images encompassing all aspects of royal duty. Paintings also served to reinforce a sense of family and history. Portraits lined the halls of royal palaces and were exchanged like snapshots with distant relatives. When the palace of El Pardo burned in 1604, destroying a considerable trove of art and decoration, Philip III commissioned paintings to replace a number of family portraits, not just of his generation or of living persons but of all persons previously represented there.[46] Artists created portraits for use in marriage negotiations, placing images of royal families in each other's collections even when negotiations ended unsuccessfully.

From an early age the royal children were the subjects of paintings. The standard portrait showed one, two, or three of the royal children, dressed in courtly clothing and perhaps holding a toy or wearing the charms typically worn during nursing, gazing seriously at the viewer. Portraits often commemorated particular events, such as one of Prince Philip and the infanta Ana by Juan Pantoja de la Cruz executed in El Escorial on the day they served as godparents for their brother Carlos (see frontispiece), or the group portrait by Bartolomé González of the three youngest children, Fernando, Margarita, and Alonso, dressed in high courtly fashion as they appeared on the day Ana's marriage contract was signed. That these portraits were seen as direct representations rather than ideal depictions is suggested by Philip III's insistence years later that Ana send him a portrait so that he could see how she had grown since leaving Spain. Their personal rather than political meaning is further implied by the fact that he had the portrait she sent hung in his private chambers and reported that her siblings stopped by to see it whenever they passed near his rooms. Death portraits were also made, as a last statement of affection or as a reminder of the inevitability of death. The queen had several such pictures painted of her month-old daughter who died in 1603, which she sent to relatives in Austria and the Netherlands.[47]

A more unusual portrait by Pantoja de la Cruz depicts Margarita as the Virgin Mary and Ana as the Angel of the Annunciation. The identity of the models and the timing of the portrait in the same year as the prince's birth led some to interpret the painting as the annunciation of the birth of a male heir. Other portraits depicting the queen and members of her family as the Holy Family at the birth of Christ and at the birth of the Virgin, along with an unusual portrait of herself pregnant, suggest that these paintings were not meant to assert the piety of the queen as much as to celebrate her pregnancies.[48]

After the infante Fernando became cardinal and archbishop of Toledo at age ten, several portraits of him in cardinal's robes were painted, in an attempt to convey a dignity of presence and seriousness of religious conviction sufficient to withstand criticism concerning the youth of the sitter. The audience for this message perhaps included the young cardinal himself as much as the people at court who considered him too young for the position, for he apparently was not by innate temperament a churchman.

A print portrait of the infante Carlos appeared as the frontispiece of a biography of Charles V written by Juan Antonio de Vera y Zúñiga, Count of La Roca, and dedicated to Carlos, probably because of their common name. In the image, the infante stands beside a table on which rest a helmet and the book of the deeds of Charles V. Dressed in armor with an incongruous ruff, a sword hanging from his belt and a feathered hat in his hand, the infante lifts his head to gaze at a portrait of his great-grandfather. The simplicity and ease of his gesture reflect the naturalness of the injunction to learn by contemplating the actions of the past and the portraits of great men. "VIRTUTEM EX ME" ([Draw] virtue from me), proclaims the motto above the emperor's image.[49]

The Larger Structure of the Royal Family

The exhortation to emulate Charles V appealed not just to the example of great deeds but also to the importance of ancestors. Beyond their immediate family, the royal children grew up with an expanded concept of family that shaped both their daily experience and their understanding of themselves in the larger world. But royal families were a mass of contradictions: relatives too distant to be true friends, long-dead ancestors honored and made present through the continuing patronage of their religious foundations, queens who came from far away, repeating in each generation the struggle to learn the customs of their new countries. Yet the central structuring nature of family in early modern political and social thought encouraged emphasis on kinship relationships. The appeal to family rhetoric and relationships was meant to cement treaties and create a spirit of cooperation in making policy and building alliances. Concepts of family helped to smooth tensions between Charles V and his brother Ferdinand and between Philip II and his cousin Emperor Maximilian II. They encouraged a united front of the various Habsburg rulers and structured ways for them to resolve their differences.[50]

While we should take care in applying modern notions of family to early modern Spain, concepts of family surrounded children at the courts of Europe. Many royal actions, especially interactions between various members of the family, can be perceived and judged on both public and private levels, with the result that actions motivated by personal affection or political strategy might look basically the same when they take place within the structure of royal government. The two senses of family—that of private experience and that of a structuring metaphor of public life—were probably inseparable for the Spanish royal children. They learned the concepts of dynastic policy through the very persons of their mother, the people who came to the Spanish court with her, and the physically distant relatives whom they addressed with terms of intimacy. Their real personal relationships with family and their experience of other extended families informed their sense of relationship with people they never met.

The importance of family can be discerned in the general habit of address in correspondence among the royal family and between the royal family and high-ranking nobles. Philip II in his letters to his daughters very seldom referred to them (or to any of his relatives) by name. Instead, he called them by their relationship to himself or his reader: "my sister," "my nephew," "my niece"; "your brother," "your grandmother," "your cousin." His letters to the Duke of Savoy illustrate this point nicely, as he shifted from calling the duke "nephew" (a distillation of a more complicated relationship—the duke's mother was the aunt of Philip's third wife, while his father was the king's first cousin through his mother) to addressing him as "son" after the duke's marriage to the king's younger daughter.[51] The infanta Isabel Clara Eugenia, writing many years later to her half-brother, Philip III, referred to her niece Ana as "my daughter-in-law" in acknowledgment of an understood relationship in the event that she herself had a son. Philip III in his letters to his daughter generally referred to the prince and princess by their titles but referred to the other children by name, perhaps reflecting the simple fact that he had too many children for the designations "your brother" or "your sister" to be clear.[52] In addition, kings of Spain addressed the grandees of Spain as "cousin," which in many cases reflected a true, though very distant, relationship.

Family also had meaning in the royal children's daily lives. Spanish royal siblings were raised in close proximity, with some separation between boys and girls as they grew older. When members of the extended family resided at court, they participated in raising the royal children. Philip II's youngest sister, Juana, Princess of Portugal, provided a measure of stability for her nephew Don Carlos and years later informally served as aya to her nieces. Another niece, Philip's fourth queen, Ana, also viewed Juana as a motherlike figure for the few years she knew her and was greatly shaken by her death in 1573. Isabel Clara Eugenia and Catalina Micaela visited Juana in the royal apartment in the Descalzas Reales, the convent she had founded, and they and their younger half-siblings did so again when another aunt, the empress María, made the convent her primary residence after 1580. They also spent a great deal of time there during the time that Philip II lived in Portugal, from 1581 to 1583.[53]

This tradition continued in the relationship that Margarita de la Cruz developed with her grandnephews and grandnieces, the children of Philip III. Archduchess Margarita, daughter of Empress María, had traveled to Spain with her mother and professed as a nun in the Descalzas Reales, while her mother simply resided in the convent. After María's death in 1603, Margarita continued several of the roles her mother had played. Having taken vows, she did not reside in the apartment where María had lived, but this remained the place where the royal children stayed when they visited.[54]

Like Juana and María, Margarita de la Cruz clearly developed personal relationships with her young relatives. Various chroniclers mention the royal family visiting the convent, and more specific insights into the nature of the relationship can be found in remaining correspondence. In November 1606 Margarita wrote the king thanking him for sending the prince to stay with her and reported how the prince had amused her, nursed, and then slept "like an angel" in his crib.[55] According to her biographer, Philip brought his children to her after their mother's death and asked the nun to perform the "offices of mother" for them. In a letter shortly thereafter, Sor Margarita offered Philip III solace and expressed her concern about his emotional state: while she agreed that he had great reason to mourn, she urged him to conform himself to God's will. A few weeks later, she wrote again, apologizing in a postscript for the boys' not having written, which suggests that the children remained with her and that she supervised some of their activity.[56]

The daily journal of the court chaplain, Diego de Guzmán, provides additional details concerning royal visits to the convent. He often recorded Philip and Margarita attending divine office there, after which the king habitually dined at the nearby house of the Duke of Lerma, while the queen remained with the nuns. Occasionally, they brought one or more of their children with them or left them there for extended periods of time when situations demanded. The longest stay that Guzmán records is that of the infanta Ana during the illness of the other children in October and November of 1609. Throughout this time the eight-year-old infanta participated in the daily life and religious services of the convent. On another occasion she resided there while ill, and her parents, in turn, altered their own scheduled travel to visit her.[57]

Other members of the larger family lived at the Spanish court for extended periods. Archdukes Rudolf and Ernst, the eldest sons of Emperor Maximilian II and Empress María, lived in Spain from 1563 until 1571. When they returned to the Empire, their brothers Albrecht (Albert) and Wenceslaus replaced them at the Spanish court. Maximilian apparently did not support his sons' living at the Spanish court for such an extended period, but he had little say in his children's upbringing during the lifetime of his own father, the Spanish-born Emperor Ferdinand. However, after Ferdinand's death in 1564, Maximilian, perhaps also influenced by María, continued the policy at a time when the increasing mental instability of Don Carlos suggested expanded roles for his own sons in Spain.[58] This investment of the two branches of the Habsburg family in each other had mixed results: Rudolf may have developed an antagonism to his Spanish relatives (even as German princes viewed him as suspiciously Hispanicized), while Albert formed his career around service to the Spanish crown, becoming Philip II's trusted governor in Portugal and, much later, as his son-in-law, ruler of the Netherlands. The reason for bringing the Austrian cousins to the court of Spain became apparent in the career of Archduke Albert. In addition to building personal ties between different branches of the royal family, the practice provided the opportunity for them to be knowledgeable participants in Spanish government.

Like his father, Philip III provided for the education of nephews at the court of Spain. The three princes of Savoy, sons of his sister Catalina, arrived in Spain in 1603. One died there in 1605, another returned to Italy in 1608, and the third, Philiberto, lived in Spain until 1611 and visited frequently thereafter, remaining connected to Spain, with appointments in the service of the crown, for the rest of his life. Philiberto's younger siblings Margarita and Tomás eventually followed him in attaching themselves to Spain, Margarita serving as titular governor of Portugal and Tomás as a general in the Thirty Years' War. This residence at the Spanish court can be seen as cementing the loyalty of half of the generation, that is, of Philiberto and two of his siblings, although it was not sufficient to ease all tension between the Duke of Savoy and his powerful Spanish relatives.

Philip III also recognized and assisted two illegitimate female relatives. During his father's reign, Ana de Austria, daughter of Don Juan, Philip II's illegitimate half-brother, had been involved, perhaps innocently, in a plot to place an imposter on the throne of Portugal. Some interpreted her subsequent residence in the abbey of Santa María la Real de Las Huelgas, near Burgos, as imprisonment by the king. Later, however, Philip III addressed her as cousin and promoted her elevation to the prestigious position of abbess of Las Huelgas. Philip III and Queen Margarita visited her at least once and corresponded with her concerning both personal matters and the business of the convent.[59] Philip also arranged the marriage of another illegitimate cousin, Juana de Austria, who wrote from her home in Italy to thank him.[60] These women were clearly recognized as family and addressed in affectionate terms, despite their distance from court and the lack of strong personal relationships.

The presence of members of the extended family at court occasionally posed problems. The imperial representative in Spain reported that Queen Margarita disliked having the princes of Savoy at the Spanish court because of their status as next in line to the throne after her own children.[61] While he does not explain the nature of the queen's concern or whether it reflected an initial reaction or an extended perception throughout the princes' residence there, the queen might have felt that their status was too close to that of her children for proper respect to be shown the latter. Indeed, elements of the relationship between Philip III and Archduke Albert and between Philip IV and Philiberto of Savoy suggest a possible "sibling rivalry" among cousins. This type of relationship was exaggerated by the fact that in each case the cousin, although of lower rank, was older than the prince.

Queen Margarita might also have been concerned about the distribution of secondary roles that members of the extended family could play. The career of Archduke Albert provides but the most outstanding example of the pattern by which Austrian cousins benefited from their dynastic ties with Spain. Margarita's mother, Maria of Bavaria, clearly saw the marriage of her daughter to the Spanish king as an opportunity for her sons as well. She campaigned actively for a variety of offices for them, proffering her son Leopold as a good candidate for archbishop of Toledo even before her daughter's engagement was finalized.[62] Margarita might have seen the princes of Savoy, who did indeed gain Spanish incomes and hold positions in Spanish government, as a danger not so much to her children as to the possible careers of her brothers. The queen, along with her cousin Margarita de la Cruz and the empress María, represented the interests of the Austrian Habsburgs not in an abstract way but in the concrete details of patronage and careers and may indeed have been influential in determining the manifestation of ideal Habsburg family rhetoric in the reign of Philip III.[63]

The royal family expressed both personal emotion and public identity by wearing mourning for relatives. The death of Queen Margarita placed the entire court in official grief—the crown paid the cost of clothing the royal households in black. In the year after her death, Philip III deeply curtailed his court activities, although the children and households took part in many normal festivities and put aside mourning for special occasions, such as the prince's birthday and Ana's first reception of the French ambassador. Philip III's prolonged mourning for his wife and his withdrawal from court each year to observe the anniversary of her death suggest strong personal feeling.[64] On the other hand, in 1589, when the royal family put on mourning for Catherine de Medici, grandmother of Philip II's daughters, the observation could not be construed as a reflection of personal affection, since they had not so much as met her, but was instead an expression of a different kind of sorrow and respect. Likewise, Philip IV and his queen, neither of whom had met Archduke Albert, withdrew from planned activities when news of his death reached them in 1621.[65] Displays of respect, interpreted as displays of emotion, thus helped shape the sense of family. Personal experiences of family helped inform these displays.

While it is hard to know the exact meaning that such terms had for individuals, members of the royal family repeatedly spoke in terms of affection and

demonstrated attachment to each other. In contrast to their near contemporaries in the courts of France, England, and Scotland, the children of Philip III
and Margarita spent considerable time together and with their parents. A few
household officials served particular children individually, but for most of their
childhood the royal children shared servants and had overlapping and fluid
households. Observers saw the children as providing the king and queen with
good company and entertainment, amazing their parents and the court with wit
and cleverness beyond their years. After the death of the queen, Philip III clearly
drew comfort from the presence of his children and appears to have spent even
more time with them.[66] His letters to the infanta Ana, written after she moved
to France, repeatedly express his desire to see her and communicate a palpable
sense of loss. He reminds her of places they had visited and experiences they
had shared. His tender description of the death of his youngest daughter in
1617 recounts his attempts to comfort the dying child and the emotions of her
remaining siblings. Ana's siblings also wrote to their sister; the infanta María in
particular expressed her hope that Ana had remembered her birthday as well as
her longing to have her there to attend plays with her.[67] María wrote to her sister
through much of her life and attempted to visit her after she herself became
queen of Hungary and later empress. Ana's correspondence with her brother
Fernando in the 1630s was interpreted by the French court in entirely political
terms but mostly provided an emotional outlet for the unhappy queen.[68] Philip
IV had to hide his face with his hat to avoid public tears when María left Madrid
for her marriage journey in 1629, while his brother Fernando wept openly. Similar emotion resonates from Philip's poignant remark years later, upon learning
of María's death, that they had always been the best of friends and had become
even better friends as they grew older.[69]

Descriptions of the royal court in the reign of Philip III contrast two major
themes: that of the court as a place for theater, dancing, and gallantry with that
of the court as a model of religious observance and patronage. Theater and the
arts contributed to a sense of majesty, while ceremony reflected a strict social
order and demonstrated to individuals where they and others fit into structures of power and influence. Religious observances shaped the activities of the
court and contributed to the patronage of art and music, while also helping to
identify royal qualities with religious virtue. The children's experience of court
was imbued with this sense of ceremony, hierarchy, religion, and majesty. The

people with whom they regularly came in contact, those who supervised and shared their activities, were particularly influential in teaching them their place in the world.

The true experience of royal childhood is hard to uncover in the available records. But although sources are more likely to give us idealized royalty than character analysis, and the costs of the households rather than the friendships nurtured in those households, we can begin to glimpse the royal children as they progressed to maturity. Ana emerges from the various accounts and descriptions as a bright but serious child who could become tongue-tied in front of strangers but participated with confident grace in theater and ceremony. Philip was an eager and enthusiastic child, embracing the arts and spectacle, fascinated by maps and curious objects, wearing his royal status with modesty. María was particularly beloved by her siblings, gracious in friendship and dignified in her public acts. Carlos was proud but mild, said to be most like his father in appearance and manner, a stickler for protocol and a writer of poems. Fernando was an energetic presence, bending himself to be a churchman but defensive of his rights as a royal brother and a patron to his friends.

The lives of the royal children became more public as they began to move toward their adult roles. Ana was the heroine of the story of the exchange of princesses; María the focus of the visit of the Prince of Wales; Fernando the subject of paintings whose focus slowly shifted from an angelic child-cardinal to a conquering war hero. Prince Philip, of course, was of greatest interest to the Spanish public, while Carlos remains the most enigmatic, accompanying his brother to masques and bullfights, a source of concern to the king's favorite, lovingly eulogized by the court at his early death. He is also depicted by Velázquez in a portrait full of haughty disdain—dressed in dark, rich, but simple clothing, a glove languidly draped from his fingers, a touch of sneer in his full lips—that seems to suggest that even the most minor members of the royal family understood the special quality of royalty that set them atop the early modern world.

Part One

Childhood

2

MASTERING THE COURT

Nobility and Household Service

The king and queen of Spain spent the summer of 1601 in the Castilian city of Valladolid, preparing the transition of the royal court to that city from Madrid and awaiting the birth of their first child. Among the many projects under way were renovations to the Duke of Lerma's home, where the duke hoped the royal child would be born, and the construction of a passageway from that house to the nearby one of Magdalena de Guzmán, Marquise del Valle. The marquise, a friend of the king's favorite who, after years of exile, had been invited back to court at the accession of Philip III, held the title of aya of the child the queen was expecting.[1] Thus the child that would be born, the infanta Ana, gained her first servant and began to shape the lives of others before she even entered the world.

The people who served the royal children within the context of the royal households were not just servants but surrogate extended families, future functionaries, ministers and advisers, and friends. Significant parts of the court rearranged around the royal children, with individuals vying for positions that could affect them and their families for years and possibly generations to come. Royal children provided expanded opportunities for women at court and meant that more children of the nobility lived at court as well. They took part in activities closely tied to the personal lives of members of their households, including hosting weddings and serving as godparents at baptisms. The composition of the households also reflected the political life of court: during the period of Lerma's favor his extended family dominated the children's households, while a few years after his retirement we can see a more balanced representation, including friends of Queen Margarita's and French elements associated with Isabel de Bourbon.

The highest-ranking person in the royal households was the king's *mayordomo mayor,* who served as a personal representative of the king in supervising all manner of business at court. All petitions and decrees passed through the mayordomo mayor's hands; he controlled entrance to and exit from the palace. Immediately under him, four *mayordomos* rotated through service on a weekly basis. They could be delegated to carry out a variety of duties connected to the needs of king and court. They attended all public appearances of the king; they inspected the kitchens and food, coordinated the king's meals, planned seating at court functions, and otherwise assisted the mayordomo mayor. Also under the mayordomo mayor's authority was the *cabellerizo mayor,* who had authority over officials of the stables and oversaw the transport of the royal family. Parallel to the mayordomo mayor was the more private (and thus potentially more powerful) service of the *sumiller de corps,* who coordinated the functions of the king's private chambers. Under his supervision were the gentlemen *de la cámara* and private secretaries, aids, keepers of the wardrobe, barbers, and shoemakers.

Beneath this highest level of the household were gentlemen *de la boca,* who served at table and accompanied the king in public, and gentlemen *de la casa,* who tended to the needs of the king and his entourage when he traveled. The various sorts of gentlemen provided the king with numerous offices to distribute among younger sons of the nobility, both Spanish and foreign. These positions, some given as titles without function, provided the men who held them with the right to be at court and made them available to perform a variety of formal and informal services for the crown.

The queen, in turn, had her own mayordomo mayor and mayordomos under him, who served in public acts and administrative functions. She also had her own master of the horse, although not an entirely separate staff under him. Women took on greater responsibility within the queen's household, including the care of her wardrobe and the supervision and protection of younger women. The highest-ranking woman of the queen's chamber was the *camarera mayor,* who had charge of the queen's goods and accounts, ordered her clothing, supervised her audiences and meals, slept in her room, and accompanied her at all times. The camarera maintained order and the moral atmosphere of the queen's household, assuring that the women at court adhered to the standards of the palace rulebooks. The women who served under her mostly held the title *dama* or *dueña*. Like the various gentlemen of the king's household, many of these women, rather than having clearly articulated duties, were present and available to carry out a variety of responsibilities as occasion demanded. The caretakers of the royal children were also members of the queen's household.

On the more humble side of court, the *contralor* received instructions from the mayordomo mayor, coordinated between branches of the court, and supervised the supplying of the kitchens. The royal kitchens, in turn, were headed by a baker and a cook, each with his own large staff. Financial matters of the households were directed to the *maestro de la cámara,* who paid salaries, and the *grefier,* who kept accounts and maintained the book of palace etiquette. Another set of officials maintained the royal collections of jewels, silver, and gold; various guards watched the doors of the palace and royal chambers; and porters managed the movement of goods both inside and outside the palace. Beneath this level of service, minor functionaries arranged such practical matters as obtaining wood and charcoal for the various residences, hunters supplied the tables, quilters sewed blankets for the royal beds, and sweepers swept the chambers, halls, and courtyards.[2]

Theoretically, the king paid all costs of maintaining the royal court, and thus all persons at court were directly tied to the crown. Many palace servants were fed, housed, and sometimes clothed at royal expense, while others received aid to cover costs and were potentially eligible for extraordinary expenses as well. But royal patronage was not a simple mechanism of service and payment. Services done or goods bought for use of the royal family were often the subjects of petitions for payment or repayment, and recompense often required an additional patron, whether noble or royal, who would plead one's cause. Individuals serving in the royal households generally received their positions on the basis of personal relationships rather than because of particular skills or training. Once they were in their positions, their compensation and claims to the resources of the crown were based on relationships as much as on their specific duties or the quality of the work done.[3] Within this system, the networks of noble families at court wielded a great deal of power, both as sources of patronage and as points of access to the royal family.

Nobles used the court to advance political careers. Whether an individual intended to serve at court for his or her whole life or to use such service as a step toward another position, proximity to the king proved essential for advancement in public life. The overlap of public and private functions resulted in two forms of political involvement at the court of Spain. The first occurred on the level of policy, in which household members participated to the extent that they were also members of councils or influenced political actors. In this case, a major household position often complimented a political appointment and was key to having the king's ear. On another level, household service helped to create the structure of court and required the presence of families. Women participated in the political life of the court of Spain primarily in this structural sense, creating an opportunity for their families to reside at court and thus close to policymaking.

Members of the nobility also gained social and cultural benefits from attendance at court, with the social benefits most easily evident in the careers of women. A court position such as lady of the queen advanced a woman's marriage prospects. Not only did the king and queen contribute to dowries for young women who married directly from the palace, they also provided dowries to women who wanted to enter convents and occasionally boarded orphaned nobility.[4] Although women usually left court service after marriage, men were often given new appointments and occasionally even titles of nobility at the time of a royally sanctioned marriage.

Most of the great families of Spain were represented in the royal households, although the major offices often settled on particular families in such a manner that they appear almost hereditary. Repetition of names across generations, such as Juan de Zúñiga senior and junior serving as *ayos* in consecutive generations, or María and Mariana Enríquez, the one serving as aya and camarera mayor in one generation and the other a dueña in the next, make the service seem even more timeless. The various Sandoval, Castro, and Rojas ancestors of the Duke of Lerma were well represented within the traditional service of the royal households. An earlier marquis of Denia and count of Lerma had served as governor of the household of Queen Juana, mother of Charles V, in Tordesillas, in which his wife and his sister, the Countess of Castro, also held offices. The third marquis, who had been a gentleman of Prince Carlos, married into the Zúñiga and Requesens family, thus increasing the family's claim to household positions. Other relatives and in-laws had served in the households of Princess Juana and of Isabel de Valois and Ana de Austria, the third and fourth wives of Philip II. The Duke of Lerma himself had come to court as a child, as a menino to Queen Isabel and Prince Carlos at about the time that Carlos was beginning to show signs of mental instability.[5]

The queen's household further expressed a variety of court and international interests through the very persons of the women who served. While the king's household could develop organically during the course of his childhood, the queen's household was created when a queen arrived from her native country. Thus, despite the overall lesser status of women at court, the queen's household in particular can be seen as a barometer of relationships at court and the standing of various noble families. In the case of Margarita de Austria, the Duke of Lerma placed first his wife and then his sister, Catalina de Zúñiga y Sandoval, Countess of Lemos, as the queen's camarera mayor, and he placed numerous other relatives and in-laws in more minor positions. He was later able to appoint another sister, Leonor de Sandoval y Rojas, Countess of Altamira, as the primary caretaker of the royal children.

The queen also retained a few Austrian women, including her childhood friend María Sidonia Riederer, whom the Spaniards soon recognized as the *privada* of the queen, and María's sister, Mariana, who arrived in 1600. María's marriage to the widowed Count of Barajas, which the queen and her friend resisted until 1603, can be interpreted through the lens of a struggle between the queen and Lerma for control of her household. But if the king or duke intended marriage to remove María from the queen's company, the attempt failed, for chroniclers continue to mention the Countess of Barajas and her sister at court functions both during Margarita's lifetime and after her death.[6]

Childhood in the Queen's Household

Behind the titles of household positions that allowed holders to wield certain types of power was the experience of stability that the royal households created for the royal children. Especially vulnerable because of the small circle of true relatives, they developed friendships and ties resembling kinship relations with persons who had their own networks of interests and family. While remaining conscious of their own special status, the children experienced the service of the nobility as a kind of extended family that sustained them despite the absences of their parents, their various separate and fluid living arrangements, and, eventually, for the children of Philip III, the death of the queen.

The royal children spent their first years under the supervision of their aya within the context of the queen's household. The aya was the first and initially the highest-ranking official assigned to the care of royal children. Her duties corresponded roughly to those of a governess, although her position was more administrative and prestigious than the term *governess* implies to modern audiences. As the children grew older, their parents also assigned them an ayo, an official who was primarily associated with boys but who likewise served the girls in certain administrative or public situations. Ayas and ayos can both be seen as general overseers of their wards' daily activities. Observers considered them in some respects teachers, as reflected in the number of texts that confuse or conflate their titles with that of *maestro*.

Rodrigo Mendez Silva, writing in the mid-seventeenth century, delved deeply into Spanish history to examine the mixed nature of ayo, maestro, and even parent in his description of the education of Fernando III: "He had no other ayo, nor teacher, than the queen [Berenguela] his virtuous, prudent, and discreet mother, who nourished him at her breast and educated him in such a manner that he emerged glorious in all and in everything triumphant."[7] Cabrera de Córdoba called Philip II the "ayo mayor" of his son, and the prince's tutor in 1617 used such terms when he urged the king to remove the prince's ayo, whom he judged lax in the performance of his duty. The biographer of Queen Margarita praised her by describing her as a true aya in the religious instruction of her children.[8]

The reference to the king and queen as "true" ayo and aya can be reversed to suggest that the ayo or aya acted as a type of surrogate parent. Mendez Silva presented Philip II as saying to his son's aya after the death of his first wife, "My son has been left without a mother, you have to be one for him."[9] Popular accounts concerning the appointment of the countess of Altamira as aya to the children of Philip III and Margarita portray the queen as saying to her, "Countess, I give you my children, for you to raise, as you have raised your own." And in a similar manner years later, after the queen's death, when the king entrusted the households of the royal children to the queen's camarera mayor, Cabrera de Córdoba describes the king as having conferred on her the "office" of mother.[10]

Most references we have to ayas are not part of theoretical discussions, as are occasional descriptions of the responsibilities of ayos, but instead appear in court chronicles and palace rulebooks. The aya functioned within the structure of the queen's household, living in the palace and participating in all aspects of the children's daily private lives. Instructions signed on July 9, 1603, for service in the queen's household indicate the range of the aya's duties. They begin with a general statement of the aya's responsibilities: "The aya of the infanta my daughter must take great care in her education and good instruction in habits, as much in spiritual as in other matters, and in that which concerns her food."[11] The rulebook required her to attend the meals, activities, and lessons of the infanta and to be present when the child woke and when she went to bed. She slept in the infanta's rooms, ordered her clothing, and distributed her worn clothing, presumably to the poor. If the infanta went out without the queen, the aya accompanied her in her coach or litter. She supervised the child's other servants and strictly controlled access to the infanta's chamber.

The infanta Ana's first teacher, on her first day of formal classes, described the infanta as already able to read, indicating that the eight-year-old had some rudimentary skills before beginning her official schooling. It was probably the aya herself who taught the infanta or supervised her acquisition of these skills as part of her general responsibility to prepare the children in a variety of practical and spiritual exercises. Despite the injunction of the palace rulebook that the infanta's aya attend lessons, the infanta's teacher never mentions her presence in his daily records, and indeed, with responsibility for all of royal children eventually falling on her shoulders, she could hardly have attended all of their lessons regularly.[12]

The choice of an aya reflected both political and personal inclinations at court, as can be seen in examples from the childhood of Philip II. The prince's parents first appointed Inés Manrique, widow of the *adelantado* of Castile, whose qualifications included connections to great families of Spain through both birth and marriage, while his second aya, Leonor Mascareñas (Mascarenhas), was a Portuguese woman not much older than the young mother of the prince, Empress Isabel. Mascareñas had previously served as a lady of Isabel's mother, Queen María of Portugal, so her presence may have had a special resonance of home for the empress.[13] Philip II demonstrated his attachment to and trust in her by calling on her to serve his eldest son, Carlos, in the same role. Although historians most commonly identify Mascareñas as aya to Philip II and Carlos, she also served Philip's sisters, the infantas María and Juana, and was attached primarily to their service between the time that Philip received his first independent household and her appointment as aya for Carlos in 1545.

The ayas appointed under Philip III reveal other political and personal patterns in the life of the court. Magdalena de Guzmán, Marquise del Valle, was named aya for the royal child expected in the autumn of 1601. Considered a friend of the Duke of Lerma's, the marquise had been out of favor in the last decades of Philip II's reign, and her rise in status at the accession of Philip III suggests that she was recalled to court as a demonstration of the change in power.[14]

But a few years later, in a confused court drama beginning in October 1603, she suddenly begged permission to retire. At first allowed to leave peaceably, she was soon after arrested at her nephew's house and all her papers confiscated. Royal agents then arrested her niece Ana de Mendoza in the palace. Shortly thereafter, two other ladies of the queen were also told to leave court, and, in a related incident officials attempted to remove Beatriz de Cardona, the Countess of Castellar, from the convent in which she had suddenly professed.[15]

The marquise remained in varying degrees of imprisonment (including seclusion at the castle of Simancas) for the next seven years. Interrogators questioned her concerning the correspondence of the queen's ladies and of the queen herself and even whether the queen was unhappy in her marriage.[16] Other questions placed the marquise within the patronage system, asking who had requested that she speak on their behalf, whether particular people had spoken against the king or the Duke of Lerma, and whether she had ever received jewels or other things of value from ministers. The marquise's explanation of one letter seems to imply problems between the queen and the Duchess of Lerma, and she described herself as telling the duke when the queen had complaints so that he could amend the problem.

As the drama played out, the Venetian ambassador speculated that the marquise had kept contact with great nobles who were out of favor, while others suggested tension between her and the Duchess of Lerma or the discomfort of the king and queen concerning her knowledge of their personal life. The imperial ambassador focused his account on the queen's feeling that her every thought and action was monitored by Lerma and his son the Duke of Uceda.[17] In the end, it seems likely that the duke had originally installed his friend as a servant of the infanta as an act of patronage and perhaps to monitor the queen's thoughts and activities, but the marquise had instead developed an independent circle of influence that the duke began to see as damaging to his own position. While the queen had developed some measure of friendship with the marquise, she was angered that a member of her household reported her thoughts to the duke and refused to come to her aid when she was arrested. In assessing her fate, it is important to note that the marquise gained her position through friendship rather than through a long tradition of service or family, which might have shielded her more effectively from the vagaries of favor and faction.

After the Marquise del Valle was forced to leave court, Cabrera de Córdoba reported speculation that the king would name the Marquise of Santa Cruz, or Doña María Henríquez, a member of the Alba family who had long been a dueña at court, or the Duchess of Vibona, who was the sister of the Duchess of Lerma, all three women of experience and standing.[18] The king and queen instead named Leonor de Sandoval y Rojas, Countess of Altamira, sister of the Duke of Lerma.

With one serving as the children's aya and the other as the queen's camarera mayor, the duke's sisters rounded out a kind of court within a court. As early as 1603 the Countess of Lemos's daughters-in-law required only the countess's permission in order to enter her rooms, an unusual situation in a court that tried to control access and the movement of women. Like her brother, she occasionally left court for extended periods of time, as when she and two of the queen's ladies summered in the town of Lerma in 1613. Her incomes from royal lands proved more flexible than those owed other women of similar standing, and occasionally the crown granted her funds for which she did not have to give an account, a gesture more often made to men performing diplomatic missions for the king.[19]

The Countess of Altamira's service as aya to the royal children did not entitle her to the unencumbered use of funds or the depth of contact with the queen that her sister enjoyed as camarera mayor. Instead, it often meant that she spent royal functions attending the children rather than taking part herself. For example, the royal chaplain noted in his journal that "all the ladies" of the court attended the 1609 Ash Wednesday service at court, yet he went to the children's rooms to mark them with ash and left an assistant to do the same for the countess, indicating that she had not been at the service.[20] Likewise, when the king and queen traveled without their children, the Countess of Altamira remained with the children, while her sister moved with the court.

Although she did not enjoy the same prestige as the camarera mayor, the aya was able to translate her connections and service into political capital for her family. Her husband, Lope Moscoso Osorio, was one of Queen Margarita's mayordomos from the time of her arrival in Spain and later served as her caballerizo mayor. Her daughters served in the queen's household and later married or took religious vows with dowries provided by the crown, while her sons obtained high offices in church and state and became particularly close to the infante Fernando. Philip III cited the countess's service as a direct reason for the granting of an ecclesiastical office to her son Melchor de Sandoval.[21]

Whatever advantages the sisters Leonor de Sandoval and Catalina de Zúñiga obviously had owing to their brother's position as king's favorite, their status was not wholly dependent on his. Precedents of service to the crown in both their family and their husbands' families were already sufficient to qualify them for the positions they held. Their use of the patronage system, in turn, provided the opportunity for their children to continue to be influential, although new conditions at court and in the larger political world eventually curtailed the effectiveness of this method in building careers.

Despite the strong position of Lerma's sister, Cabrera de Córdoba reported rumors that a new aya might be named after the birth of the prince. While at first he proffered a few names, he later wrote that it was "something that was never done" and "it is an established fact that there had never been more than one aya in the palace, and that is the Countess of Altamira." The children, however, did not always live together, so different women must have performed the duties entrusted to an aya. And indeed Cabrera de Córdoba does refer to Francisca de Córdoba as "deputy aya," and Diego de Guzmán describes Teresa de Castro, who was the Countess of Altamira's sister-in-law, as serving the "office of aya" at the baptism of Philip III's youngest daughter, Margarita Francisca.[22]

These women who occasionally took over the care of one or more of the children were all members of the queen's household. The seemingly oversized staff of noblewomen in the royal palace in part reflected the children's needs for care, supervision, and companionship, and the numbers needed grew even larger when the children lived separately from one another for short periods of time. The palace rulebook of 1603 specifically assigned two of the queen's dueñas to the service of the infanta, and it was from among these ladies that the aya could choose someone to take her place if she found herself unable to fulfill a particular duty. The title *dueña* always implied an older woman, usually a widow, who carried greater responsibility and authority than a simple *dama*, or lady. A dueña might also be called *de honor*, indicating a mostly ceremonial position, or *de retrete*, referring specifically to service in the queen's private chambers. The *etiqueta* of 1603 indicates that the two women assigned to the infanta also slept in her room, although they may have done so only in the absence of the aya. Other ladies who served the infanta slept in a "gallery," or common bedroom. The only specific duty mentioned for these women was that of making sure windows and doors of the infanta's rooms were properly regulated, except for one woman who was assigned to dress the infanta and comb and style her hair, duties performed under the strict supervision of the aya.[23] Individual women also had particular responsibilities or undertook activities that were not articulated in palace rulebooks. Doña Beatriz Guerra, for example, oversaw the transfer of jewels from storage to the queen's quarters and was noted to have returned several items to the royal storehouse after the death of the queen. Some women did handwork for household use, including Doña María de Montoya, who embroidered several altar cloths for the queen's oratory. Numerous small household items were entrusted to Doña María Abarca, several of them noted in inventories only because they had been lost.[24]

In addition to the positions of aya and the temporary position of *teniente* of the aya, the *azafata* also held an important position in the children's service. The title *azafata* can be translated as "lady of the queen's wardrobe," but the implications of the role go deeper than this description immediately suggests. The duties of an azafata are not clearly designated in the palace rulebook made for Queen Margarita but can be pieced together from various sources. Unlike the aya, who served all the children and whose position became more administrative as the number of children grew, an azafata was assigned to an individual child. Like the aya, she was appointed before the birth of a child, as indicated by the expense accounts connected with royal births and baptisms, which name specific azafatas as receiving goods or payments. Payment records, for example, designate the azafata of the infante Carlos, María Jordán, as the person to whom new mattresses for the infante and his wetnurse were to be delivered, while all the expenses associated with the birth of the short-lived infante Alonso were distributed through his azafata, María Gamarra.[25] The type of relationships these women might develop with the children is suggested by Novoa's offhand comment about Philip IV's azafata, Juana Zapata, that during Philip's early teen years she was "the one whom the prince most loved."[26] Juana Zapata had begun her palace career as a dueña de retrete of the queen on March 8, 1600, and was appointed to serve as azafata first to the infanta María (probably the short-lived child born in 1603) and then to the prince. Petitions concerning her expenses refer to her as "azafata of the prince" and indicate that her daughter also served in the queen's chamber.[27]

The intimacy of the relationship between royal children and these officials described as ladies of the wardrobe suggests that these were the women specifically designated to dress the children. Given the strict rules about who could enter the royal children's rooms, actually touching the child while dressing him or her implied a special intimacy. This person had to be above reproach, preferably an older person, as Juana Zapata certainly would have been to be named dueña of the queen in 1600. The supposition about the azafata's duties is supported by the last service that the infanta Margarita's azafata, Elvira de Guzmán, did for the child: the official description of the infanta's funeral noted that the azafata dressed the body of the seven-year-old for burial.[28]

Azafatas are generally associated with childhood for boys. The king did not have an official of this title, but Juana Zapata appears again in later documents as azafata of Queen Isabel, demonstrating that the affection and trust that Philip IV felt for his azafata continued into adulthood.[29] The azafata of the infante Carlos, María Jordán, was still residing in the palace when she died in 1625.[30] Describing her as an azafata when the infante was already in his late teens probably indicates that this had been her most prestigious appointment rather than that she continued to serve in that role. It may, however, also reflect the ways in which Carlos, even as a young adult, was treated as a child within the structure of the royal households.

Childhood azafatas sometimes continued to serve royal women in adulthood. Ursala Oempherguerin, who traveled with Queen Margarita from Austria, appears to have been her azafata. Doña Ursala's daughter also accompanied the queen to Spain, suggesting a close connection between the three women. Although Margarita did not take her aya to Spain, she remembered her in her will, along with four other women whom she described as having helped to raise her.[31] Similarly, Estefania de Villaquirán, who had previously served the infanta Catalina Micaela as dueña de retrete, was the infanta Ana's azafata by 1607. In this role she accompanied the infanta to France and remained with her there long after her other Spanish attendants were sent home.[32]

In addition to the supervisory aya and the more intimate azafata, other members of the queen's household, such as the *ama de leche,* or wetnurse, provided basic care for the children. Since theory held that moral and physical qualities of a wetnurse passed through the milk itself to the child being nursed, the wetnurse often became a permanent part of a child's life. When a royal child was expected, doctors located several potential wetnurses from among whom they could choose according to the perceived health, vigor, and virtue of the women. If doctors judged that a child was not thriving, the first remedy was to change nurses.

Since the women who served as wetnurses often were the wives of minor court functionaries or occasionally even more humble inhabitants of the immediate region where a royal child was born, the relationship with a wetnurse put the royal family in immediate contact with lower ranks of court and society. In recognition of her service, her children occasionally received dowries or positions at court that they might not otherwise have been able to access. In July 1622, for example, Philip IV granted the position of secretary of orders to Gaspar de Salcedo so that he could marry Doña Bernarda, the king's *hermana de leche,* or "sister by milk," that is, the wetnurse's daughter, who herself had a minor position in the queen's chamber. A son of María de Ibarra y Mallea like-wise petitioned to be received into royal service or, failing that, for assistance in his education, on the basis of being a "brother by milk."[33] Another ama of the prince, Gerónima Salera, received an income of 400 ducats.[34] The lesser income of 200 ducats a year to Isabel de Montoya, who had nursed both the prince and Carlos, and a single payment of 300 ducats in aid of expenses to Felipa de Villasante may indicate that these women served only briefly. Catalina de Bustamante received 300 ducats a year for being the ama of the infanta Ana and asked to have her expenses of moving from Valladolid with the court paid. Her continued attachment to the child she had nursed may be gathered from her commission of a small portrait of the infanta a few years later.[35] María Ortiz de la Harcha, in requesting the office of constable of the court for her husband, claimed that the infanta Margarita, who had been ill under the care of a previous nurse, had became healthy once she began to nurse her.[36]

As in the case of others holding such court positions, the ama might request financial aid in recognition of her services years later, or relatives might refer to her service when requesting aid. As late as 1606 Mariana de Bargas received a royal favor on the basis of having been wetnurse to Philip III. Similarly, in 1631 one of Philip IV's nurses, Gerónima Taeño, who had a pension of one hundred ducats, asked to have it transferred to her daughter. Madalena Nevada did not specify which of the children she served when she asked for the position of porter for her husband in 1608. The council reviewing royal favors was inclined to choose her out of twenty-five people petitioning to fill the vacancy, given the previous services she claimed her husband's parents had performed and the accompanying letter of support written by the Duchess of Cea at the queen's order.[37] In 1620 Philip III likewise granted the son of Isabel de Haro, who had nursed María for sixteen months, the coveted position of porter in the palace because the infanta had endorsed her ama's request.[38] Ana de Laguna requested a minor court recordkeeping position for her husband, explaining that she had served both Carlos and Fernando, "following [them] on all the journeys," for four years at great cost to herself without receiving any favors.[39]

After Queen Margarita's death, the king sent to the ladies of the palace to ask which of them wanted to return to their homes and which wanted to continue in the service of the infanta Ana and her sisters, offering great favor to those who chose to stay. They all accepted and "kissed the feet" of the king for it and then went to kiss Ana's hand. The king also reiterated the position at court of the Countess of Lemos, the queen's camarera mayor. Cabrera de Córdoba reported:

"His Majesty ordered that the Countess of Lemos should be entrusted with the raising and protection of their Highnesses, performing for them the office of mother, with all that is attached to it." The chronicler remarked that Lemos had been given this order "notwithstanding that her sister the Countess of Altamira is their aya." This last comment may have been inspired by the fact that the aya was usually seen as filling the "office" of mother. The reiteration of her office, however, ensured that the Countess of Lemos maintained a prominent position at court, a point that Cabrera de Córdoba underscores with the comment that the appointment was made "in such a manner that all the weight and care of the households of the king and their Highnesses will depend from here forward on both sisters."[40] Despite the question of which sister might be playing the role of mother, neither title was honorary, since the aya supervised the lives of the children, while the camarera oversaw the women at court.

As the queen's camarera mayor when no queen existed, Lemos was credited with running the women's quarters like a convent, an observation generally presented as a compliment.[41] She performed some duties that overlapped those of the aya. In a letter to her son in 1613 she described a charming little scene in which she placed all the children at the balcony of her brother's house and arranged for the shades that hid them to be raised at exactly the moment that the king rode into view and would see them. She also accompanied the royal children to public events, including a particularly injurious bullfight, which she recounted in the same letter.[42] By 1621 she was considered the camarera of the infanta María, a position that she probably gained sometime between the death of her sister, the aya, in 1616 and the ascendance of the household of Isabel de Bourbon as princess and queen. Although this was a lesser position than she had held previously, it indicates the survival of her prestige through the transition from the reign of Philip III to that of Philip IV. She lived in the palace itself and received visitors in her own chambers, including the cardinal-legate Barberini in 1626. Although her health was so poor that a member of the cardinal's entourage claimed that she had not left the palace in four years, she held the title of camarera mayor until her death in 1628.[43]

The Ayo and the Prince's Household

While there are few theoretical writings on the subject of ayas, several early modern writers attempted to define the qualities of an ayo. Luis Cabrera de

Córdoba, chronicler and historian of Philip II, ascribed qualities to the ayo that suggest his involvement in a variety of activities related to the social, religious, and academic training of the prince:

> The ayo needs complete virtue, a calm spirit, gentle patience, temperate qualities, perfect religion, experience of the Palace and Court, and knowledge of the prince's obligations to himself for his greatness and dignity, and to his subjects; and [the ayo] should know good letters, arts and arms, in order that he can be maestro as well.[44]

The vulnerability of this position to the dangers of patronage is suggested by Cabrera de Córdoba's reminder that

> the office of ayo is not to be given in the manner of the rest, by intercessions, gifts, demands, concerns, friendships, nor in remuneration for services; because although there may be among the ministers a good ambassador close to great princes, and a fortunate and valorous captain of armies, prudent and just governor of provinces, or [someone who] had preeminent offices in the royal household, it would not be sufficient to teach the son of the king.[45]

One discussion of ayos, which probably dates from the middle years of Philip II's reign, emphasizes the ayo's role in maintaining the physical well-being of the prince and exhorts the ayo to study the prince in order to instruct him, rather than placing himself in the position of forming the prince. Like treatises on education, the discussion offers the author opportunity to reflect on the nature of kingship and lays out qualities the ayo should encourage in the prince, ranging from religious observance to physical exercise to appreciation of both arms and letters. Beyond that, the author advises the ayo to prepare for his task by cultivating in himself the qualities he would like to teach the prince in order to have the authority necessary to instruct the prince. The ayo should build his understanding of the prince's nature, not by "consulting the stars," but by observation. He should discover what tastes and passions predominate in the prince and learn his interior inclinations by studying his modesty and the color of his face. The ayo, moreover, must have knowledge and know how to transmit it, correcting what needs to be corrected with prudence and without violence.[46]

This instruction creates the impression that the formation of a prince was a delicate matter. The qualities of the future ruler were extremely important, yet he was not to be actively molded but instead encouraged in his own nature, guided by good example, protected from bad. A prince was not to be broken to submission as other people learned discipline; instead he was to be nourished as an individual whose personality itself represented the gift of royal nature to the nation.

Rodrigo Mendez Silva, writing during the reign of Philip IV, pointed to the courtly context of the ayo's service. Prefacing his detailed list of Spanish ayos and maestros with reflections on the ancients, he assigned great philosophers as tutors and ayos to the great rulers of Greek and Roman history. While Mendez clearly intended his classical allusions to confer added prestige on his subject and perhaps felt the necessity of a pseudohumanist nod to the ancients, his vision of the duty of teachers has little to do with the instruction Socrates gave Alcibiades or the lessons Menelaos may have had for Telemachus. Instead, he focused on how the ayo should instill religion and law, obedience to parents, reverence for priests, and proper treatment of friends, family, and servants. The prince must learn to speak well, to listen attentively, to conquer his faults through reason, and to master his anger, thereby learning to give good audiences and winning the acclamation of all. Finally, he recommended the reading of histories, since they are "springs of human prudence."[47]

Although Mendez Silva does not strongly distinguish between the duties of ayo and maestro, his accounts of Spanish royalty and their teachers and guardians demonstrate a clear distinction between the types of people who held each of these titles. He sets forth a pattern of religious teachers honored by high ecclesiastical office and noble ayos who were the founders of their family's fortunes. The cases in which he mentions the ayo of a woman—those of Doña Urraca, the successor of Alonso VI, and of Isabel the Catholic—demonstrate that the appointment of an ayo reflected the political role the royal person would play rather than his or her sex. By calling Doña Berenguela the ayo, rather than the aya, of Fernando III, he also signals a difference other than gender between the offices.[48]

Letters and accounts reveal that in the children's earliest years the ayo's primary responsibility was their physical well-being. Philip II's ayos first reported on the health of the family, then on the prince's learning to read and to say his prayers, and later on the prince's progress in other areas, including learning to ride a horse.[49] Philip III's first ayo requisitioned clothing and horses both for the prince and for his sisters and nominated persons for their households.

He supervised the organization of the household that would accompany the infanta Catalina on her marriage journey to Italy, along with some aspects of the journey itself, and notified the king concerning the division of the jewels of the infantas' mother, Isabel de Valois, between her two daughters.[50]

Although one might expect that an ayo would present a flattering description of a prince, García de Toledo, the ayo of Philip II's son Carlos, reported frankly that the prince did not respect his maestro and studied unwillingly; even in jousting and fencing, "a prize is necessary to get him to do anything."[51] Philip II actively commissioned the prince's ayo and others to assess the future Philip III in 1596. Although the report this committee produced suggests that these officials felt they could speak freely, its vantage point of evaluation set the writers above the prince, and indeed some of their assessments were negative. The tone of the report suggests why Cabrera de Córdoba mentioned it a few years later as a factor in the rift between Philip III, now king, and his former tutor, García de Loaysa y Girón.[52]

Like ayas, ayos were appointed for both political and personal reasons. Philip II and his sisters were first served by Pedro González de Mendoza, the son of the fourth Duke of Infantado, who had been a member of the royal household and a churchman before he received his position. Their second ayo, Juan de Zúñiga y Avellaneda, *comendador mayor* of Castile and a member of the Council of State, was praised for his virtues but was also the husband of Empress Isabel's confidante, Estefania de Requesens. Philip II appointed their son, also Juan de Zúñiga, as Philip III's first ayo, providing him the opportunity to continue to develop his family's close relationship with the royal family. When he died suddenly in late 1586, the prince and his sister wore mourning for some days, as if for a family member, and went personally to console his wife.[53]

After Zúñiga's death, Philip II waited several months to appoint Gómez Dávila, the Marquis of Velada, as the prince's new ayo. Velada hesitated to accept the position, citing poor health and his lack of experience in government and the world. Although his friendship with Cristóbal de Moura certainly contributed to his appointment, Velada's lack of experience at court in itself may have recommended him. The king wanted no faction in the prince's quarters, which may have led him to choose an ayo without larger ambitions or an established network of associates at court. With no obligations to councils, except those involved in the prince's formation, Velada spent a great deal of time with the prince, accompanying him in a variety of activities and apparently monitoring his lessons. His extensive library, which included books on pedagogy as well as history, reflected his primary focus.[54]

Although the ayo Velada also served on the committee that evaluated the prince, he survived the transition in reigns surprisingly well, his title changing from ayo to mayordomo mayor. Some observers attributed his reappointment to his easy disposition and general charm. Perhaps his essentially nonpolitical nature worked in his favor, or he may have befriended the Duke of Lerma in the intervening years. Jerónimo de Sepúlveda claimed that when Philip III dismissed a number of ministers and household members at the beginning of his reign, only Velada thought to throw himself at the feet of the king's favorite and ask to be reinstated, which proved sufficient for him to gain his new post.[55] Although it seems too simple to suggest, as Sepúlveda apparently does, that any of Philip II's ministers could have asked for his position back and received it, the desire of Philip and Lerma to be approached in such a way is consistent with the new king's feeling that he had not been shown respect by his father's ministers. Beyond such speculations, there appeared to exist a familial feeling between the king and the marquis, suggested by small details, including the Venetian ambassador's observation that the king always danced with Velada's daughter when he did not dance with the queen.[56]

In January 1606, when the future Philip IV was not yet a year old, Cabrera de Córdoba reported speculation at court gossip concerning ayos for the prince, including the rumor that the Marquis of Villamizar was to be named ayo and mayordomo of the prince. The marquis, Juan de Sandoval, was the Duke of Lerma's brother and had been made first groomsman in September 1598 and gentleman of the king on October 16 of the same year.[57] But he died soon after he was mentioned as ayo. The chronicler does not mention other candidates for the position until August of the following year, when rumor floated the name of Philip II's former minister Juan de Idiáquez. That there was no immediate appointment, however, suggests that earlier discussions reflected long-range planning and that the prince, while a young child, could comfortably continue to be raised in the household of the queen.

Five years later, Cabrera de Córdoba again mentioned Idiáquez as a candidate for sumiller de corps of the prince and gentleman of the king, or if not that, then "deputy" of the ayo and of the mayordomo mayor.[58] Shortly thereafter, the king instead named his favorite, the Duke of Lerma, as ayo of the young prince. If we consider that the ayo's responsibilities included social instruction and the teaching of practical skills, the choice of Lerma is significant. Who better to instruct the heir to the throne in the intricacies of court life than the man who had dominated the royal court since the accession of Philip III? But if we consider the wider political goals of education under an ayo, the skills that Lerma brought to the office were of mixed value in preparing a prince for his full responsibilities. While his knowledge of the structure of court was perhaps unsurpassed, his experience and interest in foreign affairs seems to have been limited.

As in earlier generations, Lerma's responsibility as the prince's ayo extended to serving the other children as well. In the years following his appointment, we can glimpse the duke riding between Madrid and other places to escort the prince and his siblings.[59] One well-recorded example of Lerma's activities as ayo involved assisting the prince in staging a theatrical extravaganza in the town of Lerma in 1614. The duke himself had been providing other entertainment during the same week for the court, but he played a supporting role in this production, while the nine-year-old prince acted, directed, and stage-managed. The prince made specific choices for the cast, including one man (most of the actors were women), Andrés de Alcocer, whom he particularly liked for his unique wit. Accounts of the play identify Lerma not as the king's favorite but as the prince's ayo and present him as encouraging and supporting the prince's own interests.[60] The apparent success of this week of events may have encouraged the duke to stage an even greater extravaganza in Lerma in 1617, a last hollow grasp at power rather than a triumph.

Despite such notable events, the Duke of Lerma was apparently lax in his performance as ayo. That his brother rather than he himself had been the first candidate for the position suggests that he originally saw the appointment as patronage that strengthened his family rather than as integral to maintaining his own influence at court. By the time he accepted the position, however, he likely felt that he could not trust it to anyone else. He nonetheless appeared dissatisfied with the role and dedicated little energy to it. The king's favorite may indeed have been somewhat taken aback that his prestigious new position interfered with his own freedom of movement. Previously, he had often spent considerable time away from court, whether summering with his daughters and sister in the town of Lerma, attending to his own religious patronage, including a convent he founded in Valdemoro, or withdrawing to nurse bouts of melancholy.[61] While providing supervision for the royal children, however, he was notably absent from the king and less able to choose the time and place of his own attendance at court.

Like the aya, the ayo occasionally required assistance in fulfilling his duty. On one occasion, the Count of Lemos, son of the camarera mayor and the duke's son-in-law, took charge of bringing the prince to join his parents where they had been traveling, a duty usually entrusted to the ayo or a mayordomo.[62] When Lerma excused himself, due to illness, from the last portion of the infanta Ana's wedding journey in 1615, his son the Duke of Uceda performed the office of ayo. His malady was sufficiently minor to allow him to dance one last time with Ana during festivities in Burgos and to accompany the entourage at least as far as the king did. He later claimed that he had feigned illness to avoid contact with French officials, but he may in fact have chosen the king's company at such a tender moment over attendance at the ceremonial event.

Lerma's eventual departure from court appears to have been intimately linked to his removal from the position of ayo and provides a dramatic demonstration of how public and private needs of the royal family influenced the king's understanding of the priorities of court. Perhaps a year and a half prior to the duke's dismissal, the prince's tutor complained to the king that the favorite devoted insufficient care to his obligations as ayo to the prince. This criticism was relayed to the duke, who attempted to put himself in the prince's good graces by showering him with gifts and providing special meals from his own kitchen. The king recognized Lerma's poor performance and sought to rid his son's household of the very elements of a patronage system that had shaped his own. He first requested and then demanded the retirement of his friend, who reluctantly complied.[63]

Perhaps opponents of the duke brought these problems to the king's attention in the hope that pointing out the damage to the prince's education would wake the king to the dangers of Lerma's dominant position at court. Earlier attempts to open his eyes had not carried the weight of the threat to his child's well-being and, by extension, his country's future. The duke may have been otherwise pushing the limits of his friendship with the king. He reportedly attempted to place himself in the rank of ruling families by contemplating the marriage of his grandson to a daughter of the Duke of Savoy. Philip III refused permission, and Lerma ceased negotiations without complaint, claiming that he would rather be a good servant than a relative.[64]

While the Duke of Uceda inherited the majority of Lerma's offices, he did not become ayo of the prince when his father was dismissed. This fell to the Count of Paredes, who according to one source held the position "a few days" but probably served during the entire interim from the dismissal of Lerma in September 1618 until the appointment of Baltasar de Zúñiga in 1619.[65] The Countess of Paredes, along with the Count of Barajas, had served as guardian for the children of Philip II during his absence in Portugal. Philip III thus drew on the structure of court service and on the safety of precedent when he appointed the son of his former caretaker in the uncertain months after the departure of his favorite.

The appointment of Baltasar de Zúñiga as ayo to the prince represented a shift from a court-focused education to an emphasis on the larger political world. The younger son of the Count of Monterrey, Zúñiga had been active in the military and diplomatic service of Spain for more than three decades. Having served in the Great Armada against England and then as a diplomat in Rome, Flanders, and the Holy Roman Empire, he had recently returned to Madrid, where he was beginning to take an active role in the Council of State. The choice of an ayo with extensive knowledge of foreign policy may be seen as a reflection of a stage in the prince's development, although the choice of this particular ayo also indicates a change in approach to government on the part of the king. Others clearly perceived the implication of his appointment and directed advice to him as ayo.[66] For Zúñiga, the rewards for holding the position clearly intertwined with advancement in government positions. On his accession Philip IV made Baltasar de Zúñiga his top adviser on foreign matters, a position he held for a perhaps lamentably short period, until his death in 1622.

Although Lerma and Paredes served the infantes Carlos and Fernando, evidence does not suggest that Zúñiga did. At the time of their father's death, when the infantes were fourteen and twelve years old, their brother appointed new officials for their service. The infante Carlos continued to spend his daily life in close proximity to the king, and the officials attached to the two elder brothers overlapped in a structure that clearly reflected Philip's superior position. On July 15, 1621, among several men who took the oath as gentlemen of the king's chamber was Alonso de Bracamonte y Guzmán, Count of Peñaranda de Bracamonte, "with attendance on the lord infante Don Carlos, as ayo."[67]

When Bracamonte died less than a year later, Philip IV named his mayordomo Francisco Fernández de Córdoba, Count of Alcaudete, granting him "title of ayo of the lord infante Don Carlos, and of the chamber of His Majesty, and that he enjoy the salary of a mayordomo, and two titles in Italy for aid to his expense; and when they give His Highness a household, the title of his Mayordomo mayor."[68] In this way, the king gave the count a position, allowing him to keep his present income in addition to his new income, and a future income that would equal his two present ones, all in anticipation of a future, more prestigious appointment.

In March 1629 Philip IV made clear both the career and financial rewards that Fernández de Córdoba received for his service to the crown: "The king appointed the count of Alcaudete to his Council of State, and [granted] his income after his days to his grandson or granddaughter; and the salary of ayo and mayordomo mayor that he enjoys for his days, and after that my lady the countess his wife [may] enjoy them as her own." Appointing Alcaudete to the Council of State may have been an attempt to keep him at court, for palace documents indicate that he had asked permission to retire in January 1629, citing his advanced age.[69]

While Fernando had a household, at least partly ecclesiastical, before the death of his father, he does not appear to have had his own ayo until his brother appointed the Marquis of Malpica as ayo and mayordomo on July 15, 1621, the same day that Bracamonte was appointed as ayo for Carlos. The marquis, Francisco Barroso de Rivera, does not appear to have held any other court office. His son, Baltasar de Rivera, however, had been named a gentleman de la boca to the king within days of the accession of Philip IV, and on the day his father was made ayo he received the title Count of Navalmoral. Like Alcaudete, Malpica was eventually named to the Council of State, but he died only days after the appointment, on September 12, 1625.[70]

Children at Court

In addition to the officials and servants directly responsible for the children, various members of the households and other government officials also participated directly in the lives of the children. The queen's mayordomo, the Count of Casarrubios, attended the celebration of the infanta María's third birthday and helped her make the traditional offering of coins, while the Count of Arcos served at the celebration of Ana's eighth birthday.[71] In 1607, when the prince had a rash on his feet that the doctors were unable to cure, Doña María Gasca, the wife of Councilor of State Francisco de Contreras, took the matter in hand and was able to solve the problem. When the prince was too ill during Corpus Christi in 1613 to join the rest of the family at San Lorenzo, he was entertained in Madrid by the president of the Council of Castile, who took him to his house and set him at a window to watch the procession.[72]

Nobles also took the opportunity to entertain the royal family and court. In

November 1609 the Duke of Feria presented a *sortija,* a contest or demonstration of riding skills in which participants passed the tip of a lance through rings while galloping at full speed, in Madrid's plaza mayor, the two eldest infantas watching with their parents from the windows of the panadería.[73] The Marquis of Cañete gave a luxurious reception for the royal children and the ladies of the palace at his home in honor of Corpus Christi in 1617. He spared no expense for the occasion, showering his guests with gifts and decorating his house with portraits of the entire royal family, including Ana and her husband, and of the Duke of Lerma and the Duke of Uceda and their relative the archbishop of Toledo, Bernardo de Rojas y Sandoval.[74]

The occasions when members of the royal family lived separately for extended periods of time made a sizeable royal staff necessary. The queen's household accounts, which included expenditures for the children, reveal the complicated pattern of residence for the year 1610, when royal journeys were planned around the birth of an infanta in Lerma and the illness of the prince in the city of Aranda del Duero. Having rendezvoused with the queen and the infantas Ana and María in the town of Lerma, where the queen intended to give birth, the king sent the Countess of Altamira and the Count of Pliego, mayordomo of the queen, to escort the prince from Madrid to Lerma. The two younger boys, on the other hand, stayed in the palace of Madrid with another of the queen's mayordomos, the Count of Arcos, and the dueña Francisca de Córdoba.

Illness forced Prince Philip to halt his journey in Aranda del Duero and miss the festivities surrounding the birth in Lerma. Lacking suitable housing close to Aranda, the king and queen moved to nearby Ventosilla to facilitate frequent visits. When continued illness prolonged the prince's stay, his parents moved to cramped quarters in the city, while the infantas remained in Lerma, along with several of the queen's ladies and the queen's mayordomo mayor, the Marquis de la Laguna. The towns of Aranda and Lerma lent money to the court to support the queen's household during this extended period. The queen herself, having spent the critical weeks of the prince's illness at his side, began, once he was out of immediate danger, to move back and forth visiting her children, including the daughter born only weeks prior.

When the prince's condition improved somewhat, his parents left him to convalesce in Aranda under the care of the Marquis de la Laguna and went to Burgos in fulfillment of a vow they had made for his health. Stopping in Lerma to visit María, who in the meantime also had fallen ill, they traveled on to San

Lorenzo and Madrid, leaving the Countess of Altamira and the queen's mayordomo, the Count of Castelmellor, to care for her. The infantas Ana and Margarita traveled separately to San Lorenzo with ladies of the queen's household.[75]

Similar arrangements the following year had the queen sometimes accompanied by one or more of her children when she moved between palaces and
the children often traveling separately from her, in various groupings, between
Madrid, San Lorenzo, Lerma, Aranda, Alcala, and Aranjuez. Which children
traveled depended on their health, housing, and activities planned for the
journey. The youngest children, for example, were more likely to remain in a
single residence for extended periods.[76] After the queen's death, Philip III was
particularly inclined to take Ana and Philip with him. The youngest children,
Fernando and Margarita, did not participate and apparently were not present
for the extended festivities planned in Lerma in 1614. From about 1618 the king
increasingly took his eldest son with him when he hunted. The prince, the princess, and María accompanied him to Portugal in 1619, while the infantes Carlos
and Fernando remained in the palace of Madrid under the supervision of the
Duke of Infantado and the Count of Benavente.[77]

Occasionally, the royal children took part in activities closely tied to the personal lives of members of their households. While nobles sponsored weddings
of lesser servants, the king and queen themselves often hosted the marriage
ceremonies of their high-ranking servants, ladies, and officials. In 1608 Prince
Philip and Ana, aged three and six and a half, officially sponsored the wedding
of Juan Fernández de Velasco, constable of Castile, and Juana de Córdoba y
Aragon, one of the queen's ladies, in the oratory of the queen. The queen and
king apparently were not present, but the prince and infanta provided a pleasant
picture for the assembled company and carried out their functions properly,
the prince wearing a sword (presumably an appropriately small one) and the
infanta hosting the bride for the traditional dinner.[78] Not long after that, at the
marriage of the sister of the queen's best friend, the seven-year-old infanta Ana
attended her first court dance.[79] Ana also participated in ceremonies that tied
the royal family closer to the Duke of Lerma's family, serving alongside her
father as godparent at the baptism of the Duke of Uceda's son and as sponsor at
the wedding of Uceda's young daughter to the admiral of Castile. She and her
father served as *padrinos* for the baptism of the Count del Cid, carried out with
all the ostentation of a state event, since the child was both a grandson of the
Duke of Lerma and the first male child born in the house of Infantado in thirty

years.[80] After the death of the queen, the infanta Ana became even more active in such events, taking the role her mother would have played.

Beyond practical arrangements and entertainment, the households helped the royal children build connections with the nobility, including young boys who served as pages and meninos. The pattern of sending children to be raised at court can be traced throughout Europe as a method of training the next generation. This practice not only taught proper behavior and etiquette but also created ties between the young nobles and between them and the royal family that served both throughout their lives.[81] Ideally, the ayo and older men appointed to the service of the royal children earned their trust and provided through their very persons a continuity in the transition from childhood to adulthood. Acquaintance with younger nobles then provided the next set of persons from among whom the future king could choose his officials, persons whose qualities he knew from his own experience. Both older and younger men in the prince's household thus served to provide stability and continuity in government, just as the women of the queen's household had provided stability during childhood.

The position of page was common throughout western Europe, although the duties and prestige associated with it varied. In Spain, pages could be attached to any number of different persons—to the king, the queen, or any of the children as they grew older and to such people as Philiberto of Savoy during his seven-year residence in the court of Spain. Housed together in residences supplied by the crown, with their own ayo, Latin master, and teachers for dancing, fencing, and riding, the royal pages served the households on a rotating basis, each young man reporting weekly to the caballerizo mayor of the king, who supervised their activities and education.[82] Originally only the sons of grandees served as royal pages, but the pages attached to the households of Queen Margarita and Philip IV as prince included a mix of the sons of great and lesser nobles and foreigners. Two pages were assigned to the prince in 1611, one in 1613 and in 1614, and thirteen in 1615, on the occasion of his marriage. Among the earliest were Luis Laso, son of the Count of los Arcos, and Diego Melchor Luis de Acuña. Later additions to the prince's household included a son of the Count of Oñate, Beltrán de Guevara, whose brother Phelipe was not a page but a menino, the son of an Italian marquis, and the son of the *corregidor* of Madrid, brother of the principal royal chaplain.[83]

Despite the apparent prestige carried by the title of page in earlier generations, by the reign of Philip III pages did not have regular personal contact with the prince or study under the same teacher as he.[84] Instead, meninos continued this tradition and experienced closer contact with the prince. *Menino* was a title of Portuguese origin that appeared in Spain after the marriage of Isabel of Portugal and Charles V in 1526. Originally a title equivalent to *page,* usage began to differentiate between the two during the marriage of María of Portugal and Philip II. The position gained prestige during Philip II's residence in Portugal in the early 1580s, according to Antonio Hurtado de Mendoza, who reported that "since Philip II returned from Portugal, any Portuguese, even if of moderate fortune, if noble, insists on being a menino."[85]

This revision of the roles of children at court gave the king and queen greater flexibility in choosing their children's closest companions and limiting their numbers, as when Philip II reduced the number of meninos attending his son to eight because he considered them a bad influence on the prince.[86] While young men from a variety of backgrounds became pages, meninos and *meninas* were most often the children of high-ranking household officials, thus reinforcing the presence at court of families with a tradition of service in royal households. Likewise, while meninos were usually the sons of great nobles, patronage offered a few exceptions to the rules; for example, the son of Rodrigo Calderón, the famously successful creature of the Duke of Lerma, was also identified as a menino.[87] The traditional title of page, on the other hand, while no longer providing significant personal contact with the prince, still allowed young men to enter the service of the crown and provided experience and familiarity with other figures at court who could aid them as patrons in their futures careers.

Young girls also filled the ranks of the nobility at court, serving as playmates to the royal children in their early years and in minor ceremonial roles in service of the queen, acting in plays and taking part in religious observances. Since the young girls who became meninas were usually the daughters of high-ranking women within the queen's household, their being received as meninas or ladies often simply formalized an already somewhat regular presence. Occasionally, as an act of charity, the royal households received an orphaned girl as a menina or a lady, providing a sort of welfare system for noblewomen whose status within the family networks had suddenly become unclear. A notable example of such accommodations is the king's grant of the titles of menina and menino to the children of Baltasar de Zúñiga after the minister and his widow died within a few months of each other. Indeed, Zúñiga's family had already resided in the palace: Philip IV had urged his widow to remain in the palace in the queen's service after her husband's death and in turn granted household offices to the children so that they also retained palace residence.[88]

Behind the web of court positions that benefited multiple members of particular families was the reality of entire families living at court. The longtime dueña Mariana Enríquez had the company of her granddaughter Mariana de Velasco, who served as menina; when the young woman died in the palace on April 1, 1620, another granddaughter, Catalina Enríquez de Velasco, was named menina on April 4. While the Count of Oñate's sons were, as we have seen, page and menino, his daughter, Ana María de Guevara, was a menina. Margarita de Tavara, who had been a lady of Queen Margarita until 1600, returned to court as a dueña in 1617, at the same time that her daughter, Francisca Luisa de Tavara, became a menina. Other meninas included Juana de Borja, who received her position when her grandmother, the Duchess of Gandía, returned to court as camarera mayor at the accession of Philip IV, and María de Guzman, the daughter of the Count-Duke of Olivares. Meninos included the young Count of Puñonrostro, whose mother, Ana Manrique, was a dueña de honor, and Diego de Sarmiento y Mendoza, whose mother, the Countess of Salvatierra, was *señora de honor* to María and whose brother was a gentleman de la cámara. Similarly, not only was the Count of Barajas a mayordomo of the king but his brother-in-law, the Count of Pliego, was a mayordomo of the queen and later of the prince and his siblings. His two daughters from his first marriage served the queen, as did María Sidonia's daughter, Margarita Zapata, who became a lady at court while still a child and remained in that position until her marriage in 1629.[89]

Matías de Novoa described Diego de Aragon as well regarded by the prince, because he had "grown up with him" as a menino. Yet his later career as a gentleman de la cámara of Philip III and in a minor diplomatic position under Philip IV in Italy does not suggest a particularly high level of access to the king. Diego de Sarmiento y Mendoza and Bernardo de Benavides also moved from being meninos to gentlemen de la boca in the early years of Philip IV's reign.[90] Gaspar de Tebes, likewise a menino, became the king's overseer of transport by mule and a gentleman de la boca. He later served as ambassador to Venice, the Empire, and France.[91] Both Beltrán and Phelipe de Guevara followed their father in service of the crown. Beltrán, along with his father, accompanied the infante Fernando to Flanders, while Phelipe served as his father's messenger from the imperial court in 1637 and was made gentleman de la cámara soon after.[92]

Changes in the prince's household marked key points in his life. At the time of his marriage, additional persons entered his service and an independent household was established. These changes may have been intended less to affect his day-to-day life than to support his status, given that his wife would be coming from France with a full entourage. Already at that time of these appointments, in 1615, one can detect the diminished influence of the Duke of Lerma. While Philip III provided household positions to the duke's loyal younger son, the Count of Saldaña, and his supporters the Count of Santisteban and Fernando de Borja, he also appointed the Duke of Uceda, Lerma's eldest son, who was already presenting himself as a challenge to his father's authority, and the Count of Olivares and the Count of Lumiares, who supported Uceda.

The situation at court can also be read in the playmates of the royal children. While the Duke of Lerma had been able to appoint a number of his female relatives to the household of Queen Margarita, in the spring of 1618, when the royal children performed a masque in El Pardo, none of their companions in the dance belonged to the extended Sandoval family. Francesca de Tavara and Madama Eli (a French companion of Princess Isabel), apparently dancing the men's parts alongside the royal brothers, partnered with Isabel, María, Sofía, Margarita Zapata, and Marianica de Velasco. Both Sofía, probably the Austrian-born dwarf who arrived in Spain with Mariana Riederer, and Margarita Zapata were connected to the court through the queen's friend María Sidonia.[93]

The attachment the royal children developed to individuals who served them in their households seems especially indicative of the ways in which personal and political relationships interacted in the structure of royal life. Court observers interpreted relationships formed during childhood as affectionate, but the consequences of such relationships were also political. On the one hand, this was exactly how the system was intended to function, as it introduced the prince to his future ministers, councilors, and friends. On the other, affection could influence him to offer what might be perceived as too much power to particular individuals. Most crucially, in the examples of Philip III and Philip IV, the favorite emerged from the royal household during the childhood of the king. Called *privado* or *valido,* terms implying both his position in the private world of the king and the value of his service, the favorite was a person for whom the prince developed a friendship or respect based on a close, daily relationship. Queens and younger brothers were also seen as having favorites, a styling of best friend that outside observers inevitably viewed as having political overtones.[94]

The Duke of Lerma's ability to control a great many household appointments at the height of his friendship with Philip III reflects both the strength of tradition and the power granted through personal affection. One of the reasons that he was permitted to dominate offices in the royal households was that so many of the appointments could be seen, within the normal workings of patronage networks, to be merited positions; that is, the people he placed in these positions had experience and traditions of family service that made their appointment natural. When the duke wrote his own defense of the honors granted him, he placed all advantages he had received firmly within a structure of reward for service.[95] Yet even the most minor positions were distributed with the letters of patrons attached, and the specific element that determined that Lerma would receive recognition of his service was the affection of the king.

The aftermath of Lerma's *privanza* illustrates the deep and lasting implications of control of the royal households. While the duke was eventually removed from court, and many of his closest male relatives followed, the breadth of his extended family's involvement at court and the attachment of members of the royal family to them made it impossible and unthinkable to remove all vestiges of Lerma's privanza from the political life of court. Thus the Countess of Lemos remained as the camarera mayor of the infanta María, and the sons of the Countess of Altamira remained in the affections of the infantes, especially of Fernando. If the granting of government offices had depended solely on the opinion of the king or his favorite and had not been not bound by the tradition of family networks and service or by affections of various members of the royal family rather than just those of the king, the upheavals at the beginning of the reigns of Philip III and Philip IV would have been even greater and the system would not have been as stable as it remained throughout the early modern period. It was a system that, although flawed, functioned in a logical manner in a world in which the political and personal lives of the royal family profoundly overlapped.

3

TEACHERS AND FORMAL INSTRUCTION

Traditions of Education

When the Spanish crown prince Philip began his formal studies in April 1612, he was just a seven-year-old entering the classroom for the first time. The event was the initial act in a process steeped in tradition that many learned treatises described and evaluated, yet it garnered little public comment other than restrained wonder that the king had chosen a person previously unknown to the Spanish court to be the prince's teacher. Almost two years earlier, in January 1610, the infanta Ana likewise had begun her formal education without creating a stir except in the ambitious heart of her teacher. Despite their rank and future, Philip and Ana were just children learning to read and write.

The experiences of the six children of Philip III and Margarita de Austria who survived to school age demonstrate the range of goals pursued in royal education. Tradition had established the age at which the children began study, the appropriate background for their teachers, and their general course of study. Yet the specific needs and circumstances of this generation also required adjustment in tradition and other choices that can be attributed both to parental experience and to the tastes of the early seventeenth century. Despite extensive commentary on education and the importance attached to the preparation of the prince, many decisions in the education of the royal children appear to have been made almost casually. Precedent, of both short and long duration, remained a strong influence, and the experiences of earlier generations provide insight into the evidence available concerning the formal education of the children of Philip III.

From the times of Catholic kings, the Spanish royal family appointed both humanists and churchmen of a variety of descriptions to educate their children. Such luminaries as the composer and playwright Juan del Encina, the historians Lucio Marineo Sículo and Pedro Martir de Angleria, and the poet Antonio Geraldini surrounded the heir of Isabel and Ferdinand, while Allessandro Geraldini focused particularly on the education of the infantas and wrote a treatise on the education of girls. The Dominican Diego de Deza was bishop of Salamanca when the monarchs named him tutor to the seven-year-old prince, while churchmen of more modest rank, including Pedro de Ampudia, Andrés de Miranda, and Juan de Ávila, taught the infantas.[1]

The teachers chosen for Archduke Charles of Burgundy, eventual heir of the Catholic Kings, reflect the blend of nationalities the future emperor would embody during his reign. His ayo was a nobleman from the Low Countries, Guillaume de Croy, sieur de Chièvres; his religious instructor was Adrian of Utrecht, the future pope Adrian VI; and his Spanish instructors included Luis Cabeza de Vaca and Pedro Ruiz de la Mota. The education of Charles's brother Ferdinand, designed by their grandfather Ferdinand the Catholic, focused more narrowly on Spain, reflecting his hope that his namesake grandson would rule Spain. All of Ferdinand's instructors were Spanish, among them Pedro Nuñez de Guzmán, Antonio de Rojas, and the bishop of Astorga, Alvaro Osorio de Moscoso.[2]

Philip II's first teacher with the title of maestro was Juan Martínez Siliceo, a learned man of humble origins who had studied mathematics and philosophy at Valencia, Rome, and Paris. He had returned to his native Spain and was earning a reputation at Salamanca, writing extensively on Aristotle and on mathematics and dialectics, when his scholarship brought him to the attention of Empress Isabel.[3] Philip II also studied under Juan Cristóbal Calvete de Estrella, known later for his account of the prince's journey to Flanders, and Honorato Juan, the Louvain-educated author of a Castilian-Valencian dictionary. Honorato Juan later also taught Philip II's son Carlos, as did an Augustinian monk named Juan de Muñatones, whose specific duties were to teach grammar and give religious instruction.[4] Muñatones, a court preacher and former confessor of the infantas María and Juana, had a reputation for austerity, while Honorato Juan, although the holder of an ecclesiastical title, apparently was not an instructor in religious subjects and is occasionally referred to specifically as Carlos's master of Latin.

Philip III's primary tutor was García de Loaysa y Girón. Son of the court chronicler, Pedro Girón, he had studied Latin and Greek at Salamanca and theology and philosophy at Alcalá. By the time of his appointment he was also the royal almoner and the primary royal chaplain, and he can be seen as combining the qualities of both humanist and religious tutors from earlier generations. In the prince's late teen years, observers alternatively described his cousin the archduke Albert as his ayo and tutor, an unofficial appointment that took place within the context of a small council of ministers charged with introducing the prince to political life.[5] Albert, highly knowledgeable in Spanish affairs, was well qualified to guide the prince as he entered the first stages of his political education. He should not be seen, however, as giving the prince formal lessons.

While the daughters of Isabel and Ferdinand received a rigorous education that rivaled their brother's, an educational choice shaped by their mother as a ruler in her own right, the education of infantas received less attention in subsequent generations.[6] Occasionally, the infantas shared the services of the tutor employed for the prince. While Philip II's sister María later had a teacher with more strictly religious qualifications appointed for her own service, she first studied with Siliceo, who initially reported equally on the progress of both the prince and the infanta.[7] Philip II's youngest sister, Juana, likewise benefited from the services of the teacher assigned to her nephew Carlos when he was a child of six and she was sixteen.[8] In this case, the difference in their ages highlights the fact that royal tutors were assigned according to the child's status rather than age. Surely the two would not have shared a classroom if the prince had been a teenager and the infanta a six-year-old. When Charles V sought a teacher specifically for his daughters, the stated goal of instruction was that they learn "to read and to write and to pray and a moderate amount of Latin in order to understand the Mass." The eventual candidate, Juan López de la Quadra, held a bachelor's degree, which was hardly equivalent to the education of the prince's tutor but apparently sufficient for instructing the infantas.[9]

While the Spanish court, like other European courts, had previously followed a tradition of having the prince study in the company of young nobles, Philip III appears to have been educated as a solitary student, probably because of the fears for his health that dominated his childhood. Several young men did participate with the prince in a presentation of academic discourses given for an audience of nobles and clergy in 1588, but that was an unusual event.[10] The children of Philip III, like their father, do not appear to have shared their education with nobles of the court. Pages, as we have seen, did not "enjoy the benefit of the instruction that is done for the prince,"[11] and there is little evidence to support the supposition that meninos shared a classroom with the prince, despite their proximity to him in other activities. While Philip III's poor health affected choices concerning his education, his children's experience may have been shaped in imitation of his, an example of how precedent, which conceptually implies an extended practice, could be shaped by individual experience.

As in earlier generations, educational planning focused primarily on the prince, and the king summoned a tutor to court specifically to teach the prince, while teachers for the other children were mostly chosen from among the royal chaplains. The oldest child, a daughter, started her education alone but eventually studied with her sisters, as the teacher first appointed for her gradually undertook the education of her younger sisters as well. The prince was the most solitary in his studies, although he may sometimes have shared his classroom with his brothers. In general, however, the two younger brothers were housed together, and teachers were appointed to instruct them together, except for the few specially appointed for Fernando in recognition of his position as archbishop of Toledo. These last instructors, although not of the stature of the prince's teacher, may account for the perception that Fernando was better educated than Carlos. The education of Philip III's younger sons, mostly separate from their older brother and further differentiated between the two of them, suggests that not only sex but also rank accounts for the lesser humanist emphasis in the education of daughters in the previous two generations.

Royal children, in Spain as elsewhere, traditionally began formal studies at age seven. The experience of Philip and Margarita's children shows some variation in this practice. While the prince began his studies at almost exactly age seven, his siblings began at various ages, depending not on a set agenda but on chance factors of convenience and circumstance. The infanta Ana, for example, was eight years and four months old when she began her formal education in January 1610. At that time, however, she already possessed basic reading and writing skills, most probably learned under the supervision of her aya. When her sister María joined her in the classroom for the first time on February 9, 1611, she was less than five years old.[12] Carlos and Fernando began their studies together despite a difference of nearly two years in their ages. As the oldest child and a girl, Ana continued in the casual learning environment of the household longer than her siblings did probably because her education lacked the urgency and public import of the prince's, but once the educational structure was in place, younger siblings were introduced into it at earlier developmental stages.

None of Philip III's daughters shared their brother's tutor as infantas occasionally had in earlier generations.

While Philip III's early choices of caretakers for his children seem to have been based largely on the advice of his favorite, the Duke of Lerma, he appears to have consulted his female relatives in appointing his daughters' tutor. Margarita de la Cruz, who was a cousin of both the king and the queen, apparently supported the appointment of Diego de Guzmán as tutor to the infanta Ana. The Jesuit had been closely acquainted not only with Sor Margarita but also with her mother—Philip III's grandmother and aunt—the empress María, who had been instrumental in making him the chaplain of the royal convent of the Descalzas Reales in Madrid, where both women lived. Queen Margarita was also acquainted with him through her frequent visits to the convent and her extended stay there while the king traveled to Valencia in 1603.[13] Although contemporary accounts emphasize the nun's influence in this decision, the queen's devotion to the Jesuits must have been influential. In his biography of the queen, Guzmán portrays her actively involved in the religious education of her children. In his journal, he notes her occasional presence in her daughter's classroom.[14] The education of the infantas closely paralleled the queen's own, suggesting that a mother might have particularly strong influence in structuring her daughter's education.

By the time the king named him tutor to the infanta Ana in early 1610, Guzmán, who had studied theology and canon law at Salamanca, had already left his position as chaplain of the Descalzas Reales in order to become royal chaplain and almoner. Within a year after his appointment as teacher, he welcomed the infanta María to his classroom, and he later taught the infanta Margarita Francisca as well. He did not have a reputation for extraordinary piety, as some royal chaplains did, nor for a particularly outstanding preaching ability. He was, however, firmly linked to the social network at court, not through the nobility but through the royal family itself.

Guzmán's position among the chaplains at court qualified him to be a royal teacher, but his office of principal almoner was apparently also a significant factor. Palace rulebooks written for Margarita's household in 1603 specifically indicate that the queen's almoner should teach the children.[15] An apparent mistake in these etiquetas may suggest something about the origin of this rule and perhaps of such rules in general. The order for the care of the infanta identifies her as María, although at the date of these orders there was only one living child, and her name was Ana. A repetition, or rather precursor, of this "mistake" appears in the etiquetas for Queen Ana, the fourth wife of Philip II, on which those for Margarita were clearly based, written before the birth of her daughter María.[16] The orders for Queen Ana's household may have been borrowed from a yet earlier source, perhaps those for the empress Isabel and her daughter María, Philip II's sister. The use of a specific name of an infanta within the orders reflects the fact that Spanish court practice often drew on particular events as precedents. It may be that the rule concerning the infanta's teacher likewise originated in an earlier generation when a royal tutor was the almoner and that a statement of fact came, through repetition, to be read as a rule. This rule was not strictly followed, although the primary tutor of Philip III, García de Loaysa, was indeed the almoner. Philip III's own experience in this matter thus reinforced the etiqueta, and the apparently careless repetition of an incorrect name may have served to emphasize that the king wished to follow precedent in structuring his wife's household.

The provision of the almoner as teacher also indicates the importance of this official, who advised the king and queen concerning their charitable works. The almoner may have been appointed precisely with his qualifications as tutor in mind. Nothing, however, in the journal Diego de Guzmán kept suggests that he expected this appointment. His journal entry on the day he learned of his appointment as tutor to the infanta Ana, January 9, 1610, practically bursts with pride at this new honor. He made special visits to the king, to the queen, and to Nuestra Señora de los Remedios, the image in the main chapel of the Mercedarian monastery of Madrid, thanking them all for the great favor shown him. In a formal expression of his gratitude, he kissed the hands of the eight-year-old infanta.[17]

From Guzmán we get a rare personal account of a royal tutor preparing himself for the task of teaching. Immediately after his visit to the monastery of the Merced, Guzmán went to speak with the confessor of the queen, perhaps expecting to discuss the queen's intentions for her daughter's education. The following day he attended the queen's mass to thank her again, then proceeded to the rooms of the infanta in order to speak with the Countess of Altamira, the infanta's aya. Unfortunately, he does not give a detailed account of his discussions with either the confessor or the aya, but it is clear that he spent the few days prior to beginning the lessons consulting with the people closest to his student. Later accounts, including a biography of the Countess of Altamira's son, assume that the aya and the tutors were commonly in contact concerning education of the royal children, "because of the similarity between the offices of Aya and Maestro of the prince and the infantes."[18]

Guzmán also prepared for teaching by writing a treatise on education, which the queen, following the tradition of earlier royal parents, commissioned. He mentions this work in his biography of the queen, although unfortunately he does not include the text, noting that it would be too lengthy. He either saw his instruction of the infanta as religiously based or chose to use religious themes to teach the skills she was to learn, commenting that he had written his treatise with the purpose "of teaching her some matters of devotion; from which [to teach] and in the style necessary for the instruction and service of Her Highness."[19]

Ana's first lesson began at three in the afternoon on Thursday, January 21, 1610, a fact duly noted in the royal chaplain's journal. In his description of the day, Guzmán treats the eight-year-old with the dignity of her rank, calling her "most serene lady infanta Doña Ana" and making a little speech "signifying first the esteem with which I undertook to serve her in that ministry and the desire that I had to succeed in it." The infanta responded with self-possession, as if she were used to directing the actions of adults, and a similar formality: while she herself sat in a chair at a table, she gave the chaplain permission to have a bench brought for his use. The tutor then began by telling her a little of the life of Saint Inés, since it was her feast day; afterward, he offhandedly mentions, he had the infanta read a passage from a book of Latin and another bit in a book of Castilian, which clearly indicates that while she was just beginning her formal studies, she had already been instructed in basic skills. He also had her take a pen and make some letters, although it does not seem that she yet knew how to write. The class lasted forty-five minutes, Guzmán comments, so as not to tire the infanta on her first day.[20] In the following days the lessons lasted an hour.

Guzmán's journal reveals a person struggling to define the roles he played. Continuing to serve as principal royal chaplain and almoner, he was not always certain how to balance his various duties. He developed patterns of instruction that adapted to the current activity and residence of the royal family; for a while he would teach in the mornings, and then he would switch to afternoon lessons for several weeks. Occasionally, he even taught late at night. During illnesses of one or more of his students, lessons would cease for several days. Once he notes that he had not given lessons because the girls had gone with their parents to a bullfight. Most of the time, Guzmán appears to have taught in the children's chambers, but that also varied. He sometimes gave lessons in the royal apartments of the Descalzas Reales convent or at the Duke of Lerma's Las Huertas home in Madrid. Once he reported giving lessons in the library of El Escorial. Another time he started lessons in the gallery of the palace of El Escorial, only to have the king and queen pass through and casually take the children with them.[21]

Often he asked the king whether he should accompany the court to perform his roles there or stay with Ana in order to provide her lessons. In a few cases he was told to travel with the infantas, but he was barely able to complete a day's instruction before being summoned to rejoin the king and queen. In other cases his duties as chaplain clearly took precedence over those as teacher. In the autumn of 1610, a year in which Saint James's day fell on a Sunday, the king and queen sent him to Santiago de Compostela "to earn the jubilee," that is, the particular blessings to be gained by visiting Santiago that year.[22] Accompanied by a retinue of more than twenty friars and chaplains, he began his month-long journey by way of the town of Lerma, where the queen's camarera waited to give him a gift from the queen to carry to the saint's tomb. It is not clear whether the queen and king were thought to receive direct benefit from commissioning this journey or whether they wanted him to benefit from it, which would benefit them by association. Nor is it clear whether anyone undertook to instruct the infantas during his absence.

The queen apparently wished Diego de Guzmán to teach the prince as well as her daughters and may have imagined all her children studying together under his guidance. Tradition was against such a practice, and since the queen died in October 1611, it is impossible to know whether she would have been able to influence this matter. Already in February 1611 Luis Cabrera de Córdoba reported a visit of the bishop of Cuenca to court and the general assumption that he had been summoned to be the tutor of the prince. The bishop then returned to his diocese, from which, rumor had it, he would be called when wanted, "but up to now it is not known whether they have named him for teacher of His Highness."[23] The assumption that the bishop of Cuenca would be named maestro was probably based on his previous service as teacher of Archduke Albert.[24] Perhaps, however, given the bishop's advanced age, Philip III had summoned him to court to hear his advice concerning the appointment of a tutor rather than actually to appoint him.

Close to a year later, Cabrera de Córdoba expressed the wonder of the court when the king named Galcerán Albanell to teach the prince. A Catalan knight of the order of Calatrava, Albanell was a widower whose only apparent connection to court was a son who had briefly been a page in the king's service.[25] Although the chronicler often described the court as shocked at appointments, both earlier court rumor concerning the bishop of Cuenca and the availability of qualified candidates near at hand, including Guzmán, fed the response. The king, however, had been informed of Albanell's qualities and had sent both his mayordomo mayor and Juan de Idiáquez to converse with the candidate in the months prior to his appointment. The king may indeed have purposely chosen a person with no strong ties to court and thus no association with nobles who either supported or opposed the Duke of Lerma.

Less is known about the activities of Galcerán Albanell than about those of Diego de Guzmán. Albanell became maestro of the prince on March 25, 1612, and apparently served as teacher until his consecration as archbishop of Granada in January 1621.[26] Despite his higher status as tutor to the prince, chroniclers rarely note his presence, perhaps because, unlike Guzmán, he held no offices at court other than that of maestro. While Guzmán can be seen as slowly building his position and career at court, Albanell came to court specifically to undertake the job of tutor. Observers described him as well learned but provided little evidence of his background or education. They did not describe Albanell as belonging to a religious order beyond the secular Calatrava or apply any further title to him than *caballero* at the time of his appointment as tutor to the prince in 1612.[27] A few months into his tenure, the Countess of Lemos provided an equally unrevealing assessment in a letter to her son, describing the tutor as a "very good man, certainly holy, and, they say, of very good letters."[28] Later writers credited him with a great knowledge of "eastern languages" and cited his authorship of a Latin panegyric on the marriage of Philip IV and Isabel de Bourbon and a now-lost history of Spain.[29] Despite his purported piety, he apparently did not possess religious office until late in his years as tutor of the prince. This did not prevent his appointment to high church office once his teaching days were over.

Palace records give us some glimpses into Albanell's status at court. When he began his work, he was assigned housing at court or funds equivalent to it and 200,000 maravedis a year, half in normal salary and half in aid of his expenses until an appropriate equivalent income could be assigned him. In addition, he received daily meals and certain extraordinary expenses equivalent to those of a mayordomo, as well as the services of a doctor and medicines for his personal use.[30] As the prince's tutor, Albanell received various forms of advice. An anonymous author sent him eighteen lines of Latin epigrams concerning the achievements of Philip II, enclosed in a letter specifically identifying Albanell in the address as tutor of the prince, circumstances that suggest the lines' proposed use as teaching texts.[31] More casually, the Countess of Lemos reported to her son that the tutor had shown the prince a "letra" written by someone she calls Hernandico, perhaps her grandson, as an example of good handwriting.[32]

Albanell's mayordomo, Gaspar Piquero de Menes, also participated in the education of the prince, and records relating to his service provide rare proof that the infantes studied with the prince or at least shared the tutor's services. In a memorial of his service, he called Albanell "teacher of the king and of Their Highnesses the infantes" and described his own primary work for the tutor as writing out "all the items of grammar that were given Their Highnesses."[33] Piquero de Menes, in his late twenties during his service at court, was a priest who had studied at the universities of Granada and Oviedo and taught briefly in Granada. Albanell described his abilities in glowing terms when he nominated him for a vacant benefice in Granada, although he did not mention his former servant's service in the education of the prince and the infantes.[34]

The remaining tutors of the infantes Carlos and Fernando are almost invisible at first glance. Like Guzmán, these men had other responsibilities at the court by which they were primarily identified. These tutors of the younger boys, like the tutor of their sisters, belonged to religious orders and held positions in the royal chapel. In a pattern common throughout Europe, the education of younger sons was considered less important,[35] despite high mortality rates, which might easily have resulted in a younger brother's becoming the heir.

Carlos and Fernando both received instruction from Padre Simón de Rojas, who is better known as the confessor of their sister-in-law Isabel de Bourbon. His tenure as teacher, however, predated his appointment as confessor, dating from about 1615, when the passage of the court through Valladolid for the marriage journey of the infanta Ana brought him once again to the attention of the king, who knew his reputation from the years in which the court had resided in that city. Rojas's biographer reports the great emptiness the king felt when he had to leave the friar and the rejoicing of the court when Rojas obeyed his superior's order to move to Madrid. Philip entrusted Rojas with the education of his younger sons, saying that he wanted to see them Christians more than great lords. Given this instruction and the reputation of Rojas, whose only known works are sermons and an extensive treatise on the nature of prayer, it seems likely that his program of education was primarily religious in nature. He apparently served in this position, along with performing other duties, until his death in September 1624.[36]

Despite their common early training, Carlos and Fernando do not appear to have received the same education overall. Years later, the chief minister and favorite of Philip IV commented that Carlos "has no knowledge of letters," while Fernando "has very great grounding, not only in humanist letters but also in the divine."[37] This difference in accomplishments may have stemmed from ability or inclination but is most likely attributable to Fernando's position as archbishop of Toledo. In addition to a few teachers appointed for his service alone, all of the officials holding the titles of canon or dean of the cathedral of Toledo were considered in some manner instructors of the cardinal-infante. Philip III articulated this on his deathbed when he specifically commended the education of Fernando to the governor of the archbishopric of Toledo.[38] Indeed the cathedral chapter of Toledo wrote to Philip IV just months into his reign requesting that the king send the infante Fernando to them. While they emphasized the benefit the city of Toledo would derive from having its archbishop in residence, they must have also considered it their right and duty to complete the education of their young archbishop. The king thanked them for their concern and told them he would consider the matter carefully.[39] The infante, however, was not sent to Toledo. Nonetheless, his position and his ecclesiastical household may have contributed to the form of his continued and separate education.

Three teachers of the infante Fernando appear in various accounts and records. Francisco de Salamanca, a canon of Ávila, is mentioned in household accounts of 1624. Little evidence is readily available concerning his tenure, but his appointment as teacher appears to have overlapped that of Padre Rojas. Given his position as an official of the church, his instruction may have dealt more with the young archbishop's institutional knowledge of the church.[40] Another teacher, Cristóval de Guzmán y Santoyo, was a canon at the University of Salamanca at the time of the death of Philip III. Delivering a eulogy of the king, he touched on points, including the metaphor presenting the king as the sun, that show him to have been of a similar mind to the advisers of the new king.[41] Guzmán y Santoyo resided at court by at least August 1625, when Diego de Guzmán identifies him as "doctor Guzmán, maestro of the lord infante cardinal" and reports him as preaching before the king in the royal chapel. After the departure of the cardinal-infante from Spain in 1633, the teacher was named bishop of Palencia, an office he held until his death in 1656.[42]

A third teacher connected to the household of Fernando, Bernardino Manrique de Torres y Portugal, may have taught both of the younger boys. Mentioned in a document of 1627 as a steward of the cardinal-infante and canon of Toledo, Manrique was well connected at court. The younger brother of the Count of Villardonpardo, he was also the nephew of Agustín Mexia Carrillo of the Council of State and a distant relative of the Count of Lemos. Two of his nephews were meninos of the queen. In 1627 he was appointed *sumiller de cortina,* a position with both courtly and religious implications, whose duty it was to oversee the provision and proper use of the curtain or screen used to shield the royal family from the public eye during religious services.[43]

In addition to the primary tutors, other teachers specialized in both the arts and the sciences. The Dominican painter Fray Juan Bautista Mayno taught Philip IV the art of painting. The subject matter of his most famous work, the *Recapture of Bahía,* depicting the Count-Duke of Olivares crowning Philip IV with a laurel amid scenes of war, communicates a general sense of painting as instructive and in service of the crown. The foreground of the painting, however, focuses on the scene of a man being treated for serious wounds under the watchful eyes of a group of people, suggesting that the artist had in mind moral as well as political lessons when he formulated his work.[44] While we do not know details about the nature of this instruction, Julián Gallego identifies a painting of John the Baptist as having been painted by Philip in 1619 and affirms that the king continued to paint throughout his life, citing a little-known painting depicting him in middle age seated at an easel.[45]

A variety of sources converge to yield the name of an English instructor for the infanta María. To support a request for royal aid, the widow of "Jacobo Vadefort" described him as having been maestro of the infanta, as well as an interpreter between Inquisition judges and their English prisoners. While there is no evidence that María mastered the English language, a *relación* published during the 1623 visit of the Prince of Wales reports that she began to study at that time. Francisco de Jesús placed "Jacobo de Valdesfort" as an interpreter between himself, Olivares, and Buckingham, describing him as an English Catholic who had previously been a prominent Puritan. James Howell likewise reported "Mr. Wadsworth" as teaching the infanta English, along with a Father Boniface. He may also have written a grammar for her. Elsewhere, a James Wadsworth is identified as the chaplain of Cornwallis during his 1605 visit, who, studying Catholicism while in Spain, decided to convert.[46]

Various accounts also mention dancing teachers; their work can be considered educational as much as recreational, since numerous authors comment on the value of dancing in teaching proper comportment to a king. Dominguez Ortiz refers to the Italian Julio Cesar Firrufino as a mathematics instructor for Philip IV. Firrufino's technical books on artillery focus on the underlying geometric and mathematical principles of the art and are indeed laid out as textbooks, with examination questions at the end of each section. Their dedications to captains general of the artillery rather than to the king and the identification of the author as "catedrático" of geometry and artillery suggest that the Italian may not have instructed the king personally but instead taught at Philip IV's short-lived royal academy for nobles. He may have been the "king's teacher" in that he worked for him, or the book itself may have been the instruction he gave the king.[47] A few stray references identify Francisco Roales as a royal chaplain who taught math to the infante Fernando. Although his status as a chaplain suggests a connection to Fernando's ecclesiastical office, the connection of math instruction with military instruction may suggest that Roales served when the infante was preparing to become a military commander, in his early twenties, rather than during his childhood.[48] Roales is mainly known for publishing a tract critical of the Jesuits. Its publication in Milan in 1634 may place him in the infante's entourage of that year.

One of Philip IV's most prominent teachers was the Portuguese mapmaker and engineer Juan Bautista Lavaña (João Baptista Lavanha), whom the chronicler Gil González Dávila called "maestro of Your Majesty in cosmography."[49] Lavaña had been in the service of Spanish and Portuguese kings for several decades when he became Philip IV's tutor. Born sometime in the 1550s to parents of Jewish ancestry, he may have studied in Italy at the instigation of King Sebastian of Portugal, returning to Lisbon by the time Philip II began to reside there in 1581.[50] In late 1582, in an appointment perhaps precipitated by the visit of Juan de Herrera to Lisbon that year, Philip II named Lavaña to serve the crown in matters of cosmography, geography, and topography and as reader of mathematics at court. He also assigned Lavaña an assistant and granted him an income of 400 ducats a year, housing at court, and medical provisions. This appointment, which resulted in Lavaña's becoming chair of mathematics at Herrera's Academy of Sciences in Madrid and numerous other royal appointments, including those of principal "cosmographer," royal engineer, and royal chronicler of Portugal, kept him in the employ of the Spanish crown until his death in 1624.[51]

In his will, Lavaña described himself as the teacher of "His Majesty, his father, and his grandfather, and of King Sebastian,"[52] and he may also have had close contact with Philiberto of Savoy, but his tenure as teacher of Philip IV is most easily discerned. Cortesão, in his collection of documents dealing with the lives and careers of Portuguese mapmakers, found several documents calling Lavaña the teacher of Philip IV as prince, but he provides no record that Lavaña directly instructed the other kings. Lavaña's absence from Madrid during much of the 1590s also suggests that he was not as active in the education of Philip III as he was in that of Philip IV. This pattern of evidence suggests that calling the Portuguese cartographer a royal teacher meant different things in the different reigns: kings commissioned his work, so that it instructed them even when he was not officially a teacher; he also served as a teacher at an academy designed by the king and was therefore a teacher under the king's direction; and finally, he was indeed the appointed tutor of the prince in certain subjects.

Lavaña was a dedicated scholar, known especially for his map of the kingdom of Aragon, which continued to be used well into the eighteenth century. He undertook a variety of research-intensive projects at the request of the king and at his own instigation. In 1601 Philip III asked Archduke Albert to aid Lavaña in his research in Flanders concerning the history of the royal family. This was apparently part of the same project mentioned in several Simancas documents requesting funds to publish the genealogy of the king.[53] Lavaña never finished this project, and in his will he entreated his son to take that part of the work that was clean and finished to the king, throw himself at the king's feet, and beg his pardon that the work had not been completed. With similar royal aid, Lavaña had undertaken a larger project describing all of Spain, for which he gathered a series of relaciones concerning Andalusia. As principal chronicler of the kingdom of Portugal, he also began a history of King Sebastian, and in his apparent position as coordinator of the royal journey to Portugal in 1619, he wrote an account of that journey and the festivities prepared for it. Lavaña's drafts for various genealogical tables of noble families, most of them Portuguese, also provide insight into his work, revealing the extent to which an early modern genealogist was a historian and suggesting other sources of income for the royal tutor through private commissions.[54]

In recognition of their services, royal teachers received various types of rewards in addition to whatever salary they were granted. A painter, such as Mayno, may have received no further recompense than continued patronage of his artistic projects. Firrufino, if he is to be called a teacher, received the mixed blessing of having his work on artillery so highly prized that it was considered a state secret and the king prohibited its publication for several decades. (In the prologue to his 1642 work, Firrufino explains that he had been ordered by the king not to publish his work some years earlier.) Lavaña received not only support for his work but also court appointments for his sons, one of whom continued to serve at court well into the 1640s. The royal family attended the consecration of his two daughters as nuns in the convent of the Concepción of Madrid, and two high-ranking noblewomen served as sponsors.[55] For these more specialized teachers, the completion of the formal education of their charges did not necessarily signal a change in their careers. They held other offices at court in which they continued to function, and, moreover, their presence was not so weighty as to be problematic for their students when the royal children began to play their adult roles.

The most common reward for primary academic tutors was advancement in an ecclesiastical career. Throughout the sixteenth century, tutors of the prince were rewarded with prestigious church offices. Receiving such a position did not always mean that the tutor would immediately leave court or that he would cease to have influence. Philip II's tutor Siliceo did not immediately relinquish his duties as tutor when he was named bishop of Cartagena, and years later, as archbishop of Toledo, he continued to influence the ecclesiastical policy of the crown.[56] More frequently, however, the recipient of such a position would see his influence at court decrease. García de Loaysa y Girón, named archbishop of Toledo in 1598, apparently felt, as former royal tutor and primate of Spain, that he had the moral authority to criticize aspects of the new regime. Cabrera de Córdoba, however, described a rift between the king and his former tutor and mentioned the report on Philip III's education, to which Loaysa contributed, as a factor. Although the king ostensibly held Loaysa in high regard and rewarded him for his service with the enviable position of archbishop, some court observers attributed Loaysa's death soon after the accession of Philip III to shock suffered after a public disagreement with the Duke of Lerma and his realization that he no longer had the ear of the king.[57]

It may be that Philip III and Philip IV chose to appoint royal tutors to archiepiscopal sees at a distance from court exactly for the purpose of removing the holder from a position of influence. Several months before the death of Philip III, the king appointed Galcerán Albanell archbishop of Granada. This promotion may have been related to the appointment in the previous year of Baltasar de Zúñiga as the prince's ayo, an indication of the increased emphasis on the political education of the teenaged prince. Although Albanell expressed a tolerance for the occasional or even extended absence of a prelate from his church,[58] he left for his see relatively quickly. He may have chosen to remove himself from possible conflict arising from the appointment of the new ayo, but a clue to his attitude toward court is suggested by his involvement in events leading to the Duke of Lerma's dismissal.[59] A few years prior, Albanell had apparently complained to the king about Lerma's poor performance as ayo to the prince. Taking into account that his message might be unwelcome, Albanell offered to retire, provided he received payment for his debts and service. Rather than relieving him of his position, Philip III made Albanell abbot of the nearby monastery of Alcalá el Real. This gave him an income, which was ostensibly part of his complaint, but kept him close to Madrid, where he could continue his instruction of the prince. That Albanell was kept close at hand indicates that the king had no wish to remove him from court and suggests that he hoped to satisfy the maestro's grievances on one account in order to win his silence on another. Albanell does not seem to have had any enemies at court. If he incurred the enmity of Lerma through his criticisms, the consequences were apparently minimal, since the duke left court more than two years before the tutor did. Nonetheless, Albanell chose to move rather quickly into the archbishopric granted him in September 1620.

In contrast to the apparently neutral presence of Albanell, at least one anonymous author described Diego de Guzmán as a negative influence or perhaps as a critic at court in the early years of Philip IV's reign. His appointment to the archbishopric of Seville on July 30, 1625, therefore, may represent both a reward for service and an attempt to remove him from court. Indeed, the speed with which his several offices and incomes were distributed among others, at least two of them relatives of the king's favorite, emphasizes the advantage to some in his leaving the court.[60] In 1625 Guzmán's sole remaining student at court was the infanta María, and his journal provides no evidence to indicate that she was still receiving active instruction at age nineteen. Although Guzmán expressed great satisfaction at receiving the prestigious archbishopric, he did not seem at all anxious to leave Madrid. While undoubtedly a man of the cloth, he had always functioned within the social confines of Madrid. He had built his career based on connections, and he noted that the happiest years of his life had been those spent as chaplain of the Descalzas Reales.[61] So it was that more than a year later, on November 22, 1626, a chronicler of the royal court, Jerónimo Gascón de Torquemada, reported that "the archbishop of Seville, Don Diego de Guzmán, departed from this court for his church in Seville; very much against his will, for he regretted very deeply having to leave the court and palace."[62]

Even after leaving royal service, both Guzmán and Albanell maintained ties to the court. Albanell felt that his moral influence obligated him to express his concern over the activities of Philip IV. In a letter to the new king's favorite that was widely copied and circulated by critics of the new regime, the former tutor admonished the favorite for countenancing the young king's incognito nighttime excursions into the city. His advice in this matter echoed mirrors of princes in asserting the king's duty to be an exemplar of good behavior.[63] Albanell also maintained a steady correspondence with the king over issues of his see. These letters allow us a glimpse into the uncompromising personality of the archbishop. In the early months of his tenure, he argued with the city of Granada over the allocation of the charitable resources of the archbishopric and requested that the king specifically order the president and chancellery of Granada to respect their new archbishop. He continued to employ a somewhat didactic tone toward the king, explaining, for example, that the most learned men might not be the best candidates for certain available benefices in rural parishes and reminding the king of his duty to help the archbishop reward his servants with ecclesiastical offices.[64]

Guzmán's continued ties to court took a more courtly form: he dedicated a book he had commissioned on the life of the sainted king Fernando III to the infante Fernando.[65] In addition, he remained sufficiently in the mind of the court to be named to accompany the infanta María on her marriage journey in 1630. As in earlier cases, however, the presence of the teacher appears to have posed a difficulty for the king during the transition from instruction to rule. Perhaps the continued presence of any official who had been in a position of personal authority over the prince or his siblings during childhood created a tension between respect and power. Granting high office to a former teacher allowed the king to diminish the authority of the teacher without dishonoring him. The removal of each of these people from court may have aided the transition of their students from childhood to adulthood.

Texts and Methods of Teaching

One wonders what a mathematician and philosopher, such as Juan Martínez Siliceo, and doctors of theology and canon law, such as García de Loaysa y Girón and Diego de Guzmán, did when faced with the task of teaching a seven-year-old child to read and write. In general, it appears that royal tutors did not conceptualize a difference between instructing children and instructing adults, although evidence of teaching methods scattered among the experiences of the generations does suggest some adjustment to the needs of childhood.

In an instruction written for the education of his nephews, Albert and Wenceslaus, during the time they resided at the Spanish court, Philip II provided a course of study that emphasized the Latin classics, especially Cicero, Terence, and a Latin history of Alexander the Great. Translation exercises focused particularly on the letters of Cicero, considered the height of Latin eloquence. Philip indicated that the archdukes should speak Latin throughout the hours of study, although he also designated time for writing in German and Spanish. On Sundays and festival days, the archdukes read the religious works of Luis de Granada and various chronicles rather than classical works.[66]

Traces of this instruction can be found throughout the experiences of several generations. The daily schedule of Don Carlos as described by the prince's ayo is similar in many aspects to that followed by the archdukes, including set times for prayer and structured conversation, suggesting a standard set of activities for male royal children.[67] Likewise, the historians Lucio Marineo Sículo and Pedro Martir de Angleria engaged Prince Juan in literary conversation, while Maestro Siliceo reported in 1540 that the future Philip II "has progressed in speaking Latin enough that no other language is spoken in all of the time of study."[68] Honorato Juan became the prince's teacher through an almost casual arrangement in which he and the humanist Juan Ginés de Sepúlveda discussed topics in Latin in the prince's presence, with the intention of increasing his appreciation of the language.[69] But Honorato Juan had also studied at the University of Louvain under Vives. If he employed Vives's techniques once he was named tutor, Philip in this period would have found himself keeping notebooks and writing rather than focusing on the spoken word as Siliceo had done. If we may further infer some of Juan's pedagogical concerns from his writings, his authorship of a Castilian-Valencian dictionary implies an interest in language and in the problem of separate kingdoms under one crown, both of use to a prince such as the future Philip II.[70]

While Latin was often spoken in the classroom, vernacular languages in particular were taught through exposure to strong speakers, often within the context of the household. The daughters of Philip II and Isabel de Valois learned French from two ladies in their mother's household, Mesdemoiselles de Sainct-Ana and de Sainct-Legier. The queen's entourage also provided a French tutor, Matthieu Bossulus, to the prince Don Carlos.[71] A similar matter of convenience brought about Philip III's study of French under Jehan Lhermite. Like the French instructors of the prince's elder half-siblings, this instructor's primary identification at court was not as a teacher. Years later, in repeated petitions for aid and then for payment of that aid, he cited his "long and loyal service and particularly for instruction in the French language," while court documents continued to describe him simply as a former member of the royal household.[72] We have already seen that María learned English, not from a teacher skilled in the subject, but from a native speaker whose primary duty was as an interpreter for the Inquisition.

Siliceo also used texts prepared by Barnabé de Busto, maestro of the pages in the palace. Busto, an able and accomplished scholar who had translated Erasmus's *Institutio* into Spanish, had been actively involved in teaching for many years. Although his works apparently no longer exist, their titles—*Introduciones grammaticas* (1533) and *Arte para aprender a leer y escrivir* (1535)—suggest that they were practical and basic texts.[73] A few books also suggest some of the methods used to instruct the children of Philip II: Pedro de Guevara's *Arte general y breve,* drawing on the work of Raimund Lull, and his *Nueva y sutil invención,* presenting grammar in the form of games, were both designed to teach the infantas Catalina Micaela and Isabel Clara Eugenia. Lull's art, more a method of organizing thought to reveal truth and for the purpose of meditation than a method of teaching, becomes, in Guevara's work, a charming set of charts, wheels, and verses of knowledge that may have been used to structure lessons.[74] Another lesson presented as a game involved the use of multicolored cards, which the humanist Pedro Simón Abril described as a tool for teaching Prince Diego to read and write miraculously quickly.[75]

In addition to learning lessons in the form of games, the royal children were also rewarded for their studies. This can be seen in a negative light, as when Don Carlos's ayo commented that the prince did not listen to his tutor and would not even joust or fence unless he was offered a reward.[76] His brother, Philip III, reacted more positively on such occasions as an essay competition with his meninos in which, perhaps not surprisingly, he won two first prizes.[77] Another prize resulted from a private bet made by the eight-year-old prince with his tutor concerning whether he could memorize all the nominatives in a given Latin lesson before their next meeting, a feat he accomplished by waking up before dawn on the appointed day and studying in bed. Despite the obvious spirit shown by the young prince in this episode, the chronicler recording the incident commented that it revealed his obedience, suggesting observers' preoccupation with the prince's acquisition of this quality.[78]

We have some evidence of the future Philip III's learning process in an exercise book preserved in the Biblioteca Nacional in Madrid.[79] Written mostly in the summer of 1588, the book contains early versions of Philip III's rubric. Here we can see his childish hand first copying out rules of Latin grammar, then a short version of the instruction of Saint Louis to his son and selections from Aristotle in Latin and Spanish. The book has margins marked in pencil, probably prepared by the tutor or his assistant. Within the grammar, which is written in Spanish, is a note in a mature hand—"this means that each name ending in A is of the feminine gender such as . . ."—that appears to be a correction. This note is then dutifully repeated by the prince each time he comes to a similar need to explain, suggesting that Philip had written a portion of the lesson, which was then corrected before he continued. On the final page of this exercise is the date "23 jullio" written three times and crossed out twice. In the *Institutiones* of Saint Louis, red and then gold lettering is used to highlight the first letter of each phrase. The switch in colors suggests that the copying work was completed over time, as does a date of "18 de Agosto 1588 S. Lorenzo" on the first page and "yo el príncipe 24 de Setiembre 1588 S. L." on the final page. These various dates suggest that this notebook was an ongoing work assigned to the prince from July to September 1588 (by chance the months in which the Spanish Armada sailed against England). Alternatively, it is possible, given the improvement in handwriting from the earlier to later exercises, that the notations of July are from a previous year, after which the notebook was put aside and resumed some time later.

A published edition of Julius Caesar with Philip III's handwritten notes in the margin is listed in the inventory of the portion of the royal library that merged with the Biblioteca Nacional of Spain. We can assume that Philip III's scholarship in Latin reached the level necessary to read Julius Caesar in the original; the king may even have translated it as a teenager. Philip also translated select letters of Cicero, as had his cousins Albert and Wenceslaus, an assignment that may allow us to assume other parallels between the education that Philip II designed for his son and that he designed for his nephews.[80]

Translations also played an important part in Philip IV's education, although his major effort in this regard took place outside the formal classroom. Philip IV undertook an extensive project, a translation of Guicciardini's history of

Italy, when he was already king. Among the many reasons he cited for this project was the desire to learn Italian. The king valued the study of language highly. In his introduction to the translation, he commented that he had learned and knew well all the languages of Spain—"mine, the Aragonese, the Catalan, and the Portuguese"—so that his subjects would not be obligated to learn his language in order to bring their concerns to him. In addition, since he hoped to visit his subjects in Flanders someday, he learned French, "studying it and ordering that some servants in my house that knew it spoke to me continually in it; a mode that is, in my judgment, very beneficial for understanding any foreign language."[81] By his account, he learned to understand French well but to speak it only moderately well. Although he mentions the advantage of having members of his household speak French, he does not mention his French wife as a source of knowledge of the language.

But Philip emphasized his effort to learn Italian, "for that part of Europe being so illustrious, as is known, and having emerged from those provinces such great subjects in all professions, and also since [Italian] is commonly used and almost ordinary in Germany and in all its hereditary states that for reasons of blood and public policy concern me." Philip claimed that even without these personal ties and political reasons, he would have studied Italian in order to read its literature and so chose to translate a work of Italian history in order to increase his understanding of the language. Philip IV chose Guicciardini in particular for his elegant and concise language and in order to continue the favor shown to the historian and his descendants by Charles V and Philip II. Although he eventually translated the entire twenty volumes of Guicciardini's history, he originally focused on volumes 8 and 9, which had not yet been translated. These volumes suited him especially well, "because the materials they treat are generous, illustrious, noble, and worthy of being known by persons who occupy a position similar to mine."[82]

Beyond naming various benefits to be gained from translating, the king provided further insight into royal education in an epilogue to his translation, identifying several books that had helped him learn the duties of a king. While he mentions having studied literature and works of philosophy, the books he specifically names are all histories, most of them based on the reigns of particular kings. In addition to histories of twelve particular reigns, he lists two volumes of "Varones Ilustres," one by Fernán Pérez de Guzmán, appended to the history of Juan II, and one by Hernando del Pulgar, histories of "both Indies," of Flanders and the war in Flanders, of France, of Germany and its wars, of the Roman campaign, and of the history and schism of England, by which he must have meant the famous work by the Jesuit Pedro de Rivadeneira, and finally Roman histories by Livy, Tacitus, and Lucian.[83]

Philip also expressed his interest in geography, a subject closely related to history, as a method of learning the nature of a country. Perhaps having such a noted scholar as Juan Bautista Lavaña teach him the subject encouraged his particular interest in it. The works of Lavaña comprise a few of the known textbooks used by Philip IV and perhaps by his siblings. His "Descripción del universo" (Description of the universe) and "Compendio de la geographia" (Compendium of geography) focus in a scholarly way on the physical description of his subjects.[84] The first of these, dedicated to the prince at San Lorenzo in 1612, is a beautifully illustrated discussion of the earth and the heavens, beginning with an explication of the mathematical knowledge that underlies observation of the physical world and moving through measurements of the seasons and movements of the sun to descriptions of the spheres that held earth and heaven together. The geography treatise, a simpler text, provides a detailed description of all the known world, naming rivers and mountains in remote parts of Asia and the Americas, while ignoring political and national designations. His reliable map of Aragon, although published for a wider audience, can also be seen as an invaluable tool for the education of his royal student.

The journal of the tutor Diego de Guzmán reveals a lively interest in the places he visited and suggests that he too put a high value on the study of history. During the royal family's extended residence in Segovia in the summer of 1609, Guzmán compiled and presented to the king a short history of the city, including descriptions of its founding myths and its religious institutions, an apparently spontaneous act that suggests his already existing interest in research and instruction. Like his short history of Segovia, the subjects Guzmán taught appear occasionally to have been chosen through chance association, just as his first lesson began with the story of Saint Inés, not because of particular lessons to be learned, but because it was the saint's day. A list of books he took with him on a royal journey of 1612 suggest other subjects he may have chosen to present to his students. These include devotional works, a history of Spain, a *Filosofía moral de principes* (probably the work by Juan de Torres), works of Rivadeneira, Seneca, Livy, and Ovid, a French grammar and unnamed French books, the *Confessions* of Saint Augustine, and *Amadis of Gaul*.[85] Unless the tutor packed these books entirely for his own use, we can assume that his young charges had begun to learn Latin and that the infanta Ana, who months earlier had been officially contracted to marry the king of France, was learning the language of her future home. In addition, the inclusion of *Amadis of Gaul* encourages one to think that the royal family indulged in recreational reading and shared some popular reading interests.

Padre Rojas also taught the infantes through historical example, although his examples were religious as well. He began by explaining the lives of saintly Spanish royalty to the infantes: San Hermenegildo, praised for placing greater value on his religion than on the throne of Spain; King Fernando III, glorifying heaven by ridding the kingdom of so many Moors and consecrating their temples to God; and Queen Isabel of Portugal, noted for her great charity and her personal tending of the poor and ill. If the infantes were not called to such heroic works, he noted, they could at least give alms to the poor. From these he moved to the examples of Saint Isabel, queen of Hungary, whose journey to Santiago he hoped would instill in them devotion to relics, and of the "Spanish" emperor, Theodosius, who was willing to suffer the penance prescribed by Ambrose, bishop of Milan. In an interesting acknowledgment of the potentially international nature of the future roles of the infantes, Rojas also taught them the lives of saints of other countries in which they might be called to serve. In these lessons, he also chose royal saints, such as Heinrich in the house of Bavaria, Leopold in Austria, and Amadeo in Savoy, so that the lessons had the double impact of religious and familial example.[86] He was able to find an example from almost every country of Europe, demonstrating the range of careers considered possible for the infantes. Rojas is presented as telling his students these stories rather than assigning reading. The only specific book mentioned as playing a role in the instruction of the infantes was *Tratado de la excelencia del sacrificio de la ley evangelica,* by the Trinitarian Diego de Guzmán (not the Jesuit tutor of the same name), a text on the meaning of the Mass, published in 1594 and dedicated to García de Loaysa, the tutor of Philip III.

Other books that the royal children could reasonably be expected to have known are those listed in an inventory made of their mother's books after her death.[87] This list contains more than three hundred books, divided mostly among subjects in religion and history. Of the religious books, some are devotional, while others include saints' lives, guides to moral behavior, and Christian philosophy, which as a group can be seen as books aimed to instruct and improve the individual. The books of history, as well as related subjects in geography, reveal a strong Spanish focus and a secondary attention to Habsburg lands in general. Family members figure prominently among the histories and among accounts of funeral speeches and eulogies. Several histories of religious orders also appear, most of them primarily Spanish, as are most of the saints whose lives are recorded. A few German-language books serve as reminders of the queen's native land, but the very small sums assigned to them suggest that they were books of personal rather than monetary value or, alternatively, that the assessors of the queen's estate attached little value to German works.

Several works in Queen Margarita's library duplicate books identified by Philip IV as important to his own education. Of particular note is Rivadeneira's history of the schism in England, since Philip IV later faced the question of Spain's relationship with England on a level that particularly addressed the question of religion when he considered the possible marriage of his sister to an English prince. Rivadeneira also wrote a tract on the virtues of a Christian prince, which Philip IV most likely read. Diego de Guzmán took books by this author with him on the royal journey in 1612, suggesting the likelihood that the infanta María also eventually read the account of the schism, which may have informed her own opinions on the English marriage.

The preponderance of history books in the various lists of texts indicates an important approach to royal education. Both theory and practice recognized the study of history as an important method of instruction, combining learning through example with learning through aphorisms. When a young prince learned the stories of his grandparents, he developed both a pride in achievements to which he had a personal connection and a more general sense of strategy, policy, and admirable personal qualities. Given the usefulness of such lessons, it is not surprising that numerous royal tutors wrote books of history, including García de Loaysa y Girón's histories of the Gothic kingdom and of the church in Toledo and Galcerán Albanell's "Historia de España compendiada," no longer extant.

Despite the popularity of historical study among authors of treatises on education, few of these works analyze the lessons to be learned from such study.[88] While theoretically humanists viewed history as a treasury of examples for moral philosophy, its role in practice appears more concrete. Philip IV comments on the usefulness of history to a king as follows: "Reading histories also seemed very essential to me in pursuing my purposes, since they are the true school in which the Prince and King will find examples to follow, cases to note, and ways to guide the business of his Monarchy to good results."[89] For Philip as for others, it was as if the stories were simply to be presented and absorbed. The lessons to be learned were not abstract. Instead, the student filed them away for use when he or she encountered similar situations. This approach to the uses of history reflects not humanist theories of moral education but the overwhelming interest in precedent within the early modern decision-making process and indeed the stake that royal government had in maintaining a static view of history and the structures of power depicted in it. In this conceptualization of history, drawing attention to a specific historical event was meant directly to address current problems. Counselors of the king cited particular events to support arguments for following a particular policy, as when the Council of State reminded the king of the fate of Catherine of Aragon in England in order to argue against the marriage of the infanta María to the Prince of Wales or when Iñigo de Cárdenas, ambassador to France, suggested that the infanta Ana read the life of Isabel the Catholic to prepare herself for becoming queen of France. In a similar manner, Philip III commended to Ana the biography of her mother, Margarita de Austria, written by her teacher Diego de Guzmán, thus providing her with a concrete guide in motherhood, religious life, and queenly resignation.[90]

The conceptualization of the biography of Margarita as a specific teaching tool overlaps a separate category of texts written with the individual in mind in order to prepare him or her for a particular role. These include the instruction written for Ana by her father as she prepared to go to France, the "Gran Memorial" written for the young Philip IV by the Count-Duke of Olivares, an instruction for Fernando concerning his duties as archbishop, and an instruction for María written by her brother as she prepared for her marriage to the king of Hungary.

Other works were dedicated to individuals based on common names, but it is less apparent how Carlos was to be guided by a biography of his great grandfather, Emperor Charles V, or Fernando by the life of his ancestor Fernando III, since neither of the infantes was called to be king, and indeed some ministers felt the need to remind them that their status was below that of the king. More direct in their implications are the works dedicated directly to the prince. Ranging from political advice to general philosophy, they include both *arbitrista* literature addressing particular subjects and works within the traditional mirrors of princes.

But these works dedicated to or intended for an individual were not incorporated into formal study. They should instead be placed within a context of preparation for the political roles that each member of the royal family would eventually play. It was then, when specific roles were established, in the concrete environment of political life, that the next stage of royal training took place. When Philip IV referred to his translation of Guicciardini's history of Italy as unusual, it was not because royalty did not undertake such study but because he was doing it as an adult and when already king. By presenting such activity as unusual in an adult, the king recognized that formal education was considered part of childhood. The end of the formal royal education was usually marked by the transition to one's adult role.

4

DEFENDERS OF THE FAITH

Personal and Public Belief

During the Easter celebrations of 1578 the chronicler Luis Cabrera de Córdoba recounted, Philip II performed a ritual of washing the feet of thirteen poor men on Holy Thursday. In tears, prostrating himself before the poor, the king insisted the queen do so as well, despite her very advanced pregnancy. The child later born was Philip III, and thus, the chronicler concludes, the future king "began to practice acts of religion and piety" before he was even born, "signifying that he would be as he is, most religious and most zealous in the service of God, having begun with the sanctity with which . . . his father finished."[1]

Another observer, Jerónimo de Sepúlveda, a monk at San Lorenzo, called the ritual a "strange spectacle" the first time he saw it. He noted its observance in several different years, providing details of Philip II kissing the poor men's feet after washing them and giving the men a lavish meal, cloth to dress themselves in the coming year, and a purse of coins for each. Prince Philip's conscious participation in the ritual began in 1587, when he was nine years old.[2] Following the example of his father, and his grandfather as well, Philip continued the tradition for the rest of his life.[3]

The Spanish royal family's devotion to the Catholic Church played a crucial part in its public identity. Biographies and chronicles alike supported the pious image of the royal family, weaving accounts of religious observance into a tapestry of individual action and actions repeated across generations. Concretely, the children developed their religious identities through participation from a young age in religious ritual and under the influence and guidance of their confessors. As the children grew older, the role of confessors became increasingly political, as they accompanied queens to foreign lands and advised kings on matters both religious and secular.

In general, royal families throughout Europe entered the early modern era as patrons of the church, a pattern based both on a sacral concept of kingship and on the struggle to lessen papal influence in the various kingdoms. Within Spain, the identification of the crown with religious mission gained additional authority under Isabel and Ferdinand, since a crusading spirit energized the project of removing the last Islamic kingdom from the peninsula. With the advent of the Reformation, Charles V, as Holy Roman Emperor, fought wars over religion in central Europe, and the sense of crusade expanded to include threats to orthodoxy. A similar blend of political and religious goals, expressed with a zeal that did not differentiate between infidel and heretic threats, fueled Philip II's military campaigns against the Ottoman Empire and the Protestants of England, France, and the Netherlands. Spanish kings took seriously their personalized role as leaders in religious thought: even when Philip II allied with the pope, he generally saw himself as a more reliable defender of the faith than the pope himself.

Within this context, the Spanish royal court was a great center for patronage of religious orders and institutions and of particularly noteworthy individuals. Priests and friars of all descriptions served the royal court as preachers, almoners, personal counselors, confessors, censors, and teachers and were well represented within the networks of royal and noble patronage. The theological controversies debated among the various orders spilled into the royal court and found advocates there. Members of the royal family added their voices to debates over the patron saint of Spain and doctrines such as that of the Immaculate Conception, which Philip III reportedly vowed to support as he lay deathly ill in 1619.[4] Princess Juana, encouraged by her attachment to the later saint Francisco de Borja, whom she had known since childhood, actually took Jesuit vows.[5]

Philip III and Margarita de Austria both saw religious patronage as central to the concept of royalty. They considered themselves obliged to provide pious example in their daily lives, to use political policy to support religious ideals, and to play personal leadership roles in religious patronage. The court transformed religious ceremony into a social event. According to Sepúlveda, the religious observances at the royal court were such that it "appeared more a house of religion than a palace of a king: so much that there was not a grandee in Spain that would not want to put his daughter in the palace; for her to be raised where such virtues were taught."[6]

The major royal religious institutions founded in the reign of Philip III are associated with the queen rather than the king. Margarita undertook two large projects, founding the convent of La Encarnación practically on the palace grounds in Madrid and a Jesuit college in Salamanca. With these foundations Queen Margarita not only expressed her faith but also established herself as a patron in one of the ways considered most appropriate to royal women. In this aspect of her life, she followed the examples of her mother, who was the patron of a convent on the grounds of the archducal palace in Graz, and Princess Juana, whose Descalzas Reales had become one of the major female religious institutions in Madrid. The prestige of the latter institution may have contributed to Margarita's desire to establish a similar foundation, the type of project that could provide royal women with a lasting reputation parallel to the prestige associated with kings through their great monuments.[7]

Philip III did not found a major monastery in his own name nor choose a monumental act of piety as had his father in building El Escorial. However, although La Encarnación was considered the work of Margarita, Philip III was equally involved in its foundation and continued to support it and other such projects of hers after her death both as a pious act and in her memory. In addition, during her lifetime he followed his wife's pattern of piety, consisting largely of frequent visits to various religious houses and numerous small bequests to institutions and persons, including present and former lesser servants of the crown, orphans, widows, and poor monks and nuns.[8] His support for other institutions, including those founded by relatives of the Duke of Lerma in the town of Lerma, followed a similar pattern, in which the king, with perhaps excessive modesty, attached his extensive charitable works to the patronage of others.

The members of the royal family had somewhat differing daily observances. The king often attended large formal services accompanied by councilors of state, high-ranking ecclesiastics, and visiting and resident ambassadors. Otherwise, he might hear Mass in his oratory, scheduled casually around the other activities of the day. For example, he called the royal chaplain to his rooms very early in the day if he intended to go hunting later. The queen usually heard two masses daily in her private oratory, said by her confessor or by the royal chaplain. In the week prior to the birth of Fernando, in 1609, she expressed her anxieties regarding the birth by hearing a Marian Mass for her first mass in hopes of a good birth and for the second a requiem. The queen habitually attended divine office at convents and shared the nuns' meal afterward, both when she was in residence at the palace and when traveling.[9]

Like their father, Philip III's children began to learn their roles as religious patrons in their earliest childhood, participating in ceremonies and observing the example of their parents. The queen's contemporary biographer described her as instructing her children in their first prayers and devotions. In addition, one or more of her children occasionally attended her daily mass, and on more formal occasions the entire family attended public services together, often viewing them from the chancel or from behind a screen or partial curtain. A more common daily pattern would have one of the royal chaplains saying mass for the children and attending their meals to offer the benediction. The masses the children heard alone were generally shorter, as suggested by the principal almoner, who described leaving the service held for the king after the gospel reading, attending mass in the prince's chapel from start to finish, and returning to the king's mass before the sermon ended. The mass said for the prince may not have included a sermon, which may account for the significant difference in duration between the two.[10]

The royal children can also be glimpsed taking part in liturgical festivals, such as those for Palm Sunday and Corpus Christi, and accompanying their parents on visits to convents and monasteries. In 1609 the children participated with their parents in weeklong services and processions devoted to Our Lady of Atocha in appeal for rain. In 1611 the family together watched *autos sacramentales* presented on carts in the street outside the Trinitarian church next to the Duke of Lerma's house. When the family visited Segovia in 1609, the king and queen employed almost every day in visiting convents and monasteries, although evenings saw the occasional play performed in the Alcazar. During many of these visits, the eight-year-old infanta Ana accompanied her parents, while the four-year-old prince did so somewhat less regularly. On one occasion, the king and queen also climbed to the top of an orchard to visit a hermit whose home was set into the rocky hillside.[11]

Birthdays too were the occasion for charity as much as celebration. From early childhood, members of the royal family performed a special ceremony on their birthdays, giving gold escudos equal in number to their years to charity. Primarily a religious ritual rather than a celebration, the occasion's formality could vary according to circumstances. On his fourth birthday, the prince heard a short sermon in his own chapel and then, at the proper moment, was provided by the almoner with five escudos to give as the "offering of his years." The court preacher, Doctor Gamarra, conducted a similar service for the infante Carlos's second birthday, although the child himself may not have participated. By her third birthday, the infanta María appears to have been an active participant, kneeling to give her offering on a pillow supplied by the Count of Casarrubios, mayordomo of the queen. The infanta Ana spent her tenth birthday ill in bed, while her confessor directed the ceremony of the coins.[12]

For the king's birthday in 1609 an extensive musical program was presented in the royal chapel, perhaps more elaborate than usual because his birthday that year fell on Tuesday of Holy Week. The king performed the ceremony of the escudos in a smaller oratory, where the almoner again provided the king with the proper number of coins. The queen's birthday, falling on December 25, inspired a somewhat different charitable act: in 1609 she clothed six couples, each of whom had a newborn child, clearly a Christmas commemoration of the Holy Family; the following year, she clothed seven couples and their newborns. The numbers in each year mirrored the number of children she herself had borne, suggesting her method of adding personal significance to her birthday observation.[13]

The queen similarly observed the March 25 festival of the Annunciation, or Incarnation, with a ceremony in which the infanta Ana began to participate at age nine. For this observation, servants placed tables in the outer hall of the queen's chambers, and nine poor women, having confessed and taken Communion, were brought in for the queen and her ladies to feed. When the women were seated, Margarita and her eldest daughter entered from the queen's chamber. The infanta sat on a chair placed next to her mother, apparently simply watching as her mother chose one of the poor women to serve, while the queen's ladies served the remaining women the various dishes of the meal. It was all done as it had been the previous year, noted the royal chaplain, who was present to say grace. After the dinner, the queen gave each of the women items of clothing and a purse of money. The queen and Ana then departed into the queen's chamber, followed by the mayordomos and the chaplain.[14]

When Cabrera de Córdoba notes, in the year after the queen's death, that

Ana continued her mother's tradition on the March festival of Our Lady, we know from Guzmán's description of previous years what is meant. That year, the observance fell on the same day that Ana had her first audience with the French ambassador, negotiations recently having been concluded for her marriage to Louis XIII. Ana thus honored her mother's particular manifestation of faith on the very day in which she began a new relationship with her future country, a perhaps unconscious affirmation of her particular Spanish, Catholic, and Habsburg identity. Ana continued her mother's practice for at least a few years, as did María some years later.[15]

In the early years of his reign, Philip IV performed his father's rituals somewhat sporadically. There is no record in the royal chapel journal of his doing so in 1624, and in 1625 the chaplain noted that he gave Communion to the poor on Holy Thursday, but there is no mention of the washing of feet or any participation by the king. The chaplain's notes concerning certain festivals that had not been celebrated, such as the days honoring Saint Roque and Saint Louis in August 1625, add to the sense that religious practice at court had changed.[16] Descriptions of religious activities in those years communicate a greater aura of festival than of devotion. Several years later, however, Philip IV did participate more actively in such pious rituals, pointing to another contributing factor in the pattern of religious observance—the age of the individual. The life cycles of members of the royal family clearly affected their practices. Typically, a young person, while constantly involved in religious activities that defined his or her daily life, treated them as a part of the natural order of things, while an older person, having experienced grief, illness, or, for women, the risks associated with pregnancy, developed a deeper concept of the central place of religion in his or her life. One of the most influential examples of this effect occurred in the last years of Philip II's reign, when the king, having suffered personal and political losses over the course of many years, now in constant pain and unable to travel far, set a tone and pattern of devotional activity that continued well into the next reign.

In general, observing the same patterns of religious patronage and practice as one's parents carried a positive message of continuity and definition by association. The continued celebration of obsequies for ancestors also reinforced reverence for the family, an effect that perhaps bordered on the superstitious when no member of the family personally remembered the person thus honored. It may, indeed, have become a burden to the individual and to the structure of belief, demanding methods of religious observance that hindered the emergence of new forms of devotion. This, rather than lack of devotion, may have inspired Philip IV late in his reign to sweep away the observation of numerous anniversary services for many previous generations of the royal family.[17]

Advisers and Saints

Within a concept of royalty that placed a high value on religious identity, the confessor played a key formative role. The confessor functioned as a personal adviser in his duty as spiritual counselor and might also be a political adviser, as, for instance, when he served on a council or privately advised the king concerning the religious and sometimes not so religious aspects of policymaking. In addition to hearing confession and prescribing penance, he said private Mass, administered Communion, and instructed a person, whether child or adult, concerning his or her duties and ethical obligations. He might discuss religious writings with the penitent or suggest devotional reading or advise about forms of charity to undertake. On the most personal of levels, the adherence of a royal person to a confessor implied the ability of the confessor to discipline. While this quality was not absolute, it acknowledged an area in which a royal person could and should be corrected.

The understanding that a confessor acted as an adviser concerned authors evaluating the duties of royal confessors. In September 1610 Juan de Ribera, calling himself archpriest of Valencia, wrote to Philip III regarding the qualities of a king's confessor. Ribera comments generally that the king needed a confessor because no man is perfect and indeed the good of all Spain required that the king have a good confessor. He treats the office of confessor as a ministry of state and argues that the king should have two theologians "of known virtue and doctrine" on his staff in addition to the confessor. Why, he asks, when the king has so many advisers, should he have only one in the ministry of the conscience? By treating the office as a ministry of state, however, Ribera did not mean that confessors should serve on *juntas* or councils; in fact, he called such commitments distractions from their central responsibility: "It is necessary for the confessor to be knowledgeable, and to be knowledgeable it is not enough to have studied, but [to continue] to study, and thus when they become confessors they are learned but in a short time they cease to be so, occupied in business of accounts and state." He describes an occasion when he and the vice-chancellor Covarrubias wanted to talk with Philip III's confessor, Fray Gaspar de Córdoba, while the king was presiding over the Corts in Valencia, and were told three or four times that he could not give them an audience because he was busy with juntas.[18]

Ribera warns against changing confessors, comparing it to changing doctors just as the doctor has obtained understanding of a person's composition. In addition, a confessor should never leave his office to become a bishop. Here, Ribera presents the confessor's career as an exception to the expectation of advancement through service at court and bases his argument on tradition, claiming that he had only heard of one confessor becoming a bishop, Fray Bernardo de Fresneda. But in this Ribera misrepresented practice, for the careers of numerous confessors demonstrate that they, like other court officials, experienced the advantages of royal patronage.

A later treatment of the subject, addressed to the confessor of Philip IV, defends the confessor's role as an adviser to the king. The anonymous author of this work urges the confessor to advise the king on a specific matter, which he does not clearly state, concerning the crown of Aragon. The confessor, he writes, has the duty to speak to the king about injustice: "It is the obligation of the confessor, whom God has placed as guard over the conscience of the king and auditor of all the Presidents and councils, to put before His Majesty examples of Sacred Scripture and doctrine of the Holy Fathers in order that the Holy fear of God obliges him to maintain his vassals in justice. . . . In one who has the obligation to speak, silence is damaging and even a mortal sin."[19] This author also draws on examples from history to prove his point, comparing the present situation to Raymond Peñafort's leaving Jayme I in Mallorca when the king would not follow his counsel, or to Francisco Ximenez de Cisneros's requiring Isabel the Catholic to promise obedience before he would become her confessor. In a more contemporary example, he praises Fray Francisco de Jesús for arguing against the proposed marriage of the infanta María to the Protestant Prince of Wales despite the pope's willingness to sanction it.[20]

With these examples of prominent churchmen, the author, like Ribera, highlights the importance of a monarch's having a learned man for a confessor. If the confessor is not to give his opinion, he argues, any simple priest capable of giving absolution would do. Yet confessors had always been men of the finest virtue. Philip IV, moreover, had urged his ministers to speak freely and correct him "even if it appears to you that it would be in matters against my taste . . . I require that my ministers speak clearly and do not let me err"—an argument that excuses both the advising activity of the confessor and that of the author himself.[21]

In addition to consulting privately with confessors, kings called juntas of theologians to advise on particular matters, one of the most famous being the Junta Grande constituted to advise Philip IV concerning the marriage of his sister to the Prince of Wales. Significantly, the specific question addressed by the theologians in that case was whether arranging the marriage would be detrimental to the conscience of the king, so that this junta could be seen as serving the expanded function of the confessor. This sense of the confessor and the junta served to provide justifications for policy and protected the king from error but also constrained him.

Although Spanish kings had employed confessors belonging to other orders—most notably, Philip II confessed with a Franciscan, Bernardo de Fresneda, for almost two decades—they showed a preference for Dominicans, probably in recognition of their status as the oldest Spanish order.[22] Philip III, however, appointed only Dominicans for his service, following the example of his father's last decades. Subsequently, observers held it as an age-old tradition that the king would confess only with Dominicans.[23] Philip III had five different confessors during his reign, which may have inspired Ribera's advice that a person not change confessor often. He confessed under the direction of Antonio de Cáceres during his teen years, but shortly after his accession to the throne he appointed Cáceres to a bishopric and removed him from court. His subsequent confessors were Gaspar de Córdoba (1599–1604), who died in office, Diego Mardones (1604–6), who left service to become a bishop, Jerónimo Javierre (1606–8), who also died in office, and Luis de Aliaga (1608–21). Philip III used confessors recommended by his favorite, the Duke of Lerma, including two, Diego de Mardones and Luis de Aliaga, who had previously served the duke himself in that capacity. We may assume that Lerma advocated the change or at least the choice in these cases. However, Aliaga, who served last and held the position the longest, turned against the duke and may have been instrumental in his dismissal.[24] The longer tenure of Aliaga may suggest that Philip looked for different qualities than the first appointees possessed and that the king and his minister differed concerning what was important in a confessor.

Luis de Aliaga argued, in response to Ribera, that the king was better served by a single confessor who kept confidences than by a committee of conscience treating morality as a matter open to debate. The confessor's duty to advise the king made him vulnerable to criticism based on his perceived political role, and indeed Aliaga not only advised the king in private but also participated regularly in juntas, many held in his cell in Santo Domingo, and commented on consultas of the Council of State. Aliaga was criticized before the death of Philip III, and he was forced to leave court after the king died.[25] Even though he came to oppose Lerma, this did not sufficiently disassociate him in the popular mind from the fallen favorite or, more simply, from the charge of being politically active. His critics also suggested that he lacked the education proper in a king's confessor and that he occasionally neglected his duties. The king, however, had considered himself well served by his confessor, which may suggest that he valued qualities other than those primarily described in confessors, perhaps indeed spiritual qualities rather than ones that came from education.

Fewer contemporary authors wrote about the ideal qualities of a queen's confessor, but many assumed that the confessor exerted a great deal of influence. Although the queen's confessor was less involved in public life than the king's, his position at court did have political ramifications, and his appointment could carry a political message.[26] The often extensive discussions of queens' confessors during marriage negotiations reflect his assumed influence as well as the total balance of religious patronage at court. The choice also affected the queen personally: if chosen by her husband, the confessor helped to introduce the queen to her adopted country; if chosen by her native court, he could provide a link to home. Indeed, when a queen was able to bring her confessor from her native land, she was more likely to retain the same confessor all her life.

The religious order of the queen's confessor created conflict between Spain and Austria during marriage negotiations on more than one occasion. Spaniards claimed that Spanish queens traditionally confessed with a Franciscan confessor. The strict application of this rule may be as doubtful as that of the king confessing with a Dominican, but the argument reappeared several times in seventeenth-century discussions concerning confessors for Spanish queens. The Austrian branch of the Habsburg family, however, tended to appoint Jesuit confessors for both men and women. The Spanish-born Emperor Ferdinand I, along with his daughter Magdalena and his daughter-in-law María, sister of Philip II, had been among the first great patrons of the Jesuit order in Austria. Ferdinand's youngest son, Karl of Styria, in part because of the influence of his wife, Maria, the daughter of Duke Albrecht V of Bavaria, also became a major patron.[27] Karl and Maria's daughter, Margarita de Austria, first became attached to the Jesuits during her childhood in Graz, where she grew up in the shadow of the Jesuit house founded by her parents. The influence of her parents shaped her patronage of the Jesuits, including the founding of a Jesuit college in Salamanca, and also played a role in establishing the patronage her brother, the future emperor Ferdinand II, gave to the order.[28]

Margarita took with her to Spain as confessor the Jesuit Richard Haller, called Ricardo Aller by most Spanish sources. On arriving in Spain, the young queen encountered a variety of Spanish court and family structures that converged in a struggle over the composition of her household. One point of contention was her confessor, originally meant only to accompany her to Spain, where he would be replaced by a Spanish Franciscan. She was able to argue successfully, however, that she needed to keep her Jesuit confessor because he spoke German and she had not yet mastered Spanish well enough to confess in that language.[29] Once Haller was established at court, there were no further attempts to remove him.

Concern over the queen's confessor reflected the perception that a personal adviser with the weight of religious authority would have great influence on a royal person. But the etiquetas of 1603 suggest a further implication: they direct that the queen's confessor should also confess her children.[30] This directive reflects the understood and intended involvement of the queen in the religious formation of her children, as well as the structure by which the royal children were served by their mother's household. However, if the queen's confessor was not Spanish, he represented a foreign influence on the children in this sensitive area. Perhaps this is another reason why Spanish officials tried to replace Margarita's German confessor, and indeed the children of Philip III did not confess with their mother's confessor, despite the official precedent.

A royal child began to practice the rite of confession at about age seven, the same age that saw the appointment of his or her first teacher. The first recorded confessor for the children was the Franciscan Francisco de Arriba, who served the infanta Ana. In addition to avoiding having the infanta confess with a non-Spaniard, the choice of a confessor other than the queen's also allowed Ana to begin her religious life with a Franciscan rather than a Jesuit. Arriba was the infanta's confessor at least by 1611, when he is mentioned among those at the deathwatch for Queen Margarita. In 1616 he described himself as having given "eight years of service"; if he was a confessor during all of that time, then the 1608 starting date would be consistent with Ana's beginning to confess at age seven. Although he does not appear to have had the title of court preacher, he also occasionally preached during services for the royal family.[31]

The man whom Philip III chose as his seven-year-old daughter's confessor had much in common with the confessors of the highest-ranking royal persons and officials. Born outside of Almazán in the late 1540s or early 1550s, he entered the Franciscan order in Valladolid around 1563, and after preliminary study of the arts and philosophy, he earned a place in the school of theology at the college of Peter and Paul at Alcalá. Over the next several years, he taught at various schools, including the University of Coimbra, probably in the 1580s, when the unification of Spain and Portugal brought about a greater exchange of scholars between the two kingdoms. By 1593 the Franciscan had returned to teach in Valladolid, where he attempted to add a conciliatory voice to the debate raging between Jesuits and Dominicans over the doctrine of grace published in 1588 by the Jesuit Luis de Molina. A few years later he was brought into the government of his order, and in the capacity of representative of the province he traveled to Rome for the general chapter meeting of 1600. He spent the next few years in various offices within the government of the Franciscan order until his appointment as confessor to the infanta, probably in late 1608.[32]

Although generally the Franciscan is identified as the infanta Ana's confessor, payment records indicate further responsibilities. Just as some officials appointed to serve the prince actually served all of the royal children, Ana's confessor appears to have served all or some of her younger siblings for at least a while. However, when Arriba is called confessor of "sus Altezas," his salary is noted as 225,000 maravedis per year, while a payment of January 10, 1614, calls him confessor of "the queen of France" with a salary of 600 ducats, which is equivalent to the salary of the prince's confessor in the same year.[33] Arriba appears, therefore, to have served all of the children except the prince, but through separate appointments for Ana and her remaining siblings. This appointment was attached to Ana's service rather than to the prince's probably because the act of confession depended directly on the ability of the child to participate, and Ana, as eldest, was the first capable of confessing and communing.

Once Philip III concluded negotiations for Ana's marriage to the French king Louis XIII, the confessor's role was perceived as increasingly political. The French court, for example, saw him as a reasonable point of access to the infanta. On one occasion, French officials entrusted a package intended for Philip III to a Franciscan to give to the infanta's confessor, who could then give it to Ana in order for her to present it to her father. The plan went awry when the Franciscan could not locate Arriba, who was staying at the palace rather than at the Franciscan house during an illness of the infanta.[34] In this particular case the purpose of sending the package to the infanta was not to gain her endorsement of its contents but to underline the connection between Ana and the French court.

Philip III discussed Ana's relationship to her confessor in his farewell instruction to her. Advising Ana to keep her Franciscan confessor unless her husband desired otherwise, he expressed more concern with the domestic peace of his daughter's house than with asserting Spanish practice. The confessor also played an important role in protecting the infanta from dangerous influences that might infect her thoughts and the purity of her religion; the king instructed his daughter not to accept every book given to her but instead to read only those approved by her confessor.[35]

When the Council of State discussed Ana's entourage in May 1615, members apparently considered naming a new confessor for the infanta. In view of the uncertain religious situation in France, the council envisioned Ana's influence in religious matters as potentially significant. The cardinal of Toledo, Bernardo de Rojas, advocated that the king assemble a junta to write an instruction for the infanta dealing primarily with religious issues, and "that which matters most is a confessor of much virtue and good attributes of knowledge and conscience and thus it is proper to place particular care in this choice."[36] If these comments expressed doubts about the current confessor, they had little effect, for Ana herself insisted on keeping her confessor, and Arriba accompanied her to France, along with his "companion," a confessor for members of her household, and several minor officials of the chapel.[37]

Although the Spanish ambassador praised Arriba, the confessor did not have an easy tenure in France. While he had previously been a legitimate point of access to the infanta, once they settled in France, his importance in this respect faded. He aroused French suspicions when a doctor at court attempted to arrange an interview through the confessor's aide in order to warn Ana and the king against the queen mother's government. Arriba received a strong warning from Spain and was told to ask the advice of the ambassador if further questions of audiences arose.[38] Marveling at the infanta's ability to navigate the waters between Spanish and French attendants in her household, Arriba may have indicated the source of his own difficulties. During his first summer in France, he complained to the Duke of Lerma that the French showed him no respect: "Eight years of service," he wrote, "has as its reward the mockery with which the French ask why I am addressed with titles of honor when I have no more [office] than that of confessor."[39]

The confessor may not, in fact, have been fulfilling the service Philip III had charged him with. His letters of complaint to Lerma state that he would not be in France were it not by the duke's order and imply that the advice he gave to the infanta proceeded from the duke alone. His concerns for the spiritual and practical comfort of the infanta were overshadowed by the contempt he sensed from the French and the political situation at the court. While Philip III imagined the confessor advising his daughter on such delicate matters as what books might be harmful to her religion and reputation, the confessor was preoccupied with the mockery of the French and his own diminished status.

Although Philip III was aware of Arriba's complaints, he did not allow him to return to Spain when difficulties arose. The king's choice may have had little to do with his evaluation of the confessor's personal qualities. In the summer of 1618, when Arriba requested permission to return to Spain, the king saw the coming expulsion of the infanta's Spanish household and forestalled her total abandonment by refusing the request.[40] Within a few months, the French did indeed reorganize her household, and Ana retained the services of only one Spanish woman and her confessor. Shortly after the death of Philip III in 1621, however, the confessor too returned to Spain. While his return appears to have been simply part of the overall French disengagement of Ana's Spanish entourage, it is possible that the confessor himself instigated his own return, receiving the permission previously denied him only through the transition in reigns that precipitated so many other changes. Before Arriba even reached Madrid, the new king rewarded him for his service by appointing him bishop of Ciudad Rodrigo.[41]

Although his siblings apparently shared a confessor, the prince had his own confessor by separate appointment. If the understanding concerning the age at which confession should start was strictly observed, the prince would not have confessed with Arriba at all before the appointment of his first confessor just weeks after his seventh birthday. The future Philip IV's first assigned confessor, Joseph González, received the title in May 1612. He had already informally begun his duties prior to his appointment, for his expenses of 600 ducats a year began on April 20, which was the first day he confessed the prince. Cabrera de Córdoba identifies González as the Duke of Lerma's confessor as early as 1609, a position he still held when he began to serve the prince. Diego de Guzmán further identifies González as a court preacher, and Simancas documents refer to him as a provincial of the Dominican order.[42] The appointment of a confessor for the prince alone may, of course, reflect his rank, although it may also reflect the preference for Dominicans as confessors of kings, while the Franciscan padre Arriba was appropriate for a future queen.

Cabrera de Córdoba provides us with an example of how a confessor might take advantage of daily interaction to instruct a child. He described the prince's (or possibly the king's) confessor explaining to the future Philip IV the meaning of the Order of the Golden Fleece. Not quite eight years old, the prince received the *tusón de oro* (Golden Fleece), the symbol of membership in the Burgundian pseudochivalric order, on the Festival of the Three Kings, 1613. The chronicler reported: "His Highness was so pleased that he went to show the Fleece to the meninos, and asked his father if he had any obligation to wear it; and when he said no, the confessor, who happened to be present, told him that that lamb stood for Our Lord, and thus he had the obligation to be a very great Christian."[43] Although the confessor's impromptu lesson reveals misunderstanding of the symbolism of the fleece, and at the very least simplification of its relation to service, the king expressed satisfaction with his message.

González retained the office of confessor for only a few years. By 1616 the prince's confessor was the Dominican Fray Antonio de Sotomayor. With an illustrious career already behind him, Sotomayor provides an excellent example of the education and experience thought necessary in a king's confessor. He had been both a student and a teacher at the *colegio* of San Gregorio in Valladolid and had taught at the universities of Salamanca and Santiago de Compostela. From 1608 to 1615 he had held increasingly prestigious positions within the Dominican order and been successively appointed prior of important monasteries in Salamanca and Toledo, leading to his unanimous election as a provincial of his order in 1615.[44]

In a summary of his service to the church, written in 1634, Sotomayor described himself as having been appointed confessor to all three of the sons of Philip III. After the accession of Philip IV, he noted, he had continued in this office, beginning a few years later to serve Queen Isabel in this capacity as well. The infanta María also confessed with him numerous times, although he did not claim that as an official appointment.[45] If the younger boys had previously confessed with Padre Arriba, the infanta Ana's departure for France in 1615 would have necessitated the appointment of a new confessor for them. Although Sotomayor does not specify that he no longer confessed the infantes after the accession of Philip IV, he says that he confessed them for six years, which would be consistent with an appointment beginning in 1615 and ending in 1621. The appointment of Sotomayor to serve all three sons of Philip III suggests that the order of the confessor rather than the rank of the prince had been the reason for the prince to have his own confessor in earlier years.

By 1619, during the royal journey to Portugal, the infanta María had her own confessor, Juan de Santa María. Having studied law at Salamanca, the Franciscan friar had also served as a confessor at the Descalzas Reales and was a court preacher by 1615, when he published his *República y política cristiana,* a widely popular work that went into five editions within a decade of publication and was translated almost immediately into Italian and by 1632 into French and English as well.[46] The book was commonly understood to have contributed to the atmosphere of reform that encouraged Philip III to dismiss his favorite in 1618. Matías de Novoa criticized the friar as a troublemaker, an accusation supported, from Novoa's point of view, by his implicit criticism of the type of government through privileges that dominated the reign of Philip III during the mid-teens.[47] Nevertheless, he remained a prominent ecclesiastical member of court during the transition in reigns, and indeed Philip IV was reported to have consulted his book when planning reforms early in the reign.

By early 1623 Juan de Santa María had died, and the Franciscan Juan Venido became the infanta's confessor. Few records remain to give us insight into the new confessor, although Venido, like Arriba, had been active in the government of the Franciscan order and was serving as *comisario general* of the Indies in 1622.[48] He served on the junta of theologians that considered María's marriage to the Prince of Wales, and as the infanta's confessor he guided her through the process in which she considered whether to embrace a role as advocate of Catholicism in England or enter a convent rather than marry. Queen Isabel also confessed with Venido on at least two occasions, an unusual occurrence explained by the illness of her own confessor during a time when the queen was also ill, late in a difficult pregnancy.[49]

Juan Venido apparently was still serving in 1626, when, during the course of negotiations for María's marriage to the future emperor Ferdinand III, the infanta's confessor became a focus of discussion. The imperial ambassador stated the Austrian court's preference for Jesuit confessors and relayed Ferdinand II's observation that the special mission of the Jesuits to combat heresy had earned them great prestige. Since everyone at the imperial court had Jesuit confessors, he argued, it would appear odd for the infanta to confess differently. Furthermore, since the order had originated in Spain, it seemed particularly damaging to its reputation that a Spanish infanta would choose a confessor of another order. The emperor further hoped to persuade María by citing the example of her mother's devotion to her Jesuit confessor despite Spanish traditions. The only novelty she would find, he somewhat disingenuously pointed out, was in the habit, which was not the substance of a confessor.[50]

In that same year, Ferdinand II nominated the Jesuit padre Ambrosio de Peñalossa for the position of confessor to his future daughter-in-law. Peñalossa appears to have been an ideal candidate. A native of Spain, he had studied for several years in Vienna, winning a reputation as a scholar. He had, moreover, recently taught Spanish to the emperor's son, María's future husband. Recognizing Peñalossa's unique qualifications and acknowledging the usefulness of his acquaintance with German custom, the emperor had removed him from his position as professor of theology at the University of Vienna and sent him to Spain.[51] But the Spanish court was not prepared simply to accept this appointment.

Venido died, probably in 1627, and rather than accept Peñalossa, María began to confess with another Franciscan, Diego de Quiroga.[52] Like Peñalossa, Quiroga had had international experience. After an obscure early career that may have included military service during which he was imprisoned and narrowly escaped execution in France, Quiroga joined the Capuchins in 1598. Moving quickly into the hierarchy of the order, he became involved in founding monasteries in Madrid, Toledo, and Salamanca and held the title of provincial of the Capuchin order in Valencia from 1615 to 1618 and in Castile from 1622 to 1627. During the second decade of the century, he preached at least twice at functions attended by the royal family in Capuchin houses. Quiroga became more deeply involved in politics when he was called to Madrid in 1621 by Jacinto Casal, who, as both imperial extraordinary ambassador and papal legate, had come to urge Philip IV to increase Spanish aid to Austria. In 1622 Quiroga traveled to Vienna as Casal's representative, with a letter of introduction that may have exaggerated his place of confidence at court but placed him permanently within the ranks of persons involved in international religious politics. When he returned to Madrid the following year, Quiroga joined the junta of theologians who advised Philip IV on the potential marriage alliance with England, being among those who opposed this marriage from the beginning. Sometime within the next few years he was named confessor of the infanta.

The matter of María's confessor was again discussed almost two years later, when marriage negotiations were almost completed and the king circulated the question among members of the junta in charge of assembling the infanta's household. The political implications of the patronage of religious orders emerge clearly in the discussion. The Austrian court opposed Quiroga specifically because he was Franciscan, "their order being so dependent and attached to the duke of Bavaria." On the other hand, the Company of Jesus was the order "most esteemed in Germany . . . with which all of the imperial house have confessed and confess." This identification of particular religious orders with political entities meant that a Franciscan at the imperial court would immediately be seen as a partisan of Bavaria. But the Spanish resistance to Peñalossa appears to have come, not from overtly political sources, but directly from the infanta, she "having shown . . . more inclination to confess with Fray Diego de Quiroga than with a religious of the Company."[53]

Most members of the junta felt that the infanta should be able to take whomever she wanted as confessor, although they expressed the hope that she could be convinced to accept Peñalossa. While they would have liked to please the emperor, they presented the naming of the confessor as primarily a personal issue. The Marquis of Flores Dávila emphasized the importance of the comfort of her soul, while Agustín Mexía focused on the rights of the queen, saying that "one cannot deprive the lady queen of Hungary of the free will to confess with whom she has inclination." Those who urged the king to encourage his sister to choose Peñalossa argued that if the entire imperial family confessed with Jesuits, the infanta, by insisting on Quiroga, would distance herself from her new family in a crucial way. But none of them wanted to deny her the final choice. Fernando Girón especially felt that once the imperial family knew Quiroga, they would respect María's good judgment in choosing him. Several members of the junta suggested that Peñalossa be honored in some other way if he was not appointed her confessor. Proponents of both sides used the example of Margarita of Austria to support their arguments, the Austrians pointing out that she had used a Jesuit confessor and the Spaniards countering that she had been allowed to make her own choice.

If the diplomatic exchange can be seen as a conflict, María instigated it. The infanta must have been confident of her rights, despite the pressure of her future in-laws and some of her brother's councilors. Her brother, moreover, either supported her decision or bowed to her wishes, while offering a form of compromise. On the back of the report of the junta, he noted briefly, "I have named Quiroga and in his absence my sister will choose a confessor of the

Company, and [I have named] Peñalossa for my preacher and hers."[54] Quiroga
accompanied the infanta to Austria in 1630 and remained her confessor for the
rest of her life.

By the time the infanta and her entourage left Spain, Quiroga had been re-
cruited as a political emissary as well. Letters of the Count-Duke of Olivares to
Quiroga reflect a strong vision of the confessor's possible role.[55] Whether or not
this intention affected his appointment, Quiroga's letters often provided points
of discussion in the Council of State, and he, along with the rejected Peñalossa,
is understood to have been close to the heart of the politics of the Empire.[56]
After the death of the infanta, by then empress, in 1646, Quiroga remained at
the imperial court until his appointment as part of the entourage assembled for
María's daughter, the archduchess Mariana, when she traveled to Spain to marry
Philip IV. During that journey, the king again expressed his confidence in the
friar by naming him confessor to the surviving daughter of his first marriage,
the infanta María Teresa.[57]

Following the same pattern as Queen Margarita and her daughters, the
French princess Isabel de Bourbon took a confessor with her when she went to
Spain to marry Prince Philip in 1615. A Jesuit, he appears in court documents
under several variations of his name but never became enough of a presence
at court to merit more than passing mention. He departed court in late 1621 as
part of the same series of events that cost the infanta Ana her Spanish confessor.[58] Whatever pain Isabel may have experienced concerning the loss of her
confessor was perhaps mitigated by the appointment of one of the most noted
holy men at court, Simón de Rojas, as his replacement.

Long a presence in the religious life of the court and well known among
noble benefactors, Simón de Rojas was a Trinitarian of great piety with whom
the royal family had become acquainted when the court resided in Valladolid.
He had studied at Salamanca from 1573 to 1580 and taught at the cathedral
school in Toledo for seven years. Sometime in the 1590s he had moved to Valladolid, where the royal court also moved in 1600. After the court left Valladolid
in 1606, members of the royal family continued to visit him when they passed
nearby. He moved permanently to Madrid in 1615 at the request of Philip III
and lived in an austere cell in the monastery of the Trinitarians next to the Las
Huertas estate of the Duke of Lerma.

Rojas was intimately involved in the lives of the royal family by 1611, when he
was present at the deathbed of Queen Margarita in El Escorial. Some accounts

portray him as having miraculously revived her near the moment of death, enabling her to receive extreme unction with full consciousness.[59] Although Diego de Guzmán did not particularly credit Rojas with this blessing, the chaplain confirms Rojas's presence at Margarita's deathbed in his journal, which describes the all-night vigil held by Guzmán, the queen's confessor and his companion, and Padre Rojas. Starting at the oratory in the antechamber of the queen's room, a larger gathering of priests, including the infanta Ana's confessor and monks from the monastery of San Lorenzo de El Escorial, along with members of court, processed to the church to attend the consecration of the Sacrament prepared for the queen. When the blessed unction was brought in, the dying queen asked what it was. She was told, and when asked if she wished to receive it, she said yes. Margarita had already lost most of her physical senses, but the chaplain noted, as writers of the time always took pains to indicate, that she was fully conscious for the Sacrament. The small gathering who held the vigil were joined in the morning by a few others, including Ana's confessor, who said devotions and prayers. They said the commendation of the soul twice, and as they began the third time, they saw the queen's chest heave, and giving two gasps, she died.[60]

According to Rojas's biographer, when Philip III wanted to reward him for his service to the queen in her final hours, the friar asked for the king's aid in founding the congregation of Ave María, a devotional organization that among its charitable activities operated an early modern version of a soup kitchen that still functions today in Madrid.[61] Whatever the immediate inspiration for royal patronage of "the slaves of Ave María," the congregation quickly became a focus of noble patronage as well. Biographies of Rojas and the accounts of people who supported his good works or went to him for help read like a who's who of court society.[62] The response of the nobility particularly reveals the social nature of charitable activity at court and suggests both the public awe before a person perceived as particularly saintly and the desire to follow the royal lead in patronage. Interest in the activities of the friar spanned the social classes, from poor servants of the crown to the Countess of Lemos, Queen Margarita's camarera mayor. The congregation accessed the highest levels of patronage through the countess, who wrote to her son, the Spanish representative in Rome, on behalf of the Ave María in 1612. She praised Rojas, whom she described as "a very holy friar . . . well known for the great devotion that he has to Our Lady," and urged her son to gain the official approval of the pope for this new manifestation of Marian devotion.[63]

The appointment of Rojas as Isabel's confessor in 1621 placed her at the center of patronage of the friar's activity. Despite her high rank, her reputation profited as much as his from their association. The prestige she gained by having an acclaimed holy man as confessor lent an additional luster to her transition in the same year from princess to queen.

When he became confessor, Rojas was already serving the infantes Carlos and Fernando as teacher, and the relationship between Isabel and him can also be understood as that of student and teacher. "Father," his biographer presented her as saying, "I put myself in your hands, for you not only to care for my soul but also to advise me in all matters that you understand would serve Our Lord and please the king." The friar responded by proposing that the queen tell him her problems and concerns before confessing so that he could advise her on each before attending to confession, in which he should only talk of the rites of penitence. Rojas also persuaded the queen to give up her books, especially her French ones, and read only the devotional and doctrinal works that he recommended. He encouraged her to see "that all creatures are open books, in which we can continually read, and draw much fruit from their lesson."[64]

Rojas's talent as a confessor can be seen in his unique ability to comfort and in his practice of listening to the queen's troubles, whether they were sins or not. Under Rojas's care, his biographer maintains, Isabel attained a serenity that had previously eluded her. The biographer explores this quality with great sensitivity, presenting the Trinitarian as understanding that her earlier experience of confession had not eased the queen's mind but instead had increased her spiritual anxiety and suffering. Rojas was able to penetrate this condition, which had descended like a physical illness on the queen, and develop the trust necessary to solve this basic psychic or spiritual problem.

The source of Rojas's ability is suggested by his only known published work, an extensive treatise on the qualities and uses of prayer. *Tratado de la oración y sus grandezas* clarifies that his was not a preaching ministry but a ministry of prayer. In the treatise he examines three types of prayer: brief, directed requests; meditation; and contemplation, which he differentiates from meditation as a search for the beauty, wisdom, kindness, and perfection of God, which only God himself can master. Sin weighs men down and makes them susceptible to death, making prayer a vital daily act that brings consolation and prepares the soul for Christ. He compares the active with the contemplative life, arguing for the necessity of both, although he values contemplation more highly. Prayer, he states, makes the soul wise and teaches more than books can. This privileging of the wisdom of the soul over books suggests his approach to teaching and confession, and in what we can see as a clarification of the biographer's comment that Rojas thought all creatures were open books, the treatise states that all creation teaches human beings to love, and especially to love their God.[65]

The confessor's insistence on the removal of French books may appear to be a harsh rather than an admirable measure, seemingly depriving the queen of a possible source of comfort. The measure, however, which echoes the injunction of Philip III to his eldest daughter to read only the books her confessor approved, actually served two potentially useful functions: not only did it protect a queen from ideas inappropriate in themselves or coming from inappropriate sources, a useful protection for a young queen establishing herself in a foreign land, but it also served to remind her that she no longer belonged to the country of her origin, a realization that may have been hard but was necessary for her own good.

Despite his position as the queen's confessor, Rojas continued to lead an austere life at the Trinitarian monastery in Madrid. His biographers demonstrate his great modesty by mentioning his refusal of honors and present the friar as embarrassed by any deference shown to him. When Rojas became Isabel's confessor, he refused the standard payment and services given to confessors. Isabel persuaded him to accept the monetary part of his wages and give it to charity in her name as he saw fit. She was not able to persuade him to accept the use of royal carriages to travel to the palace from his monastery. He insisted upon remaining at liberty to serve the poor and visit hospitals, a proposition the king accepted despite fears that the friar might bring the diseases of the poor into the palace.

One biographer used the distinctions and honors of the royal court to highlight Rojas's humility. During an illness of the queen, the friar was sitting next to her bed when the king and several high-ranking courtiers entered. The confessor stood for the king to take his chair, but the king ordered him to remain seated and sat on the edge of the queen's bed rather than take Fray Simón's chair, while the rest of the entourage remained standing. On another occasion, it took the urging of the Countess of Altamira to get Rojas to accept a gift the king had given him. This self-conscious modesty also is evident in his refusal to call Isabel "child," the standard address a confessor uses for penitents.[66] While we need not doubt Fray Simón's humility, perceptions of it depended on expectations of court manners and the ways in which religious patronage intertwined with social life. The eagerness of authors to connect the friar with the great figures of court is indicative of a system that combined social, political, and religious patronage into an all-inclusive power structure. But while the long lists of nobles affected by his miracles heightened his reputation, they did so within a system of values that he himself disdained.

At Rojas's deathbed in 1624, people gathered to view the holy man in what was described as a "miraculous" coma and scrambled to claim his possessions as relics. Even the queen ordered humble articles from his cell sent to her. His piety and service so impressed Isabel that she herself led the movement for his canonization and wrote letters in support of it. Among the attributes mentioned in the canonization process were miracles of Rojas's knowing when someone needed his aid and traveling long distances impossibly quickly in order to help, as well as numerous others connected with cures or with easing the pain of childbirth. He was also credited with predicting the sex of the queen's children, counseling her to accept the birth of numerous daughters as God's will.[67] If the types of miracles attributed to saints reflect their personal nature, we can infer that Rojas practiced a consoling ministry, one that focused on easing pain and relieving physical and spiritual need. In the year after her confessor's death and just two days before the birth of yet another short-lived daughter, Isabel made her first visit to the monastery in which Rojas had lived. With a five-voice *Salve Regina* setting the devotional tone, she visited the chapel where he was buried, clearly in search of the comfort he had provided her in earlier years.[68]

After the death of Simón de Rojas, the queen began to confess with her husband's confessor, a practice she probably continued the rest of her life. Although the new confessor did not possess the saintly reputation and presence of Rojas, he aided the queen in her next transition to a more mature and political presence. Sotomayor developed a friendly relationship with Isabel and often remained at court with her during the absences of the king. His admiration of her is apparent in his letters to the king written during her regency in the summer of 1643.[69]

Another royal confessor who became a major figure at court was the Jesuit Jerónimo de Florencia, who became a court preacher in March 1609.[70] A noted speaker, Florencia was often mentioned by Diego de Guzmán as having preached on particular occasions. One chronicler of the time suggests Florencia's involvement in factional struggles at court in 1618, when, in the months before the Duke of Lerma's dismissal, he carried out a thankless commission from the archbishop of Toledo to intercede with the king on the duke's behalf, a task the archbishop, Lerma's kinsman, could no longer bring himself to perform.[71]

Like Rojas at the side of Margarita, Florencia attended the deathbed of Philip III. It was, in fact, after hearing Florencia preach that Philip took to his bed, ill and filled with remorse at his failures. Tension between Florencia and the king's confessor implies that Florencia did not often attend the king in the royal chamber itself, but Philip III apparently deemed the sermon a special sign that he needed Florencia's guidance. It may be that, as at the deathbed of Margarita, several of the royal preachers and chaplains gathered during such a serious illness, but it is also clear that the two men served different functions in the king's last hours. While the confessor Aliaga comforted him, the court preacher Florencia begged the king to give orders for the future governing of his state. An anonymous contemporary description of the scene reads like a struggle between Dominicans, embodied by Aliaga, and Jesuits, in the person of Florencia, for the future of Spain. Perhaps it is significant in that regard that Aliaga was forced to leave court after the death of his patron, while Florencia's role expanded as a result of his presence at the deathbed. Philip III especially commended the cardinal-infante Fernando to Florencia's care, inspiring Philip IV to name Florencia confessor to both his brothers.[72]

Florencia's published works, combined with his popularity as a preacher, suggest the possibility of a royal confessor and preacher playing a role in binding together the religious practice of court and country. A collection of his sermons published in 1624 and dedicated to the infantes is devoted to Marian themes.[73] Philip III had originally commissioned the book, directing that Florencia should write it in Spanish rather than Latin in order to reach a wider audience. The introduction to this two-volume work places the Jesuit firmly within the patronage network of court, as he expressed his hope that the infantes would read the sermons with pleasure and implicitly asked for their favor. Judging from his admonition for them to learn from the life of Mary, he clearly intended his books as a teaching tool, although the sermons themselves address a general audience rather than examining how the virtues of the Virgin specifically applied to the infantes' lives and concerns. Florencia's thinking can be further inferred from another publication, entitled *Práctica de la frequencia de la sagrada comunión,* which he dedicated to Queen Isabel in 1622.[74] Just as his sermons reached a larger audience, this volume suggests Florencia's role in the larger community and his participation in the movement to urge the faithful to commune more frequently.

A letter of 1625 places Florencia within the networks of court patronage.

Agreeing with other members of a junta to reform Fernando's household, he became exuberant in his praise of the king's favorite, the Count-Duke of Olivares. Wishing him spiritual and temporal prosperity, he calls himself his chaplain "and servant so attached and passionate in your service as recognized in the honor that, since the beginning of your privanza and conforming to your Greatness, you have done me at every opportunity." His analysis of the need for reform seems in accord with the count-duke's, emphasizing the necessity that the household budget be within the infante's incomes. He implied the necessity of the king and the infante understanding the basic financial reason for reform.[75] However, nothing in Florencia's comment suggests that he shared the count-duke's belief that the infante should be convinced of his lower status; instead, it demonstrates that he considered the desire to express the dignity of the infante through his household appropriate, even if the expenses were now deemed extravagant.

The infantes continued to share the same confessor until at least January 1625, when Diego de Guzmán referred collectively to their confessor. The following August, however, he referred to Florencia as specifically Carlos's confessor. However, Florencia had not been among the entourage when Carlos accompanied Philip IV on a journey to Andalusia in the previous year, the king's confessor serving the infante.[76] Within the next few years, Carlos began to confess with the Dominican Domingo Cano, perhaps at the same time that the friar's *limpieza* (purity of blood) was confirmed as part of the process to make him a royal preacher in 1627. Cano remained Carlos's confessor for the rest of the infante's life and was awarded the bishopric of Cádiz in recognition of his service in February 1633, after the young man's death.[77]

Florencia became rector of the Jesuit-supervised court academy in 1628 and a royal censor of historical publications in late 1630. He may have continued to serve as Fernando's confessor, although he did not accompany the cardinal-infante when he left Madrid in 1632 to begin his journey to the Low Countries. By then Fernando's confessor was Juan de San Agustín, perhaps more able than the aging Florencia to accompany the cardinal-infante on the dangerous journey north and to carry out the duties of messenger, as he was occasionally required to do. Juan de San Agustín, an Augustinian as his name suggests, was a court preacher by 1623, when he participated in the Junta Grande and was one of three clergymen who consulted privately with the infanta María concerning her proposed marriage. A description of festivities in 1627 in honor of Saint

Teresa as patron of Spain identified him as rector of the college of Doña María de Aragon in Madrid.[78]

The confessors of the king and the cardinal-infante both undertook tasks whose relation to their religious offices are less than readily apparent. From summer 1632 to spring 1633, as he prepared in Barcelona for his journey to the Netherlands, the infante corresponded with the king's confessor concerning such practical matters as the proper provisioning of ships, while the infante's confessor wrote to the count-duke on matters concerning the infante's household, commenting on an official not given proper recognition for his services and the possible loss of the services of another official on account of illness.[79]

In December 1632 the infante entrusted Juan de San Agustín with a diplomatic mission to Madrid. He instructed him, first of all, to assure the king of the infante's own zeal in the service of the crown, a gesture that may have been simply a formality but may also have served to reassure the king that the questions the confessor would present to the Council of State were posed in the interest of hastening the infante's mission. Sending the confessor in person may have been intended to underline the urgency of the infante's requests or simply to expedite the matter through the services of a single-minded messenger.[80]

In March 1633 the king wrote to his brother's confessor and the Count of Oñate, who was serving as an adviser to the infante, instructing them to discourage Fernando from returning to Madrid. They were to emphasize that such an action would be contrary to the king's will.[81] That this message was entrusted to both Fernando's political adviser and his spiritual adviser demonstrates the blend of political and personal meanings of duty in royal lives. Confessors could appropriately discuss with penitents matters of personal duty, which for member of the royal family included political considerations. Yet, clearly, political advisers might also remind royal persons of their duty. Indeed members of the royal family often received similar advice and injunctions to duty from their confessors, from one another, and from writers on the education of princes anxious to provide a balance to the wide implications of royal power.

Within the context of the court, it would have required great effort on the part of confessors, especially the king's, to remain nonpolitical. The recognition Padre Florencia received at court was such that a chronicler reported his death with the comment, "He died like an apostle."[82] But despite the respect accorded to Florencia, no movement emerged to canonize him as happened in the case of Simón de Rojas, Isabel's confessor. While certainly the nomination of a confessor for sainthood represents an exception rather than a rule, it is revealing of the religious values at court to examine the differences between the two men and to question why Rojas was nominated and Florencia was not.

Florencia, despite his reputation for piety, worked within the social network of court. Like the king's confessor, he served on various committees and juntas. His position as confessor to Fernando probably led directly to such worldly matters as his service on the committee to reform the household of the cardinal-infante in 1624. His friendly relationship with the king's favorite probably contributed to the string of public responsibilities he undertook in the 1620s. But while the court supported a system of patronage that linked respect to honors received, it gave even greater respect to a person who disdained the rewards of service. Rojas's biographer noted his refusal of his confessor's salary and lingered on stories that revealed his modesty. Although the system of patronage surrounded Rojas for the last three decades of his life, he had consistently resisted any personal honor or worldly appointment that could have proceeded from it. While the city and court of Madrid honored both men, a sincere devotion distinguished between the two and recognized the extraordinary actions of Rojas.

No such hagiographical references exist for the life of Philip IV's primary confessor. The political qualities necessary to a king's confessor may have precluded such a saintly image. Philip IV, as king, remained loyal to his childhood confessor, Antonio de Sotomayor. He named the confessor to the committee on reform that he established a week after inheriting the throne, and three years he later appointed him to the Council of State. In subsequent years the confessor joined the Supreme Council of the Inquisition, of which he was inquisitor general for a few years, and the Council of War. He also held the posts of *comisario de la Cruzada,* abbot of Santander and Alcalá el Real, and archbishop of Damascus.[83]

The king's favorite, Gaspar de Guzmán, Count of Olivares and Duke of San Lucar, does not appear to have concerned himself with the king's confessor as Philip III's favorite had. Relying on Jesuit confessors himself, he did not attempt to promote his own confessor to the position of confessor of the king. While he could not have ignored the confessor as a link to the king, the count-duke's approach to the role of favorite focused on policy rather than patronage and remained more political than cultural. He relied less on controlling the king's life than on persuading the king of his need for political guidance.

In the early 1640s, when Antonio de Sotomayor was well into his eighties, Philip IV began employing other confessors during several long absences from Madrid. While it may have been that Sotomayor's advanced age limited his ability to travel, the shift in practice may also have been linked to the king's process of reshaping the court and disentangling himself from the policies of his favorite, who had left court in 1643, or indeed to the rising importance in his life of the nun Sor María de Agreda. Philip's correspondence with her is deeply reminiscent of the relationship of confessor and penitent, underlined by his frequent interjections of the words *I confess* and his injunction to her to tell him what she really thought, reflecting the classic statement of the confessor's duty to tell the prince the truth.[84]

The qualities of the various early-seventeenth-century Spanish royal confessors indicate the various meanings of religion in the public and private lives of the royal family. One of these meanings was institutionally based. The perception that the king's confessor should be Dominican, while the queen's was traditionally Franciscan, suggests a balance of royal patronage of the religious orders that, over time, became a conscious program. The rising influence of the Jesuit order in the second half of the sixteenth century disturbed that balance, perhaps accounting for the arguments that ensued over the use of Jesuit confessors, a conflict that otherwise seems difficult to explain, given the Spanish origin of the order. The Spanish court could, however, employ some flexibility, for it supported all major religious orders, unlike the smaller courts of Germany and the imperial court, which limited themselves to one major patronage. The confessors of the royal family ranged throughout the major Spanish religious orders. But while queens and lesser sons might choose Franciscans, Jesuits, or even Trinitarians and Augustinians, kings continued to rely primarily on Dominicans.

The scholarship and reputation of confessors also suggest the variety of roles they played. The qualities sought in a confessor reflected the situation of the individual. Both Ana and María took with them confessors whose education especially equipped them to help the young women remain orthodox in their beliefs. Rojas, however, served Isabel through a great and selfless piety rather than through his education. Philip III, strong in his assurance of his own faith, had the option of taking a confessor of lesser education and obscure social background, but whose spirituality or other qualities personally pleased him, as in the case of Aliaga. Philip IV, in choosing Sor María de Agreda as a type of confessor later in life, followed this pattern of privileging his personal spiritual needs over the traditional qualities of a confessor, perhaps unaware that his choices were leading him in the same direction that his father and grandfather had taken.

The patronage of the different orders and of numerous religious institutions deeply affected royal image. In the early years of his reign, Philip IV moved away from the great emphasis on piety that had shaped the public image of Philip III, but he continued patronage of religious institutions and individuals, both to support social leadership and to maintain the traditions of earlier generations. The role of the confessor within this network existed at the intersection of public and private religious duties. In many ways, confession should be the most private part of a person's life, but the public nature of royal life demanded that the confessor too be a public figure. The careers of the various confessors of the Spanish royal family thus reveal different aspects of religion as an element of royal image and power: Rojas was noted for profound piety, Sotomayor for political activity, and Quiroga as a symbol of the rights of a queen, yet all illuminate functions of the confessor within the early modern construct of royalty.

Part Two

Transitions to Adulthood

5

COURTSHIP AND MARRIAGE

"Seeing you with new obligations of state that God has given you," wrote Philip III to his eldest daughter as she prepared to travel to France to become its queen, "I did not want to fail you at your departure in my office of true father, advising you of some matters that I judge worthy of your consideration." Thus the king of Spain began his instruction to his daughter in recognition that her marriage established her political identity and began the fulfillment of her promise "as daughter of such hopes and expectations."[1]

Marriage played a central role within the structure of early modern monarchies, bridging personal and public issues of royal life, creating real families while indicating the alliances rulers chose to make. Family alliances had built the kingdoms of early modern Europe, and family rhetoric continued to color interactions between countries. Although monarchy privileged male rule, its basis in family relationships often resulted in women's holding considerable influence, traditionally through the natural advising role of a mother or wife but at other times as the best alternative to relegating power outside the family. While other roles existed for women, marriage was the platform on which the majority of such roles were built.

Rulers used marriages strategically to seal treaties and, in some cases, to prevent other countries from forming alliances. The number of marriages commonly considered for any given royal child indicates that negotiations expressed not just political reality but also political possibilities. Within a given generation, however, chance circumstances such as the number of male or female children in a family or the age of potential spouses limited possible alliances.

Among available spouses, royal families had to consider seriously each option and occasionally to appear to consider marriages from diplomatic courtesy or strategy. Because of the larger implications, the various European courts closely monitored one another's marriage plans.

Royal parents negotiated their children's marriages almost from the moment of their birth. While this was particularly true of daughters and the heir to the throne, Spanish diplomatic correspondence touched on possible marriages for the infante Carlos when he was barely a year old. On a personal level, however, decisions regarding marriage affected women much more deeply than men. Marriage was the defining moment in a young woman's life. Not only did it place her into her adult role but it usually required her to change nationalities and often separated her from her family, both physically and politically, for the rest of her life.

While the true value of exchanging women between countries remained largely unexplored, faith in the ability of this system to accomplish tremendous goals ranged widely in the early seventeenth century, and the complexity of the benefits each side expected to receive from such alliances goes far toward explaining the tension attending marriage negotiations and the rumors that characterized the process. Despite the often unsatisfying results of the system, alliances thus formed could have very real ramifications, almost automatically increasing the exchange of persons between the two countries and occasionally resulting in changes in the sovereign control of territories.

Token of an Unlikely Peace

Negotiations for the double marriage of the infanta Ana to Louis XIII of France and Prince Philip to the French king's sister Isabel dominated diplomatic discussion between Spain and France in the years 1611 to 1615. The birth of Ana and Louis within days of each other in the autumn of 1601 suggested to some that the match between Spain and France was divinely ordained. This coincidence, however, did not smooth the negotiations. Discord between the two countries was of long standing, and it was not improved by the marriage of Philip II and Isabel de Valois, which had sealed the treaty of Cateau-Cambrésis in 1559, and only patched by the Peace of Vervins in the final months of Philip's reign. Although Henry IV of France listened to proposals for a marriage alliance with Spain, it was probably only his death that allowed a window of good relations to open long enough for negotiations to actually take place. The tension apparent in the negotiations reflected the precarious nature of this opportunity and the conflicting needs of the two sides. Spain tried to keep the negotiations secret until the matter was settled in order to avoid unnecessary ruptures in other diplomatic relationships, while the French queen mother, Marie de Medici, as regent after the death of Henry IV, wanted to have the marriages settled and publicized because of her own difficult position, with her husband's cousins openly critical of her government and struggling for power.

That this proposed match had implications for other countries became apparent early in the negotiations, when the ambassador Iñigo de Cárdenas reported the Duke of Savoy's anger over rumors of the betrothal of Prince Philip to Isabel, since the duke felt that he had a prior claim to the hand of the eldest French princess for his heir, the Prince of Piedmont.[2] Savoy already suspected the motivations of Philip III, his brother-in-law, in the realm of marriage policy, accusing him of trying to control the marriages of the duke's own daughters, an accusation that appears to have been at least partly justified.[3] Tension between the two escalated as the duke reportedly investigated whether Philip II had had the right to give the Low Countries to Isabel Clara to the exclusion of her sister Catalina, Duchess of Savoy.[4] Savoyard agents warned Protestants in France and the Netherlands that a Spanish-French alliance would work against them, and they attempted to interest the English in a marriage that was perhaps more of a ploy than set policy. The Spanish Council of State, concerned that France would have a foothold in Italy if the French princess married the Prince of Piedmont, expressed wonder that Savoy did not see the danger. Further, rumors flew at the French court that Spain and France were not only planning the double marriage but also plotting the division of Savoy's territories. Marie de Medici protested that if there had been discussions of this sort, they had occurred during the lifetime of her husband, when she was excluded from the political process. She also used such reasoning to deny any responsibility for a previous understanding between France and Savoy.[5]

The queen mother herself contributed to the cycle of rumor, letting slip that she had told the English ambassador that the marriages with Spain were not settled. Others speculated that James I had requested Isabel's hand for the Prince of Wales, and the English envoy mentioned to the queen that Spain had at one time spoken of an English marriage for Ana. The Spanish representative Cárdenas assumed that the English were trying to break the Spanish-French alliance, and in a partially coded letter he reported the English ambassador's assertion that the English had a written offer of Ana's hand for the Prince of Wales, and if not her, then the second daughter of the Spanish king. Cárdenas claimed that he had told the ambassador not to speak of his fantasies, but he nonetheless wrote to the Spanish ambassador in England to inquire about the matter.[6]

While more substantive issues were also being discussed, most crucially the renunciation of Ana's rights to the Spanish throne, the circulating rumors may have served their purpose and forced Philip III to clarify his position. The Italian Marquis of Campiglia, apparently acting unofficially on Spain's behalf, understood Marie de Medici's impatience to conclude negotiations as a desire "to close the mouth and deprive of all hope" those who urged a different match. The queen mother, he noted, had asked him if he had written to Spain about this matter, suggesting that she had specifically tried to communicate this point, an indication of her true commitment to a Spanish match. He suggested that reaching an agreement would improve relations with France, after which one could delay the actual "exchange of princesses."[7]

Accordingly, the two sides soon concluded the official marriage contracts, and the major issue of negotiation became the timing of the infanta's arrival in France. The queen mother and her ministers wanted Ana sent to them as soon as possible to settle the matter and prove to Protestant subjects that the Spanish marriage would not alter the crown's policy toward them. The Spaniards, on the other hand, wanted to delay the actual marriage for both political and personal reasons. Philip III considered Ana too young to marry and expressed concern about her physical health and the health of her children. The Duke of Lerma ordered Cárdenas to clarify that there would be no exchange before Ana turned thirteen, which would have set the earliest date in the autumn of 1614. Even though the French princess was even younger, Marie was not concerned for the health of her daughter, probably since she did not envision sexual relations beginning for the young couples until at least a few years after the marriages. In the case of her son and Ana, she offered to delay the consummation of their marriage until they were both fifteen.[8] In addition to such concerns, the Habsburg family could look to the experience of Philip's great great aunt Margaret of Burgundy, who had been sent as a three-year-old to the French court to be the future bride of Charles VIII, only to be repudiated and sent home at age thirteen. If the infanta were older when she arrived, her personal authority would increase and the possibility that she would be neglected would decrease. Moreover, she would be a better representative of her native country. Whatever his motivations, the

Spanish king waited more than a year after the betrothal before asking his representative in Rome to request the pope's dispensation for the Spanish prince to marry despite his youth, an essential part of the double-marriage agreement.[9]

The Spanish court and ambassador implemented the strategy of extending the time, so that with various excuses the exchange of princesses was postponed from the official date of the marriage agreement in July 1612 until October 1615. The diplomatic correspondence in those years provides some evidence of how the Spanish and French rulers prepared their daughters for their new roles. Marie de Medici suggested that in the time between the capitulations and the exchange of princesses Ana should add a Frenchwoman to her household to help her learn French. Campiglia explained that Marie herself "experienced the greatest difficulty and almost impossibility in learning this language and in adjusting herself to the customs here, so different from those of Spain and Italy," and thus hoped that such difficulty could be alleviated by having Ana begin to learn French immediately.[10] Although no Frenchwoman appears in records concerning the infanta's ladies in the next few years, a French grammar and a few unspecified French books appear on a list of books that Ana's teacher took with him on a journey of 1612. She also received an occasional visit from the wife of the French ambassador. In 1615, just months before the exchange of princesses would finally take place, the Spanish Council of State was still urging that she be well instructed in French, although whether this indicated inadequate instruction prior to that point is unclear.[11]

Isabel de Bourbon began to learn the language of her future home even before the marriages were settled. Cárdenas employed code to inform the king that Isabel was learning Spanish from a Flemish cleric and worried that that might imply that an agreement had been made. Marie countered that her younger children, the Duke of Orleans and the second princess, were also learning Spanish, and Italian as well. This, the ambassador observed, was "to disguise" that Isabel was being prepared to go to Spain.[12] Whatever language instruction she received, in August 1615, a few months before the final exchange of princesses, the French queen instructed the Spanish ambassador to choose two minor officials for Princess Isabel's service. Seeking Philip III's permission to do so, Cárdenas also asked whether he could "choose one of them that could serve as interpreter between Her Highness and the prince."[13]

The instruction Ana de Austria received in the manners of the French court and that Isabel de Bourbon received in the manners of the Spanish court can be said to have begun in the interactions each had with representatives of her future country. When the future queen of France first met with the French ambassador shortly after the marriage agreement was finalized in March 1612, she could not respond to his greetings. Her father answered for her, explaining on her behalf that the crowds had overwhelmed her and made her nervous. But the following summer she successfully presided over the elaborate reception of a special ambassador, the Duke of Mayenne, who visited Spain to express French condolences on the death of her mother and conclude the formal marriage contract. The Spanish ambassador advised that all of Mayenne's retinue should have access to the infanta's chamber, to an extent greater than Spaniards of equivalent rank. Not only would this please the French but it would provide all the more witnesses to give positive reports of the "queen infanta" to the queen mother, who closely questioned anyone who came from Spain.[14] Ana wore black and few jewels in her first meeting with Mayenne, but a few weeks later, on the day the marriage contract was signed, the king of Spain, his children, and the court put aside their mourning clothes as an expression of pleasure in the visit. The French ambassador and much of his entourage likewise expressed their satisfaction by dressing in the Spanish style. Pressing into the infanta's chambers with a disorder much remarked by Spanish observers, they were greeted by the eleven-year-old in the company of her household, without other members of the royal family present. The French went away impressed, and Mayenne was heard extravagantly praising the infanta as he exited the chambers. The Spaniards further signaled their association with the French by holding a special observance of the feast of Saint Louis a few days later.[15]

At the same time that Mayenne set out on his official condolence call, the Duke of Pastrana paid a reciprocal visit as Spanish special ambassador to the French court. During court festivities held in honor of his visit, Marie de Medici urged Pastrana to take her daughter's hand and dance, but the duke stiffly refused, on the grounds that it would not be allowed in Spain. The French, presented in the Spanish accounts as impressed and amazed, were perhaps also amused at the excessive dignity of the Spaniard, who would neither eat nor sit in his princess's presence. While Spanish etiquette did indeed allow nobles of such stature as Pastrana to dance with royalty, the situation was not resolved until the queen ordered her daughter to invite the duke to dance, an offer he did not refuse.[16] The Spanish ambassador was not simply insisting on ceremony; he was also instructing his future princess and queen on her position in the formal world of the Spanish court. Formality, a quality that the French court was commonly seen as lacking, created a bulwark against disorder and showed each person his place.

The Spanish king and councils encouraged Ana to make positive contact with Marie de Medici. All the court had been impressed, wrote the Spanish ambassador, by a letter from Ana to the queen mother, and the queen had been particularly pleased that Ana addressed her as "mother." In addition, Princess Isabel had received a letter from Prince Philip, and Cárdenas reported that she had accepted it very gracefully, asking after the health of the king and sending her aya to ask her mother if she should open the letter. The Spanish emphasis on the queen mother reflects their perception of the power structure but may have been shortsighted in creating the proper relationship between the infanta and her future husband. Louis XIII did not take well that his mother received a letter from Ana when he received nothing. The problem of dealing with a child king thus added another dimension to diplomatic concerns. At first, ambassador Cárdenas seems almost to have gloated that Louis had not "made demonstration with the Infanta Queen," while Prince Philip had been "very gallant" toward Isabel. A week later, however, beginning to sense a problem, he suggested that a band of cloth indicating the infanta's colors, which the French court had requested, be sent specifically to the young king, not to the queen.[17]

While Cárdenas continued to promote delay, the focus of diplomatic conversation shifted to the composition of households. The creation of a household for a royal woman traveling to marry abroad involved issues of both comfort and honor. Households always came under close scrutiny from the receiving country because of the influx of foreign presence and the expense to the crown. The discussions at the French and Spanish courts, moreover, reveal a further clash of goals and understanding. The French in general stressed the person of Ana, while the Spanish envisioned a wider exchange between the countries, part of which would take place through the people who served the infanta. French officials assured the Spanish ambassador that Ana "would be absolute mistress of her house and do in it whatever she wanted and confer offices with the same authority and freedom Her Highness Madame Isabel would have in Spain,"[18] but the Spanish and French households were styled differently, complicating the quest for agreement on entourages and their exact duties.

In May 1613 Philip III chose Ana Manrique, the Dowager Countess of Puñonrostro, as camarera mayor for his daughter. The countess had been a close friend of Philip III's mother and more recently had served as dueña of honor in the household of Queen Margarita.[19] In August of the same year, however, the French were inclined to give the position that Cárdenas equated with camarera mayor to the Countess of Soissons, the wife of one of Marie's critics and a rival for the regency, and suggested that the Countess of Puñonrostro have the title of aya until the marriage of Ana and Louis was consummated. Cárdenas attempted to interpret the difference as meaning that the Spanish aya would serve in private chambers and the French "camarera" would serve in public acts. The French, however, saw the title as a way to rid themselves of this childhood attendant once Ana reached adulthood. Although Cárdenas urged that the appointment of the Countess of Puñonrostro be permanent, by early 1614 he was warning Philip III that Ana's household would be run in the French style. Concerning the possibility of her keeping the Spanish style, "it is not to be spoken of because they will not allow it in any manner; the queen infanta should enter her kingdom and show that she wants to be served by the French and that she takes pleasure in them and in this."[20]

More than a year later, when Cárdenas announced that the widow of the constable of France had been named the infanta's lady of honor, he did not clearly state what he must have known, namely, that in French royal households the lady of honor was the highest-ranking female official. Various members of the Spanish Council of State expressed impatience. The Duke of Lerma, commenting that Cárdenas "is a very good gentleman but so confused in his style," warned the ambassador that the countess "is not a person to go under the hand of another, nor can I follow what benefit is to be expected from her attendance there if they do not make use [of this position]." While other councilors focused on issues of honor and reciprocity, the king's confessor urged giving France satisfaction on this issue, since resisting it might serve the infanta's needs less well. The king, who appears to have increasingly comprehended the difficulties facing his daughter, accepted the appointment of the lady of honor, suggesting that the Countess of Puñonrostro serve only in private, while the French lady would serve in public functions.[21]

Shortly before Ana and her entourage actually began the journey to France, the Countess of Puñonrostro died unexpectedly. In what must have been a disconcertingly abrupt appointment, the king named Inés Enriques de Sandoval, Countess de la Torre, to replace her. Although the Countess de la Torre may have been equally qualified for the appointment, the negotiations of status had specifically focused on the person of the Countess of Puñonrostro, and thus the planning of months and years was marred by the replacement. The change may, in fact, have contributed to the great difficulties the Countess de la Torre herself encountered in France.

Among the other women appointed to accompany Ana were several whom the infanta would have known through their prior service to her mother and herself. The most prominent of these was the dueña of honor Francisca de Córdoba, who had acted as aya during absences of the Countess of Altamira, although she too died before the journey began. Less prominent but equally important was Estefanía Romero de Villaquirán, the infanta Ana's azafata. Her husband, Rodrigo de Castro, had served Archduke Albert as an auditor, and she had been a dueña in the household of the infanta Catalina, Duchess of Savoy, at the time of Catalina's death in 1597. She probably returned to Spain with the entourage of Queen Margarita in 1599. Her appointment to accompany Ana to France continued not only her own service to the crown but also that of her family, for her daughters and son also traveled to France with offices in the queen's household.[22]

A Father's Advice

Philip III had a few specific goals for the double marriage with France, which he expressed in the instruction he gave to Ana when she left on her wedding journey.[23] The king recognized his daughter's marriage as giving her "new obligations of state," yet he placed these obligations, not within a political context, but within the context of the personal sphere he thought appropriate to a queen. He emphasized that she should build her personal authority, win her husband's love, and support the true religion. The specific issues he brought to her attention were matters accomplished through long-term influence and of a general nature rather than affecting particular policies. By far the potentially most controversial of these goals was that she encourage the establishment of the Inquisition in France in order to combat heresy, but even this he presented simply as something she should keep in mind in the event that, with time, circumstances favored it.

Philip III considered religious patronage and advocacy a legitimate activity for a queen but recognized the difficulty of involving his daughter in the specific issues then facing religiously split France. In one of the final council meetings on the subject of Ana's entourage, the cardinal of Toledo urged particular attention to the choice of confessor and recommended that a junta be formed to advise her "concerning all that she ought to do and say in matters of religion and the rest, undertaking the good and the observance of our holy faith in that kingdom." The king's response showed more restraint than might be expected from a man history has painted as a blindly religious politician. He recognized the importance of sending good advisers in the service of God, but he declined to appoint a junta to decide this issue, since such an action "could give [the French] reason to think and throw them into new suspicions, particularly the Huguenots and those who do not desire these weddings, a thing that will foment their disquiet."[24]

The king emphasized that the infanta should build and preserve her reputation. While her religious patronage was a good in and of itself, it was also a key element of her public persona. Her father advised her to participate in public religious ceremonies and to honor all persons of religious orders and other holy people. Urging her to exhibit devotion to the Holy Sacrament, Philip suggested that if she encountered processions of the Host in the streets, it would be good if, at least once, she could accompany it, and otherwise she should descend from the coach to adore the Host while it passed and do what she could to see that it was carried with proper decorum. This advice, reflecting his own experience as well as images from family history, indicates that Philip saw such actions as important to both male and female royalty. The good derived from this act was public as well as private; not only did it reflect her own faith and show proper respect but it set a good example. Philip specifically laid out the mixed nature of this type of act as a motivation for her charitable activity: "This will aid you much in gaining the heart of God and of vassals."[25]

Philip III presented Ana's household as a reflection of her own reputation and authority. He warned that her servants must exhibit spotless religious practice. It was not their place, he noted, to enter into religious debate; they should simply believe. He advised her to choose friends whose friendship would help her, avoid gossip and flatterers, and keep her household modestly and economically. Within her household, she should not allow any type of "frivolity or profanity, even if it is the custom of the land." In effect, the Spanish king expected his daughter to hold herself to a higher standard of behavior than that of her new country in order to support her faith and her authority. Philip warned her not to get drawn into the flirtations popular in court literature but generally discouraged at the Spanish court. "Do not allow," he wrote, "anyone to lose the respect owed you; nor consent that this material be spoken in front of you, nor that it be discussed whether you are pretty or not." He hoped she would respond to such matters as her mother had, which opens a small window into Margarita's experiences at the Spanish court, about which we unfortunately know little.

In other matters that affected both her private life and her public image, Philip also encouraged Ana to keep modest habits. He instructed her to avoid excessive novelties and amusements and not to play cards unless it particularly pleased her husband or mother-in-law. She should avoid luxury and instead work with her hands or embroider, which, he commented, she did so well. She should hide her emotions as much as possible, an action "very appropriate of monarchs." She should speak little and think carefully about everything she said. In these matters Philip articulated the reserve and austerity that both Spanish and Austrian Habsburgs cultivated to accentuate the special dignity of the royal family.

Tying together biological and political goals of both of the French-Spanish marriages, Philip advised his daughter that obeying and pleasing her husband was the way to win his heart, and from this would be "born the great benefits that are expected from these marriages." He stressed the central importance of the personal relationship for the achievement of all goals, "because if the conformity of spirit is not good, it will serve no other union." Ana's relationship with her mother-in-law also occupied a central place in his thoughts. Take counsel with her, the king advised, and respect her experience and her prudence. Consider her your mother, he wrote, placing the importance of her opinion next to that of her son's on several issues.

Philip III juxtaposed the advice that Ana treat Marie de Medici as mother with an exhortation to look to the example of her own mother. The vision of mother presented here comprises two roles: one, the counseling, experienced woman whose position in the structure of court made her essential to her daughter-in-law's comfort; the other, a saintly and much-loved model for her daughter to emulate not only in her marriage and in the modesty of her personal life but also in raising her children. The manner in which Ana was to consider Marie de Medici mother echoes how ayas were considered to fill the "office" of mother, while the influence of Margarita de Austria provided Ana with a spiritual guide in her personal and religious life.

Philip advised his daughter to take advice from wise, prudent, experienced men but warned her not to involve herself with questions of justice or government unless her husband specifically requested her to do so. Philip probably envisioned the possibility of Ana serving as governor during absences of her husband. Women served as short- and long-term regents often enough that one might expect a young royal woman to receive instruction in such work. If such preparation existed, however, it was not the place of a king to instruct his daughter if she were regent in a foreign country. Philip expected Ana in such a situation to rely on the experience of others and to incline toward mercy and clemency, instincts "very appropriate to your heart and estate."

The other political injunctions of Philip III's instruction also focused on Ana's personal relationships. He encouraged her to correspond with her aunt, Isabel Clara, governor of the Low Countries, and to procure good relations between them and France. His only specific direction was that she attempt to ensure that France not assist "his" rebels. He further encouraged her to correspond with her relatives in Germany, with the emperor and empress and with other Catholic princes, but did not attach particular goals to this correspondence, instead urging her to remember them for family relationships rather than for their rank, especially commending to her attention her aunts who were nuns. In his letters to her after her marriage, Philip III continued to advise his daughter to correspond with his sister, although he mentioned only their personal relationship and the goodness that merited Ana's love.[26]

With the same delicacy he had used in refraining from giving specific political advice in matters of a regency, Philip recognized his daughter's changing nationality, calling France her country and Spain his throughout the instruction. If God allowed war between the two countries, there was no question that she would remain French. She would do her public duty, although he hoped she might privately pray for peace and order sermons advocating peace.[27] This shift in understanding must have been difficult in some respects, for in the following year the king reassured his daughter that he understood the conditions of her Frenchness and apologized apparently for having teased her about being French: "I was amused that [my] complaint of [your] being very French on the outside would disturb you; it is good that you are, but I believe that inside you are Spanish, and since I said it as a joke, you may pardon me for it."[28]

In addition to his own instruction, Philip III commissioned a short work from Padre Simón de Rojas that echoed the king's ideas in matters related to the infanta's religious observances and her relationship with her husband. Rojas warned her even more forcefully than the king had that she faced a great internal battle and that if circumstances demanded, she had to "forget being a daughter and show she is a wife."[29] The king further warned his daughter to be careful not to read everything given to her but instead to wait for the approval of her confessor, since people might present her with books in order to introduce wrong ideas into her household and "even into the souls" of her entourage. But he did commend two other works to his daughter's attention, urging her to read them and his instruction occasionally. These were the instruction that Saint Louis, king of France, had given to his son and the biography of Margarita de Austria written by Ana's tutor, Diego de Guzmán.

The instruction of Saint Louis was a well-circulated and almost canonical text for royal education. Influenced by Augustine in particular, it presented the world in a constant struggle of good and evil, with the king bearing ultimate responsibility for all that happened in his kingdom. It offered an image of pious and modest yet strong kingship that resonated with Habsburg ideals.[30] This Spanish invocation of a French king should not be considered strange, both considering its general popularity and since the Castilian-born mother of Saint Louis was credited with the exemplary moral training of her son. Philip can also, however, be seen as giving his daughter a model that would be acceptable to the French.

Philip's recommendation that Ana read the biography of her mother echoes ambassador Cárdenas's suggestion, made amidst frustrating diplomatic discussions in May 1615, that the Spanish Council of State encourage Ana to read the life of Isabel the Catholic.[31] Given its timing and context, this recommendation appears to have derived from an ill-defined desire to assert Spanish authority and identity. Cárdenas did not specify what he hoped Ana would learn from the example of Spain's strongest queen, and no particular evidence indicates that his advice was followed. But Philip III in effect answered his ambassador's advice with a far more appropriate recommendation: the biography of his own queen, Margarita de Austria.[32] Written by Diego de Guzmán, who knew not only his subject but also his intended reader, this biography was more than a simple tribute to Philip's beloved queen; it specified the tools his daughter needed to be happy. It is much clearer what the young queen could gain from the example of her mother, who showed herself devoted to her husband and family, generous to charity and friends, firm in her faith, pliable to Spanish custom, and generally satisfied to stay out of political life. The eventual satisfaction and happiness that Margarita found in her marriage and in her role as queen came not from an insistence on her rights, which had brought her only grief in her early years at the Spanish court, but in her acceptance of her husband's rule and of Spanish tradition. The comfort she found in religion and in her children was a lesson to Ana to focus on the proper scope of the life of a queen, but it also offered a key

to discovering the true path of power available to women in early modern political life. Philip III knew this and spoke from his own experience, for he himself
felt the influence of his queen long after her death and may indeed have envisioned a great deal of power for his daughter through this method of influence.

Ana herself, although we cannot know her immediate understanding of this
instruction, had been old enough at the time of her mother's death to remember
her clearly and would have been able to use her memories to tie the biography
to reality and reinforce its advice. One of her last actions in her native country,
on the way to France as her entourage stopped in Burgos to celebrate her wedding, was to commission the court artist Bartolomé González to paint a portrait
of her mother as Saint Margarita,[33] a token of her respect for her mother and her
intention to keep her example always before her.

First Years at the French Court

In late summer of 1615 the infanta Ana made the rounds of the convents of Madrid, taking leave of the nuns and the sacred images of her home. A few weeks
later, the royal family traveled to Burgos, where on October 16 the king and his
children heard Mass at the monastery of San Agustín and Ana renounced her
right to the throne of Spain. Fireworks, masques, and dancing filled the night.
Two days later the betrothal took place, with the archbishop of Burgos presiding. Ana and Prince Philip wore white—his marriage was being celebrated in
France, as his wife's entourage made its way to the exchange—while their father
wore black. Close to six hundred people came to glimpse the king, Ana, and
Philip as they ate in public, and in the evening there were more festivities. Days
later, the king took leave of his daughter outside the town of Irun, with tears
on both sides. The queen then departed with her entourage for the banks of the
Bidasoa River, on the border with France. An elaborate ceremony placed Ana
on one side of the river and Isabel on the other, each seated on an open barge.
The gentlemen of the Spanish court kissed Ana's hand, followed by the ladies,
whom Ana embraced one by one. The barges then were taken out into the river,
the queen of France and the princess of Spain embraced briefly, and the boats
moved on, taking each young woman to her own future.[34]

Ana appears to have begun some aspects of her relations with the French
well. In June 1616 her confessor remarked that "Spanish and French attend to the
service of the queen; it amazes me the serenity and prudent equality with which

Her Majesty treats and favors both these parts that do not easily harmonize."[35] But within months she was deprived of the service of many of the Spaniards who had accompanied her. The French court did not observe the same religious rituals that had been the stable core of her existence since childhood, and while she had danced and loved theater in Spain, the public ceremonies and entertainments in France had a disorderly quality to which she could not immediately adapt. In addition, many people interpreted the reserve her father had urged on her as "appropriate to monarchs" as simple coldness. The French court simply did not function as the Spanish court did, and much of the training she had received from childhood did not immediately serve her in her new country.

The cornerstone of her position in France, the relationship with her husband, also did not function in the way her father had envisioned. Louis XIII, young and proud but somewhat awkward, appeared uncomfortable in her presence. Moreover, after the much publicized and politically necessary consummation of their marriage soon after the infanta's arrival, the king seemed little inclined to sexual relations and seldom resided in the same palace as his wife.[36]

The Spanish council initially continued to dwell on the relationship between Ana and the queen mother: Philip warned his daughter not to give anyone cause to say she was "dry" with her mother-in-law. The Duke of Lerma was almost dismissive of the problems between the young king and queen, attributing them to the king's youth. The ambassador echoed this assessment, a sentiment that could not have pleased Louis and was even more problematic given the increasingly poor relationship between the king and his mother. Based on this assessment, however, Lerma and Monteleon gave reasonably sound advice: Ana should do all she could to please her husband, and the problems would pass as he matured.[37]

Beyond Ana's personal relation with the king, she and her household could be seen as a manifestation of Marie's policies, which may account for the apparent hostility toward the Spaniards and the fairly swift movement to dismiss many of them. Philip III's responses to these difficulties suggest that he put his daughter's comfort not only before politics but occasionally before questions of her rights and the honor due her rank. Concerning one report on problems at the French court, Philip declined to comment on the substance of discussion in the Council of State or to give advice on the central issue of whether the infanta's confessor should give audiences but noted that the council should emphasize to the ambassador, now the Duke of Monteleon, to "always strive [to procure] peace between those monarchs and my daughter."[38] While his comment appears unresponsive to a crucial question, it served to override lesser issues and refocused the council on his primary concern.

Other problems that arose in Ana's first years in France were resolved through a mix of concession and defense of honor. When the French appeared to insist that Ana dress "a la francesa," Cárdenas, now retired outside of Madrid, cited extensive precedent to argue that queens could choose their own style of dress but advised that perhaps Philip III should write to his daughter suggesting that she dress in the French style more often. Opinions apparently differed concerning this course of action: the Duke of Lerma crossed out the proffered compromise in Cárdenas's memorial, while the king expressed his hope that his daughter could dress in the French style without exposing her breasts. When the French complained about Ana's nurse sleeping in her rooms, Cárdenas suggested that they simply concede this point. Isabel too was encouraged to ease Ana's situation by writing to her mother and especially by informing her firsthand of the good treatment she herself received.[39]

Although he protested a further dismissal of Spanish attendants in 1618, Philip III urged his daughter to accept the situation and encouraged her to believe that no one intended to offend her. He was inclined to make no further complaint, because his ambassador assured him that the "very night the attendants left," the French king would sleep with his wife. Thus, expulsion of the attendants would decrease the tension between the royal couple and allow for the development of Ana's proper position at court. Within a short while, Ana bid good-bye to all but one of her remaining women, her azafata, Estefanía de Villaquirán.[40]

And apparently the relationship between the young king and queen of France did improve. They began to live in closer proximity and to have fairly regular sexual relations. Although Philip III no longer spoke of the advantages to Spain of his daughter's presence in Paris, his joy at the trust Louis showed in making her regent during a prolonged absence from Paris is apparent in a letter of 1620. It was an assignment, moreover, that she accomplished with a dignity and popular acclaim that suggest the success of her political training. Relations between the king and queen worsened again in 1622, however, when Ana suffered a miscarriage that Louis blamed on reckless behavior, and never truly improved despite reconciliations long enough to conceive two sons in the late 1630s.[41]

During this time, Ana can be seen to have been following her father's advice as best she could. Resisting attempts to involve her in political matters, she settled into a daily life that included both the frivolity of court and her custom from childhood of visiting convents regularly. A French translation of Diego de Guzmán's biography of her mother appeared in 1620, perhaps under her patronage. Patterning her actions after her mother's in matters large and small, she moved a community of nuns near to the royal palace so that she could visit often and have an apartment there for herself as a retreat.[42] Her status, however, remained a concern until she gave birth to her first child, the future Louis XIV, in 1638, at age thirty-seven, in the twenty-third year of her marriage. Her role as mother eventually placed her in a position to exert political influence through her relationships in the manner her father imagined.

By contrast to her sister-in-law, the young Isabel de Bourbon quickly blended into the daily life of the Spanish court. Once in her adopted country, she fulfilled some of the functions of a queen while holding the title of princess. Although she was married to the prince, she often served as hostess at events for which her father-in-law was the host, and in some cases she was inadvertently called queen, perhaps because her household was in effect the queen's household. She can also be seen as replacing the infanta Ana in the daily life of the court; palace activities and observers paired her with the infanta María as often as with her husband. Over the next few years, several of her French ladies married Spanish nobles, ensuring that they would have a permanent place in Spain rather than be vulnerable to expulsion.[43]

The consummation of Isabel and Philip's marriage five years after her arrival in Spain provides a marked contrast to accounts of Louis and Ana having sexual relations the night of their official wedding, although it too received public mention. In November 1620 Gerónimo Gascón de Torquemada noted in his *Gaçeta* two significant facts about the young Isabel: on November 21 he described the princess as celebrating her eighteenth birthday by "putting on *chapines*," that is, by beginning to wear the type of shoes worn by adult women, as opposed to the type worn by girls; and four days later he reported that the prince and princess had consummated their marriage.[44] The chronicler drew no specific connection between the two events, but they are clearly linked: Isabel was an adult when her marriage was consummated.

Negotiation and Ceremony

The infanta María's experience demonstrates other aspects of royal marriage and the decision-making process. Two marriage possibilities for Philip III's youngest surviving daughter advanced to the stage of direct negotiations, both of them initially discussed by her father but concluded by her brother. The first of these proposed marriages occasioned the visit of Charles, Prince of Wales, to the court of Spain in 1623. The pomp with which the Spanish court entertained the young prince contrasts sharply with María's eventual wedding to her cousin, the king of Hungary and future emperor Ferdinand III, celebrated in her brother's chamber with only minimal witnesses.

The Spanish court considered other marriages for María as well. One of the earliest was the match eventually made for her sister. The French originally asked not for the eldest daughter of Philip III but for the second, an indication that they had indeed intended to make an alliance with Savoy, since with this request they could reasonably give Spain their second daughter as well, reserving their eldest for a Savoyard marriage. For a few years after Spain's diplomatic conflict with Savoy over the French marriage, rumors circulated that Savoy had been advised by various parties to mend relations with Spain and ask for María's hand, but such discussions apparently never reached official levels.[45]

Both Spain and France considered an alliance with England. Indeed, perceived French interest in such a match may have encouraged the Spanish to take the matter more seriously. The Treaty of London in 1604 set the stage for negotiations, and that same year Queen Anne of England reportedly privately discussed with the Spanish ambassador the marriage of her eldest son Henry and the infanta Ana. The ambassador identified religion as the major point of conflict, and while that aspect of a Spanish marriage might not have disturbed the crypto-Catholic Anne, the suggestion that Henry would have to be raised Catholic to satisfy Spain probably closed immediate discussion. When the English raised the matter more formally in 1611, Philip III demurred, saying that negotiations with France were too advanced to consider an English match for Ana, although he noted that he had more than one daughter. In the next few years, discussions continued intermittently, remaining sufficiently active that the Spanish king appointed a junta of theologians to consider the implications of the marriage.[46] In early 1618 Philip III acknowledged his ambassador's report of rumors at the French court concerning an Anglo-Spanish match. In August of the same year, he authorized Diego de la Fuente, confessor of the Count of Gondomar, his ambassador in London, to remain in England during the ambassador's absence so that negotiations would not stall simply because the English had no one with whom to talk.[47]

In the following year, the Spanish king also began to discuss a new marriage alliance with his Austrian relatives. By 1619, religious and political tensions in the Empire had descended into war, and a marriage would have been a sign of Spanish commitment to the conflict. However, this marriage offered Philip III the prospect of sending his daughter to a friendly court at a time when he was beginning to understand the personal impact on the infanta Ana of the unhappy alliance with France. Although relations with Vienna did not necessarily achieve the ideal assumed by the rhetoric of family relations, the two branches of the Habsburg family were in greater accord with each other than either was with other powerful countries.

The earliest discussion of the Austrian match closely followed the death of the childless Emperor Matthias in March 1619. By early April the Count of Frankenburg and Sor Margarita de la Cruz were both pressing for response to the proposal of Ferdinand of Styria, brother of the Spanish queen Margarita de Austria and at that time king of Bohemia and Hungary, of a match between his eldest son and the infanta María. Implying that he understood Philip III's consideration of the English match to be a diplomatic ploy, the count asked for a clear statement of Spain's intentions and offered the Spanish king a brief history lesson on the dangers of marrying outside of Catholicism and the importance of the two houses of Austria strengthening each other. Placing the decision within larger interconnected goals, he described the king of Hungary as putting himself and his children at Philip's disposal and proposed Ferdinand's daughter, the archduchess Anna Maria, as an alternative bride for the Prince of Wales, which would allow María to marry Ferdinand's eldest son, the archduke Johann Karl. The following year, Ferdinand again relied on family rhetoric to press his suit, entrusting Sor Margarita to negotiate the marriages of his children "as if she were their mother." By then the discussion of the match had shifted focus, with King Ferdinand having become emperor, bringing the imperial title into the Styrian line and, since the death of his eldest son, making his second son, Ferdinand, the proposed spouse.[48]

Contemporaries claimed that Philip III had decided against an English marriage by 1620 and clearly repudiated it on his deathbed, but Philip IV nonetheless kept his options open. While the imperial ambassador, encouraged by Margarita de la Cruz, attempted to start a conversation and Philip's ambassador to the Empire bid his time waiting for instructions from the new king, the Spanish representative in London, the Count of Gondomar, continued to build a personal relationship with the English prince and to encourage his interest in a Spanish match.[49] Both Spain and England understood religion as the major impediment to the marriage; while various Spanish authors discussed the propriety of the match, James I offered a list of concessions to the infanta's religion, shaped by the diplomatic discussion of the preceding years, which was sent to Pope Gregory XV for his consideration.[50] Gregory, in response, consistently intensified the prestige of the infanta's entourage and the requirements for their protection and that of other English Catholics. When James allowed for a private chapel for the infanta in the palace, staffed with clergy chosen by the Spanish and completely under the infanta's control, the pope proposed that a full church in London be set aside for her use, under the direction of a Catholic bishop and with free entrance allowed for all Catholics.

Enthusiasm over the prospects of the match ran high when the Duke of Alburquerque met with the pope and cardinals in February 1623. Several prominent cardinals supported the marriage, with the stipulation that England make a public edict of tolerance for Catholics. At the same time, ambassadors of France and Venice argued against giving dispensation for the marriage, since they preferred a French alliance with England. English Catholics in France, however, reportedly supported an Anglo-Spanish match, believing that it would better aid their cause.[51]

While Gregory XV and some Spanish theologians dreamed of mass conversions of the English, James may simply have wanted to balance the marriage of his daughter to a Protestant with the marriage of his son to a Catholic, thereby offering himself as a broker of peace in central Europe.[52] Although James's offers appear generous, it may have been impossible to reach the degree of compromise that would have guaranteed the goals of each side. It may be that the Spaniards realized this but preferred not to be the first to disengage from negotiations. Keeping discussion open allowed a variety of ongoing diplomatic exchanges; moreover, it prevented the French from forming their own such alliance with England.

The Prince of Wales may not have had any of these diplomatic complexities in mind when he traveled incognito to meet his supposed Spanish fiancée in early 1623. Encouraged by Gondomar and his friend and his father's minister, the Duke of Buckingham, he had romantic notions about wooing his own bride and apparently felt his presence would encourage Spain to conclude negotiations and proceed with the union. His arrival sent the Spanish court into a frenzy of activity. Recently proclaimed sumptuary laws were largely thrown to the winds[53] in favor of an opulent program of entertainment and festivity designed to demonstrate the hospitality and wealth of Spain and cover the tension of the negotiations. From March 7 to September 2, the Prince of Wales attended theater and tournaments, hunted with the king and his brothers, had a series of formal interviews with the infanta, and endured, with a forbearance perhaps encouraged by his limited Spanish, the earnest ministrations of a variety of theologians, intent on his conversion.

Meanwhile, the Spanish Council of State actively debated the marriage, and the king ordered a public meeting of royal chaplains and confessors, provincials of religious orders, and professors of theology.[54] This junta of theologians, called the Junta Grande, considered many of the same issues that Philip III's juntas had addressed but focused primarily on setting out the conditions under which Philip IV could with good conscience sanction the marriage. The theologians proclaimed four necessary conditions: that the Spaniards wait a year after the betrothal to be sure that edicts of toleration for the infanta's religion were published in England; that María and especially any non-Catholic descendant be excluded from the succession to the Spanish throne; that some protections be guaranteed for Irish Catholics; and that the infanta be informed of all that had been agreed, "without using any type of force or threat, [so that] she can judge if the said marriage is good, using her liberty in choosing to celebrate the wedding or not, and this too the committee holds as a necessary condition of Your Majesty's oath."[55] They did not consider any other points necessary, although they recommended that the infanta guide the education of her children and that their ayo be Catholic.

The major argument in favor of the match was that María would be a positive influence in ensuring the good treatment of English Catholics and perhaps even in returning the whole country to Catholicism. The Spaniards hoped, moreover, that the marriage would encourage England to help Spain against the Dutch rebels, just as England hoped to gain Spanish aid in regaining lands belonging to James's son-in-law, the Elector Palatine Frederick V. One anonymous opinion hoped for economic advantage emerging from good relations with the English, imagining the establishment of trading companies between England, Spain, and Germany and even holding out the hope that England could be persuaded to withdraw from the Americas.[56]

While many of the theologians remained optimistic about the benefits of the marriage, several felt strongly that its success depended on the conversion of the prince. At first, officials had considered Charles's arrival in Madrid proof that he meant to convert, a perception not discouraged by the prince's unwillingness to express himself clearly on religious matters. But since they now considered his conversion unlikely, many despaired of the infanta's children being anything other than heretics.[57] One observer warned that marrying his sister to a heretic would damage Philip IV's reputation, as Charles V's toleration of Henry VIII's treatment of Catherine of Aragon had (at least in that observer's interpretation) hurt his. Moreover, he noted, although the infanta's faith was beyond reproach, she was young, and there would be many people who would try to corrupt her. And while the Bible gave examples of concubines encouraging kings to err, few had been thus encouraged to shift from error to the truth, and indeed wives did not have the same rule over the passions that concubines had. In addition to citing the sad case of Catherine of Aragon, an example that haunted the thoughts of many Spanish observers, this author doubted whether the infanta would truly be allowed to keep her Spanish and thus Catholic entourage, given what had happened to the infanta Ana in France.[58]

In this atmosphere, the Spanish crown asked for an increasing number of guarantees from the prince and the king of England. While earlier agreements had allowed María the choice of Catholic wetnurses for her children, the Spaniards now took as a starting point that María should be allowed to raise her children as she saw fit, which would include overseeing their religious education, until age ten or twelve. They also proposed that both bride and dowry should remain in Spain until James implemented all conditions of the treaty or even that the infanta and the Prince of Wales reside in Spain until their first child was born. In the face of all this, one can sense the frustration of the king of England when, asked again what security he could give that the marriage would not be dissolved, he replied simply that his honor would have to suffice.[59]

Although Spanish negotiators may have been upping the ante in hopes that England would withdraw from the match, Philip IV began to prepare his sister for her possible future. He sent two of his court preachers and the bishop of Segovia to discuss privately with the infanta her obligations in her "new state in which there were so many dangers to fear."[60] At public events, the infanta was associated with the prince by wearing his colors. She also sponsored a festival at the English Catholic seminary in Madrid during Charles's visit, thus acknowledging a new connection to England while affirming her devotion to her faith.[61] On a practical level, María and her ladies were learning English—

perhaps significantly, from an English convert to Catholicism, who was also serving as an interpreter between Olivares and Buckingham.[62]

Beyond considerations of state, the Prince of Wales's visit brought the marriage negotiations into the arena of public debate. Given the length of his stay, it is hardly surprising that numerous accounts of the festivities made it into the popular press, along with verses by poets of great and small talents and discussions of the propriety of the match, such as one that presented kings and queens in heaven considering the issues. Rumor even held that the queen's confessor, the prophetic Simón de Rojas, who had been mentioned as a candidate to accompany María, had predicted that neither of them would ever see England.[63]

But some stories were less direct in their content. A series of events, rumors, and observations reflected the underlying tensions of the visit. And here we begin to see differences in English and Spanish accounts, many of which have to do with the style and ceremony of the two courts. While one English account has the infanta blushing with "love and affection" the first time she saw the prince and the Spanish crowds cheering the prince for his gallantry, saying that he deserved to have the infanta "thrown into his arms the night he came," Spanish accounts see the infanta as appropriately reserved and the same crowds as cheering the prince's conversion, which was the general interpretation of his purpose in coming to Madrid in person.[64]

Early modern courts and individuals made use of protocol in a variety of ways. Spaniards of the time saw ceremony as fulfilling a concrete function within daily life. Protocol created order, allowed everyone to know his or her place in a crowded court, and, what is more, provided for the safety of royal persons. In contrast, the court of James I, in which Charles grew up, has generally been described as casual and somewhat inelegant. Indeed, the English prince and the Duke of Buckingham reported themselves outclassed by the Spaniards. The Spaniards, in turn, found the English rude, especially Buckingham, citing his leaning forward in public to stare at the infanta and his familiarity with Charles, which included sitting at the prince's table in his dressing gown and occasionally standing with his back turned to him. The English court also allowed a greater degree of lighthearted interplay between men and women at court. Spanish court etiquette, by contrast, allowed Charles only formal public audiences with the infanta, and he chafed at the lack of private communication. One incident that demonstrated this contrast was related by the Venetian ambassador: when, at a formal meeting with the royal family on Easter Day, Charles strayed from the prepared text of his greeting to the infanta and began to declare his emotions, while the queen registered disapproval and onlookers whispered among themselves, the infanta did not acknowledge the prince's gesture but answered him with a prepared reply, as if he had done nothing of note.[65]

Protocol became the central issue in a particular episode in which the prince attempted to make contact with the infanta when she took a walk in the gardens of the Casa de Campo, a royal retreat just outside Madrid. The Spanish sources tell us that María was exercising for her health, as recommended by her doctor, while an English source describes the infanta as going out to collect "maydew." She had with her, of course, a number of ladies, and guards walked several paces in advance of and behind her retinue. According to English sources, the Prince of Wales scaled a wall in order to join her, having been denied entrance at the gate.[66]

English sources report Charles's attempt as a gallant gesture and present the infanta as having "screeched" and run away, a description that may have encouraged later historians to describe the infanta as "strictly secluded" and unused to the company of men.[67] Spanish sources indeed credit María with a more dignified reaction, presenting her as an exemplar of correct conduct. In these sources, the infanta, either unaware of the prince's presence or choosing to ignore him, resolutely continued her walk and took turns that kept him out of her sight, while he attempted to talk his way past the officials meant to protect her privacy. Finally, the young man ceded to an official's entreaties to depart. Gascón de Torquemada ends his short account of the event with the following statement: "But the Lady Infanta never turned her head nor took notice, instead she continued her stroll."[68] Perhaps the most trustworthy account of the incident, given by the queen's mayordomo and principal guard for the walk, Don Pedro de Granada, has the Prince of Wales not scaling a wall but entering the park through the gardens attached to his room in the palace. Accompanied by some ten or twelve men, the prince clearly unnerved the guard, who certainly very seldom had to enforce the rules of etiquette upon a person of such high status. As soon as he saw the prince and his men from a distance, Granada asked the infanta to return in the direction from which she had come. The infanta, without comment, turned and left. The prince, after first not acknowledging the guard and then attempting to subvert his authority by turning as if to leave by a distant exit, finally left by a nearby gate. The guard called for a coach and himself paced back and forth in front of the gate until the infanta had returned safely to her quarters.[69]

Spanish sources implicitly present the infanta María as teaching the prince a lesson about the Spanish court. Her response was an appropriate one, for lapses in proper behavior could have serious consequences. On a similar walk in 1625 María's sister Ana encountered a situation that increased the suspicions of her husband and strengthened the French rumor that linked her romantically to the same Duke of Buckingham who had previously accompanied Prince Charles to Madrid and now was in Paris to conclude negotiations for Charles to marry Henrietta Maria. While on a formal stroll with a larger group, the French queen and the English duke momentarily wandered out of sight of the others. The people following heard a cry and rounded the corner to find the queen visibly upset and the duke disappearing down the path. Buckingham apparently had attempted to take some liberty with the queen, perhaps a stolen kiss or a brief embrace. While Ana could very easily be seen as faultless, especially given that she cried out, it nonetheless reflected badly on her and could have been avoided if she had not allowed herself to be alone, however briefly, with the duke.[70]

Beyond providing examples of contrasts between English and Spanish protocol, accounts also differ in their understanding of the infanta's response to the proposed marriage. The English ambassador, the Earl of Bristol, claimed that María had initially resisted the marriage, owing to the influence of her confessor, but that after his death a new confessor had inspired her with a vision of returning England to the church.[71] Francisco de Jesús suggests that María's initial reservations concerning the marriage reflected not a rejection of the matter as a whole but her assessment that conditions offered to Catholics in England were insufficient. Some saw the infanta as rejecting the match, preferring to enter a convent rather than marry. Popular tradition presented her as making this choice herself. The early modern observer found such an explanation more satisfying than reasons of state and chose to see members of the royal family acting as individuals in the very political realm of marriage. Indeed, diplomatic strategy may have taken this into account, for there was also some suggestion that María's resistance was part of a strategy originally developed under Philip III to provide the king with an escape from the marriage agreement that would appear to be a magnanimous bowing to his daughter's sensibilities. Whatever her personal involvement in such a plan might have been, the infanta apparently reserved the right to enter a convent up until the time of the actual wedding. After the prince's departure, however, María would not let anyone question her affection for him, suggesting that she intended to play the role given her, although she later blamed Olivares and Gondomar for having "done mischief" to herself and the king.[72]

Historians too have tended to get caught up in the romance of the story, interpreting María's response on the basis of emotion and personality.[73] But understanding her personality or her temper is not necessary for analyzing her reaction: if indeed she had reservations about the marriage, they were certainly shared by the Council of State and by other members of her family. Rather than look to emotion to explain her actions, we should look to her training as a champion of religion and exemplar of propriety. It is difficult to know the extent of María's refusal or whether she would have gone through with the marriage if it came to that, but she played her part with the gravity her father described as "appropriate to monarchs." During Charles's last visit with her, they spoke for close to half an hour, with Ambassador Bristol serving as interpreter. She responded with the "seriousness and modesty that a person so grave and prudent ought to follow in public acts." She asked him to visit a certain nun along his route and deliver a letter, a mission that seems incongruous with the prince's own mood and intentions concerning his journey. Finally, she commended the English Catholics to his care.[74] To the end, she indicated that her role was shaped by her religion, not by romantic notions.

Contemporaries and historians also offer a variety of speculations regarding Charles's intentions. While some have seen his journey as a gesture of independence from his father, others have seen it as a strategic ploy designed to push the Spaniards to admit that they had never intended the marriage to take place. Alternatively, if one thought the intention was to force the Spanish hand in regard to the Palatinate, then Charles's actions can be seen not as a failure but as a "bold cavalry charge."[75] The English ambassador came to see the whole adventure as a conspiracy on the part of Buckingham and certain members of the prince's household to convert the prince.[76] Whatever his motives, Charles patterned his actions on stories of royal life, including his own parents' courtship, but showed a basic misunderstanding of the reality of diplomacy and policymaking. Marriage negotiations required the resolution of complex issues and were invariably time consuming, often started when a child was young and not concluded until the child was a teenager. The prince, by taking active control and demanding resolution by his presence, probably undermined the possibility of success. As the Spanish showered him with gifts and entertainment, reflecting proper ceremony, not their diplomatic opinions, he could not perceive that the underlying negotiations were working against him.

Although documents were signed at an official betrothal ceremony, it is still difficult to evaluate the intentions of either side. The wide range of advantages suggested by the marriage rendered it worthy of consideration, and while Spanish faith in the power of a marriage to solve a wide range of religious issues can be seen as naive, the ambitious Spanish policy was balanced by the apparent English willingness to promise anything in order to procure the alliance. Despite a reportedly affectionate personal farewell between the king and the prince, Charles left having made an agreement that could not be kept and perhaps, at that point, one that he had no interest in trying to keep. In England, James I remained briefly interested in the match, but Charles and Buckingham worked against it and encouraged an anti-Spanish policy. By March 1624 the match had been officially terminated.

The Making of an Empress

Only a few months after the departure of the Prince of Wales, the imperial ambassador again began to sound the waters of Spanish opinion regarding an Austrian match. The negotiations for such a marriage were not as complicated as those surrounding the English match. The political issues, although wide in their implications, were perceived as a simple strengthening of a preexisting alliance. Despite arguments over the order of the queen's confessor, religious issues played only a small part in negotiations, since both the emperor and the Spanish king were unquestionably champions of the Catholic faith. The Spaniards debated, however, whether to postpone the marriage until the groom could be named king of the Romans, the office understood as that of emperor-elect. He already held the title of king of Hungary, but this kingship was directly subsumed by the emperor, so the Council of State urged, first, that he be given a particular province to govern directly and, second, that he be named king of the Romans. The council discussed the new status of the infanta after her engagement and suggested that she should be called "Majesty" and treated as an official state guest, but Philip IV chose to postpone any change in treatment of his sister, arguing that it might give the impression that all issues of the alliance were settled, thus decreasing the urgency for the imperial court to resolve the election of Ferdinand as king of the Romans.[77]

The contract with the emperor proceeded despite the lack of resolution on this issue. In contrast to the negotiations with England, the announcement of the engagement garnered no special occasion, made as if for convenience on the same day as the baptism of the Spanish princess María Eugenia, on June 7, 1626. Earlier in the day, the imperial ambassador made his first official visit to the infanta María, now addressed as queen of Hungary. María received the ambassador and his entourage without other members of the royal family present and was accompanied by them to the infanta's baptism. As a sign of her new identity, she wore a little hat "in the German style" for the occasion.[78]

The Council of State also began to discuss the composition of María's entourage. While the French court had rejected a Spanish camarera mayor for Ana, the imperial court did not argue about the definition of the office. Perhaps the numerous years of interchange between the Spanish and the Austrian Habsburgs had brought about mutual understanding. The choice of camarera was further eased by the existence of a family formed through the marriage of a respected Austrian diplomat and a high-ranking Spanish woman. The favored candidate was the Marquise of Mondéjar, Beatriz de Cardona. She was the daughter of Margarita de Cardona, the camarera mayor of the empress María, and Adam Dietrichstein, the imperial representative in Spain during the central years of the reign of Philip II, as well as the ayo and mayordomo mayor of Archdukes Rudolf and Ernst. Her brother was Cardinal Dietrichstein. The nomination of the Marquise of Mondéjar met with the almost reverential approval of the Spanish Council of State. The imperial court also applauded the nomination, not only for the marquise's outstanding personal qualities but especially "because she knows the two languages, the customs and practices of both courts, and in the one and the other place she has so many relatives."[79] Having Austrian relatives not only provided her connections, prestige, and knowledge of customs but also diminished perception of her as a foreign influence or as a burden to the imperial court.

The king asked the Council of State to comment on naming the imperial ambassador Franz Christoph Khevenhüller, the Count of Frankenburg, as mayordomo mayor. Like the marquise, the count came from a family experienced in international service: he was the son of Hans Khevenhüller, who had served the empress María as mayordomo mayor for many years, and he himself had been the imperial ambassador. While enthusiastic in their endorsement of the marquise, a few members of the council commented on their lack of choice in the matter of the mayordomo mayor. But a cover note, perhaps written by Philip IV's valido, the Count-Duke of Olivares, comments, "I understand from a sure source that the emperor would be glad if this ambassador were given the office of mayordomo mayor of the queen of Hungary and if the Marquise of Mondéjar were named camarera mayor."[80]

The king, however, resisted somewhat the pleasure of the emperor and perhaps of his own favorite, naming the marquise but noting that "in respect to the mayordomo mayor I will keep looking." In the end, neither the Marquise of Mondéjar (who had subsequently died) nor the Count of Frankenburg served in María's household. The camarera mayor was instead the Countess of Siruela, identified elsewhere as Victoria Pacheco Colonna, daughter of a respected Spanish-Italian family.[81] In the summer of 1628 the Council of State also debated the qualifications and resources of several great nobles and prelates, choosing one of each to accompany María on the journey. Among noblemen, they eventually chose the Duke of Alba, an honor he would live to regret during the long and expensive journey. While the noble escort received an *ayuda de costa* for the journey, the prelate would not receive any subsidy, which accounted for the prominence of the topic of wealth in the council's discussion of an ecclesiastical escort. Proposed were the bishop of Sigüenza, the cardinal Moscoso (Lerma's nephew), and the archbishop of Seville. Despite Moscoso's wealth, the king chose the archbishop of Seville, Diego de Guzmán, the former teacher of the infantas. One can imagine Guzmán, who had at least initially considered moving to Seville an exile, as overwhelmed with the honor of escorting his former pupil, just as he had been when he was named tutor almost twenty years earlier. He made a grand entrance into Madrid in December 1629 and was appointed to the Council of State a few days later.[82] It was a joyful reunion with the court for the elderly archbishop, whose fate was to die in Italy, several months into the journey.

The Council of State took special care to specify the nationality of members of María's household. The queen required a Spanish secretary and a Spanish doctor for her personal service, as well as several Spanish women, among them three damas, an azafata, and two assistants in the chamber. These women would be joined by several Austrian women once María reached a convenient point on the journey to her new country. A few members of her entourage needed to speak both Spanish and German, including one designated simply as an "official" and four others whose duties of buying goods, keeping accounts, and directing staff would require them to interact both with the Spanish infanta and with German speakers at the imperial court. Several other minor officials—a tailor, cooks, a "personal washer," and six porters to carry sedan chairs—may have been intended to ease the infanta's transition from home or to provide services that were not customary in Austria. Of the eighty-some persons who would serve the infanta in her new country, the negotiated agreement allowed between twenty-five and thirty to be Spanish.[83]

Several persons in the entourage had served previously in similar positions, many of them in the household of Prince Philiberto. Others were children of people who served the king and queen in similar capacities. The significant overlap of personal and diplomatic service so notable in the Khevenhüller and Dietrichstein families can be seen in the appointment of the Marquis of Cadreita, who was to serve both as one of María's mayordomos during the journey and as the new Spanish ambassador to the imperial court. The imperial ambassador, the Count of Frankenburg, also accompanied María, although not with an official title in her service, as did the Baroness of Par. These two persons, both experienced in international service, were available to ease the infanta's transition in her new country.[84]

Following patterns of service from other contexts, several families provided more than one member of the household. The Countess of Siruela took with her both her daughter, Leonor de Velasco, a lady of the queen, and her son, listed among the "mayordomos mayores, gentlemen, and other servants," but without an official title or official duties. Despite his lack of household office, the young count was available to carry out official functions, including serving as messenger between the infanta and her husband before their formal meeting.[85] The Marquis of Ariça served as menino, and his elder half-brother, Juan de Palafox, later a prolific author of sacred, historical, and political works, went as a chaplain and the queen's principal almoner. Two of Diego de Guzmán's nephews also traveled with the entourage, apparently in their uncle's service rather than the queen's, and among the ladies of the chamber was Isabel de Quiroga, who may have been the sister or niece of the father confessor. Juan de Soto was an assistant in the queen's oratory, and Ana María de Soto, María's azafata since earliest childhood, accompanied her in that role. Years later, Ana María de Soto returned to Spain with María's daughter Mariana, continuing the exchange of Spanish and Austrian culture and customs through the very persons of the women who served royalty.[86]

Philip IV, in his instructions to the Marquis of Cadreita concerning his service as ambassador to the imperial court, emphasized personal elements in the success of his sister's marriage and of the diplomatic mission. He urged the ambassador to establish himself close to the king of Hungary, taking care not to make the emperor's ministers envious of him. He should, most of all, attempt to encourage good communication between father and son and advise the king not to differ with the emperor. The queen, his sister, he noted, understood very well the attention she should give to the pleasure and service of the emperor, the empress, and the king, her husband. If, by chance, these relationships did not function as they should, the ambassador should, with "all ingenuity," counsel the queen to adjust herself to her husband's will and give satisfaction to the emperor and empress.[87] These instructions suggest that Philip IV, like his father, placed personal relationships at the center of the success of the marriage alliance and the diplomatic benefits it was intended to procure. He emphasized the importance of an absolute concordance between the wills of husband and wife, and he urged the wife to conform to the husband's will in order to procure that end. Like his sister Ana and, indeed, his own wife, María had to please not just her husband but also his parents, whose acceptance of the new daughter affected both diplomatic success and personal happiness. In all of these comments, Philip develops concepts of the function of marriage that may derive both from his parents and from his own experiences and those of his elder sister.

The king's instructions to the infanta herself suggest that he imagined his sister taking a more active part in political discussion than he admitted to his ambassador. When directly addressing her, he called her his best ambassador and did not hesitate to share with her his assessment of the relationships between Spain and various entities within the Empire. Advising her first of all to remain always in full accordance with her husband—just as, he noted, he had always advised their sister, the queen of France—he then argued that she could nonetheless always take his part because the interests of the king of Hungary, the emperor, and himself had always to be united. She must never believe, or even hear, any word spoken against the unity of the three. Citing a recent example with which he seemed to assume she was familiar, he announced the trial of a person who had written lies, apparently about discord among the three. His advice goes to the heart of the ideal of family relations: both sides needed to realize and assume that they were united, "closing the door completely" to other thoughts so that all persons would know such talk would not be tolerated. Otherwise peace would be impossible.[88]

Having settled this point and provided a very practical interpretation of its usefulness, Philip turned to diplomatic issues, assigning his sister the power to commit his services to his uncle and brother-in-law. On that basis, he informed her about several aspects of his international policy, writing frankly about disagreements with the Empire over Mantua and Monferrat and about his need of the emperor's assistance against rebels in the Low Countries. In regard to the journey itself, he gave a similarly frank, although not as detailed, evaluation of Spain's relations with various Italian states, noting especially that she should show great consideration to the Duke of Savoy, for even though he was of lesser rank, their blood tie with his children and the mutual obligations between them and the duke demanded her esteem. In the details of these relations, the king again expressed his sense that his sister was his representative as she made her way through Italy. Last among the Italian powers the king mentioned the pope, to whom the infanta should show due reverence, although he candidly acknowledged that the pope was also a secular prince with whom the king of Spain did not always agree.

The king also shared with María his thoughts on family issues. He expressed hope that their brother Carlos would marry the emperor's daughter and urged her to ascertain what the emperor might be willing to bestow on his daughter as dowry in such a marriage. Concerning the career of the infante Fernando he also looked to the Empire, but he said he would inform her about this at the proper time, at which point she could help in that project. He urged her to see that her husband was sworn king of the Romans as soon as possible, reminding her that this was part of the wedding agreement, although it had not yet been done. Briefly commending the electors of Bavaria and Saxony and the ecclesiastical electors to her, as well as all religious matters, he advised her to treat their aunt, the infanta Isabel, governor of the Low Countries, as mother, taking her advice in all matters, and to develop good relations with their cousins. In mentioning the empress, he did not echo Philip III's admonition to Ana to consider Marie de Medici a mother by suggesting that María think of Eleanore Gonzaga, the emperor's second wife, as her mother. Instead he noted that she should show that she esteemed Eleanore but that, if possible, she should encourage the emperor to be more partial to the house of Austria than to that of Mantua.

The king urged his sister to continue to employ the Burgundian household, that is, the structure and etiquette used at the Spanish court since the time of Charles V. He considered this style appropriate to the dignity of an infanta of Castile, a matter that he saw as beneficial both to her and to her new family, as well as a favor to him that would help avoid the problems that had been encountered in France.

Finally, the king noted a change in diplomatic usage among the imperial ambassadors of which he heartily disapproved and placed on his sister the burden of informing the imperial ambassador and the court of his displeasure. The method of negotiating through threat, which he accused the imperial ambassadors of employing, could by itself, he noted, be enough to undermine all their relations if it continued. Ending his instructions on this rather ominous note, he cautioned his sister once more to maintain the "circumspection of Spain," and he closed by wishing her many happy years.

The great ceremony surrounding the exchange of princesses with France and the failed marriage negotiations with England contrasts tellingly with the simplicity of María's wedding, which took place in the king's chamber with only the infantes, the queen, and a few nobles in attendance. Other than the ambassador, a representative from the Empire was not even necessary, since the infante Carlos acted as proxy for the king of Hungary. The bride asked Philip's permission before taking her vows, and the queen of Spain yielded place of precedence to the queen of Hungary, gestures described by contemporary accounts in such personal and charming terms that one would not guess they were the product of years in planning.[89] Although the simplicity of the ceremony might be explained by the financial difficulties of both Spain and Austria, it also suggests that a sure alliance did not require the pomp of an unsure one.

The Spanish crown intended the journey, too, to be fairly simple, despite the large entourage. Attempts to contain costs were, however, undermined by various changes in itinerary to avoid reported outbreaks of plague and war-torn areas. As the journey through northern Spain and Italy lengthened from weeks to months to more than a year, María visited convents, made formal entries into various cities, was an honored guest at entertainments, and even had occasion to sit for one last portrait by Velázquez, who was traveling separately in Italy.[90] Various arguments over ceremonial and service also marked the journey. Some of these disagreements reflected the difficulty of determining precedent during the various stages of a complex journey, such as when the Count of Barajas and Barcelona officials disagreed concerning who could wear hats during a reception or when a planned ceremony at the border of Aragon and Catalonia was dropped because the governor of Catalonia did not appear at the designated time.[91] More serious was the Duke of Alba's refusal to serve his household position, claiming that he had come to accompany the queen, not to serve as mayordomo mayor. He also objected to the Countess of Siruela being treated with courtesy equal to his—hers based on office, his for being a grandee—and entered Barcelona separately rather than accept placement inferior to that of the viceroy. Although María ordered him to serve his office, she transferred most of the work of mayordomo mayor to the Count of Barajas, and lack of definitive orders from Madrid encouraged the duke to persist in his interpretation of his position. All through the four months the entourage stayed in Naples, Alba and the Duke of Alcalá, viceroy of Naples, argued over who should have precedence in ceremony.[92]

María charmed the crowds in Barcelona by entering the city in an open sedan chair and glancing around to all sides with obvious pleasure. In this case, unlike her father's "reserve appropriate to monarchs" or her brother's reputed habit of watching entire plays without a single movement of his head, María communicated her pleasure. Her version of royal fortitude included watching dances performed for her from eight in the evening to four in the morning without leaving her seat, appearing engrossed and happy the entire time. On another occasion, she learned a lesson about ceremony when she treated Cardinal Dietrichstein too formally. Accustomed to the greater simplicity of the Austrian court, the cardinal left his first interview with her dissatisfied. The confessor Quiroga informed the infanta of the problem and, eager to correct the unintended slight, she drew out the cardinal's next visit with extended conversation, questions, and compliments.[93] Regarding ceremony in general, she choose according to what was needed: when the city of Lérida sent to ask in what form they should receive her, María requested that they forgo an elaborate entry rather than wait for preparations; but when the arguments of the Dukes of Alba and Alcalá resulted in a less than satisfactory entrance into Naples, María ordered an elaborate ceremonial exit from the city to satisfy the requirements of her own prestige.[94]

Like her mother three decades earlier, María took advantage of the opportunity her journey offered to visit a number of holy places. Putting on walking shoes, she hiked up to the hermitages in the heights of Monserrat. Although she tried to arrange to visit without being seen publicly, the crowds that gathered to see her return to the monastery served to increase her reputation, since everyone was impressed with her energy and spirit. But these activities clearly had personal meaning for the infanta, who was noticeably moved by the Marian image at Monserrat and gave her best jewel to Our Lady of Loreto in Italy. Throughout the journey, she confessed and communed often, and the day after the festival of the Annunciation, she and her ladies served a meal to nine poor women, as had been her mother's practice. On Holy Thursday she did the same for twelve poor men, washing the feet of a child among them rather than those of an adult as her father or brother would have done.[95]

Unlike her sister Ana, María found herself in the embrace of family both during her journey and when she arrived in her new country. Her brothers accompanied her as far as Zaragoza and after days of festivities left without saying good-bye, out of excess rather than deficit of emotion. Although disappointed in her hopes of seeing her sister in Marseilles, she disembarked in Livorna, where her mother's sister, the widowed Grand Duchess of Tuscany, came out to meet her with her son, whose looks and manners reminded the Spaniards of Philip IV. In Trieste her uncle the archduke Leopold came to greet her and escort her over the mountains. When the king of Hungary and his brother slipped in among the welcoming Austrians not far from Vienna, she recognized the king, partly because his brother looked so much like her own brother Fernando and partly because her husband dressed in the Spanish style for the occasion. When she arrived at the imperial palace, the entire family came to greet her and accompanied her to her chambers, where they chatted casually for some time. Like his Spanish relatives in such private moments, the emperor was not one to hide his feelings: he was very pleased with his new daughter-in-law and watched in pleasure as María and Ferdinand conversed in Spanish. "Look," he commented to his companions, "how my daughter and the king are becoming friends."[96]

The journey to central Europe represented the final and not inconsequential step of a larger journey. The young queen of Hungary had learned the lessons of her upbringing and her experiences. She had previously shown both dignity and resolve in dealing with the prospect of marriage to a prince she considered a heretic and in arguing to retain the confessor of her choice. Now she experienced a journey that revealed high spirits, flexibility in dealing with people and events, and a natural graciousness that suited her well in her role of queen and later empress.

Both daughters and the daughter-in-law of Philip III developed political identities beyond those of simple tokens of diplomatic alliance. They embraced the roles that the seventeenth century offered royal women, taking the possibilities and molding them to their own use. Ana de Austria and Isabel de Bourbon both served as regents in their adopted countries, Ana for several years during the minority of the Sun King, Louis XIV, and Isabel for a shorter period, from the summer of 1643 to the autumn of 1644. Ana's hard lessons in the early years of her life at the French court taught her that beyond all doubt she was French. As regent of France, she commanded a war against her brother's kingdom and arranged yet another unhappy marriage of a Spanish infanta in France. The infanta María, first as queen of Hungary, then as empress in the Holy Roman Empire, served a more conventional queenship. Like her great aunt, great-grandmother, and namesake, she was credited with the behind-the-scenes influence that was the pride of queens and occasionally the fear of politicians. This type of influence, born of political marriages that purposely placed foreign queens at the heart of royal courts in all countries, was the normal lot of queens within the personal world of the monarchy in the early modern state.

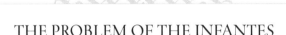

THE PROBLEM OF THE INFANTES

Precedents and Opportunities

While public and private rejoicing greeted the birth of second and third sons to Philip III and Queen Margarita, the royal brothers eventually occasioned anxiety as much as joy at the Spanish court. Philip III considered several options for his younger sons' careers when they were still young and began to implement his decisions in the few years prior to his death. When he died in March of 1621, however, Carlos and Fernando were only thirteen and eleven, and the final task of defining their careers fell to their brother Philip IV and his favorite, the Count-Duke of Olivares. The question of the infantes' roles at court and in the larger world deeply concerned Olivares, who in particular cautioned the king about factions forming around them. But the valido's heightened anxiety was not the only source of concern about the brothers. King and favorite faced a more basic problem: since the mid-fifteenth century, no generation of the Spanish royal family except Charles V (who was not, in any case, raised in Spain) and his brother Ferdinand had included legitimate sons other than the heir who survived to adulthood; precedent defined practice at the Spanish court, yet there was no direct experience on which to base decisions concerning the brothers of the king.

Seeking models to help Philip IV shape his brothers' careers, Spaniards could not rely on the unsettling examples of late medieval Castile and Aragon or of contemporary France, where the existence of royal brothers had led to civil war. Three generations earlier, Charles V had preempted tensions with his brother by sending Ferdinand to the Empire before he himself took power in Spain, and he had avoided further conflict by providing him with his own territories in central Europe. The unusually large amount of European land newly under Habsburg control in that generation had facilitated the development of a strong supporting role for Ferdinand. While relations between the brothers clearly had not been ideal, Ferdinand's strict adherence to the concept of family politics had kept peace between them.[1] The roles available to Philip IV's brothers more closely suggest comparison to the careers of various royal cousins and Don Juan, the illegitimate brother of Philip II. These comparisons place the choices most effectively within Spanish practice and suggest the perceived rank of the brothers. Moreover, the similarities in their careers highlight how the lack of brothers in the previous generation had encouraged the employment of cousins in key Spanish roles, a practice that had temporarily strengthened the ties between different branches of the Habsburg extended family.

When Philip III and then Philip IV planned the careers of the infantes Carlos and Fernando, they clearly looked to the precedent of Don Juan, Archduke Albert, and Philiberto of Savoy. Carlos was appointed both *general del mar,* as his great-uncle Don Juan and his cousin Philiberto had been, and governor of Portugal, as Albert had been, although he did not live long enough to serve actively in either position. Fernando's ascent to the rank of cardinal and the archbishopric of Toledo echoes Albert's rise in the service of the Spanish crown through ecclesiastical office. His eventual transfer to govern the Netherlands also parallels Albert's career both in the specific appointment and in his movement away from the church, although Fernando was not required, as Albert had been, to marry and give up his ecclesiastical office. His experience and eventual reputation can also be compared to those of Don Juan, who persuaded Philip II to appoint him to military commands instead of pursuing the ecclesiastical career their father had envisioned.

Although neither infante married, there does not seem to have been any suggestion that they should not marry, as there had been in the case of Ferdinand, whom advisers had encouraged Charles V not to allow to marry for fear of providing challenges to the inheritance of imperial lands.[2] As early as 1608, when Carlos was not yet a year old, Philip provided two sets of instructions to the Spanish ambassador to France, Pedro de Toledo y Osorio, concerning a possible marriage alliance with France. His "public" instruction allowed the ambassador to speak only of the prince's marriage, and then not officially, but the secret instruction also mentioned the possible marriages of the infanta María to the dauphin and of Carlos to the second daughter of Henry IV and Marie de Medici. Philip III described these discussions to Pedro de Toledo as having been advanced by the French, whose ambassador in Spain "has opened conversation many times about the marriages of my children with those of that king." The papal nuncio in Madrid had also suggested the match, "expressing great urgency in the matter."[3]

The Netherlands figured in both sets of negotiations. Spain accused France of supporting rebels in the Netherlands, while France was concerned about having Spanish forces on two borders. While negotiations for the prince's marriage opened an opportunity to discuss these matters, Carlos's marriage addressed the issue directly, as it involved the potential separation of the Netherlands from Spain, with Carlos and his proposed French wife invested as governors. By this time it was clear that the archdukes Albert and Isabel Clara would not have children to inherit the governorship, leaving Philip III to address the same questions that his father had addressed concerning the Low Countries.

Despite the focus of his instruction on the marriage and proposed alliance, Philip advocated a studied display of disinterest in the matter. The ambassador should not introduce the subject himself; if someone else introduced it, he could comment on the possibility of a marriage between the Spanish prince and the eldest French princess, but he should present himself as speaking his own thoughts, with no authorization from the king. Regarding Carlos's marriage and the Netherlands, the ambassador should hazard no opinion, however unofficial, on the matter, but simply say that he would relay the matter to the king, while recommending that the French attempt to procure the obedience of rebels in the Low Countries and the free practice of Catholicism. Before any discussion, the ambassador should emphasize Philip III's disappointment with the French king's failure to ease the situation in the Low Countries. France had in fact formed a league with the rebel provinces, but Philip presented himself as yielding to the pope and the good of the church by sending an ambassador rather than an army to France. The central place of the Low Countries in the consideration of Carlos's marriage is also indicated by the Spanish ambassador's correspondence with Archduke Albert during these negotiations.[4]

It was not the French, however, but the papal nuncio in Paris who initiated conversation concerning the marriage of Carlos to the second daughter of Henry IV. This apparently spontaneous act was actually instigated by the Spanish ambassador, who described the nuncio's audience to Philip III and reported that he had arranged for the nuncio "of his own accord" to introduce the subject.[5] This statement may clarify a point in Pedro de Toledo's instructions telling him to attempt to arrange a discreet meeting with the nuncio in France before he spoke with the French king. A papal letter the ambassador was to deliver to the nuncio may have instructed him to introduce the subject of a marriage alliance, thus opening discussion, while maintaining the impression of Spanish disinterest. The pope's involvement in the matter, expressed both through his letters and through his nuncios in Madrid and Paris, indicates once again the range of issues perceived to be part of marriage politics and especially the place of religion as a key element of these particular negotiations.

The following year, the Spanish ambassador in Paris, now Iñigo de Cárdenas, reported rumors that Henry IV wanted to contract his son to the Duke of Lorraine's daughter, who was his heir. The territory of Lorraine was strategically located on the edge of France, and the duke hesitated to ally with either France or Spain, fearing that his brother, the Duke of Vaudémont, would side with the rejected party against him and deprive his daughter of her inheritance. Philip III instructed his special ambassador to France to take advantage of the duke's anxiety and discourage him from allying with the French and to point out that the king of Spain had "other children beside the prince."[6] Cárdenas followed this logic as well and shaped his vision of the match to the concerns of Lorraine, noting that he thought the match right for Carlos rather than the prince because the duke wanted to be connected with Spain, not subsumed by it. In July 1611 Cárdenas met with the Duke of Lorraine, and that night he found himself unable to sleep for thinking of the possibility of Carlos marrying the duke's daughter: "I confess it has made me turn more than twice on my pillow with a good fever, desiring her for the lord infante Don Carlos."[7] The match haunted the ambassador's thoughts, although he saw the age of the infante and the tension that had existed between Lorraine and Henry IV and threatened to continue under Louis XIII as reasons to proceed slowly.

Carlos's marriage prospects again figured in diplomatic discussions in November 1613, when Cárdenas reported the rumor that Philip III had offered his protection to Princess María, the three-year-old presumed heiress of Monferrat and granddaughter of the Duke of Savoy, in order to control the duchy and later to marry her to the infante Carlos.[8] This assertion apparently did not reflect

Spanish policy, however, but instead derived from rumors floated by Savoy's agents in attempts to establish a foothold in discussions.

In 1611 the Spanish representative at the imperial court, Baltasar de Zúñiga, was also considering the future of the infantes and flirting with the idea of proposing one of them as king of Bohemia. Children should be invited to the Spanish court from Germany, Flanders, and Bohemia, he advised, to serve as meninos and aid the brothers in learning the languages of these countries.[9] In the following year, Rodrigo Calderón, writing from the Low Countries, also spoke of a possible future for one of the infantes in the Empire. Zúñiga, he reported, was on his way to the imperial elections taking place after the death of Rudolf II. Calderón's proposal was immediate and more specific than Zúñiga's had been: envisioning the election of Archduke Albert as emperor, he speculated that since Albert had no children, Carlos could then be named king of the Romans and thus his successor to the imperial throne. One could reasonably assume that Albert might be elected; he was, after all, the brother of the recently deceased emperor. Once the election was secured, all of the archduke's years of service to Spain and his obligations to and love for the king suggested that he would be "very pleased with the proposal [to name the infante king of the Romans] and foster it as much as he could."[10]

To our eyes, however, Albert looks more Spanish than Austrian and had been attached to Spanish interests too long for the German princes to have found him an attractive candidate. Indeed, if the more experienced Zúñiga had not hinted at such a plan earlier, one could easily ascribe Calderón's vision to simplicity of perception.[11] However inconceivable it may seem in hindsight, this course of events seemed plausible to the Spanish court, resting on the basic structure of royal power that placed status above other considerations. The further notion of the infantes serving in some capacity in the Empire was not at all extravagant, since Austrian cousins had prospered in Spain, and Zúñiga's advice for them to learn the languages of the Empire would have been equally useful for other positions they might have held. The success of Austrian archdukes in Spain, however, had come in a generation in which the Spanish dynasty had a deficit of male offspring, while the Austrian Habsburgs had numerous sons. The imperial crown, in any case, went to another of Rudolf's brothers, Matthias, and in the next transition, that of 1619, passed to Ferdinand II, head of the junior branch of the imperial family founded by Karl of Styria, brother of the emperor Maximilian II and father of the Spanish queen Margarita. Even as late as this

election, Albert remained an acknowledged player, making an official renunciation of his rights to the imperial succession.

Other than marriage possibilities, little discernible discussion concerning
Carlos's career occurred during the lifetime of his father. The lack of plans for
the infante may reflect the fact that so many heirs to the throne had died in
Philip III's generation: the king may have seen the elder infante as security, given
the poor health of the prince. For his youngest surviving son, however, Philip
planned a potentially powerful career in the church. Following in the footsteps
of Archduke Albert, the infante Fernando became archbishop of Toledo. Unlike
Albert, he did not first build a career but instead was nominated at age nine.
This decision could just as easily indicate either that he was considered the more
capable of the two younger brothers or that he was considered the more expend-
able. Widely perceived as the most avidly military of the boys and described by
some observers as vehemently opposed to an ecclesiastical career, Fernando
had little say in the matter. Whatever reasoning determined the younger infante's career, the choice was not based on personal inclinations or abilities,
but on the intersection of immediate needs and patterns set by tradition.

The decision to make Fernando archbishop of Toledo and a cardinal has also
been linked to the Duke of Lerma's ambitions. Some contemporaries suggested
that Lerma aspired to high church office during the decline of his power as
favorite in order to protect himself from prosecution for misuse of power.[12] He
had, however, spoken previously of retiring into religious life, perhaps as early
as 1606. In addition to affording protection from prosecution, the income of
the archbishopric may have been attractive to the duke, given the pattern of a
career that had amassed great wealth for himself and his family. It was, after all,
the death in 1618 of his great uncle, Bernardo de Sandoval, who presumably had
received the position at least in part through Lerma's influence, that left vacant
the see of Toledo; Lerma may indeed have envisioned his own retirement to
the most prestigious ecclesiastical office in Spain. Only the appointment of a
person of yet higher rank, an infante of Spain, could provide the king a suitably
graceful excuse to deny his friend the archbishopric.[13]

Fernando's nomination was not unopposed, and it provoked arguments
about the propriety of appointing someone so young. Pope Paul V suggested to
Philip III that it would be better for the care of his people's souls to find a more
clearly qualified person, and he also expressed concerns about granting concessions concerning age or preparation that had not been granted in Germany or

France, thus setting precedents that might be dangerous in countries faced with a greater threat of heresy. The Spanish king persisted, however, citing examples of precocious appointments in earlier centuries and noting that the education of infantes of Spain had always been notably religious and above reproach.[14] Despite his reservations, the pope also granted Philip's request to make Fernando a cardinal. The news arrived during the 1619 royal journey to Portugal, an event duly noted in the accounts of the journey, since an expenditure of one thousand ducats was authorized to reward "the messenger of His Holiness . . . who brought the news of the cardinalate of His Highness."[15]

To compensate for the infante's youth, it was stipulated that the archbishopric would be governed by an ecclesiastical administrator until Fernando reached the age of thirty. Despite this provision, Fernando undertook several duties related to his office and received an ecclesiastical household. Within a few years, he was signing some of the business papers of the archbishopric, which were countersigned by his secretary, Pedro Fernández Navarrete.[16] He gained ecclesiastical incomes, and the Council of State researched his proper titles and treatment.[17] Chroniclers described him as being instructed in his duties and noted that he wore clerical dress on some public occasions. Despite his youth, observers considered him a major patron of Simón de Rojas's congregation of Ave María from early in its existence, and on December 8, 1623, the infante co-officiated with Cardinal Zapata at the baptism of his niece, Margarita María Catalina.[18]

On public occasions, the infante's office appears to have curtailed his involvement in court activities. While the royal chaplain described gala festivities for María's nineteenth and Carlos's eighteenth birthday in 1625, Fernando heard Mass for his sixteenth birthday in the same year in his own chambers, by himself. Often in the early years of the reign of Philip IV, when the infante Carlos rode with the king in masques and tournaments, Fernando watched from a balcony with his sister and sister-in-law, as during the festivities held for the Prince of Wales in August 1623. On this occasion, color effectively defined the relationships and conditions of the royal entourage: the king and Carlos were associated with each other by wearing black, the Prince of Wales wore white, María wore the colors of the Prince of Wales, and Fernando wore "Roman purple," that is, the color associated with his ecclesiastical rank.[19] Likewise, Carlos usually accompanied Philip when he traveled, while Fernando remained at court.

On other occasions, however, the younger infante played a more active role because of his title; for example, in his capacity as lord of Alcalá de Henares, which belonged to the archdiocese of Toledo, he oversaw the reception of his uncle, Archduke Karl, in 1624 and the visit of the cardinal-legate Federico Barberini in 1626. On one occasion he woke at four in the morning to go to Alcalá for a festival transferring the Host from the main church of the city to a parish, at which the king and Carlos made an appearance much later in the morning, at ten o'clock. Similar responsibilities were implied when Fernando authorized the bishop-elect of Rosana to execute the orders and other pontifical acts for the beatification of Francisco de Borja, although the infante himself does not appear to have taken an active role. On another occasion, however, the king and Carlos took part in the procession and mass celebrated at the Descalzas Reales for the canonization of Isabel de Portugal, while Fernando and the queen stayed in the palace with María, who was ill. Fernando, indeed, participated in processions less often than his brothers, suggesting that processions were considered primarily public rather than devotional acts.[20]

Perceptions of the Brothers

When Philip III died in 1621, Andrés Almansa y Mendoza conceptualized the transformation of Philip IV's relationship to his brothers by presenting the new king as saying to them that "if until now he had had them for brothers, now he would cherish them as sons, and that they would see the many things that he would do for them."[21] He became their father in the theoretical sense that the king was the father of all his subjects and in the practical sense that a father provided his sons with the necessities of life and with careers. The laudatory biography of the infante Fernando by Pedro Gonçalez de Salcedo y Butrón, also struck a positive chord and emphasized the way in which the brothers worked together for the good of the crown. Calling Philip III "the Saint" and Philip IV "the Great," he gave Fernando the title "the Heroic." Of Philip III he wrote, "For reward of his virtues it was enough to leave such sons . . . since he assured his crown with the government of the one and the daring of the other."[22]

But these conceptualizations of the brothers' respective roles did not alter the fact that the close equality of the three in age and rank raised concerns. During the lifetime of Philip III, another writer posited that the natural modesty of the infantes made problems unlikely, but he was not confident that there was no risk: "Because the blood of infantes and of princes is the same, with difficulty they are habituated to the humility of being vassals." For this reason, he continued, it was necessary to educate the infantes properly in their roles, giving them "servants separate from those of the prince, reduced to the point that they naturally respect him like the father himself, not finding themselves in any matter equal to him, not in goods nor in ceremonies nor in clothing, so that in these exteriors as in the rest they are habituated to inferiority."[23]

Despite their royal blood, he continued, infantes could be raised with a correct understanding of their roles through proper training from their earliest years. Religion and customs combined to teach them loyalty. The call to duty, so consistent and attractive in the philosophy of Habsburg dynastic politics, becomes, in this writer's hands, simply a tool to keep the young infantes in their place: "The customs in which each person is raised are so powerful that animals by nature ferocious by this remedy live in domestication . . . and if [the infantes] are settled in this during the childhood years . . . if this is supplemented by placing near to them grave wise men of good zeal, loyalty, and prudence who would gently build in them the determination that they are inferior," there would be nothing to fear. Furthermore, these wise servants would encourage the infantes to see their lesser situation "as true and Christian doctrine," reflecting not political considerations but instead the service of God, thus rendering them capable of fulfilling their obligations. Toward these ends, the servants of the infantes should be older men without dependent children so that their intent would be solely to serve the infantes rather than to advance their sons' or indeed their own careers.[24]

While the author of this tract shared some of the concerns of the future favorite, the Count-Duke of Olivares does not appear to have written this work, although the author could conceivably have been his uncle, Baltasar de Zúñiga, who clearly influenced the count-duke's thought. Despite having concerns similar to the count-duke's later concerns regarding the infantes, however, the author of this work found the presence of an adult prince at the court of Spain equally inconvenient. Indeed, the situation he addressed differed considerably from that which the count-duke faced a few years later, when the infantes were the brothers, not the sons, of the king.

Olivares's earliest attributed reference to the subject of the infantes appears in the second section of his "Gran Memorial" of 1624.[25] Placing the infantes among the nobility, he asserted that previously infantes had never been treated as they now were, a statement that he does not fully explain. While their position served a good purpose in that it humbled the grandees, the infantes should show the king as much deference as the grandees did; that is, while the infantes properly ranked above the grandees, the distance between them and the king remained the same as between king and grandees: there was a difference looking up the scale of rank but not looking down.

The count-duke warned against appointing persons to the infantes' households who might have their own agendas. His stated purpose was political: he wanted no communication between the infantes and people who did not fully support the king's policy. The effect of such an order, however, would be to close the infantes off from patronage cycles and deny them the opportunity to petition on a servant's or friend's behalf, shutting down the personal relationships on which court careers, for better or worse, were based. Olivares further suggests that their income should be not great but large enough that no other resources would be needed. Similar preoccupations underlie prohibitions in palace etiquetas against members of royal households receiving goods from outside sources, provisions aimed at focusing dependence and patronage on the crown. This recommendation from Olivares thus reduced the brothers to the level of household members or possibly to the level of potentially bribable officials. The count-duke's harsh closing metaphor of the king treating his brothers with open arms but bridle in hand is a telling contrast with the gentle phrasing of Habsburg family documents. It may well have struck the young king that way, given his prolonged silence on the matter.

The favorite wrote increasingly tersely on the matter of the infantes in subsequent years. He devoted a paper to the subject the following year, another in 1627, and yet another as late as 1632, if the ages of the infantes are accurately given. The frustration of the count-duke is apparent, and he does not bother to hide his criticisms of the treatment he received from Fernando or his dismissive assessment of Carlos.

The careers of the infantes figured more prominently in the 1625 paper.[26] Again, Carlos's marriage was considered the key to his career, and although the count-duke blithely asserted that either of the infantes could be engaged, he identified specific possibilities only for Carlos. A match in Lorraine was again mentioned, although this time the proposed bride was the sister of the Duchess of Lorraine, the child whose inheritance had so enticed Ambassador Cárdenas in earlier years. The count-duke was not enthusiastic about this alliance but preferred it to matches in Mantua, Savoy, or Florence, dismissing those possibilities on account of poor dowries. He did not envision any of these marriages as providing a title for Carlos but instead imagined him ruling for his brother in Sicily, in Naples, or on the frontiers of Africa. Olivares emphasized the importance of the infante's mayordomo mayor, for Carlos would not actually be trusted to rule: nothing would be done without instruction from Madrid.

Olivares's suggestion that Carlos would be ruled by his mayordomo contrasts sharply with his assessment of Fernando's position: Fernando, he said, should be encouraged to set his sights on the papacy. Encouraging him in this idea would be simple, according to the favorite, for the infante was vain and proud. Focusing his ambition in such a way would encourage him to develop a true interest in an ecclesiastical career. Alternatively, or in the meantime, the cardinal-infante could be sent to the Empire, to finish his training at the imperial court.[27]

Even though the matter of the infantes had been officially resolved by the summer of 1632, Olivares wrote once again on the subject, perhaps worried that the decisions, although made, might not be carried out.[28] The count-duke emphasized the numerous times he had given the king advice in this matter and the great importance he attached to it now that the infantes had reached full adulthood. He claimed that he had not previously considered it a pressing matter, although the tone of his earlier memoranda on the subject suggests that he chose this stance to cover his impatience because the king had not acted on his advice. Careful study of the infantes' inclinations and information acquired from their attendants, he commented, had shaped his advice. The count-duke reiterated the placement of the infantes among the grandees, which he had laid out in previous documents, as the accepted mode of treatment, a repetition that itself suggests that his point of view may not necessarily have been widely shared. Given this rank, he considered the friendship of the king with his brothers inappropriate: the infantes were "passing from brothers to friends, more than is permitted in such persons." In addition, the great expense of the cardinal-infante's granting favors, many linked to the charitable resources and offices of the archbishopric of Toledo, and the huge entourage that followed him when he went out disturbed the favorite of the king.

Among the entourage, Olivares complained specifically about one of the cardinal-infante's gentlemen, Antonio de Moscoso, whom he identified as "absolute master of the favor of the infante Don Fernando." Moscoso was the son of the Countess of Altamira, who had raised the royal children from an early age. His brother, Melchor de Moscoso, *camarlengo* to Fernando since 1622, had been appointed bishop of Segovia, probably in order to remove him from the

company of the infante, who held him in high regard.[29] Fernando had apparently transferred his affections to Antonio. Olivares presented the infante Carlos
as following Fernando's lead in depending on Moscoso, although he also dwelt
on the influence of Carlos's old friend the admiral of Castile, Juan Alonso Enríquez de Cabrera, the Duke of Medina de Ríoseco, who had recently returned
to court after years of exile precipitated by his perceived influence on the elder
infante. The admiral and Moscoso, Olivares noted, were not only relatives but
also friends, a combination he clearly saw as dangerous.

The count-duke proposed to separate the brothers from each other and from
their favorites. The eventual destination of Fernando would be Flanders, which
would allow the removal of some of his retinue, thus serving the double purpose
of separating the infante from Moscoso and relieving the royal finances of the
expenses of his oversized household. Judging the project of sending Fernando
to Flanders premature, the count-duke proposed that the king and his brothers
should first travel to Barcelona to open the Corts and that Fernando should
stay to oversee its completion. His household, however, would be reduced for
travel. Olivares predicted that Moscoso, when he saw himself deprived of access
to the resources of the archbishopric of Toledo and furthermore being a man
accustomed to life at court and little given to travel, would voluntarily withdraw from the service of the crown. Carlos, for his part, would be kept close
to the king and removed from the influence of Fernando and the admiral, who
would be given an assignment in foreign provinces designed to last an extended
period of time. This project, which would revolve around organizing an army
to accompany Fernando, was clearly busy work from the point of view of the
count-duke, who did not intend to move Fernando out of Barcelona quickly.

One senses from these papers that the real threat posed by the infantes was
not to the well-being of the state but to the position of the count-duke himself.
The affection between the king and his brothers interfered with the king's reliance on his favorite. Knowing that his own power was based on the favor of the
king, gained through the structure of household service, Olivares suspected any
household official of having ambitions to power. Antonio de Moscoso's relation
to the Duke of Lerma—as a son of the Countess of Altamira, he was Lerma's
nephew—probably encouraged the count-duke in imagining that he could have
no motive other than building his personal fortune. Olivares's concern with this
relationship between friendship and power led to confrontations with Fernando.
When Moscoso was denied an important office in Fernando's household, the

infante refused to believe that the decision had come from the king rather than from the favorite. Furthermore, when Olivares showed the infante a letter from the infanta Isabel Clara advising that the Low Countries would disapprove if Fernando brought a Spanish privado to Flanders, the infante did not try to hide his emotion: "His anger was notable," the count-duke reported, "and turning on me, he said this was my doing and that I was the author of this deed."[30]

If Olivares could dismiss the younger brothers of the king and demand that they be taught their inferior position, other authors were quick to praise the brothers and to depict their roles as necessary to the crown. Like Almansa y Mendoza seeing Philip as father to his brothers and Salcedo presenting Philip and Fernando as twin pillars of the government, other observers credited the brothers with a position based on the proper relations between family members. Chroniclers, moreover, eagerly presented the brothers as active and popular public figures.

Ana de Castro Egas's short biography of Philip III, dedicated to the infante Fernando, provides brief but revealing insights into the personalities of the younger brothers. Castro's comments appear to be based on a personal knowledge of the infantes; evidently, she had served in the household of the children, probably beginning shortly before the birth of Carlos. She characterizes the elder infante as prudent and liberal, lamenting his lack of resources and openly acknowledging his role as successor to his brother. Ignoring the common convention of presenting Fernando as unusually pious, she refers to him as being from childhood "gallantly inclined to arms" and indicates that only his great sense of obedience to his father encouraged him to accept his office in the church. She, in fact, questions whether the king chose the best person for this role, but she praises the infante's personal devotion, which led him to turn from his own inclinations: "He adjusted his mind to the vocation by obedience: in a manner that, [although he was] by his own taste a soldier, it appeared that he was born to be an ecclesiastic."[31]

Carrying the theme further, Salcedo's biography of Fernando, written shortly after Fernando's success at the battle of Nördlingen, makes no mention of the infante's identity as archbishop. He makes a few facile comments about Fernando's education "balancing the learned with the military, since arms and letters were the forge of the crown that the world builds him," and echoing Ana de Castro, he emphasizes the infante's devotion to the hunt rather than his piety. He also presents Fernando as properly reverent toward his brother and respectful of his rank. Suggesting a way in which a member of the royal family might instruct the public, he relates a story of Fernando's reaction to a portrait of his brother unveiled in Brussels: "His Highness looked at the portrait of His Majesty, venerating it with just bows, so that everyone would know the reverence that he had for his brother, and that which he would give the original when he gave so much to his portrait."[32] He presents Fernando as teaching the world "the reverence that is owed his king"; just as he was to learn from the examples of his ancestors and classical history, ordinary people were supposed to learn from him.

Ana de Castro's praise of both younger brothers may place her in a possible faction of the infantes, but politics does not appear to have inspired the dedication of her book to Fernando. Instead she notes "the inclination that I have toward Your Highness since I knew you as a child," suggesting the motivation of an affection informed both by close contact and by idealization.[33] Her personal ties to the infantes and her lament over Carlos's lack of resources suggest, however, that the deprivations the infantes experienced could provoke opposition to the crown on the basis of personal affection.

The disgruntled courtier Matías de Novoa more pointedly declined to praise Philip IV and his favorite. Dedicating the first volumes of his account of court life to Fernando, he praised the younger infante as a great son of a great father, while making no mention of Philip IV. Where Olivares saw disobedience and even conspiracy on the part of the infantes, Novoa saw deprivation of their rights and honor, claiming that they were not allowed so much as to keep a horse. In his view, Philip IV planned his sister's marriage and his brothers' careers solely for the purpose of removing them from court. Any friend they had was dismissed, and any person added to their household became a spy. Despite all provocation, however, the brothers were obedient to the king.[34]

The King Decides

Whatever the perceptions and realities of factions at court, the royal brothers maintained an image of family affection. The surviving records are silent about any possible antagonism between them. Despite the urging of the count-duke, the king was slow to respond to his minister's concerns. The silence seems to reflect the gap between the king's attitude toward his brothers, based on personal affection and encouraged by set concepts of relations between members of the royal family, and the not always respectful anxieties of the favorite.

Some changes took place in the households of the infantes shortly after their brother became king. These changes were purely structural, since, in effect, the infantes had previously shared the household of their brother, but while infantes could share the services of the prince's household, they would not, in general, share those of the king's. A king did not have an ayo, while the younger infantes still required one. The appointment of the Count of Peñaranda de Bracamonte and, after his death, the Count of Alcaudete as ayos to Carlos and the appointment of the Marquis of Malpica as ayo to Fernando emphasized that the two infantes were not yet fully adults.

An official searching in 1707 for precedents for the treatment of the children of Philip V, unable to find evidence of any household for Carlos, wrote: "During his tutelage he had no further household . . . since he lived in the company of his brothers."[35] Carlos, indeed, practically shared the king's rooms in the palace of Madrid: after the death of his father, Philip IV emptied the room Philip III had used as an oratory, adjacent to the king's chambers, in order to create new sleeping quarters for the infante.[36] Carlos shared the services of Philip's household, since they were almost always together, while Fernando spent more of his time apart from his brothers. Carlos also ate regularly at the king's table, while Fernando's status when he ate with his brothers was that of guest.[37] The same researcher thought that Fernando, too, had only limited service, but subsequent documents suggest the existence of a separate household for Fernando. Moreover, in March 1625, when all three brothers resided at Aranjuez, the king ordered: "I have resolved that [during] the time that he will be in Aranjuez this year, those officials that would attend to my service, attend also to that of the cardinal-infante my brother,"[38] an order that would hardly have been necessary if Fernando regularly shared the service of his brother's household.

Philip IV did plan a household for Carlos, although it was always perceived as a future plan and never fully established, as reflected in the phrasing of several appointments. In 1624 the royal tutor Juan Bautista Lavaña requested that one of his sons be named a groom in the stables of the infante "when his household is set." Juan Fernández de Córdoba described himself in a memorial of 1627 as a gentleman de la boca of the king and a mayordomo of Carlos.[39] In November 1629 Francisco Fernández de Córdoba, who had been granted the offices of *primer caballerizo* and gentleman of the chamber of the infante Carlos, found himself still in financial difficulties, "since up to now the household of His Highness has not been put in place."[40] As late as May 1632 the king appointed

Beltrán de Guevara, the youngest son of the Count of Oñate, gentleman of the chamber of Carlos "for when the household is established, and in the meantime, so that he would not be idle, he will serve the same office for the lord infante Don Fernando." When the infante Carlos died, only a few months after this appointment, the person making arrangements for the funeral was the Marquis of Torres, referred to as "Mayordomo of the king, the one that attended His Highness,"[41] which suggests that Carlos continued until his death to live within the structure of the king's household.

Carlos not only shared the service of the king's servants but also shared with him the secretarial services of Juan de Urbino, who had previously been in the service of the princes of Savoy, while the cardinal-infante had a secretary attached exclusively to his service as early as 1620. The appointment of Beltrán de Guevara, which honored Carlos as the older of the younger brothers but provided service for Fernando, particularly demonstrates the difference in the two brothers' treatment. Fernando's household at that time also included musicians, a kitchen staff, and pages with their own teachers of Latin, dancing, and fencing.[42]

Early in his reign, the new king made several additions to Fernando's household. In June 1622 eighteen new officials were appointed, including five mayordomos, seven gentlemen of the chamber, and four with the title camarlengo, a type of ecclesiastical chamberlain. The appointments made the following month further indicate the mix of court and church offices in Fernando's house: eleven gentlemen de la boca, seven caballerizos, thirteen chaplains, and two counselors of the chamber, who were also theologians. These appointees included three sons of the Countess of Altamira, several titled nobles, at least two men who had grown up as meninos at the court, numerous sons of the greater nobility, and several learned doctors. Of the seven offices in the royal stables, two went to women who served in the queen's chamber, for them to bestow on their future husbands.[43] While the king later removed individuals from the household of the cardinal-infante and tension apparently developed between the king's brothers and his favorite, in the first several years of the reign of Philip IV, there is very little evidence to suggest that the king saw harm in attaching people to the service of Fernando.

Nonetheless, in 1624 Philip IV did order reform in Fernando's household. The alterations, however, did not focus only on the cardinal-infante's household but instead constituted part of the general attempt at fiscal responsibility that had begun with the new reign and was renewed after a period of extravagance during the visit of the Prince of Wales in 1623. The households of the king and queen were also undergoing reorganization, with the model for the queen's household taken from the etiquetas written for Queen Ana in 1575, which had also been a year of financial reform. Noting that the infante had been granted a household appropriate to his person and dignity but that time had proved his income insufficient to support his staff, the king ordered a junta to consider the reduction of his brother's entourage in the summer of 1624. We have little evidence of Fernando's thoughts on the matter, although the records of the junta indicate one objection: the king noted that after showing the proposed reform to his brother, he had agreed to reinstate certain funds for the infante's stables, ordering that his brother's favorite mares not be sold. Of the numerous changes made in the household, only the reduction of his stables appears to have concerned the young cardinal.[44]

The differences in the households of the two infantes were based on a variety of factors. Most importantly, service attached to Fernando reflected the honor and functions of his archiepiscopal office. In addition, however, the appointment and implementation of his household can be seen as a product of his entering his adult role, even though the entrance into that role began while he was still a child. Carlos, on the other hand, never reached this stage in his career despite his years. While Fernando was being prepared for his ecclesiastical career, Carlos continued to function as a specialized member of the king's household. Indeed, the royal chaplain commonly referred to the king as being accompanied by "Carlos and the gentlemen of the chamber," as if the infante filled a specific household office.

In 1624 the king usually heard private Mass daily with both his brothers, but when he attended public sermons and processions, such as the Epiphany service, only Carlos was mentioned, first among the accompaniment of ambassadors, grandees, and household members. When the royal chaplain wrote of "the king and his brother," he almost exclusively meant the king and Carlos, although references to Carlos and "his brother" meant Carlos and Fernando. The two older brothers hunted together, sometimes with the king rising early and leaving instructions for Carlos to follow when he woke. They participated in *monterías,* in which wild animals were captured and corralled for an enclosed hunt, and they often "went to the countryside to kill rabbits," as the chaplain bluntly described it. The cardinal-infante hunted by himself, sometimes following the same schedule as his brothers, but separately, and when the three hunted together, the royal chaplain made a point of repeating "all three together," as if to highlight the unusualness of the event. Indeed, the chaplain often seems to have included Fernando as an afterthought, in one case making a full entry in his journal about having said Mass for Carlos, then adding at the end that Fernando had been there too.[45]

Despite his lack of a household, the elder infante also spent time by himself, traveling to country palaces to hunt and to San Lorenzo de El Escorial for his health. During a prolonged bout of recurring fevers lasting from October to December 1624, Carlos went to San Lorenzo accompanied by the Count of Puebla de Montalban, one of the king's mayordomos, and a few of the king's gentlemen of the chamber. Breaking up the journey, he slept at La Torre de la Parada, the aptly named halfway point between Madrid and San Lorenzo. The following day, the king joined him for a meal, and then the infante proceeded to San Lorenzo, while the king hunted. Although the infante felt well enough on some days to hunt with the king, he continued to experience fevers serious enough to concern Fernando, who sent the Count of Navalmoral, son of his ayo, Malpica, to ask after Carlos's health. As the illness progressed, Philip and Fernando expressed their concern by hearing Mass with their brother in the king's chamber, having removed a portrait of Fernando from the "galería de m[edi]odía" in order to set up an oratory, which allowed Carlos to listen to the service from bed, while his brothers sat on cushions on the floor. The follow-ing week, Carlos heard Mass in his room, while his brothers attended services together—one of the very few occasions recorded by the royal chaplain when Philip and Fernando heard Mass together without their brother being present.[46]

The king and his brothers also played pelota together, including an occasion when a ball hit Carlos in the face. The elder infante rode with the Count-Duke of Olivares in an impromptu masque to celebrate the birth of the infanta María de la Presentación in 1625. The royal family attended such events as bullfights in the plaza mayor (although the infanta María, like her mother, often found reasons to absent herself from such occasions), and the king and Carlos partici-pated in *juegos de cañas* (mock tournaments).[47] The king occasionally entrusted his brother with large amounts of money for matters in his service and specified that the infante should never be asked to account for how the money was spent.[48]

While at first Carlos seems to be a cipher, his life is not undiscoverable. If one wanted to trace his activities, it would not be difficult to find a great deal about how he spent his days, especially since he spent so much of his time with the king. Novoa considered him a vigilant observer of royal customs, possessing the princely ability to mask his feelings, including his regret at the dismissal of his friend the admiral. A Venetian ambassador presented him as a staunch advocate of María during the visit of the Prince of Wales, expressing his doubt that Charles would convert and his fear that the king and favorite were endangering her by considering the marriage.[49]

Less clear are the roles he could play within the patronage structures of court. The answer to this question, as well as some elements of his personality, can be deduced from advice given to him by the count-duke in 1624 concerning the conduct of audiences.[50] The tract implies that the infante regularly received official visits, contradicting the image of his isolation. The favorite employs a gentler, more friendly tone here than one might expect based on the comments he elsewhere addressed to the king regarding his brothers, perhaps reflecting the count-duke's concentration in this paper on the even more important task of humbling the nobility. Noting that he gave the infante advice out of his love and desire to serve, the count-duke also sent an original letter in which Philip II requested Juan de Idiáquez's advice on a question of etiquette as proof that even great men needed advice and asked counsel from people they trusted. Taking the opportunity to provide general advice as well, the count-duke recommended that the infante observe temperance and moderation in jests, avoid indecent entertainments and actions, and ride and apply himself to virtuous exercises and matters.

Arriving at his main point, Olivares urged the infante not to feel badly about experiencing difficulty in speaking with ambassadors or vassals he did not know. This happened, the favorite assured him, because of his modesty and lack of experience, and for no other reason. As proof that the infante was not alone in his difficulties, the count-duke presented himself as awkward and nervous when speaking, as breaking into a sweat at the very thought of making a public statement and fearful of falling down while bowing. To overcome this type of problem, the infante should first of all remember that only the king and queen and the king's eldest son (when he had one) outranked the infante. Just as Olivares presented himself as writing down what he wanted to say in order to overcome nervousness, he recommended that the infante memorize stock responses to particular types of circumstances. To this end, he provided the infante with appropriate questions and replies to address to ambassadors and vassals, mostly inquiries concerning the health of ambassadors' masters and vassals' families and congratulations on royal favors received. When individuals requested favors, he should be certain that he and the king concurred before discussing them with vassals, and when asked, he should offer to speak to the king about vassals' requests, assuring them that they would receive what was just. In other matters, the infante could speak to vassals as he would to his gentlemen of the chamber, presumably meaning with the same level of familiarity or formality. Finally, the favorite advised, the infante needed to overcome his fear of erring, being assured that no man lived who did not make mistakes.

The image of the infante that emerges from this tract recalls the assessment of his father made by his teachers in 1596, in which they commented specifically on individuals leaving audiences with the prince unsatisfied: like his father, Carlos appears to have been somewhat hindered by awkwardness. He was, in fact, said to resemble his father and even to have been his father's favorite among his children.[51] These observations may cover a polite but negative assessment of the infante, given that history has not been kind in its judgment of Philip III. Carlos, as we have seen, was also said by the count-duke "not to have knowledge of letters," while Fernando "has very great grounding, not only in humanist letters but also in the divine,"[52] statements suggesting that the brothers either had been exposed to different levels of education or possessed different levels of intellectual ability. Matías de Novoa also recognized this difference in learning between the infantes, attributing it to differences in their inclinations rather than in their abilities. Indeed, he noted that the elder infante wrote poetry, calling some of his writings "the most extraordinary of our times," although few poems identified as his have survived.[53] Fernando, however, had apparently enjoyed the benefit of greater education because of his ecclesiastical office and the learned men who gathered around him as a result.

Despite general praise of Fernando's abilities, a candid assessment by the president of the Council of Castile, Fernando de Contreras, suggests that there were lapses in the younger infante's education.[54] Contreras is careful to point out in introducing and concluding his remarks that he was specifically asked to discuss the issue: matters relating to the infante had been discussed in the council, and Philip IV had asked Contreras to write down his thoughts. To better complete his assignment, he consulted several treatises, both secular and ecclesiastical, on education of princes—he mentions Augustine, Gregory, and Thomas Aquinas—but he also intended to speak his own mind. Commenting on Fernando's high birth and the dignity of his office, second only to that of the pope, he writes generally about the infante's need to understand his office.

Saint Thomas, he says, cited the need for both knowledge and kindness, and to acquire those, one had to have sound understanding and an inclination to the good, which the infante had, making him "fertile ground" that if well cultivated would bring forth good and if badly cultivated would bring thorns and thistles. Contreras delineates areas of knowledge, from great letters to theology and canon law, that would enable Fernando to clarify mysteries and convince nonbelievers. Fernando did not have to be the greatest scholar in the world, but he should not leave all religious matters to the ministers who served and aided him. Those who depended on others to tell them what to say and think would not have real power, and in addition, they would lose the esteem, love, and obedience of their subjects. If his conscience did not lead him to undertake the necessary study, his reputation would demand it.

Having laid out the importance of the office, Contreras turns to the specifics of the infante's experience. The infante, he notes, was almost fourteen, a very dangerous age, open to influences, good or bad. One had to study the principles of grammar and the arts in youth in order to be capable of acquiring knowledge in other areas when one reached the age of understanding. But the infante apparently was not applying himself to his studies: his fine mind and memory should have allowed him to learn Latin in a year but he had been at it for three years and still did not have the better part of basic grammar. The problem, according to Contreras, was that the infante did not take the time to study: on some days he spent an hour and a half at it, on others just an hour, and on still other days he did not study at all. What with spending time going out to the country (presumably hunting) and other activities with the king, Fernando was right where he had started, forgetting what he was taught amid all the other things he was doing.

Getting to specifics, Contreras recommends that Fernando spend at least three hours a day at his studies, dividing the time between learning new lessons and reviewing and exercises. He should have meninos to study with him—by learning and doing exercises together, they would help each other, especially as the lessons got more difficult. He should be led in daily devotions and be shown only virtuous entertainment. His teachers should attend him every day; employing metaphors of medicine and gardening, Contreras suggests that they learn the best medicine by knowing the illness and get to know the various flowers of the infante's potential, trimming the branches of bad inclinations. Contreras presents this as an urgent matter and notes that if the infante became too accustomed to the habits of chivalry and secular nobility, it would be very difficult to introduce the style of an ecclesiastical prince. He suggests that the king emphasize to his brother that it would please him if he studied. "No one," he comments, "other than your Majesty has the authority to take this matter in hand."[55]

As Fernando approached adulthood, another instruction concerning the duties of archbishop was written for him, perhaps by the members of his religious household.[56] With this mostly abstract document, the writers apparently hoped to convince Fernando of his key role in the Catholic Church and perhaps encourage him to take a more active role in his office. Liberally sprinkled with Latin quoted from various popes, the Council of Trent, a few ancients, including Aristotle, and a few contemporary theorists on royal rule, such as Padre Juan Márquez, the instruction explores the administration of the archbishopric, focusing especially on the important business of appointing persons to ecclesiastical office.

After generally discussing the eminence of the archbishopric of Toledo, asserting the promise that the infante had shown since childhood and the importance of his personal involvement in the government of Toledo, urging him to do nothing to displease God and not to listen to men who had only their own interests at heart, the authors of this instruction turn to their central concern about the granting of offices. Quoting heavily from the decisions of the Council of Trent, they outline the qualities necessary in the recipient of a benefice, noting the importance of the candidate's spirituality and merits, putting the service of the divine cult and the reward of virtue before considerations of blood or friendship. They warn against youthful appointments and appointments of persons who will not serve actively, noting especially those who excused themselves by saying that they were attending the infante—"as if," the authors observe, "there were a lack of others to serve you." The Council of Trent had decreed that holders of such offices should reside in their churches (that is, in their dioceses) and serve in their own persons. In addition, they highlight problems of plurality of benefices and of persons who undertook and left ecclesiastical office lightly, presumably as if it were simply another career ladder. While they imply that Fernando was setting a bad example, apparently he erred not in his own absence as much as by allowing his canons to be absent. A prelate, they comment in passing, who appoints someone who he knows will not be ordained and actively serve shares the blame for the disservice and damage done to the church.[57]

Another misuse of the system involved persons requesting an office that was not yet vacant, that is, anticipating the vacancy, through death—as the authors put it, before the present holder had so much as had a headache. While it was permissible to promise a person that he would receive a position when circumstances allowed, and people should be confident that a "law of gratefulness" existed between a lord and those who served him, office seekers must know that reward for service functioned on merit. If this standard were known and followed, the infante could avoid both disservice to the church and the inconveniences and fatigue involved in responding to excessive petitions.[58]

This instruction for Fernando echoes treatises on the qualities of the prince in a few striking points. Concern over misuse in the granting of offices parallels the problem of excess *mercedes* (favors) at the royal court. Two references to the promise Fernando had shown since childhood also suggest that, like the prince, he was seen as having inherent qualities that enabled him to fulfill his office well. Within the context of the church, Fernando's royal blood equipped him for leadership in the same way that royal blood endowed the king with qualities that enabled him to rule. He had it in his veins to lead, to choose ministers well and honor them properly. Just as treatises seldom criticized the prince, the authors do not direct their criticism of the way in which the archdiocese functioned at the infante, although they present him as the person who could set problems right. Reflecting contemporary discussion of favorites, they remind him that although some persons might say that certain aspects of the administration could easily be performed by others, the responsibility did not belong to the administrator, but to him. They recommend examples from history for him to follow.[59]

The parallel between the specific critiques of the administration of the archdiocese and those made of the royal court in the same era suggest that Fernando was indeed running the archbishopric as a species of court in itself. Like a well-trained patron, Fernando attempted to bestow the extensive offices of the archbishopric of Toledo on his friends and servants. Among these was Melchor de Moscoso, the first of the two brothers to raise the ire of the count-duke, who collected the titles of sumiller de cortina, principal chaplain of the Chapel of the New Kings in Toledo, and archbishop of Segovia and requested that the various appointments be accompanied by special privileges of nonresidence, exemption from providing proof of purity of blood, and the right to receive incomes from all three posts.[60]

Despite such interest in the activities and training of the young archbishop, Fernando's appointment to the archiepiscopal see of Toledo did not actually solve the problem of establishing his career. Although he undertook many roles on the basis of his title and requested in his will to be buried in the cathedral, it does not appear that the king and his brother ever seriously considered that he would live in his see and govern it. Throughout his youth and adulthood, a series of administrators oversaw the archbishopric, although they also held titles of their own that potentially interfered with their attention to all duties. The first of these, Alvaro de Villegas, often resided at court and became active in matters not touching on the archbishopric. He preached the sermon of the obsequies of Philip III at the convent of La Encarnación in May 1621. He effected a reconciliation between Fernando and Olivares after the illness of the king in 1627, according to Novoa, and witnessed the king's will during that period.[61]

While Carlos struggled with awkwardness and Fernando learned to be a patron in his own court, Philip IV considered other prospects regarding their service to the crown. "Among the infinite things that I owe to Our Lord," he addressed a special junta in 1626,

> it appears to me very much to the service of His powerful and pious hand to have given me two brothers . . . and as much as I owe Him that much more Our Lord obliges me to arrange their place and greater good by whatever means available; and it appears to me already the season, given the age they are approaching, to take considered opinions concerning the suitable path on which to send them, and the means and the form to address the business on which so much depends.

He thus ordered an unnamed person, certainly the count-duke, to convene a secret junta, calling together the Marquis of Monteclaros, Fernando Girón, the Marquis of La Hinojosa, the Count of Monterrey, Fray Iñigo de Brizuela (Archduke Albert's former confessor, now president of the Council of Flanders), the king's confessor, Fray Antonio de Sotomayor, Juan de Villela, and Diego Mexía. He added that the report could be written "in your hand; for in no manner are these materials and papers to be trusted to anyone else."[62]

The junta's discussion is partially preserved in notes made by the Marquis of Montesclaros.[63] While these notes contain much the same information that appears in the count-duke's final paper on the infantes, they lack the tone of urgency and the vaguely disrespectful commentary. The junta differentiated less between the possible careers of the two brothers, considering either eligible for a career in Flanders. They mentioned marriage only for Carlos and alternatively pictured him at the head of an army. They weighed the dangers of assigning him positions in which he had no experience, such as "prince" of the sea, but concluded that the selection of appropriate lieutenants would be sufficient to guarantee the safety of the assignment. Concerning sending Carlos to Flanders, Montesclaros noted and then crossed out that the infante would be educated in matters there by the infanta Isabel, perhaps rejecting a characterization of the relationship that might appear to place Isabel's influence above the king's. Closer to home, they considered the governorship of Portugal for Carlos and the diocese of Oran for Fernando.

The junta offered a variety of precedents that might inspire Fernando in a religious career, including that of Cardinal Jimenez. In addition to the notion that encouraging him to aspire to be pope might awaken his ambition in the church, the junta briefly considered training him for the office of inquisitor general. Its rejection of the latter is instructive of the difference between roles that might be the ecclesiastical equivalent of rule and ones that required rigorous theological training. Without insulting the infante, Montesclaros noted, "we can say he does not have the right qualities" to be inquisitor and that his appointment could cause scandal. One might consider it an insult to the papacy that the committee would encourage Fernando to aspire to it without those qualities, but one might also note that the position it rejected was the one that was in the king's power to confer.

In the following year the junta met again to discuss preparations for the infante Carlos to go to Portugal, with the titles of governor and captain general of the sea.[64] Probably because of his age—he was not quite twenty—the junta agreed that his mayordomo mayor had to be a person of great authority in whom the king had perfect confidence. The mayordomo would both serve Carlos in his daily activities and discuss all dispatches and resolutions with him, offering counsel and guidance. If the mayordomo mayor did not serve this function, Montesclaros observed, another high office would have to be added to the infante's household. It was therefore in the interest of consolidating personal and political influences on the infante that the junta proposed combining the positions of mayordomo mayor and lieutenant of the captain general in a single person. This appointment, however, threatened the positions of two nobles, the Count of Portalegre, who by tradition held the office of mayordomo mayor to the ruler of Portugal, and the Marquis of Santa Cruz, whose service as de facto captain general gave him a claim to the position of lieutenant. The junta did not want to deprive Santa Cruz of his duties but proposed to subvert Portalegre's claim by appointing a household for the infante immediately, thus establishing a contrary claim to this office. In this, they looked to the example of Archduke Albert, who as governor of Portugal had had a personal mayordomo mayor rather than the traditionally designated Portalegre. Given the authority necessary for this position, the junta proposed to appoint a member of the Council of State and nominated the Count of Monterrey, the Marquis of La Hinojosa, Fernando Girón, Diego Mexía, and the Marquis of Montesclaros.

Although the junta concluded that combining the offices of lieutenant and mayordomo mayor was useful, it stopped short of endorsing the consolidation of the offices of sumiller de corps and caballerizo mayor into the service of the mayordomo mayor, noting that that would concentrate too much power in a single person. The junta hoped to place ministers from the Council of War in these positions so that their duties would overlap personal and state service, just as those of the mayordomo did. Although the junta clearly intended the mayordomo mayor to control all the subjects of discussion, these ministers should offer advice on the matters the mayordomo mayor proposed and any other information or analysis they could. The junta nominated the Marquis of La Puebla, the Marquis of La Veita, the Count of La Puebla, Pedro Pacheco, and Luis Brabo de Acuña, with the Count of Monterrey adding the Marquis of Frómista to the list.

Despite the activity of 1626 and 1627, Philip IV was not yet ready to resolve the question of his brothers' careers. Indeed, given the ages of the infantes, who were in their late teens, immediate decisions were not required. Palace intrigues during a serious illness of the king in 1627, accompanied by the uncomfortable perception that courtiers were anticipating the death of the king by attaching themselves to his brothers, served more to upset the favorite than to prompt the king to activity.[65] The apparent change in Philip IV's attitude toward planning the careers of his brothers occurred a few years later and may be directly attributed to the birth of a healthy son in 1629. Until the birth of Prince Baltasar Carlos, the infante Carlos was in effect heir to the throne; although the queen had given birth to several daughters in those years, each holding the title of princess, none of them had lived long. With the birth and apparent health of his nephew, Carlos no longer had a defined role. In addition, the infanta María's marriage by proxy in 1629 allowed the king to turn his attention to his other siblings. Although the polite phrasing of state and family rhetoric may disguise rancor, both the king's reluctance to reach a decision regarding his brothers and the timing of the final phase of decision making appear to have been motivated not by fear of the dangers his brothers might present but instead by circumstances of age and the increased necessity of providing them with independent roles given the king's new focus on his son.

On January 23, 1629, the chronicler Gascón de Torquemada reported the first appearance of the king's brothers in the Council of State. The tone of his announcement indicates that this was perceived as a turning point in the careers of the younger brothers, as if they would henceforth attend and participate regularly in council. A description of the day by Antonio Hurtado de Mendoza, however, suggests a more ceremonial event, as if this were their introduction into public life, not the start of specific careers. Hurtado de Mendoza's description reveals that it was not a regular meeting of the council, which indeed would normally not include even the king, but a meeting in the king's chambers of a smaller group of key councilors, presidents of councils, and *maestros de campo*, who would offer reports. The king sat in a chair against the wall, with a table in front of him, while chairs for the infantes were placed "on the far side of the desk, in the back corner," and the councilors sat on a bench facing the king and his brothers. The king apparently improvised the treatment his brothers would receive, directing that when councilors bowed to him, they should also make a small bow to the infantes, and that when the infantes spoke, members of the council should remove their hats, as they did when the king spoke. Mendoza intended his record of this event to provide guidelines for proper deportment in council to people who might need them, thus serving the function of establishing precedent and proper usage.[66] There is, however, little evidence to suggest that the infantes attended council meetings often enough to require preparation of a formal rulebook.

Later in the same year Philip, still pondering several options for his brothers' careers, wrote to his sister that he expected to place both of them in the Empire. He imagined Carlos marrying a daughter of the emperor and hoped that María would be in a position to ascertain what the emperor might settle on his daughter, presumably either as dowry or as a territory for them to rule. Concerning Fernando, he still felt that it was not yet time to make a final decision, although he may have been considering an ecclesiastical office within the Empire, perhaps an electorship.[67]

By April of 1631, however, Philip IV had reached conclusions regarding his brothers' careers. If he had indeed seriously considered possibilities in the

Empire, he had since completely changed his thinking. Noting that the "blind obstinacy and arrogance of rebels, fostered and assisted by the church's enemies and mine, has reached such excess that they begin in both Indies to disquiet this Monarchy," he resolved to send Carlos to Portugal and Fernando to the Low Countries. Calling Lisbon the "principal fortification of Spain, particularly in maritime matters," he stressed its importance in the maintenance of all his empire and named Carlos viceroy, captain general of the kingdoms of Portugal, India, and Africa, and "Generalissimo" of the sea. Of Fernando he noted only that "he will go to assist the most serene infanta," perhaps deeming unnecessary any further comment on the circumstances.[68]

In September 1631 a council convened to discuss Fernando's journey. The poor health of the aging infanta Isabel Clara, the unsettled nature of the political situation in France, and the recent flight of the French queen mother and her younger son to the court of Brussels all demanded the immediate presence of a new governor. The council, however, expressed concern about the safety of the infante, considering the uncertainty of the roads he would travel and the unhealthiness of the places where he might stay. The Count of Oñate cited María's journey as an example of how difficult it was to overcome such challenges. Although the consensus ruled against sending Fernando immediately, the Count of La Puebla suggested that he go to Barcelona "in order to await the right opportunity so that he could make his voyage with more brevity." In a second report of the same date, the council considered possible routes for the infante's journey. After discussions of routes through Italy, by sea, and even through France, the Count of La Puebla suggested that the journey be delayed, "without announcing it," until spring, when at least some of the risks of travel would be diminished.

In his response, the king cited both his concern for the health of his brother and the costs that delays could cause, "since the example of the queen of Hungary, my sister, and the great expense that her delay caused is so fresh," and ordered the Duke of Feria to inquire about the healthiness of places through which the infante might travel.[69] The king, concurring with the opinion of the Count of La Puebla in matters of embarcation and timing, delayed the official announcement of Fernando's appointment and took advantage of the opportunity to go to Barcelona himself.

Both infantes accompanied the king to Barcelona for the Corts of 1632. While there, on May 12, Carlos took the oath of office as general of the sea. Philip and

Carlos left Catalonia for Madrid a few days later, leaving Fernando to supervise the Corts. The infante Carlos, for his part, was preparing for his own journey to Portugal. Although Novoa claimed that Philip IV had begun to introduce Carlos to government by having him read dispatches from Germany, Flanders, and Italy, little evidence remains of the preparation the infante received for his new role or how active his brother intended his participation in government to be. A basic household was assembled for his journey in 1631, at about the same time as the junta met to discuss the cardinal-infante's journey to Flanders.[70] Plans apparently developed parallel to those for Fernando but were never finalized. Just weeks after Carlos and the king returned to Madrid, the infante suddenly fell ill and died six days later, on July 30, surrounded by the most renowned holy images and relics that the city of Madrid could offer. The king, who could not bring himself to look at his brother's body or to attend the mass said later the same day, was now bereft of all his siblings. Except for a brief and formal meeting with the queen of France in 1660, he would not see any of them again.[71]

From Cardinal to General

For the moment, Fernando's appointment as successor to the infanta Isabel awaited formal announcement. In the meantime he served as the king's "deputy and captain general" in Catalonia and the counties of Rosellón and Cerdaña. The cardinal-infante spent several months in Barcelona while he prepared for the journey, assembling his staff and household with the aid of the king and the royal councils in Madrid, learning proper treatment of the officials and princes he would encounter, and defining the role he intended to play.[72]

The Council of State assembled a brief set of points in May 1632, outlining issues to be addressed in an instruction for the infante concerning government, his household, and persons and places he should visit. A response to these points does not answer these questions as much as it indicates what sources should be consulted concerning each one, directing issues both to juntas and to particular precedents. The precedents mentioned help to place Fernando within the hierarchy of the royal family: one was the experience of the archduke in Lisbon, presumably Albert, and the other the example of the queen's household, which may refer either to the general practice of the queen's house, which seems to emphasize Fernando's lesser status, or to the example of the queen of Hungary during her stay in Barcelona.[73]

Later in the year, the council incorporated most of these points into a set of instructions concerning the government of Aragon, from convening the Corts to the infante's service as viceroy.[74] The instructions gave the infante general guidelines for his own conduct, both in the business of government and in the treatment of others, degrees of respect, and public presentation. After years of being reminded of his inferior status, he was being encouraged to conduct himself with the full dignity of royalty. The instruction advised him to use a *cortina* if he attended public Mass and to employ macebearers, "as does the king." It informed him that viceroys of Aragon usually attended meetings of councils but that to protect the decency of his person and avoid the "embarazo" of being personally present, he could order little windows cut into the council rooms, through which he could hear what transpired, as had his brother in Madrid. In addition, the councils should consult with him through written communication, and any minister who desired an audience should present, prior to the meeting, a written statement of what he wished to discuss. Otherwise, Fernando was advised to undertake activities that emphasized his public nature, such as visiting jails during holy seasons, for the sense of justice and comfort such action conveyed, and inspecting the frontiers. Correspondents writing about matters in Catalonia, moreover, should adjust the etiquette of their requests to reflect the respect owed Fernando, and in military matters, levies, and sending funds to Italy the infante's orders should be executed as if they had come from the king, although if possible he should inform the king beforehand or as soon as possible afterwards. The infante was also given fairly extensive rights to grant favors, although, again, he should try to consult with the king beforehand.

The instruction gave the cardinal-infante the right to name his own juntas in consultation with the Count of Oñate, although the council set the basic guidelines, drawing from the cardinal-infante's notably experienced entourage. In the ordinary business of state the infante should consult Oñate, the Duke of Cardona, the Marquis of Montenegro, the Marquis d'Este, and his confessor. In juntas of war he should include the Count of Santa Clara, who was in charge of the artillery, the Baron of Watteville,[75] and the attendant gentlemen of the chamber. The juntas of finance and of the household should include Oñate, d'Este, and Fernando's confessor. Oñate was also to supervise and govern the household, while Martín de Axpe had charge of the papers. In the absence of the infante, Cardona carried the title governor of arms, but orders for the military had to be directed through Montenegro. At about the same time that the council assembled these guidelines, the king sent Francisco de Irarrázabal y Andia, an experienced military man newly named Marquis of Valparaíso and a member of the Council of War, to assist in military decisions.[76]

The rest of the instruction dealt with particular details of government. Fernando's correspondence from September 1632 until his departure for Italy in the spring of 1633 concerned concrete issues of outfitting galleys, paying accounts, and dealing with levies, soldiers, and personnel. His work included forwarding requests to the king, occasionally with his own assessments of a petition's worth. He expressed concern about the raising of troops that were to accompany him, asking Madrid for guidance on all these matters but also offering his own opinions and insights.[77] It is clear from this correspondence that Fernando did not intend to be a mere figurehead, but an active governor.

One of the key matters to be settled was the final composition of his household and councils. The Marquis of Villafranca requested not to be named deputy general of the sea, arguing that he should be named to the Council of State in order to carry the prestige he needed to serve the infante. The members of the council, although shocked at the audacity of a person requesting such an honor, were nonetheless not shocked enough to remove the marquis, whom they obviously considered an indispensable part of the diplomatic entourage. A year later, the king granted the marquis's request for a seat on the Council of State, although the infante was instructed not to inform him until the day he embarked for Italy.[78]

Another key member of the entourage, the Count of Oñate, asked to be removed from the service of the infante only weeks before the final departure. Citing his poor health and his many years of service, which he numbered at forty-five, the count pointed out that the best quality of a king was knowing when and how to reward his servants. The Council of State, however, advised the king to order that one of the galleys be left behind for the count if the danger was that great, ignoring Oñate's implication that considering his advanced years he might never be well enough to withstand the dangers inherent in further foreign service and sea travel. Although the members of the council indicated that they would follow the judgment of doctors concerning the count's health, Oñate's presence and experience appeared so important that they could not conceive of simply letting him retire.[79]

Concerns about honor and illness also affected other members of the household. At Fernando's instigation, the infante's confessor informed the count-duke that Alonso Carrillo felt insufficiently recognized for his services and feared that he was out of favor. He also expressed concern that Luis Laso had been ill and could not participate in the journey if it began soon. "And the same would happen although in different degree," said the confessor, "if Don Manuel Guzmán fell ill and no one would be left here but an ecclesiastic steward."[80]

Fernando offered his own opinion concerning adjustments to his entourage, noting that he preferred Montenegro to the Duke of Feria as his principal adviser. His primary motivation was not so much to retain Montenegro as to have a person who was "more of a soldier" than Feria with whom to consult. While the Council of State and Olivares saw this suggestion as verging on disobedience, the infante offered that one had to listen to many opinions and that it was inescapable that there would occasionally be disagreements. Reiterating that he would always listen to counsel, he rejected the apparent suggestion that he simply follow the advice of Feria and asserted his own ability to decide what best served the king.[81]

In December 1632 the cardinal-infante, apparently frustrated by his continued delay in Barcelona, sent his confessor to Madrid with a list of questions to be resolved by the appropriate councils. Urging his confessor to assure the king of his zeal in his duty, he commanded him to carry out the mission with all haste. While earlier instructions had stressed the business of Aragon, Fernando was eager to move on to the true goal, Flanders, and asked a series of questions concerning the three central issues of his journey: how to prepare to govern Flanders, the nature of his role in Italy, and the governance of his household. While he clearly considered the last point important, the rigor of his questions concerning Flanders and the armies he was helping to raise reveals his deep involvement in the details of his job. Juan de San Agustín must have made this point clearly, for the response he brought back also emphasized these questions to an extent not previously seen in Fernando's instructions.[82]

At about the same time, Villafranca expressed different types of concerns about the journey. In his view, the army being assembled would not be ready when the infante arrived in Italy, which would delay his departure for points north for an undetermined length of time. Villafranca urged the king to announce only that the infante was traveling to Milan and to appoint him to an office there that would allow him to remain in Italy as long as necessary without damage to his reputation. This reasoning apparently underlay increasingly insistent requests that Fernando be made imperial vicar general of Italy. The infante apparently supported the marquis's requests and his policy, for he himself wrote to request further favors on the marquis's behalf weeks before the scheduled departure from Barcelona.[83]

The success of the infante's journey also depended on his visits with princes along his route and his proper relations with them. Of crucial importance was his cousin Vitorio Amadeo of Savoy. The king himself wrote to his brother concerning how to interact with their cousin, describing Philip II's treatment of the Duke of Savoy and drawing on the precedent of their father's treatment of Prince Philiberto and, finally, recalling the directions he himself had been given as a child. Indicating the importance of these matters of ceremony, Fernando wrote back confirming his instructions, which he summarized as "excluding equality [of treatment] I should try not to discontent the duke," and implying that proper treatment would be key to the success of his mission.[84]

Fernando also expressed concern about the nature of his titles and argued for his appointment as vicar of Italy. In a graceful, well-argued letter of January 1633, Fernando offered his own interpretation of his estate and provided insight into the necessity of the questions of etiquette that he had raised elsewhere. He rejected the use of the journey of the infanta Isabel Clara through Italy as a precedent for his journey, arguing that although in Castile infantes and infantas garnered equal respect, it would not be so in Italy. He instead compared his condition to that of Ferdinand, the brother of Charles V, who had made a similar journey through Italy, a comparison that nicely evokes his perception of his own rank and dignity.[85] He perceived the respect he would receive and indeed the success of his journey as dependent on the clear definition of his role and the authority he carried. Without such designation, he would not even know how to address princes along his route; he would be paralyzed.

As late as March 1633 a flurry of activity surrounded reports that the cardinal-infante planned to return to Madrid. The infante was probably motivated by impatience to start the journey rather than by a regression from earlier plans. The Council of State, having heard letters from Villafranca on the matter, advised the king to write in his own hand, a ploy perhaps guaranteed to get the attention of Fernando's advisers. The king did indeed write, urging Oñate and the infante's confessor to talk some sense into the infante and impress upon him that his return to Madrid would be thoroughly contrary to the will of the king. To Villafranca he wrote in more practical terms about getting the journey under way. He noted the great prospects he saw in his service but implied that the marquis's own activities had postponed the journey. The prospect of Fernando's returning to Madrid may also have been the reason that the king issued new orders, also in his own hand, for the cardinal-infante to travel to Flanders.[86] If Fernando intended his threat to return to Madrid as a ploy to get his journey under way, it worked. There could now be no question among his staff about the king's intentions, and indeed once the king had reiterated his position so personally, the journey could not help but become a priority of state.

Even when Fernando left Spain, it had not yet been publicly announced that his eventual destination was Flanders. Chronicles presented him as appointed to govern Milan.[87] The instruction of March 1633 stressed the preservation of religion as the reason for the infante's journey. The cardinal-infante may have been perceived as equipped for this task through his religious office, but there could have been no doubt in the infante's mind that his purpose was a military one. He had spent close to a year in Barcelona learning how to be a military commander. Among the Council of State papers concerning Fernando during this time, only one reference to his ecclesiastical responsibilities survives: on September 16, 1632, a packet of five reports concerning the archbishopric of Toledo were forwarded to the cardinal-infante with the request that he inform the bishop-governor what procedure to follow in the event that some matter demanded immediate resolution.[88]

Fernando left for Italy and the Low Countries with a much-reduced entourage. Perhaps recalling the experience of the infanta María and the expense and inconvenience of her stay in Italy, he traveled with a streamlined staff that included few of the ecclesiastical trappings of his 1624 establishment. Although his entourage might appear sizeable to modern observers, it was tiny compared with the grand household he had had ten years earlier and contained few ceremonial offices. It included the reluctant Count of Oñate, with the titles mayordomo mayor and principal minister, his son Beltrán de Guevara, the same young man who previously had been officially attached to Carlos's service, the Prince of Montenegro, the Marquis d'Este, the Marquis of Orani, son of the Duke of Pastrana, and Valeriano Esfondrato, Count of La Rivera. Except for Beltrán de Guevara, all of these men had diplomatic experience, particularly in Italy. Martín de Axpe continued in his service as secretary for both the Council of State and the Council of War. One mayordomo, Luis Laso de la Vega, three chaplains and an equal number of groomsmen, eight pages, six aides and one secretary de la cámara, and a few assorted minor officials completed the entourage. Not mentioned in the official records was Antonio de Moscoso. Nonetheless, his reported death at Innsbruck in August 1634 indicates that the count-duke had not been able to drive the infante's friend and privado from his service.[89]

The importance of this journey as a turning point in Fernando's life is clear. On April 11, 1633, the infante set sail from Barcelona, never to return to Spain. After more than a year in Italy he traveled north, arriving at Lake Como in soldier's uniform at the head of seventeen thousand infantry and six thousand horsemen.[90] Although he continued to be called cardinal-infante, he was soon depicted as a hero of the battle of Nördlingen, in which a combined Spanish and imperial army rousted Swedish forces from southern Germany. His journey through the Empire to the Netherlands was celebrated in a book illustrated with beautiful prints immortalizing the contrasting qualities of angelic yellow-haired cardinal and heroic soldier.[91] As governor of the Netherlands, he experienced numerous military successes against both Dutch rebels and France, but while these actions built his reputation as a royal hero, they were not sufficient to preserve the territories intact for Spain.

Despite the successes of Fernando's career, the position of Philip IV's younger brothers within the Spanish monarchy was never truly settled. The royal brothers remained a source of anxiety for Spanish writers eager to prove the devotion and love between the king and his brothers, but while popular accounts seemed to suggest that the admirable personalities of the infantes removed concerns, the private writings of councilors suggested that nothing could overcome the danger inherent in having relatives so close in rank to the king.

Contemporary accounts present Carlos as leading an active life and credit him with the love of the populace, but palace politics, education, documentation, and the traditional concerns of history conspire to render him a historical nonentity. From this silence historians have reached a variety of conclusions about the personality and ability of the infante, resulting in evaluations ranging from Stradling's comment that Carlos wisely "kept his own counsel" to Elliott's characterization of him as "shy" and "retarded."[92] Another sort of document, the portrait of the infante by Velázquez, suggests a haughty self-possession hardly in keeping with the historical characterization. This figure more closely reflects the man who rode next to the king in games and processions and went hunting despite his fevers.

The cardinal-infante, rather than Carlos, captured the imagination of later generations. Fernando's image as hero, so reminiscent of his great uncle Don

Juan, suggests that the best arena for a brother of a king was in the wider world, where he had more opportunity to prove himself and to shape himself to the roles and image of his own inclination. It also suggests that the way to resolve the question of the status of the king's brother was to remove him from court and place him in a position in which the training, patronage, and sense of royal identity that made him a threat and source of faction at his brother's court could become an asset in service of crown and country.

7

"EL PRÍNCIPE INSTRUIDO"

Texts and Models

Twelve years into his reign, Philip IV completed a translation of books 8 and 9 of Guicciardini's history of Italy, which he had started several years earlier when already king. He described his intentions in undertaking the project in an epilogue, asserting that "this work has not been superfluous, but necessary and indispensable" for his own ability to rule.[1] He explained that when he inherited the throne he had not been prepared for the obligations of kingship, specifically lamenting the tutelage cut short by his father's death, and expressed the wish to set an example for his own son. He intended the translation itself to be part of that example, an illustration of how a king could seek to educate himself and learn what teachers could not teach. Above all, he emphasized his desire to gain mental discipline through the translation and useful knowledge through reading. Other royal persons are known to have translated various works, but Philip characterized this type of work as unusual for a reigning monarch and was perhaps unique in his perception of its critical role in teaching how to rule.

At the time he finished his translation and wrote the epilogue, Philip IV was emerging from the first phases of a struggle to define himself as king. Having come to the throne at a young age, he thought of kingship as a skill to be learned. But while he had many eager teachers and advisers, the ultimate responsibility was his, and his own understanding of royal duty would determine what kind of king he was. Other sources of legitimate authority placed restraints on a king, but he could wield a considerable amount of power independently and mold the form of government, as seen in the varying degrees to which Spanish kings relied on councils, juntas, nobles, ministers, secretaries, or favorites, according to their tastes and particular circumstances. His notion of kingship consciously and unconsciously included elements that would shape his image through political, religious, and cultural patronage and through public display.

In navigating the different issues of kingship, Philip had a variety of authors willing to advise him. A long tradition of mirrors of princes had established central questions concerning the nature of kingly rule. As monarchs in the late medieval period consolidated power, so that the idea of an all-powerful king seemed attainable, treatises began to reflect the desire to contain royal power through structures such as councils and through more subtle arguments asserting the necessity of individual morality and other personal qualities in a king. Over the generations, one can see the development of political thought in the works published during the formative years of the monarch or in times of particular crisis. Treatises such as Martín de Córdoba's *Jardín de nobles doncellas,* written for Isabel the Catholic, and Erasmus's *Institutio principis christiani,* written for the future emperor Charles V, offered both an outline of moral formation and practical advice, while the royal preacher and speechwriter Antonio de Guevara found popular as well as scholarly and royal audiences for his *Libro aureo del emperador Marco Aurelio* and *Relox de príncipes* and further works that examined both the good qualities of princes and the nature of the royal court and the favorite.[2]

During the reign of Philip II, such works as Fadrique Furió Ceriol's *Consejo y consejeros del príncipe,* Juan Ginés de Sepúlveda's *De rego et rego officio,* and Bartolomé Felipe's *Tratado del consejo y de los consejeros de los príncipes* emphasized the structure of government and the choice of advisers. Treatises also increasingly recognized that the king should earn the confidence and devotion of the people. Earlier works tended to consider this a question of the king showing himself to his people in public acts, whether in dispensing justice and demonstrating piety or in dancing and horsemanship, thus building his reputation and gaining admiration of his person. Later thought evolved to acknowledge the manipulation of image through literature, arts, and public display. Through these acts, the king reaffirmed the aura of majesty as a separate quality that placed him above other sorts of persons, thus conceding him the right to rule.

The majesty of display also gave way to its opposite, the majesty of distance, which allowed the concept of the king to permeate events when the king himself could not be seen, a style of kingship that historians have described as the "invisible king."[3] Associated in Spain with the desire of an individual, Philip II, for solitude, this conceptualization of kingship used ceremony and ideology to set the king apart from other persons, relying on his office and reputation rather than his person to command public respect. While royal practice moved in this direction, theorists did not necessarily accept this separation of the king's two persons. They continued to argue that the king should be seen and understood the public actions of the king not just as a way to win the affection of the people but also as an instruction to them.[4]

Another branch of theorists focused on the person rather than the image of the king, emphasizing the king's religion as a guarantor both of good rule and of the Catholicism of the nation. The Jesuit Pedro de Rivadeneira's *Tratado de la religión y virtudes que debe tener el príncipe cristiano* (1595), written when Philip III was in his mid-teens, continued the tradition of directing such treatises to a prince during his adolescence.[5] Unlike Erasmus, Rivadeneira did not take "Christian prince" as a general assumption, but as a blueprint for government based on Christian thought as opposed to ideas of expedience and reason of state associated with Machiavelli. He dismissed the idea of using religion to fool people and presented a vision of a king who could not rule a moral people unless he himself was moral. Rivadeneira also offered advice on a variety of practical issues, some of them reflecting standard concerns growing out of the nature of court-based political life and others perhaps inspired by current abuses. Since no man could have full understanding nor entirely balance his passions, he argued, a prince had to have wise councilors, men of great experience and great charity granted the freedom to say what they thought to their prince. His references to classical and current political thought do not suggest an outlook limited by religious orthodoxy, but a closely considered argument concerning the interaction of personal belief and public responsibility.[6]

If Rivadeneira's work marked Philip III's youth, Juan de Santa María's *República y política cristiana* (1615) addressed the king in the maturity of his reign and at a time of perceived crisis. Less rigorously argued than Rivadeneira's book and less subtle in its understanding of how the king's morality affected good government, it struck an even stronger moral tone. Presenting kingship as an office, Santa María emphasized the duties of the king and the structure of government, with its councils and ministers as extensions of the king. The king should ask advice when he did not know the solution to a problem, and thus he needed to know how to choose ministers, how to comport himself with these ministers, and perhaps most crucially, how to take counsel. Considering at length the role of favorites, Santa María attempted to redefine the term to signify a trusted minister.[7] Like many other authors of such treatises, Juan de Santa María wrote based on his own experience. A Franciscan royal preacher and the confessor of the infanta María, he was actively involved in the religious matters of court. He not only criticized Lerma but also reportedly participated in a 1620 attempt to remove the Duke of Uceda and the confessor Aliaga from their positions in the king's favor and promote in their stead Philiberto of Savoy, whose candidacy might have been thought to solve the problem of favorites by drawing on family relationships.[8]

Neither Rivadeneira nor Santa María, both of whom were caught up in concrete political and religious concerns, developed questions of the king's majesty or described public actions designed to win the hearts of the people. Indeed, they focused more on the duties of kingship than on its glories and admonished the king as much as they praised him. The "Tratado del príncipe instruido," addressed to the future Philip IV when he was in his mid-teens, apparently by Francisco de Aragon, focuses more directly on the ways princes learned their craft.[9] Familiar with the general literature on the subject and apparently influenced by Juan de Santa María in his metaphors for kingship and analysis of the favorite, his treatment and conclusions differ from those of Santa María and have a more worldly and courtly tone. Although he touches on religious matters and asserts that Prince Philip should be a model to other princes of devotion to the pope, he leaves the subject quickly and urges the prince to remain aware of his own secular and royal jurisdiction.

Using images of physical sustenance, the "Príncipe instruido" addresses the moral and physical health of the prince in a striking balance of the personal and biological realities of royal power and considers how the prince passed through the four ages of man in ways both similar to and different from other men's experiences. While the first stage, infancy, was easily addressed, since good results depended mainly on choosing good caretakers, the emphasis should be on discovering the nature of the prince rather than on forming it. The blessings of wise old age were apparent, since "in kings, there is no decrepitude, but perfection and even greater with more advanced age."[10] The more problematic stages were adolescence and young adulthood. In these stages, the supervisors of the prince's activities needed to build his understanding carefully and begin to gauge what kind of ruler he would be by observing whether he liked the sounds of the hunt, how he dealt with the games and fights of his meninos, and how he treated his companions and shared with them.

The author recommended that the prince read the histories of his four immediate predecessors but also proposed his own work as an immediate guide and explored the ways in which the court itself prepared a prince to rule. Unlike the general injunctions of treatise writers to read history to uncover role models, he specifically tied its use to the prince's ability to understand documents of state and meant reading to serve more immediately as a tool for developing an understanding of current issues. From his other studies, the prince should learn not only to write and figure but also to understand Latin, and ideally French and Italian as well, so that as king he could speak with ambassadors, both pleasing them and aiding secret negotiations. Among princely arts, equestrian skills figured prominently, but dancing and playing musical instruments also contributed to the grace and good disposition of the prince, while studying fine art, including learning to draw, opened his understanding to all the liberal arts "so necessary in a perfect prince."[11] Among more practical arts, the prince should understand surveying, and through it geography and cosmography, the navigational charts, and the placement of all the seas and lands. This knowledge would enable him to study both his own and his enemies' territories and thus to understand the reports of his generals and his councilors of state and war on his own, without asking others to explain.

All of these lessons in reading, dancing, horsemanship, geography, language, and history are presented as preparation for carrying a sword. Addressing the subject at length, the author recognized both the practical and the symbolic uses of the sword, both of which the prince must be old enough to comprehend before he was entrusted with the object itself, perhaps at age sixteen or eighteen.[12] First, the prince must carry a sword because all (noble)men carried swords, and he must above all be a man. Ordinary men, however, used the sword to defend faith and king, as well as their own personal honor. The king did not have the obligation to defend such things with his person but instead carried the sword to represent them at a higher level, that of justice.

The "Príncipe instruido" also posits *romances* sung at entertainments as a form of instruction that impressed important matters on the spirit of the prince without long discourses. This activity supplemented rather than replaced reading history, as suggested by a story depicting Philip II, inspired by a song about Alvaro de Luna, the favorite of King Juan of Castile, asking the future Philip

III whether he had read the history of Luna and what he thought of it. The prince's actual knowledge of the event is thus presented as coming from his reading, while the more riveting experience of listening to a ballad provided the occasion for discussion and reflection. At other times, inspiring stories and songs offered appropriate criticisms of the king, such as the story of Alfonso de Alburquerque, ordered a second time to travel to the Indies, letting the instruction the king had handed him fall into the sea, saying that "the true instruction was his experience and his honor."[13] These examples, unexpectedly vivid in a way that suggests the author's personal knowledge of them, were intended to fortify the spirit of the prince through emotional response to stories.

Although certain emotions could properly be instilled in the prince, his passions had such wide repercussions that he simply should not have them. His clemency too should have its limits, and above all—here the author suddenly shifts from the abstract to the practical—the king should show balance in his liberality, not overdoing the granting of favors, especially those that endangered royal income. The prince must learn that he should not do everything he wanted simply because he had it within his power to do so, but instead must govern by established laws. The prince earned the love of vassals through governing by law and respecting the various local laws. Just as plants and animals grew differently in different climates, the author noted, people of different kingdoms had different natures and qualities and thus required different governments. The prince needed to understand these differences and to have "the nature of wax" in order to be what the different regions and traditions of his kingdoms required.[14]

Having set out these several basic ideas, the author turned to the question of favorites. Recognizing the favorite as something more than a trusted minister, he implicitly rejected Santa María's redefinition of the term but struggled to define the role a favorite should play. He posed the question whether a privado should be a great noble or a man of lesser quality, noting that rank conferred status but that education, often lacking in the great nobility, was necessary if one was to do the true work of governing. As an example he pointed out that Philip II, toward the end of his life, divided the business of state into parts and put each under the charge of persons of the highest trust: Juan de Idiáquez, Cristóbal de Moura, the Count of Chinchón, and the secretary Mateo Vázquez. But these, the author noted, should not be called privados, even though each met privately with the king in his appointed hour and should properly be considered a privado.

The king should choose a favorite as he chose a viceroy or a lieutenant, for the qualities suited to the position, yet he chose the favorite through friendship, and that too was essential, for the king had to trust him fully. Like all men, the king needed to be social and to enjoy friendships, or he would lose the most essential part of being human. The favorite, for his part, should always have the king's best interest at heart, and toward that end he should reduce his dependents and accept favors only from the king. Despite the political role allowed the privado in this discussion, he should not be involved in matters of justice nor favor causes or persons publicly or privately. Doing so would make him unpopular and would be poor repayment for the king's friendship. He should instead simply take it for his greatest prize that he had the first place in the king's favor and recognize that if the king paid him excessive favor or relied too much on his advice, the king's own reputation would be damaged.

Throughout this discussion, the author knowingly treaded the line between ideal and reality. Many of his concerns about the ideal privado reflected criticisms of the Duke of Lerma. Further, he described the odd situation of a prince having two favorites, even though these be father and son, a clear reference to the struggle between Lerma and his son, the Duke of Uceda, for the favor of Philip III. The resulting tension could put public matters in a dangerous state, and therefore the king ought to choose one or the other.[15] The author then gave the potential favorite—whether he intended Lerma, Uceda, or some ideal person—several points of advice on keeping his privanza, accompanied by a copy of the letter of advice that the Count of Portalegre had sent to the Duke of Lerma in 1600 and a summary of a conversation he himself had had with the duke, then Marquis of Denia, as they rode together from El Pardo to Madrid after the obsequies of Philip II. His advice had in common with that of Portalegre and others the observation that favor is brief and that a valiant and prudent king will eventually put aside a privado.

Having already spent more pages on this issue than on any other, the author proceeded to consider which privado had enjoyed the best career. Although the author had dismissed the definition of the three great ministers and the secretary of Philip II as favorites, the prudent king had, nonetheless, had a privado, and that, of course, was "the great" Ruy Gómez de Silva. Expressing respect for the Portuguese courtier bordering on hagiography, the author outlined the qualities of the perfect privado. First, Ruy Gómez had been extremely prudent and discreet and had known how to judge a person's quality. Charles V had loved him as well, the author claimed, and had urged Philip II to keep him close rather than send him on diplomatic missions. Listing examples of the favorite's talents, the author concluded that Ruy Gómez had been the best privado of "our times" and that although Philip II had had other privados after Ruy Gómez died, none could compare to him.[16]

In placing such emphasis on the subject of the favorite, the author echoed the concerns of many writers of the time. During the reign of Philip III, when the Duke of Lerma emerged as the undisputed favorite of the king, many Spaniards searched for precedents that supported the use of a favorite. Mateo Renzi's "Tratado de el Privado Perfecto" presented the "office" of favorite as a benign and useful institution, offering praise and advice.[17] Others searched recent history to prove the prior existence of favorites. Many focused on Ruy Gómez de Silva as the favorite of Philip II, while others presented Diego de Córdoba as the king's friend and Cristóbal de Moura as a favorite in the final years of the reign.[18] Some writers defended the choice of a favorite by indicating that the previous king himself had made the choice for his son, as the author of the "Príncipe instruido" described the emperor Charles V specifically recommending Ruy Gómez de Silva to his son (although the empress had a greater influence on Gomez's early career).[19] Ana de Castro presented the return of the Marquis of Denia, later Duke of Lerma, to court during the lifetime of Philip II as proof of the late king's approval of him, a point also argued by Matías de Novoa.[20] The same reasoning can, of course, be applied to the role of Philip III in shaping his son's reign. He was the one who appointed Gaspar de Guzmán, the future Count-Duke of Olivares, to the same offices in the prince's chamber that the Duke of Lerma had held in the household of Philip III as prince.

Both Juan de Santa María and the author of the "Príncipe instruido," as we have seen, discussed whether ministers should be considered favorites, but arguments for this definition should be seen as attempts to remake the system, since the term clearly indicated a person who played a role beyond that of a valued minister. Rather than being simply a minister, the favorite straddled the line between the public and natural persons of the king, and between the concepts of common and ideal friendship, the first based on clientage structures, the second on genuine affection. The prominent consideration of the favorite within discussions of the nature of the king gets to the very heart of early modern anxiety concerning the person of the king.

Anxiety concerning innovations in the structure of royal rule is also reflected in the emphasis observers placed on the downfall of the favorite. These discussions point to the essential problem of the favorite: his position did not depend on either of the structures of early modern power; he received his "title" neither by merit, as reward for service, nor by inheritance. The king, first and foremost, had his power through inheritance, and the nobility likewise passed down titles in this way. Furthermore, individuals at court had a sense of their rights to certain offices or rewards, mounting arguments for reward from a sense of contract. Sometimes successive generations of a family served in similar positions in a way that appeared to constitute an almost inherited right. Other professions also gained a right to position through various methods of training. Among the numerous officials at court, only the favorite did not earn his position by any traditional structure. This in itself may have made the practice appear to be a novelty, despite the appearance of favorites in many earlier generations. The favorite existed outside of the structures of court intended to create stability.

Father and Son

From his earliest years, activities at court centered on the future Philip IV in ways of which he was perhaps unaware. The ceremonies in which he received the oath of allegiance as future ruler and the emblem of the Order of the Golden Fleece were rituals designed specifically for the prince, although they also had value for those observing him. Observers did not pretend that the prince understood these activities, pointing out that he slept during the oath taking and treated the emblem of the fleece as if it were a toy. Even events not meant for his particular edification tended to be overshadowed by his presence and actions, as when he disrupted the baptisms of two of his younger siblings, one by crying every bit as much as the sister who was being baptized and the other by demanding to be taken to his parents, who were watching the ceremony in which he was participating.[21]

While Philip III had been dressed in what were described as children's underclothes until he became king, he had felt it below his dignity and did not impose such treatment on his son.[22] The prince often dressed in child-sized versions of adult clothing, even to the point of wearing a sword, perhaps a merely decorative one, at age two and a half, on the occasion of the infante Carlos's baptism, and at age three, when he served as the official sponsor for the wedding of two nobles that took place in the queen's oratory.[23] The king actively involved him in religious ritual, took him hunting from an early age, and encouraged his participation in theater and court festivities. We can glimpse the future king dancing, holding mock tournaments with his brothers, and directing theatrical productions.

The future Philip IV married earlier than his father had, in 1615, when he was ten years old. In the five years before he and his wife began to have sexual relations, her role at court and her relationship to Prince Philip closely paralleled those of his sister. Although Spanish negotiators did not mention the prince's age as a reason to delay the marriages, the delay in consummation of the marriage was surely based on the age of the prince as much as or more than on the age of the princess. While threats to the health of a girl who began sexual relations too early might be more apparent, the potential problems for a boy who began married life at age ten were also grave; indeed it was feared that early sexual activity might weaken a growing boy.

The Spanish court may also have considered respect between husband and wife a factor in determining the age at which the prince should begin true married life or indeed hoped that the couple could become friends in the intervening years. In September 1617, when the twelve-year-old prince experienced his first extended absence from his wife, he spent his spare time writing daily letters to her.[24] By the following year, at least, the prince had developed a romantic interest in his wife, expressed in a poem praising her beauty and accusing her of mistreating him. While the poem follows a classic courtesy form blaming the beloved for cruelty, the courtier who preserved it claimed that it had been inspired by the princess's refusing to let the prince kiss her.[25]

As had been the case with the princess, consummation of the marriage was a sign that the prince had reached adulthood. While Gascon de Torquemada had juxtaposed Isabel's beginning to wear women's shoes with the consummation of their marriage, Gonzalo Céspedes y Meneses juxtaposed the consummation on November 25 and Philip's introduction to reading consultas of the Council of Castile on December 4.[26]

In addition to his attachment to his wife, whom he was assumed to love, and his siblings, for whom he clearly expressed affection, chroniclers noted the prince's attachment to various members of his household and reported as a matter of course that he had favorites among them. In 1611, when the Duke of Sessa was ordered to retire to his lands, it was generally understood that Philip's growing affection for the duke had raised concerns that he was becoming "too familiar" with the prince, which might lead to a lack of respect. At the same time, other members of court were forbidden the casual access to the prince's quarters that they had previously enjoyed, apparently to avoid similar problems. To the extent that such dismissals reflected the Duke of Lerma's agency, they limited access to the prince and reduced the opportunity for persons other than the favorite's nominees to become close to members of the royal family. The prince, however, had some influence concerning the composition of his household, for it was apparently at his insistence that he retained the services of his azafata, Juana Zapata, described by Novoa as the "one whom the prince most loved," even after all other women had been removed from his service as he entered adolescence.[27]

In 1618 the true struggle for the affection of the prince began, and with it, although no one could yet know it, the first phase of the transition in reigns as well. In what has been termed the "revolution of the keys," two major figures in the prince's household were ordered to relinquish the keys that gave them access to the prince's chamber. One of these was Fernando de Borja, a distant relative of the king's favorite whom Novoa then considered the favorite of the prince. The other was the Count of Lemos, the son of Queen Margarita's cama-rera mayor and the Duke of Lerma's nephew but also his son-in-law, who had returned from royal service in Italy a few years prior. While Borja was given a position in the government of Aragon, Lemos, after a brief conference with the king in which he blamed all problems on himself and attempted to have others reinstated, begged leave to retire to his estates. Both men had begun to side with Lerma in a mounting struggle between the duke and his eldest son, the Duke of Uceda. Also asked to leave were Juana Zapata, her son-in-law, who was the keeper of the prince's wardrobe, and three other men. It was in the aftermath of this struggle that Lerma himself departed court in the early fall of 1618. The apparent victory of the Uceda faction was not, however, complete, for Lemos had the chance to explain his departure personally to the prince, and Juana Zapata answered the prince's questions before she left, blaming Uceda, the king's confessor, and the Count of Olivares, who had relayed information about the prince's chamber to Uceda.[28]

Prince Philip had at least some affection for his father's favorite. When Lerma departed from court, the prince, who was then thirteen, was one of the last people to take leave of him. Calling from his chambers to the duke, who was in the gardens of San Lorenzo, the prince invited him to join him in his room, where they spoke for a quarter-hour. The duke then gave the prince the final gift of a small chain and left him "affected and even with some tears," and soon after that he left court forever.[29] When, not long after this, Philip III ordered carriages for a journey without indicating where he intended to go, gossip at court posited that the destination was the town of Lerma and reported that the prince had expressed hope that the rumor was true.[30] Although the royal party did not go to Lerma, the king, the prince, and Prince Philiberto did indeed meet the duke on this journey. While the prince and his cousin hunted, the king, Lerma, and Uceda met concerning business related to the infanta Ana. In a letter written during the same meeting, the Duke of Uceda attempted to disguise the dismissal of his father by noting to the Spanish ambassador in France that his father had gone to Lerma, "as he usually has in other years."[31] In the following year, when the king fell seriously ill, the prince was thought to retain enough affection for Lerma that rumor proclaimed he would recall the duke and make him first minister if the king died. The king continued to write to the duke, while the prince sent his regards through the Count of Saldaña.[32] By the time he became king, however, whatever affection Philip IV had for his father's favorite had cooled sufficiently that he deprived him of considerable incomes he had from the crown.

With the dismissal of Lerma, Philip III embarked upon a more active, public style of rule. Whether in response to the work of Santa María, the influence of his confessor, or simply his own assessment of the state of his kingdom, Philip III began to change his mode of governing in early 1619. It was also at this time that the political education of the future Philip IV began in earnest. While it is easy to connect this shift in education to the new style of government, the prince was reaching his mid-teens, the age at which both Philip II and Philip III had first been introduced to the details of the art of governing. Philip III's apprenticeship was not the active and extended exposure to government that his own father had enjoyed, but by 1596 he was witnessing the daily activities of the king, presiding over both religious and court ceremonies, attending some meetings of councils and the Junta de Gobierno, and signing documents for his father.[33] Circumstances limited his preparation of his own son even more; nonetheless, it was not nonexistent.

The long-delayed journey to Portugal marked the true beginning of the prince's political education. Claiming Portugal in 1580 after the death of his nephew Sebastian, Philip II had attached great significance to the position of Portugal within the Spanish monarchy and emphasized its importance by residing in Lisbon for two years and by showing favor to Portuguese nobles both during his residence there and after his return to Madrid. In the early years of Philip III's reign the Portuguese campaigned repeatedly for the king to visit the kingdom, offering generous grants to pay the cost of the journey. Despite repeated reports of planned journeys, Philip III delayed visiting Portugal until 1619. Neither the king nor his favorite considered Portugal central to the monarchy. In addition, Philip III apparently had a difficult relationship with his father's former minister Cristóbal de Moura, who served as viceroy in Portugal from 1599 until his death in 1613. The Duke of Lerma may also have wanted to diminish the influence of the more experienced statesman, and since Philip III clearly had made this appointment with the intention of removing Moura from court, king and favorite may have ignored Portugal partially in order to ignore Moura. It was only after Moura's death and Lerma's dismissal that the king undertook to visit Portugal.[34]

The king, the prince, the princess, and the infanta María left Madrid in April 1619, having first attended a memorial service for Emperor Matthias in the Descalzas Reales.[35] Passing through Trujillo and Mérida, they arrived at Badajoz, where they observed obsequies for Matthias for a second time but where they must also have recognized the loss so many years prior of Queen Ana, the mother of Philip III. Visiting monasteries and convents along the way, they followed a pattern not significantly different from that which guided journeys closer to Madrid.

Throughout Portugal, the royal family was greeted by allegorical figures, triumphal arches, dances, and masques meant to convey the history, prosperity, and devotion of the Portuguese. In the city of Lisbon itself, presentations prominently featured the figures of the kings of Portugal, ending with the first king who had ruled both Spain and Portugal, Philip II of Spain and Philip I of Portugal. The Portuguese seemed eager to demonstrate to the king and prince that while they were now part of the Spanish monarchy, they held their own separate history in high regard. Philip III, having viewed the extensive tributes of Lisbon with the prince, returned the next day with the princess and the infanta María to examine the images and epigrams at a more leisurely pace. As if to allow himself the pleasure and instruction of viewing them yet again, he commissioned his Portuguese chronicler (and the prince's tutor in mathematics and cosmography) to write an account of the journey, complete with detailed drawings of the figures and arches, which Philip IV later ordered published.[36]

While in Portugal, Prince Philip saw his father maintaining a more active schedule than usual, not only taking part in numerous ceremonial occasions but also listening to philosophical disputes and attending a meeting of the Portuguese royal council, as had been the custom of earlier kings of Portugal.[37] To further emphasize the changes occurring in the prince's education during this journey, the king appointed a new ayo, Baltasar de Zúñiga, who had been in the diplomatic service of the Spanish crown for all of his adult life. After a period of apprenticeship with his uncle, the second Count of Olivares, who was the Spanish ambassador in Rome, Zúñiga had served as the crown's representative to Brussels, Paris, and the imperial court. Returning to Madrid in 1617, he had become a councilor of state.[38] With the appointment of this accomplished person as ayo to the prince, Philip III appears to have followed his dismissal of his favorite in the previous year with a decisive shift in focus. Soon, in addition, the prince began to read reports from the different parts of the Spanish kingdoms and ambassadors' letters from foreign lands.[39]

Shortly after the journey to Portugal, one observer recommended another way to expand the education of the prince, focusing particularly on the dynamics of an anticipated long period in which there would be an adult crown prince at the court of Spain. The author of the "Discursos admirables" chose the day the prince began "the conjugal life" (1620) as the starting point for his discussion of the adult roles of the prince as well as those of his brothers.[40] Having first considered the problem of the infantes, the author turned to the prince, for as the future Philip IV approached his mid-teens, his immediate role was no clearer than that of his brothers. With his father in his early forties, there was no reason to expect that the prince would inherit the throne soon. The author feared the effects of a too-courtly existence on the growing prince and advocated filling the prince's household with older men, those of the court as well as soldiers and men with experience of all the states of the monarchy. He presented these men as a battery of instructors, teaching what was impossible to learn from "one master alone."

The reading of history, he commented, was all very well and good, but the prince needed to learn from experience. Turning from the question of education within the household to education in the field of action, the author advocated seizing the advantages of having a prince close to fully grown: Prince Philip should be sent to the Low Countries, for his own good and for that of the monarchy. How fortunate, the author claimed, to have one Philip to rule Spain and another to send on such a mission. He contemplated how different things would have been if Philip II had had a son to send to Flanders rather than the Duke of Alba and imagined sending the prince with his wife and family, with good ministers and validos, to govern. He apparently considered it only a minor inconvenience that Archduke Albert still ruled there and did not even address the infanta Isabel Clara's claim. Instead, he wrote as if neither was of sufficient stature to satisfy the people there, who had always begged for a ruler of the blood.

The benefits of the changes made by the king and the luxury of a long apprenticeship imagined by the authors of the "Príncipe instruido" and the "Discursos admirables" were curtailed by the sudden death of Philip III in 1621. On his deathbed, the king gave his son his last counsel, along with "buenos documentos" that were to guide him in good government and a sealed private instruction.[41] In giving his son the latter document, which apparently is not extant, Philip III followed his father and grandfather in providing his son with a particular instruction. The "buenos documentos" included a copy of the same instruction of Saint Louis to his son that the king had given the infanta Ana when she began her marriage journey. In this action as well he followed his father's example, for the dying Philip II had likewise commended this document to his son, as his father had commended it to him.[42] In addition to giving him the written documents, the king enjoined his son to continue patronage of charitable works, especially those of his mother. This injunction, although it has helped shape the image of the king, should not be seen as a special reflection of the piety of Philip III, for Philip II on his deathbed similarly admonished his son to serve God foremost.

Certainly, as prince and as king Philip IV did not suffer for lack of advice. In addition to mirrors of princes providing him with general guidelines, writers advised on various subjects within plays, poems, and *arbitrios,* so that a wide variety of authors can be seen as the "would-be tutors" of the king.[43] It is difficult to know how much of this material Philip IV actually saw. At the time of his father's death, he is reported to have said that he had read "a book by a good author that said that kings did not need privados but good councilors."[44] Rumor held that the book in question was Juan de Santa María's treatise on Christian rule. Santa María followed up the general advice of his 1615 book with a paper written six days into the new reign advocating a rather partisan dismissal of persons from office.[45]

In the epilogue to his translation of Guicciardini years later, Philip IV commented movingly on the personal and political impact of his father's death. He described as part of the natural order of things that children, including himself as a child, were mischievous and undisciplined. He did not explicitly say what brought about the transition from the age of frivolousness to the age of true learning but implied that this transition occurred naturally. When he himself was still in this period of life, he continued, he had lost his father, "a father whom I loved dearly and a master whom I served with all love, loyalty, and submission." At just sixteen he had been unprepared for the obligations that faced him. He blamed not his father but his own age for his lack of preparation: "I remained . . . with very little or no information of what I ought to do in such a great position, since for my few years the king, my lord, who is in heaven, could not introduce me near to his person in the business of this monarchy. . . . I found myself, as I have said, without any knowledge of what I ought to do, in the middle of this ocean of difficulties and sea of confusions."[46]

The young king had then undertaken to learn to be king with the same enthusiasm that everyone had previously seen him learn "the exercises of a knight." He presented the task he had had before him, of learning to be king, in a disarmingly practical sense and wrote as if his readers, too, might find themselves in the position of having to learn to rule: "All these notices are of benefit to the persons that occupy the position which I hold."[47] Yet it is clear that he had considered kingship an enormous and at times overwhelming task and one that he had questioned his ability to fulfill.

King and Favorite

Great excitement greeted the new reign, and public mourning was tinged with anxiety and optimism concerning the opportunity for change. But the transition from the reign of Philip III to that of Philip IV was also fraught with a particular anxiety, heightened by the youth of the king and by the policy and factional shifts that had already been taking place in the previous years. Francisco de Quevedo, writing from temporary retirement, captured the energy of the transition, with its bewildering array of appointments, dismissals, and arrests.[48] Caught up in the turbulence of the transition were such court figures as the Duke of Osuna, accused of misuse of office while viceroy of Naples, and Rodrigo Calderón, the former favorite's favorite, already imprisoned at the time of the death of Philip III. A few of these changes, such as the dismissal and later imprisonment of the Duke of Uceda and the appointment of Juana Zapata as azafata for the child the queen was expecting in the spring of 1621, probably stemmed directly from the personal desires of the king. One author speculated that such personal reasons also led to Philip IV's resolution not to show clemency to Rodrigo Calderón, since he knew the pain that this protégé of Lerma had caused his mother.[49] Other appointments, such as the recall of the Duchess of Gandía, who had been Queen Margarita's first camarera mayor, as camarera mayor of Queen Isabel and of the Marquise del Valle as aya of the expected royal child, were clearly intended to express the new ruler's desire to reverse injustices of the previous reign and may have been ordered by the king at the prodding of older members of court, since he himself would not have remembered the events that had led to these dismissals.[50] Other than these appointments, which appear to have been based on the affections of the king or his desire to appear just, the changes at court had much to do with the agenda of the new favorite in consolidating his power and eliminating the last vestiges of the Duke of Lerma's privanza.

Despite the significant dismissals, more persons in the service of the crown retained their positions than lost them. Palace records indicate that dozens of gentlemen de la cámara and de la boca renewed the oath of office for the positions they had held under Philip III, the queen's chamber was untouched except for additions and a few French ladies who returned to France based on issues stemming from international politics rather than court factions, and the royal chapel remained unchanged except for the dismissal and later banishment of the dead king's confessor. In addition, numerous lesser officials and servants, ranging from pages and stablehands to laundresses, cooks, and sweepers, continued to serve in the palace and court in a seamless transition from old to new reign.[51]

Amid the turmoil and continuity of the transition, we can discern a few details of the sixteen-year-old king's accommodating himself to his new role. One description of the scene at the deathbed of Philip III describes the prince not shedding a tear, while his sister María sobbed for all to see, actions apparently considered admirable in both cases. Another author presented the new king as assuring his brothers of his fatherlike love for them.[52] Throughout the events of the next several weeks, Philip IV put on a graceful show of kingly habits. In accordance with family practice, he withdrew to the royal apartment at the monastery of San Jerónimo. His brother Carlos accompanied him, while his wife, sister, and younger brother went to the Descalzas Reales. After almost a month's seclusion, he emerged on May 2 to accept the greetings of the various councils and attend obsequies for his father in the church of San Jerónimo. A week later the new king officially entered Madrid. His mount for this occasion, a white horse with black livery, was escorted from the palace of Madrid by a grand accompaniment of pages, macebearers, *regidores,* and the corregidor of Madrid, followed by grandees, nobles, and gentlemen riding in groups of four. When this escort, all in black except for the corregidor and his lieutenant, arrived at San Jerónimo, on the eastern outskirts of Madrid, the king mounted the horse and rode into Madrid and across the city to the palace under a great canopy of white brocade, sustained by sixteen golden poles carried by the regidores.[53]

Within several days of these events, the king presided at a dinner at which he publicly granted the Count of Olivares the grandeeship long coveted by his family.[54] Conferring grandee status served to recognize Olivares as the favorite and was the culmination of several years of factional struggle at the Spanish court, divided along the lines of noble family networks. The level of faction at court created by Lerma's rise to power spawned a complementary reaction at his fall. On the one hand, the traditions of royal service in Lerma's family had made his monopolization of power seem almost natural. On the other, his position had, in one generation, created the expectation that the king would have a favorite. But the family network brought to power at the beginning of the reign of Philip IV did not have the same depth of ties at court. Although Olivares's forebears and Zúñiga personally had served for years in the diplomatic service, they had very little experience in the royal households. Olivares and Zúñiga prospered almost entirely through personal attachment to the king, that is, not through a structure in which their monopolization of power might be presented as the natural outgrowth of tradition. Without the backing of a family tradition of service at court, their power relied all the more on the favor of the king.

Although theorists posited friendship as the basis of the favorite's influence, the balance of political influence and personal sentiment varied in the creation of favorites. Perhaps the most complete overlap of these elements occurred in the career of the Duke of Lerma, who was clearly both the king's closest friend and his chief minister. Lerma can be seen as having gained a place in Philip III's favor by building up the confidence of the prince, a pattern seen in other young kings, including James VI/I, Louis XIII, and, in the late seventeenth century, Carlos II. Philip III had a genuine deep affection for Lerma that did not cease when he dismissed his friend from court.[55]

But if Philip III's choice of favorites appears to have been based on true friendship, little evidence suggests that Philip IV considered Olivares a personal friend. While still prince, he insulted the count, inspiring him to offer to withdraw from service, and heard his beloved Juana Zapata blame the count for her own dismissal. In the early years of his reign he apparently disregarded the count-duke's advice concerning the younger royal brothers and treated with indifference the possibility that Olivares might retire because of poor health.[56] Indeed, if any person appeared to be the best friend of the king, it was his brother Carlos. The young king perceived himself to need a guide, however, and in that respect the favorite was clearly the Count-Duke of Olivares.

Olivares entered the unofficial office of favorite determined to differentiate his actions from those of Philip III's favorite, in effect attempting to take up the redefinition of favorite suggested by Rivadeneira, Santa María, and the author of the "Príncipe instruido." He disliked being called valido or privado but still retained, at least initially, household positions similar to those that had been the basis of the Duke of Lerma's power. Despite his intentions, however, the negative perception of the favorite crystallized under Olivares in a way that it had not under Lerma. Olivares's lack of an entrenched family network in court service and his determination to curtail royal grants and honors affected people who had previously found ways to work within the system or at least remain undamaged by it. A structure that could withstand the abuse of patronage could not survive the curtailment of it.

According to J. H. Elliott, Philip IV's education at the time of his accession was "hopelessly inadequate."[57] While the king himself seems to say as much in his epilogue to the translation of Guicciardini, he exaggerated his ignorance. The talents of his primary teachers, Galcerán Albanell and Juan Bautista Lavaña, can hardly be so easily dismissed; indeed, Philip specifically identifies geography, one of Lavaña's specialties, not only as a favorite subject but also as a key tool for developing his understanding of the world. On all sides, Philip IV was urged to read history, and Olivares was hardly unique in exhorting the young king to look to the example of his grandfather and other predecessors. The impressive reading list described in Philip's epilogue, which Elliott assumes Olivares helped construct, could easily have been assembled by his tutor, his confessor, or his father, or by himself through perusal of the works recommended by treatise writers. Indeed, although he had access to the riches of the library at El Escorial, enough of the books he read had been present in his mother's library to argue that even a modest collection could suggest his reading program. His inspiration to translate Guicciardini, which Elliott also attributes to Olivares's educational plan, may have come from a number of sources, including the example of his cousin Philiberto of Savoy, who dedicated his translation of the chronicles of Philip Commines to the king in 1624.

The influence of the count-duke in the king's education is most easily detected in the specifics of political policy and administration. In addition to the official records of Olivares's administration, a number of papers survive that the favorite intended more specifically as teaching texts, beginning with his short work written a few months into the new reign on the necessity of limiting royal favors, a theme popular in the thought of the era.[58] Olivares continued his instruction of the king in his "Gran Memorial" of 1624, in which he outlined not only the structure of the monarchy but his approach to administrative, constitutional, and economic reforms. While parts of this paper present factual information about the different realms and other parts delineate a concept of kingship and power, the document as a whole has the tone of a lesson, as do many of the papers written by Olivares for the king, underlined in this case by an introductory statement in which he reminds the king of his youth.[59] Olivares's conceptualization of the king as a kind of student and the papers he produced on various political subjects may also reflect the count-duke's own learning process. Given his lack of personal experience in foreign policy, he, as much as the king, may have been under the tutelage of Baltasar de Zúñiga in the late years of Philip III's reign.

Although it is likely that Philip's political education, at least prior to the appointment of Zúñiga as ayo, was indeed lacking—he was, after all, only fourteen at the time of the appointment—it is less obvious that his cultural education had been neglected. Philip's interest in history, geography, and art predate the ascent of Olivares, as does his familiarity with the work of Lope de Vega and Antonio Hurtado de Mendoza. He grew up surrounded by the impressive royal art collection, assembled mostly by Philip II. Philip III's court painters, if not at the forefront of artistic invention, were nonetheless kept busy in the royal employ. Indeed, the Duke of Lerma, for all his shortcomings as ayo, would have been the ideal person to introduce the prince to artistic patronage, since he himself was one of the greatest patrons of the arts in early-seventeenth-century Europe.[60] It is difficult, therefore, to comprehend the artistic tastes of the king as purely reflecting a plan on the part of the count-duke to focus attention on the king as an example to the nobility or to imagine Olivares as orchestrating the theater of court, with the king simply "warming to his part."[61]

Philip IV, in his epilogue to the translation of Guicciardini, does not mention any other person's influence on the course of study he chose to undertake. He presents himself as acting alone in devising the program of reading, setting the timetable of his undertaking active involvement in government, and deciding to cut a window into the council chamber in order to listen to and learn from council meetings. It may be that the king recognized Olivares's aid with his reference to ministers who had helped him. Our understanding of the central role of the favorite might make the lack of specific mention appear an omission, but the king may simply have been expressing the truth that, in the end, it was the king who had to act and that any other person's input was secondary. The lack of specific mention may indeed reflect an underlying struggle between Philip IV and the count-duke over the shaping of the reign and the credit for its achievements.

The count-duke, indeed, continued to see Philip as a student long after that was acceptable to the king. As late as 1627, in a letter to the infanta Isabel, Olivares referred to the twenty-two-year-old king as a boy and complained that he could not persuade him to work. In 1629 he professed himself shocked that the king had written a state paper by himself.[62] By his own account, he was pleasantly impressed by Philip's talent and erudition, although one cannot help but wonder about the true effect of the king's effort on Olivares given that the judgment he expressed in the paper differed from that of the favorite. Disagreements between Philip and Olivares continued to surface throughout the late 1620s and the 1630s, with Olivares occasionally expressing impatience at the king's habits and interpreting his ideas not as opinions but as signs of stubbornness and youth. The king clearly did not simply yield to the opinions of the privado, although he considered him an anchor and perhaps an indispensable shield.

The King His Own Teacher

Philip IV grew into his part as king, a process probably both helped and hindered by the count-duke. While Philip III had followed the pattern set by his own father of not appearing often in public, descriptions of public events in the early years of Philip IV's reign reflect the types of display that establish the poise and public presence of the king. Although he often gave audiences without so much as turning his head, numerous descriptions of public events suggest that

the king also participated in exactly the types of activities traditionally recommended to win the hearts of the people. The early years of the reign abounded
in masques, bullfights, and entrances.

The visit of the Prince of Wales offered Philip IV an extended opportunity
for this type of kingly display. While his political assessment of the English marriage remains unclear, Philip IV treated the prince with all the dignity due his
rank and may indeed have been happy to have the excuse to add a few juegos
de cañas and hunting trips to his schedule. Religious processions for Easter and
Corpus Christi were conducted with particular solemnity and brilliance, both
to honor the prince and with the overt intention of speeding his conversion. In
many ways the visit was a defining moment for both Philip of Spain and Charles
of England. The journey can be seen as a personal expression of Charles's need
for independence from his father, while it furnished Philip a canvas for his own
images of majesty.[63]

But Elliott's assertion that the visit of the refined and discerning Prince
of Wales "could not fail to suggest to Philip how much he still had to learn"
concerning kingly accomplishment does not ring true. The level of cultural life
to which Philip IV was accustomed since youth argues against such a transformation. Jonathan Brown provides a more subtle reading of the assertion that
Charles had a lasting effect on Philip, suggesting that Charles's great interest
in Philip's extensive art collection helped the young king to recognize its great
value. Other authors suggest that the splendor and ceremony of the Spanish
court influenced Charles's love of courtly manners and arts. Indeed, Charles
procured, through gift and purchase, so much art that Gregorio de Andrés
mischievously suggests that the purpose of the prince's visit to Spain was not to
win a bride but to take home as many objects of art as he could carry.[64]

If the young Spanish king, adept at public ceremony, influenced the English
prince to adopt a more remote and formal style, there is some evidence that the
reverse was also true. A handful of Spanish sources describing events during the
prince's visit and in following years reported the king embracing persons who
had begun the gesture of kissing the king's hand, something it is hard to imagine
his father or grandfather doing. Philip, in his turn, had taken the cue from the
"rude" English and lightened his personal style, at least in more intimate circles.
In the next few years, more books of gallantry were printed at the court as well,
suggesting a lively banter between ladies and gentlemen and the participation
of the royal family.[65]

Philip continued to revel in activities that served both his personal enjoyment and his public image. In festivities surrounding the baptism of his son, the king not only rode in juegos de cañas but was so exhilarated by the day's events that instead of calling for his coach at the end of the day, he remained on his horse and rode back to the royal palace, lance in hand, among the people on the crowded street.[66] He attended and, in a limited way, even took part in bullfights, including one that various court figures commemorated in a collection of epigrams and romances, praising the king's skill and drawing loose connections between this physical skill and his ability to rule.[67] To facilitate such events, Philip IV developed a plaza and riding grounds at the foot of the palace, next to the gardens belonging to the Augustinian colegio of Doña María de Aragon and the convent of La Encarnación. This location, known as the "plaza of the prioress," was the scene for a magnificent celebration during the Prince of Wales's visit. Events held there could be viewed from the palace, although by 1629 a freestanding building with a balcony had been built to facilitate attendance by the royal family and members of their households.[68]

The king found both recreation and reputation in the arts as well. Increasingly, treatises included understanding and patronage of the arts among the attributes of a king, accepting humanist theories of artistic creation as a superior activity, worthy of the support of high-minded individuals. From the beginning of his reign, both amateur and professional theater abounded in court and city, accompanied by an increased interest in special effects and spectacle. The king himself reportedly wrote plays and poems that circulated under the byline "de un Ingenio de la corte" and played musical instruments, including the viol, taught to him by an English gentleman of his household named Henry Butler.[69] Contemporaries cited descriptions of the king himself painting as proof that painting was a noble art. Although some sources report this as a youthful activity, Philip IV may have painted throughout his life. He also remained a patron of the arts, actively pursuing purchases, providing a studio for Rubens when he visited, and maintaining a particularly close friendship with Velázquez, through whose career he demonstrated his own belief in the nobility of painting.[70] His major collecting activity began in the late 1620s, at about the same time that he became more politically active. The grand-scale building and decoration of the Retiro palace, on the outskirts of Madrid, in which Olivares took a strong role, was visualized as providing a stage for the theater of state. But in a more intimate project, the king added to the Torre de la Parada, on the grounds of El

Pardo, long favored by the royal family both as a hunting lodge and as a place to overnight between Madrid and San Lorenzo. In line with Philip's personal taste, the Torre was now decorated with a cycle of mythological paintings from the workshop of Rubens, religious works by Carducho, modest and delicate Velázquez portraits of the king, his brother, and his son as hunters, and the same artist's sensitive series of portraits of court buffoons and dwarfs.[71]

Philip IV also established himself as a patron of education. New interest in creating an academy for nobles at court reflected the preoccupation of both the king and his favorite with issues of education. Philip II had founded an academy at court, which included a faculty of sciences overseen by his architect Juan de Herrera, but it was opposed by the universities and suffered lack of interest on the part of the nobility. The death in 1624 of the last member of the original academy, Juan Bautista Lavaña, may have precipitated its rededication and re-design in the following year, under the auspices of the Jesuits.[72] In founding the academy, Philip IV set out his thoughts on education: "Considering that all the well-governed republics have drawn the better part of their happiness from the good education of [their] youth and although it is in their interest that this good education is provided for the common people, it matters yet more that it not be missing in the sons of princes and nobility."[73]

But while Philip II intended his academy to increase the general level of scientific inquiry in Spain under the patronage of the court, Philip IV meant to educate the nobility as a method of improving government. His thinking reflects that of an arbitrio written in 1619 by Sancho de Moncada, which placed the need for improved education of all the ruling class within a plan for the economic and political revitalization of Spain. Moncada recognized the role of the nobility in government and offered education under the control of the king as a means to ensure their success in this task. With such education centrally controlled, the prince would also have the opportunity to observe the nobles and to judge their abilities and motives.[74] Encouraging the nobility to send their sons to a royal academy could be seen as an extension of the traditional role the court played as the training ground of young nobles. But in the earlier model of sending aristocratic youth to serve at court, as it existed throughout Europe, nobles had not gone to school as such but had developed networks through social interaction and relied on a method of "education" through participation, observation, and exposure to role models.[75]

In a similar gesture of control, Philip IV placed limits on publishing of all sorts in the Junta de Reformación of 1625 and in a decree of 1627. Restrictions applied both to plays and to histories, two major instruments to move and persuade people. The stated intent of these measures was protection of morals, although one cannot but wonder if perhaps art and information had become rights reserved to royalty. Certainly the crown had, over the previous century, increasingly controlled the writing of history, so that by Philip IV's reign royal chroniclers served in large measure as propagandists and supports to the king's authority.[76]

Whatever its intended usefulness in centralizing education and influence, the patronage of learning also clearly reflected the interests of the king. From early in his reign, Philip IV established a private study and library that served as a retreat accessible only to himself and a very few members of court. Unlike the library at El Escorial, it was not composed of rarities but was a practical working collection, organized for use and pleasure. A second library, near Philip's office, likewise housed books of personal interest to the king and included an extensive map collection. Additional rooms held instruments, clocks, and oddities for the king's amusement and to demonstrate his desire to exalt the acquisition of knowledge.[77] These interests reflect a type of Renaissance and baroque kingship that saw the ruler as the patron of all knowledge. Even his translation of Guicciardini appears, despite his elaborate justification of it, intended less as a specific lesson than as a contribution to his sense of himself as a well-rounded king, knowledgeable in all subjects.

In regard to religious patronage, the new king initially did not appear to share all his parents' priorities, but he did imitate their observances and spent a great deal of time in such activity from early in his reign. He attended services daily, supported canonizations, and offered opinions in religious controversies. He and Queen Isabel participated in the baptisms of Moors, Jews, and Native Americans, as had Philip III and Queen Margarita, ceremonies that often took place in the semipublic royal chapel. A year into his reign, the royal family attended the festivities surrounding the canonizations of Isidro of Madrid, Ignatius Loyola, Francis Xavier, Teresa of Avila, and Philip Neri. In 1627 the king designated himself patron of the festival celebrating Saint Teresa as patron of Spain, thus placing the stamp of royal approval on the resolution of the controversy concerning whether Teresa or Saint James should embody the soul of the country. The first royal *auto de fé* of Philip IV's reign did not take place until 1632, celebrated by the Inquisition of Toledo in Madrid to facilitate the attendance of the king and queen.[78]

Whatever their devotional meaning to the new king, these events had a great deal in common with his other public acts. In September 1622 the king rode to the Madrileño shrine of Atocha, dressed "muy a lo soldado," to thank Our Lady of Atocha for imperial and Spanish victories in the Empire.[79] When Philip IV continued some of the devotional observances of his father, such as washing the feet of thirteen poor men on Holy Thursday, this ceremony became a more theatrical event, as in 1635, when eight gentlemen of the chamber, each with twelve attendants who were themselves of high rank, accompanied the king and assisted him in bringing meals to the table for the poor.[80]

The religious activities of the queen, inspired in part by her difficulty in carrying a healthy child to term, were also public in nature. In the late months of pregnancy she would order a novena (a series of nine devotional masses) at the major churches of Madrid following the cycle of festivals of the life of Mary. In addition to her religious activities, she contributed to artistic patronage at court by hosting theatrical events in her chambers and arranging the performance of plays for occasions such as the birthday of the king.[81]

Family also influenced Philip IV's idea of kingship and a few specific policies. His actions early in his reign suggest an attempt to balance personal and political identities. He attempted to maintain a friendly relationship with his sister Ana, regularly sending her Spanish delicacies and other gifts and in 1625 recognizing her birthday with a gala entertainment in spite of increasing hostility between Spain and France.[82] In the first weeks of his reign he enthusiastically sent coaches to escort his cousin Philiberto, who was arriving to express condolences, to Madrid. He subsequently decided, or perhaps was persuaded, that the Prince of Savoy had acted inappropriately in coming so close to Madrid without permission, and thus he denied him entrance to the court, meeting with him only very briefly in Aranjuez.[83]

Philip IV's initial policy toward his younger sister's marriage was perceived to have been influenced by his father's advice. Rumor held that Philip III had apologized on his deathbed to María for not having settled her marriage and admonished the prince, soon to be king, to make her an empress.[84] Besides considering his father's advice against the English marriage, Philip IV may have been influenced by his sister's opinion, bolstered by the voices of his junta of theologians. In other cases, Philip clearly chose to ignore plans set in place by his father, such as those for a church career for Fernando. In this instance, he was probably influenced by his brother's desire to serve in more active roles.

Indeed, Olivares's general tendency to ignore the possibility of a true career in the church for the infante reflects the attitudes of the king and his brother.

In these family matters Philip IV appears most like his father, even in the details of leave-taking, arranged in such a way as to protect the privacy of his and his siblings' emotions. When María left for her marriage journey, the infanta María and Queen Isabel took leave of each other in private, and indeed Philip IV and his brothers, having accompanied their sister as far as Zaragoza, left María without bidding her good-bye in order to avoid the possibility of public tears. After they parted, he expressed his attachment by sending gifts and even a company of actors to entertain her along the way.[85] He continued to think fondly of his sister later in life: "From childhood, we were always great friends, and with age this love increased," he wrote to María de Agreda at the time of María's death.[86] His love for his brothers likewise originated in childhood affection, and indeed the time he took to decide their careers suggests reluctance to take leave of them.

The contrast between the king and his father in their respect for marriage is notable. While his father is not known or indeed even rumored to have had sexual relationships outside of his marriage, Philip IV fathered several illegitimate children during the lifetime of his first wife. The "salidos" in which the young king engaged early in his reign were assumed to include sexual activity, as indicated by his former tutor's concern about the king's virtue and the bad example he would set by engaging in "illicit matters."[87] The period during which the prince and his wife lived separately may actually have engendered a lack of respect for marriage on the part of the prince, though it is not necessary to assume a lack of affection for the queen, since the question of their emotions in itself was never a matter submitted to any standard of proof. In addition, although the king wrote to his sister about the political meanings of personal relationships in her marriage, he seems not to have seen his own marriage in the same light. There is little evidence that he discussed political matters with his wife or consulted with her in matters related to France.

Awareness of the proper structure of royal authority also informed Philip IV's actions in regard to family. When he congratulated his sister Ana on the birth of her son, an action that appears to have surprised at least one historian,[88] he may have been expressing both a lingering affection from childhood and an acknowledgment that the birth of an heir, even to an opponent in war, affirmed the structure of royal power. He likewise affirmed the role of the larger family when he urged Fernando to take upon himself the full trappings of royalty while viceroy in Catalonia and when he called María his best ambassador in the Empire, expressing the central importance of the different branches of the family presenting a united front. Although Philip treated both of his brothers with royal dignity, he clearly expressed the true structure of power: unlike Philip III and Margarita, who declined to call their first daughter princess based on the optimism that they would soon have a son, Philip IV and Isabel had no compunction about calling one after another of their short-lived daughters princess, perhaps with the intention of emphasizing that the daughter, not the king's brother, was the heir.

International family concerns were also expressed at the Spanish court in the early years of Philip IV's reign, with visits of numerous relatives, beginning with the infanta of Modena, whose residence at Descalzas Reales had long been discussed; Archduke Karl, brother of Queen Margarita; and Don Duarte of Portugal, described sometimes as an uncle of the king but more correctly a distant cousin, often present at court festivities. In later years the Princess of Mantua, wife of Tomás of Savoy and cousin of Queen Isabel, made an extended visit to the court, as did Princess Margarita of Savoy, who later served as regent in Portugal.

Philip also learned to be king in the journeys he made in the first years of his reign. Although European kings in general were less peripatetic than they had been in earlier centuries and had less need to travel to obtain simple knowledge of their kingdoms, travel remained an important way for a king to build ties with his country and his people. Royal attendance at the assemblies of the eastern kingdoms of Spain was also necessary for the granting of taxes and the recognition of heirs. Visiting the various regions of the monarchy was seen as an effective means of dealing with their particular concerns. As early as 1622, Philip IV's former tutor urged the king to visit Aragon, citing the great affliction of his native land and the comfort the king's presence would provide. He urged the king to consider that the kingdom was his patrimony and part of his substance and therefore to treat it as a father would, listening to its concerns and respecting its privileges. He implied that this approach would ensure the quiet and peace of Catalonia. Earlier that year, Philip had received a magnificent embassy from Barcelona, which had made a grand entrance to deliver a simple message requesting that the king visit the kingdom.[89]

But the first major journey undertaken by Philip IV echoed, perhaps more closely than the new favorite might have realized, the visit Philip III had made with Lerma to Valencia early in his reign. This journey took the king and his brother Carlos to Seville and to neighboring areas and the southern seaports, where the favorite had his estates and had spent his young adulthood. Setting out with a large entourage of gentlemen, clergy, and councilors, the king and his brother spent the period from February 8 to April 18, 1624, visiting noble estates, attending plays, riding in tournaments, and touring monasteries and cathedrals.[90]

The journey to Aragon, undertaken in 1626, was more clearly a response to the concerns of the kingdom and the financial needs of the Spanish crown. According to Matías de Novoa, however, the journey was badly planned, which he blamed on the favorite. The purpose of the trip was to conduct business, with the ambitious design of undertaking the Corts in the three centers of Zaragoza, Barcelona, and Valencia, allowing little time for the more intangible benefits of a royal progress. When Fernando de Borja expressed the amazement of the city of Zaragoza that Philip was not planning a formal entry into the city, Olivares told him that the king had not come to spend his time in ceremonies. In recounting another incident, in which the admiral of Castile was temporarily deprived of his place in the king's coach in favor of the Duke of Cardona, Novoa could not contain his criticism of the count-duke, who as sumiller de corps and mayordomo mayor controlled questions of etiquette, for not arriving at a diplomatic solution by which the admiral might have been warned of the change and thus saved the embarrassment. When, shortly thereafter, the count-duke's son-in-law was appointed to a position in the king's chamber that some thought should have gone to the admiral as the gentleman of greatest seniority, the situation was handled with an equal lack of grace and provoked the admiral's withdrawal from court. While the king also earned Novoa's censure for responding badly to the situation, the count-duke clearly bore the brunt of the blame, since he controlled ceremony. This would not have happened, he concluded, under the Duke of Lerma, who had been kind and courteous and had known the proper structure of the royal court.[91]

Matías de Novoa's central critique of the court of Philip IV was that it lacked the luster and reverence at which Spaniards and others had marveled during the reign of Philip III. The courtier blamed this mostly on Olivares, calling Philip IV a prince of excellent qualities but saying that he was surrounded by persons who induced him to bad behavior. Nobles, he said, were not being rewarded for their services. Offices were given capriciously, and no one could be sure of his position. Even requesting patronage was considered an affront. "How strange," Novoa commented, "not to let anyone try to advance himself."

Among the examples he gave was his own, recounting Olivares's rudeness and fury when Novoa had asked for a position that would have been a promotion: "He told me that I did not appear to be dying of hunger."[92] As in the unfortunate matter of the admiral, the court simply lacked the grace and, with it, the order of previous years.

With Novoa's critique, we come to the central irony of the first decade of the reign of Philip IV: a young king who could invoke the aura of the public king, who appreciated art and theater and blended solemn religiosity and gallantry, was nonetheless unable to create and sustain a lustrous and mannerly court. The main figure of his reign, Olivares, was unskilled in the art of balancing the various interests of the nobility and alienated people he should have courted; he neglected the king's underlying role as natural mediator among the forces of the kingdom. Furthermore, the king himself accepted the idea that he was not educated and looked to his favorite for tutelage.

The king's performance in public events suggests that he felt confident in that sort of display. In the business of state he felt less confident, and from early in his reign he set himself a program of study. He took great pleasure in reading, in Spanish and foreign languages, on arts and letters, and "with particular and general notices of history, and geography in which with little work and great inclination I quickly rendered myself able to discuss all general matters." Although he acknowledged the arts, which he described himself as enjoying very much, his list of specific texts that he had studied contains only histories, most of them concerning Spain. Thus, all the brilliant artistic accomplishments that distinguished his reign and the gallant display of his early years are relegated by the king himself to secondary status; they were not intended to win the hearts of vassals through piety or magnificence but done primarily for personal pleasure.

Despite the stated importance of his reading program, Philip ascribed only one concrete goal to it, that of enabling him to discuss these subjects. Shifting to the necessity of knowing the facts of present events, he noted that he was not satisfied to read the summaries of diplomatic correspondence that the councils sent him but instead insisted on reading the letters himself. He clearly considered this an unusual habit and noted the extra work it entailed. A few years into his reign, he felt competent to participate in discussions of these materials and to vote "as if I were a councilor of state." Before entering such a vote, however, the king consulted "persons of my confidence" concerning the pros and cons of the issues. These confidants, one supposes, included Olivares, although his use of the plural implies others as well. In this he claimed to follow the example he had seen in the original papers of his grandfather, Philip II. Eventually, he considered himself competent to speak his mind before the Council of State itself. Six years into his reign—when Olivares was still calling him a "boy"—the king felt capable of working on his own in matters of state.[93]

Philip also intended to learn how to govern from watching his councils in action. He considered following an old Castilian tradition of kings attending meetings of the council, but being young, and the custom being out of use, he ordered windows cut into the rooms where the councils met and covered with a blind so that he could listen to the council without the members being aware of his presence. He thus hoped both to gain general knowledge of issues and to hear opinions that he might not otherwise hear. He conceived of the council as a sacred forum in which any member could speak his mind and urged his ministers to speak freely to him. He resolved to grant interviews to all who requested them, not allowing a minister to come between them. This concept may reflect both his reading, for such writers as Rivadeneira argued vigorously that councilors should be able to speak their minds, and his youth, since he deferred to the knowledge of older, more experienced men.

Other events contributed to the king's sense of readiness for a more active role in government. In 1627, the same year he identified in the epilogue as the year by which he felt himself capable, he experienced a serious illness that threatened an upheaval at court. During the illness, the count-duke, thinking it possible that the king would die, struggled to guarantee that he himself would remain in power.[94] Perhaps it was the count-duke's own activity that convinced the rest of the court that a transition was about to occur, but when individuals began to make the natural adjustments one might make in the face of such a change, the favorite bitterly blamed the households of the infantes, claiming even that vassals desired the king's death so that they would be free of Olivares. But the aftermath of the general court trauma played out less dramatically than one might expect based on the anxieties of the favorite: the king was said to possess greater serenity than before the illness; feared retributions did not occur; and he reiterated his affection for his brothers by having them present during his first post-illness meeting with Olivares. The favorite himself found it necessary to initiate a formal reconciliation with the infante Fernando.[95] The king, like his father, apparently experienced illness as an occasion for introspection and emerged with a desire to live up to the responsibilities that he had not yet properly fulfilled. Although Olivares remained close by, the king increasingly saw himself as an active participant in government.

The decisions Philip IV made within the next decade reveal an increasing confidence and a sense of his own definition of policy. His somewhat subtle resistance to the policies of his favorite, consisting on some occasions in mere silence, as in his slow response to his favorite's advice concerning his brothers, and on other occasions in defying his wishes, as when he accompanied his sister María for the first portion of her marriage journey, suggest his growing desire to remove himself from the stage of tutelage and to take full control in defining his reign.

More than any other member of the royal family, the king filled out the details of his own role. Philip IV's age at the time of his inheritance and his consequent perception of himself as unready for rule informed his concept of kingship. But the era in which he lived, as much as his own chronological age, determined this perception. He actually inherited the throne of Spain at the same age as had Charles V. Other examples, notably that of Louis XIV of France, also suggest that the inheritance of the throne by a child did not necessarily portend disaster. The perception that Philip was unready for rule may have been conveyed to him unwittingly by people who meant to educate him. The seriousness of this problem is apparent in the experience of the previous generation, in which suggestions that Philip III was unready to rule brought charges of damaging the reputation of the king against the previous king's ministers.[96] In the case of Philip IV, however, the king internalized the criticism, and the daunting examples that were supposed to humble an all-powerful king left a young king too humble at times, too anxious at other times to prove himself, too aware of the ways in which he was not powerful.

Philip IV thought of kingship as a skill to be learned, and he approached his work with seriousness and openness. At the same time, his public activities from early in his reign suggest that he had the personal presence of a king. He held royalty above other people, an attitude necessary for rule, and developed an all-encompassing range of skills and interests reminiscent of the finest Renaissance ideal. Religion too played a natural part in his self-definition as king, although this became more intrinsically woven into his nature as he matured, a pattern not uncommon in both royalty and commoners. With these skills, he was equipped to serve the function of keystone of the kingdom. But the young king saw himself as unfit for his duties, by which he clearly meant his duties in matters of state. Thus he sought to educate himself, surrounding himself with papers of state and placing the same trust in the lessons of history that treatise writers did.

If we return to Philip IV's epilogue to his translation of Guicciardini and consider it as specifically directed to the prince Baltasar Carlos, we can uncover the essential lesson that only a king could teach himself to be king. If some of Philip's narrative sounds overly modest, we must consider the possibility that he never intended anyone other than the prince to see it. The preparation that Philip felt himself to lack and the discipline that he sought to teach himself were private confessions made to his son, revelations that a king could make only to a future king and lessons that only a king could teach.

THE FUNCTION OF ROYALTY

Members of royal families did not so much learn their roles as they *were* their roles, and they served their function simply by existing. The royal family was meant to provide a stable keystone for early modern society. Such a system worked to avoid civil conflict by designating one family to bear a special quality enabling and entitling it to lead, with one member of that family exalted above all others. All court functions emphasized the rightness of this solution to the problem of power, and writers, artists, and playwrights supported it in their work, even when they criticized aspects of its operation. When it functioned properly, there was no question about who should succeed the king, and the acceptance of that fact ideally served to limit power struggles. Clearly, however, in matters both large and small, the system was at the mercy of the biological vagaries of the chosen family. By depending so heavily on things affected by chance, early modern society exposed governments to a great deal of potential turmoil.

In response to this uncertainty, continuity of practice in order to promote stability was a primary goal of the dynasty and its servants. The structure of court resisted change, as if that in itself were its purpose. This desire for stability contributed to the great and at times almost comical fear of *novedades* in the early seventeenth century. While concerns about unwarranted change were not new—as early as 1516 Erasmus had warned the prince that people do not like innovation and that any reasonable change had to be implemented gradually[1]— in the early seventeenth century they crystallized into a kind of paranoia. But despite the fear of novelties, there were constant changes in government. Philip II, for example, employed several types of government throughout his reign, balancing various conciliar and secretarial structures and relying heavily on juntas late in his life. Many changes, however, were implemented through the use of images, manners, and etiquettes rather than by altering the structure of government itself.[2] While writers of treatises began to write separately about political and personal issues of kingship, and while elsewhere in Europe governments experimented with different responses to the changing role of monarchy, Spanish practice remained attached to the forms and thoughts that had served it well throughout the sixteenth century.

Despite the family tendency toward a retiring disposition, the children of Philip III appear to have entered the larger world with confidence and self-assurance. The sense in which members of the royal family played their roles simply by existing meant that their lives were shaped by the demands of structure and stability even as they were celebrated as extraordinary individuals. From their earliest years, royal children were surrounded by a system that taught them their place in the world. The attention and service of the adults and children of the court must have struck them as the natural order of things. Examples from history reinforced the lessons of ceremony and hierarchy, while evidence of the grandeur and piety of their ancestors surrounded them in the palaces, churches, and artwork of their youth.

As the children grew, pious teachers introduced them to formal study within a tradition of religious and classical education, emphasizing historical example in a way that indicated confidence in precedent. The education of the prince was more rigorous and certainly more intensely examined, although his brothers too were encouraged in intellectual and military aspirations. The younger brothers, however, had a more religiously focused education, as did the sisters. All of the siblings, however, imbibed the theory of royalty and learned their place within its structure. Their adult roles were planned for them in a manner based on precedent but molded by current events. Marriages were planned or considered as opportunities arose rather than according to the ages of proposed spouses. Careers for the younger sons were also designed opportunistically rather than systematically. Decision making in both cases tended to be slow, reflecting both the time necessary to make prudent decisions about complex issues and the ages of the children involved.

The royal family patterned life at court according to their own life cycles. Nobles vied to serve in the households of Philip III's children and to become their closest companions. During their childhood, the number of women and children at court expanded, and they brought with them the liveliness inherent in an elite population eager to be entertained. When the royal children grew to adulthood, these persons continued to serve them, creating stability and a sense of continuity in both private and public life.

Servants and court officials moved from the service of one royal person to that of another, and after the deaths of patrons, they campaigned for new appointments as if they were theirs by right. Estefanía Romero de Villaquirán, for example, served the infantas Isabel Clara and Catalina Micaela, accompanied Catalina to Savoy, lived there twelve years, then returned to Spain in the service of Margarita de Austria when her wedding journey passed through Italy; a few years later, she became the azafata of the infanta Ana, and in 1615 she accompanied her to France, where she remained after the rest of the infanta's Spanish attendants were sent home. Likewise, most of the household of Empress María, sister of Philip II, moved into service of the Spanish king or queen after María's death in 1603, and servants of Prince Philiberto of Savoy moved after his death into the service of the infantes Carlos and Fernando. Three years after the death of Fernando, who died in 1641 while governor in the Low Countries, his attendants and councilors were ordered to return there in the service of his nephew, the illegitimate Don Juan José.[3]

These patterns of service can be seen from the point of view of the servants themselves as reflecting a need for employment and from the point of view of the king as making use of the skills and knowledge of experienced servants of the crown, but seen from the broader perspective of the structure of court, they provided a stability that withstood the dramatic but surface changes of political life. Successful transitions between reigns were embodied in persons who could ease much of the inherent tension by simply continuing in their positions. Although several high-placed figures left court at the accession of Philip IV, the majority of persons remained.

Religious institutions attached to the court also went through phases shaped by changes in the practices of the royal family and by the deaths of individual royal patrons. Queen Margarita's foundation of the convent of La Encarnación partially shifted the focus of noble patronage from the Descalzas Reales, which Princess Juana had founded. Another shift in the decline of influence of the Descalzas Reales convent coincided with the death of Margarita de la Cruz, at which point the Count-Duke of Olivares proposed tightening discipline at the convent, preventing the attendance of ambassadors there, and limiting the privileges of other types of visitors.[4] Olivares's proposal, which the Council of State, accepted without comment, indicates a desire to limit sources of patronage and influence other than the king. The count-duke proposed that the reforms of the convent of Descalzas Reales should also be extended to the convent of La Encarnación, indicating his broader desire to lessen the ability of persons to gain and express power through such institutions. Underlying these measures was a subtler agenda of separating political functions from other types of personal and religious power, a step in the process of redefining structures that reflects modern concepts of just government.

Unlike the changing fortunes of the Descalzas Reales, and despite the patronage of people attached to shifting factions at court, the popularity of Simón de Rojas's congregation of Ave María was undiminished in the transition between reigns and well into future generations. Philip IV continued his father's patronage, but the active role of the nobility in supporting this institution explains its perseverance long after the deaths of its saintly founder and its first royal patrons. The role of noble patronage in the survival of such institutions as the Ave María and the place of "servants," both high and low, in filling out the structure of court suggest ways in which royalty helped to order the lower levels of power and influence.

Just as the royal family shaped the life of court with their own lives, they experienced international relations through their own larger family relationships. While the king and his father, and his father before him, were generally native kings who had built power in various ways, his mother and their mothers were intrinsically foreigners, thus providing a wider angle of vision. By limiting their potential marriage partners to the ruling families of other countries, royal families placed themselves above the concerns of the nobility. This partly foreign position of the royal family added to their unique ability to rule and facilitated members of the royal family serving as points of interaction between their own country and the larger world.

The cosmopolitan nature of the royal family also aided royal women in serving their country through marriage. While the daughters of Philip III grew up learning the lessons of their native land, they envisioned the rest of Europe as full of relatives, their uncles on the thrones of the Empire and Savoy, their aunt and her cousin-husband governing in the Low Countries, and various aunts peopling the convents of Vienna and Graz in a pattern familiar to them from their own experience. Their concepts of family as transcending boundaries of

countries may have allowed them to accept more readily the difficult role offered to them and perhaps even to see the good in the larger structure that
placed them between countries and loyalties.

Historical representations of queen-consorts often suffer from the interpre-
tive dangers of relying on primary sources that considered them foremost as
foreigners. But while contemporary observers tended to view queens with sus-
picion, the wider views suggests that their experiences were quite similar from
country to country. They tended to suffer isolation, especially after having the
households that accompanied them removed, often more quickly than had been
negotiated. While we might feel pity for a queen such as Ana de Austria, who was
deprived of her Spanish household, we should remember that this was simply
an extreme case of a more general pattern—Isabel de Bourbon eventually lost
much of the entourage that had accompanied her from her native land, as had
Isabel de Valois in the 1560s, and the English queen Henrietta Maria de Bourbon in the 1620s.[5] Queens also commonly experienced shifts from exuberant
youth to pious later life, a process shaped by both absorption of ideals and the
rigors of repeated childbirth. Like younger brothers of kings, they often showed
themselves competent to maintain royal power when they became regents,
although contemporary evaluations of their actions tended to be skewed by
the general supposition that women could not rule except under male tutelage.

Evidence suggests that successful female regency depended on a queen-
regent's sharing the vision of royalty that placed a king unquestionably at the
top of the early modern world. A recent biographer of Mary Stuart finds her
subject badly educated on the basis that she was raised in France, a convincing
argument given that Mary's instinctive loyalties needed to be with Scotland—
although it raises the question why Mary of Guise, who was also raised in
France, was a successful regent of Scotland.[6] Comparing the situation of these
two queens, whose formative experiences were probably fairly similar, we can
discern an essential difference between the educations of a queen and a queen-
consort: a woman who was queen in her own right had to be raised with kingly
confidence, while a woman who would be a queen-consort and perhaps even
a regent had to accept a role in which she contributed to the greater power of
another person. Like that of Mary of Guise, the infanta Ana's successful regency
for her son Louis XIV grew out of an understanding of the nature of royalty
rather than a desire for independent power. A queen in her position had to
accept her place as a person who belonged in different ways to both her native

country and her adopted country and whose most important responsibility was less to either country than to her family and to maintaining the larger structure of royal power.

Younger brothers, too, learned their roles and followed them in patterns common across Europe, balancing royal privilege and lesser status. While we may be uncomfortable with the image of Ana de Austria encouraging the submissiveness of her younger son by treating him almost like a girl, doing so made sense within a context in which he had to accept his brother as his superior. Hers was a political rather than a personal choice, perhaps based both on reason and on her experience of Louis XIII's brother's plotting against him.[7] But some of what historians have described, and what contemporaries perceived, to have been palace coups were what Novoa called "crimes not against the king but against what time might bring."[8] The younger brother of the Sun King was in the middle of just such a situation during a serious illness of the king in 1658: if he did not encourage them, he was at least conscious of prominent people assembling around him. Though his grief at his brother's condition may have been tinged with a kind of guilty hope, it is nonetheless not necessary to believe that he wished for the death of his brother in order to assume that he considered the possible future.[9] When the infantes Carlos and Fernando faced a similar situation, they and prominent nobles were also assumed to be plotting, although the king supported them in the face of such accusations from his favorite.

On the other hand, despite a structure of power that decreed the lesser status of the king's brothers and attempted to inculcate this assumption in them from childhood, early modern monarchies provide numerous examples of younger sons capable of assuming power when elder brothers died, such as Henry VIII and Charles I of England and Leopold I of Austria. While Leopold's biographer describes his subject as shy and uneasy in his new position as heir because of his previous upbringing as second son, he accepts as apparently unproblematic that these qualities would be transformed in a short period into the ambition and self-assurance necessary to campaign for the imperial throne.[10] These successful transitions suggest that the proper mode of instilling a younger brother's concept of his role was not to undermine his self-esteem by convincing him of his inherent personal inferiority but to demonstrate that he had a place within the structure of royal government. With this approach, the transition from deferential younger brother to king was simply a question of accepting the role that circumstances provided.

The use of favorites also follows somewhat predictable models throughout Europe, many based on the life cycle of individuals. While historians tend to echo early modern writers in seeing the use of favorites as a sign of weakness in a king, patterns in their use suggest a structural as well as a personal origin of the role. The growing complexity of the role of the king, the great expectations focused on the king by theory, and the individual's increasing distance from the circumstances that established the structure of royal power all encouraged reliance on favorites. Styles in favorites correlate to stages of the king's career, with a favorite who functioned as a kind of strong surrogate father or indulgent older brother common early in a reign, as was the case for Louis XIII, Leopold I, and James I while he was king of Scotland only.[11] This pattern occurred in Spain as well, stretching from the example of Philip II and Ruy Gómez de Silva to that of Carlos II and his half-brother Don Juan José. Even Charles V can be seen as an undefined youth in his early years, and if we consider Guillaume de Croy as a favorite early in the reign, he was one who, moreover, had the grace to die when the emperor turned twenty-one.

These patterns in the use of favorites suggest that many kings went through an experience similar to that of Philip IV, feeling themselves ill-equipped for the enormous task of governing. Individual favorites, however, served different roles in smoothing a young king's transition into adulthood, alternatively providing personal reassurance, instruction in government, or a buffer between the king and others. Although Philip IV chose his favorite for different reasons than his father had chosen his, he followed Philip III in selecting a single favorite, and he too reached maturity in his reign when he dismissed his favorite, in the turbulent year of 1643. He was thirty-nine years old, the same age his father had been when he dismissed the Duke of Lerma and the same age Philip II had been when he began to detach himself from Ruy Gómez de Silva.

Viewed more broadly, monarchical dynasties can be seen to experience a natural life span, often based very much on biological issues, including the sex, number, and health of children. England, France, Portugal, the Netherlands, and even the Empire struggled with such challenges in the sixteenth and seventeenth centuries in ways that demanded innovation. With each change of dynasty, a dramatic chance for reorganization occurred, while in Spain authority resting in an undisturbed dynastic legacy encouraged a reliance on the precedent of earlier practice and provided a misleading illusion of strength in continuity.

Along with changing forms of government, requirements of kingship changed. Many historians have pointed out specific cases throughout seventeenth-century Europe in which royal education appears to have been incomplete or unsatisfactory. But the elements that constitute a well-educated king are themselves difficult to evaluate. In terms of formal study, James VI/I was one of the best-educated kings of early modern Europe, yet he has not been judged one of the more successful kings of his time. Louis XIV, on the other hand, had little interest in study but has been judged an eminently qualified king. Perhaps, indeed, we should consider the contrast in environments in which each grew up: James in somewhat fearful isolation, without family and with few true friends, and Louis in the center of a bustling court, under the guidance of a mature, confident mother and a surrogate father, Cardinal Mazarin, eager to instruct him. In evaluating Louis XIV, even a traumatic experience such as the Fronde can be seen as a positive influence, since the king drew conclusions from it that helped him rule effectively.[12] Such formative experiences do not guarantee a worthy king, although they are arguably more important than a classical education.

Although the structure of royal government was perhaps more important than the personality of an individual, rulers could have a significant effect on the course of history. Achieving such a result did not, however, demand that they be a strong presence. The recent biographer of Mary, Queen of Scots, puts personal evaluation at the service of political interpretation and argues that Mary's personal failings and failures made her a political failure. Even in her unenergetic government, however, the choices made by Mary Stuart as an individual had a profound effect on Scotland: her lack of interference in religion as long as she herself could hear private mass was a unique case in Reformation Europe of a ruler not demanding that her country follow her religion, a decision that helped ensure that Scotland would be Protestant.[13]

Counterfactual speculations such as those that praise Prince Henry of England and Baltasar Carlos of Spain point to our continued perception that an individual ruler might have made a significant difference in the fortunes of a country.[14] But while Roy Strong's panegyric to a lost renaissance reads partly like wishful thinking, the consequences of the loss of seventeen-year-old Baltasar Carlos are more concretely demonstrable. The qualities that Strong particularly admired in Henry reflect the active princely patronage that created an image of majesty, yet one can only speculate about whether Henry would have been a more successful ruler than his younger brother, Charles I. The survival of

Baltasar Carlos, however, would have resulted in a healthy adult son succeeding Philip IV rather than a four-year-old child of limited physical and uncertain mental capabilities, a substitution that could hardly have failed to make a significant difference in Spanish history. Thus, while personal qualities of the king may or may not have made a difference, structural issues, such as the age and health of the heir, could have had significant effect.

The latter half of the seventeenth century provides a clear example that education was not enough to make a good king if his person did not command respect. The continued importance of physical bearing to the reputation of a king is apparent in the historical treatment of Carlos II. Lack of respect for the last Spanish Habsburg king both in his day and by historians was and is largely based on his unfortunate physical appearance. Observers do not even demand a detailed history of the reign in order to assume that the king was mentally incompetent as well as physically unattractive.[15] Within the structure of early modern government, however, the failure of Carlos II was not his presumed mental deficiency but the fact that he did not produce an heir.

Biological failure is a very serious matter, yet less dramatic problems of the family had an equally devastating effect on transitions between reigns. Damage had already been done in the chance decreasing ages at which successive kings inherited the throne. The strongest Habsburg monarch of Spain, Philip II, was thirty-one years old when his father died. What is more, he kept the most talented of his father's ministers and secretaries until they too died. The preservation in this manner of the experience of the previous generation was terribly important. The dismissal of a great number of Philip II's ministers at the accession of his son was devastating to the maintenance of good government and stable policy and is probably at least somewhat attributable to the king's youth. Another set of dismissals in the last years of Philip III's reign may have removed some bad ministers but led to increased uncertainty when the king died a few years later, leaving an ill-defined ministerial structure whose two main leaders had been energized by years of factional struggle against the people who had run the king's government through most of his reign.

Extended family also affected the king's prestige, his perception of his place in the world, and his ability to be a strong international influence. When Philip III inherited the throne, he was closely connected to key international figures. Although the two had not met, the emperor was his cousin and uncle and had lived in Spain during his youth. The rulers of the Netherlands were the half-sister who had helped to guide his childhood and another cousin-uncle who had spent his formative years in the service of Philip II. His aunt and grandmother, the dowager empress, lived in a convent in Madrid and retained the authority to receive international guests and give political advice. His elder cousin also lived there, a moral presence if not as politically active as her mother. He had access to the advisers of his father, even if he rejected their council because of their insufficient show of respect. In contrast, when Philip IV became king at age sixteen, he did not know personally any of the rulers of Europe. His sister was queen of France, but she would not have a voice in government there for another twenty years. The empress was no longer living, although her daughter survived, her level of activity decreased by advancing blindness. The young king was far more isolated in the world than had been his father, who himself had been more isolated than his father.

At age sixteen Philip IV was not ready to exert the initial influence to shape his reign. Even more than in the transition to his father's reign, the issues of this transition were largely the concerns of the nobility. Lack of forceful definition by the king encouraged this tendency in the struggles at court in the early years of Philip IV's reign. Surely the nature of government itself was affected by the simple fact of the youth of the monarch; the oldest member of the royal family in residence at the palace was the queen, then eighteen years old. One historian remarked: "Fácil resultaría a Olivares manejar aquella corte de príncipes casi niños" (It would be easy for Olivares to handle that court of princes, who were almost children).[16]

History has viewed Philip III's reign as a transition from the glory of Spain to its decadence, and Philip IV's reign as the cap on that fate. This judgment has generally been so powerful that until recently the reign of Philip III has largely been deemed unworthy of study. Even the ongoing historical fascination with the decline of Spain, perhaps an even more intriguing phenomenon than its spectacular rise, has only recently inspired the examination of the reign itself in order to begin to discover its internal concerns and structures. Yet the reigns of Philip III and Philip IV saw great artistic and cultural achievement in Spain and were imbued with an ideal of selfless kingship. More interesting than viewing the seventeenth century as an age of lost power is to see it as an age that experienced contradictions in what constituted a good king, an age that still perceived the qualities of the king as a central part of good governing, while putting restraints on the king's power through concepts of personal humility and a structure balancing noble and royal and eventually ministerial power.

Whatever the judgment of history, the people of the early seventeenth century did not consider the reigns of Philip III and Philip IV insignificant. Biographies, chronicles, plays, political treatises, and religious texts abounded, and writers in ever-expanding numbers entered into discussion concerning government, the royal court, the king, and even the function of royalty. Indeed, the great variety of forms in which writers presented their ideas in itself suggests an expansion of concepts concerning public life. The prevalence of the figure of the monarch in plays reflects both a discussion of the nature of royalty and a demonstration of the use of the figure of the king to express concerns about society in general.[17]

Centuries beyond the reign of Philip IV, royal government remains a compelling structure of power. While it was challenged by the nobility in Spain, by Parliament in England, and by revolution in France, the same elements of idealized personality, precedent, and family promised a stability that have made governments and people turn again and again to royal solutions to questions of power. Even in the twentieth century, while public commentary increasingly questioned the utility of the essentially powerless English royal family, the existence of a king in Spain in 1975 allowed a transition to democratic government and modern society after decades of the Franco dictatorship. In that case an individual, Juan Carlos de Borbón y Borbón, making use of the weight of history and the particular qualities attached to royalty, was able to facilitate a transition that was by no means assured. What is more, despite the necessary support of various other elements and persons within the government, he was generally presented as executing that change by sheer force of his own personality and moral standing. He was able to do so by accessing a concept of power that, while deeply flawed, appeals to a long history of precedent for its structure and rectitude and still has the power to make its mark in the world.

Notes

CHAPTER 1

1. Kleinman, *Anne of Austria*; Dulong, *Anne d'Autriche*. There have also been numerous highly fictionalized depictions of the queen in both popular biography and literature.

2. Van der Essen, *Le Cardinal-Infant*. Aldea Vaquero, *El Cardenal Infante*, while not strictly a biography, also addresses aspects of the infante's education and training.

3. Stradling, *Philip IV and the Government of Spain*; Elliott, *Count-Duke of Olivares*.

4. Some sources and historians call her Ana María, perhaps reflecting incorrect expansions of an abbreviation of her name.

5. Stradling, *Philip IV and the Government of Spain*, 5.

6. Pinheiro da Veiga, *Fastiginia*, 95.

7. P. Williams, "Lerma, Old Castile," 395n64. On the conflict between the queen and her husband's favorite, see Pérez Martín, *Margarita de Austria*, esp. 99–148; and Sánchez, *Empress, the Queen, and the Nun*.

8. Diego de Guzmán, "Memorias del Cardenal Don Diego de Guzmán," RAH, Colección Salazar y Castro, MS 9/477, fols. 19–20; Florencia, *Sermón*, fol. 15; Soto, *Margaritas preciosas de la Iglesia*.

9. "Historia de Joan Kevenhuller de Aichelberg," BN, MS 2751, p. 967.

10. Consulta, 1620, AGS, Estado, leg. 265.

11. Antonio [Hurtado] de Mendoza, "Relación de la comedia que en Lerma representaron la Reina de Francia y sus Hermanos," BN, MS 18656, no. 49, published in Ferrer Valls, *Nobleza y espectaculo teatral*, 245–56.

12. Philip IV's response, written on consulta of 29 May 1626, AGS, Estado, leg. 2328.

13. Consultas on the treatment of the cardinal-infante, May, June, August 1620, AGS, Estado, leg. 265.

14. Document submitted to the Council of State, n.d., AGS, Estado, leg. 2645.

15. Cabrera de Córdoba, *Relaciones*, 241.

16. Cabrera de Córdoba, *Relaciones*, 512. It is not entirely clear which of the brothers was being described as the aggressor. If it was Carlos, as the phrasing and surrounding detail suggest to me, the lack of reprimand carries a very different meaning than it would if the prince were hitting his younger brother.

17. Marvick, *Louis XIII*, 30; Bingham, *Making of a King*, 84, 91; E. Williams, *Anne of Denmark*, 173.

18. Philip IV, "Epílogo breve," vii–viii.

19. See Wolf, *Louis XIV*, 26.

20. "Documentos para el oficio de Ayo del Príncipe," BN, MS 10857, fol. 101.

21. Gascón de Torquemada, *Gaçeta y nuevas*, 21; Novoa, *Historia de Felipe III*, 60:171.

22. BN, MS 2347, fols. 268–69.

23. Cabrera de Córdoba, *Relaciones*, 314, 317.

24. Cabrera de Córdoba, *Relaciones,* 288, 314, 317, 372; Guzmán, "Memorias," RAH, Colección Salazar y Castro, MS 9/476, fol. 46.

25. Guzmán, "Memorias," RAH, Colección Salazar y Castro, MS 9/477, fol. 20.

26. Cabrera de Córdoba, *Relaciones,* 406.

27. Guzmán, "Memorias," RAH, Colección Salazar y Castro, MS 9/477, fol. 162v.

28. Philip III, *Cartas de Felipe III a su hija Ana;* see, e.g., 10, 22, 36. *Compadre* can be used by the parents and godparents of a child to refer to each other, or it can also imply a godparent-godchild relationship.

29. Cabrera de Córdoba, *Relaciones,* 325–30; Vélez de Guevara, *Elogio;* Uhagón, *Relaciones históricas,* 313–26.

30. Cabrera de Córdoba, *Relaciones,* 326; Uhagón, *Relaciones históricas,* 315.

31. Vélez de Guevara, *Elogio;* Uhagón, *Relaciones históricas,* 319.

32. Ferrer Valls, *La práctica escénica cortesana,* esp. 105–42; McKendrick, *Theatre in Spain,* 209–13.

33. Ferrer Valls, *Nobleza y espectaculo teatral,* 235–44; Cabrera de Córdoba, *Relaciones,* 547. On dwarfs at the court of Spain, see Bouza Alvarez, *Locos, enanos y hombres de placer.*

34. Antonio [Hurtado] de Mendoza, "Relación de la comedia que en Lerma representaron la Reina de Francia y sus Hermanos," BN, MS 18656, no. 49. For additional details of this event, see Ferrer Valls, *La práctica escénica cortesana,* 180–89.

35. Payments for Alonso Fernández, dancing master of their highnesses, 22 May 1614, AHN, Cámara de Castilla, leg. 4420, no. 73, and 8 July 1618; AGS, CJH, leg. 556, pt. 11, no. 16; Philip III, *Cartas de Felipe III a su hija Ana,* 29, 44, 47.

36. Cabrera de Córdoba, *Relaciones,* 104, 155; Guzmán, "Memorias," RAH, Colección Salazar y Castro, MS 9/476, fol. 13.

37. Philip III to Ana de Austria, 3 April 1618, in Philip III, *Cartas de Felipe III a su hija Ana,* 43–44; Gascón de Torquemada, *Gaçeta y nuevas,* 51.

38. Ruiz Alcon, "Armaduras infantiles."

39. Echevarría Bacigalupe, *Alberto Struzzi,* 17–19. Struzzi described the set of soldiers in the short work *Imago militiae auspiciis Ambrosii Spinolae,* simultaneously published in Spanish as *Imagen de la milicia y de un ejército firme con el favor del marqués Spinola.*

40. Gascón de Torquemada, *Gaçeta y nuevas,* 56. The chronicler assures his readers that the facial hair of Prince Philiberto eventually grew back fully.

41. María of Bavaria to the Duke of Lerma, 10 December 1600, BN, MS 915, fol. 59; Sepúlveda, *Historia de varios sucesos,* 243; Guzmán, "Memorias," RAH, Colección Salazar y Castro, MSS 9/476, fols. 81v, 96, and 9/477, fol. 98; Antonio de Sotomayor to Philip IV, summer 1643, in Espinosa Rodríguez, *Fray Antonio de Sotomayor,* 72.

42. Cabrera de Córdoba, *Relaciones,* 254, 259, 342; Guzmán, "Memorias," RAH, Colección Salazar y Castro, MS 9/476, fols. 85–100.

43. Cabrera de Córdoba, *Relaciones,* 404–6, 409–13; memorial of the count of Castelmellor, mayordomo of the queen, for expenses incurred in 1610, 8 January 1619, APR, Sección Histórica, caja 81.

44. Kleinman, *Anne of Austria,* 7–8.

45. Guzmán, "Memorias," RAH, Colección Salazar y Castro, MSS 9/476, fols. 85, 86v, and 9/477, fols. 20v, 24–24v; Duke of Lerma to the Council of Finance, 28 September 1613, AGS, CJH, leg. 522.

46. Sánchez Cantón, "Noventa y siete retratos," 130; Kusche, *Juan Pantoja de la Cruz,* 34.

47. Sánchez Cantón, "Noventa y siete retratos," 139; Kusche, *Juan Pantoja de la Cruz,* 237–38; Philip III, *Cartas de Felipe III a su hija Ana,* 17, 25.

48. Kusche, *Juan Pantoja de la Cruz,* 88–92, 237; Hamann, *Die Habsburger,* 279.

49. Vera y Zúñiga, *Epitome de la vida,* frontispiece.

50. Sánchez, "Dynasty, State, and Diplomacy"; Fichtner, *Ferdinand I of Austria;* Fichtner, *Emperor Maximilian II,* 27, 45, 112; Fichtner, "Of Christian Virtue and a Practicing Prince"; Spielman, *Leopold I of Austria,* esp. 9–16.

51. Philip II, *Cartas de Felipe II a sus hijas;* Altadonna, "Cartas de Felipe II."

52. Isabel Clara Eugenia, *Correspondencia de la Infanta,* e.g., 95, 126; Philip III, *Cartas de Felipe III a su hija Ana,* e.g., 11, 15, 16.

53. Cabrera de Córdoba, *Filipe Segundo,* 2:212. Antonio de la Cueva describes a visit of the infantas to the convent in a letter to Philip II, 10 April 1570, AGS, CySR, leg. 247, no. 170.

54. Palma, *Vida de la serenissima Infanta.*

55. Margarita de la Cruz to Philip III, "dia de todos santos," BN, MS 915, fol. 117.

56. Palma, *Vida de la serenissima Infanta,* 141; Margarita de la Cruz to Philip III, 12 and 29 October 1611, BN, MS 915, fols. 94, 97. See also, e.g., Cabrera de Córdoba, *Relaciones,* 261, 274, 293, 335.

57. Guzmán, "Memorias," RAH, Colección Salazar y Castro, MS 9/476, fols. 85–100, 40.

58. Fichtner, *Emperor Maximilian II,* 43, 51.

59. One of Ana's letters to Margarita indicates that Philip and Margarita had recently visited her: Ana de Austria to Margarita, 17 March 1604, AGS, Estado, leg. 198. See Brooks, *King for Portugal.*

60. Juana de Austria to Philip III, 10 January 1603, AGS, Estado, leg. 1099, fol. 1.

61. "Historia de Joan Kevenhuller de Aichelberg," BN, MS 2751, p. 1142. These comments were reported in early 1606, although Khevenhüller's observations refer to events throughout the early years of the reign.

62. Pedro Rodríguez to Philip II, 1598, AGS, Estado, leg. 705.

63. Sánchez, *Empress, the Queen, and the Nun;* Sánchez, "Confession and Complicity," 145.

64. Cabrera de Córdoba, *Relaciones,* 473, 477, 521, 531.

65. Cabrera de Córdoba, *Filipe Segundo,* 3:365; Almansa y Mendoza, *Cartas y novedades,* 57.

66. Cabrera de Córdoba, *Relaciones,* 266, 339, 354, 411, 457, 460.

67. Philip III, *Cartas de Felipe III a su hija Ana,* esp. 18, 21–23, and "Cartas autógrafas," esp. 12–13.

68. Palafox, "Diario de la jornada," 461; Kleinman, *Anne of Austria,* 84–85; Freer, *Married Life of Anne of Austria,* 2:7.

69. Simón Díaz, *Relaciones breves,* 394; Agreda and Philip IV, *Cartas,* 108:64–65.

CHAPTER 2

1. Cabrera de Córdoba, *Relaciones,* 98–110.

2. This description of the court is drawn primarily from AGS, CJH; APR, Sección Histórica, legs. 2914 and 2923; and Hofmann, *Das spanische Hof zeremoniell.*

3. On the similar Austrian Habsburg system, see Fichtner, "Habsburg Household or Habsburg Government?"

4. "Precedentes para el recibimiento de huéspedes," 13 August 1647, APR, Sección Histórica, caja 81.

5. Feros, *Kingship and Favoritism*, 32–38; Aram, *La reina Juana*, 205–7, 210–20, 236–40; Amezúa y Mayo, *Isabel de Valois*, 3:120–21, 363–64.

6. "Damas de la Reina," APR, Sección Histórica, leg. 2914; Guzmán, *Reyna católica*, 100v, 101; Cabrera de Córdoba, *Relaciones*, 111, 163, 172, 341; Jerónimo de Sepúlveda, "Historia de varios sucesos de España," BN, MS 2577, fol. 115; Almansa y Mendoza, *Cartas y novedades*, 181.

7. Mendez Silva, *Breve, curiosa, y ajustada noticia*, fol. 66–66v.

8. Cabrera de Córdoba, *Filipe Segundo*, 4:198; "Resolución que tomó el Rey Nuestro Señor cerca de algunas cosas que importavan aesta Monarquía de su Magd. por setiembre de 1618," BN, MS 2348, fol. 403; Florencia, *Sermón*, fols. 15v–16.

9. Mendez Silva, *Breve, curiosa, y ajustada noticia*, fol. 96v.

10. Antonio de Jesús María, *D. Baltasar de Moscoso i Sandoval*, para. 24; similar wording is used concerning the appointment of the countess in another biography of Moscoso, which may suggest a common original document source: Passano de Haro, *Exemplar eterno de prelados*, 3. Cabrera de Córdoba, *Relaciones*, 453.

11. "Cédulas reales sobre el gobierno y etiqueta de la casa de la reina y officios que en ella había, Valladolid 9 Julio 1603," BN, MS 1007, fol. 7v (hereafter cited as "Cédulas reales").

12. Guzmán, "Memorias," RAH, Colección Salazar y Castro, MS 9/476, fol. 124v; "Cédulas reales," BN, MS 1007, fols. 8, 20.

13. March, "El aya del Rey" and *Niñez y juventud*, 1:23–24.

14. Fernández Martín, "La Marquesa del Valle."

15. Cabrera de Córdoba, *Relaciones*, 191, 201–2, 204, 208–9; Pérez Minguez, "La Condesa de Castellar."

16. "Declaración dada por la Marquesa del Valle en la Prision," BN, MS 18191, fols. 193–201.

17. "Relación que hizo á la república de Venecia Simón Contareni, 1605," in Cabrera de Córdoba, *Relaciones*, 577; Sepúlveda, *Historia de varios sucesos*, 318–22, 343, 345; Fernández Martín, "La Marquesa del Valle"; "Historia de Joan Kevenhuller de Aichelberg," BN, MS 2751, p. 1140.

18. Cabrera de Córdoba, *Relaciones*, 191.

19. "Cédulas reales," BN, MS 1007, fol. 9; Cabrera de Córdoba, *Relaciones*, 525; memorial of the Countess of Lemos, 13 July 1605, AGS, CJH, leg. 458, no. 12. Household accounts similarly released money for the countess without waiting for official decree. AGS, Tesoro, Inv. 24, leg. 577, fol. 13.

20. Guzmán, "Memorias," RAH, Colección Salazar y Castro, MS 9/476, fol. 14.

21. Philip III to Francisco de Castro, 3 April 1614, Archivo de la Casa de Alba, C-90, no. 10.

22. Cabrera de Córdoba, *Relaciones*, 241, 406; Guzmán, "Memorias," RAH, Colección Salazar y Castro, MS 9/477, fol. 20.

23. "Cédulas reales," BN, MS 1007.

24. Accounts of Antonio Voto (1600–1609), APR, Sección Administrativa, leg. 902.

25. Accounts of Hernando de Espejo, *guardajoyas de la reina*, APR, Sección Administrativa, leg. 902.

26. Novoa, *Historia de Felipe III*, 61:141.

27. APR, Expedientes Personales, caja 1113/32; memorial of Juana Zapata, 5 September 1609, AGS, CJH, leg. 489.

28. Account of the death of the infanta Margarita, 11 March 1617, APR, Sección Histórica, caja 56.

29. Memorials of Adransio Zapata, [1622], and Juana Zapata, 1 May 1623, AGS, Patronato Eclesiástico, legs. 106 and 107.

30. Gascón de Torquemada, *Gaçeta y nuevas,* 226.

31. Testament of Queen Margarita, 1601, AGS, Patronato Real, leg. 31–20, clauses 25 and 26. Palace documents are not clear on this but appear to place a person by the name Operguene in the queen's service in 1600. APR, Expedientes Personales, cajas 1113/32 and 759/6.

32. Documents concerning the income of Estefanía Romero de Villaquirán, June 1607 and 20 July 1607, AGS, CJH, legs. 481, no. 22, and 473, no. 13.

33. Gascón de Torquemada, *Gaçeta y nuevas,* 127; Cortés Echánove, *Nacimiento y crianza,* 40–41.

34. Payment requests of 8 August 1607, 8 June 1608, and 1608, AGS, CJH, leg. 473, no. 16; leg. 482, pt. 25, no. 42; leg. 483, pt. 21, no. 26. An income of 200 ducats in 1607 is listed in AHN, Cámara de Castilla, leg. 4418, no. 157.

35. Authorization of payments, 15 September 1605 and 6 March 1614, AGS, CJH, legs. 458 and 531, pt. 19, no. 12. It is possible that Isabel de Montoya was not a wetnurse but some other kind of nurse. Petitions of 2 October 1603, 16 September 1604, and 1606, AGS, CJH, legs. 432, 445, no. 21, and 468, no. 23; Kusche, *Juan Pantoja de la Cruz,* 263.

36. Memorial, 7 May 1616, AHN, Cámara de Castilla, leg. 4420, no. 45.

37. Grant to Mariana de Bargas, 1606, AGS, CJH, leg. 467, no. 23; Cortés Echánove, *Nacimiento y crianza,* 41; summary of memorials, 22 November 1608, AHN, Cámara de Castilla, leg. 4418, pt. 2, no. 73.

38. Cortés Echánove, *Nacimiento y crianza,* 42–44.

39. Memorial, 12 December 1612, AGS, CJH, leg. 512.

40. Cabrera de Córdoba, *Relaciones,* 452, 453.

41. Cabrera de Córdoba, *Relaciones,* 456.

42. Countess of Lemos to Francisco de Castro, 26 June 1613, Archivo de la Casa de Alba, C-58, no. 177.

43. Simón Díaz, "La estancia," 180.

44. Cabrera de Córdoba, *Filipe Segundo,* 3:202.

45. Cabrera de Córdoba, *Filipe Segundo,* 3:202.

46. "Documentos para el oficio de Ayo del Príncipe," BN, MS 10857, fols. 100–105.

47. Mendez Silva, *Breve, curiosa, y ajustada noticia,* fols. 30v–31v.

48. Mendez Silva, *Breve, curiosa, y ajustada noticia,* fols. 62v, 86v.

49. Pedro González de Mendoza to Charles V, letters apparently written in 1531, one undated, others dated 15 April, 30 April, and 20 May; Juan de Zúñiga to Charles V, 24 June 1535 and 25 February 1536; and summaries of letters of Charles V to Zúñiga, 18 May, 9 June, and 12 July 1536, in March, *Niñez y juventud,* 1:46–48, 92, and 95, respectively.

50. Consultas of Juan de Zúñiga concerning the households of the prince and infantas, Biblioteca Zabálburu, Carpeta 85, nos. 27–71.

51. García de Toledo to Charles V, 27 August 1557, in Amezúa y Mayo, "El hermano mayor"; García de Toledo to Philip II, 22 May 1558, in *Colección de documentos inéditos,* 26:408–9.

52. Cabrera de Córdoba, *Filipe Segundo,* 4:200–202, and *Relaciones,* 10.

53. Cabrera de Córdoba, *Filipe Segundo,* 3:201.

54. Martínez Hernández, "Pedagogía en palacio."

55. Sepúlveda, *Historia de varios sucesos,* 211.

56. "Relación que hizo á la república de Venecia Simón Contareni, 1605," in Cabrera de Córdoba, *Relaciones,* 568.

57. Cabrera de Córdoba, *Relaciones*, 269; "Asientos de gentilehombres," APR, Sección Histórica, leg. 2914.

58. Cabrera de Córdoba, *Relaciones*, 432.

59. See, e.g., Cabrera de Córdoba, *Relaciones*, 443, 477, 484–85; and Guzmán, "Memorias," RAH, Colección Salazar y Castro, MS 9/477, fols. 106v, 122–122v.

60. Antonio [Hurtado] de Mendoza, "Relación de la comedia que en Lerma representaron la Reina de Francia y sus Hermanos," BN, MS 18656, no. 49.

61. Guzmán, "Memorias," RAH, Colección Salazar y Castro, MS 9/476, fols. 60, 73, 106; Sánchez, *Empress, the Queen, and the Nun*, chap. 7, esp. 169–70; Feros, *Kingship and Favoritism*, 235–36.

62. Cabrera de Córdoba, *Relaciones*, 402.

63. "Resolución que tomó el Rey Nuestro Señor cerca de algunas cosas que importavan aesta monarquía de su Magd. por setiembre de 1618," BN, MS 2348, fols. 401–4.

64. Pérez Bustamante, *La España de Felipe III*, 150.

65. Céspedes y Meneses, *Primera parte de la historia*, 16. Novoa thought Uceda received all of Lerma's offices, including that of ayo. He also describes Paredes as leaving court in disgust, since as the "most senior" gentleman, he considered himself entitled to the position. *Historia de Felipe III*, 61:196–97.

66. "Apuntamientos politicos," BN, MS 5873. While some sources describe this advice as directed toward Olivares in 1629, this copy clearly indicates that it was intended for and in fact given to Zúñiga, "ayo que fue del Rey nro sr." It may have been rewritten later as advice to Olivares.

67. Gascón de Torquemada, *Gaçeta y nuevas*, 104.

68. Gascón de Torquemada, *Gaçeta y nuevas*, 133. Palace documents list Alcaudete as a mayordomo from 1610 to 1629, having taken the oath as mayordomo of the queen in February 1610 and of the prince in October 1615. APR, Expedientes Personales, caja 24/17.

69. Gascón de Torquemada, *Gaçeta y nuevas*, 297; memorial of the service of Francisco Fernández de Córdoba, APR, Expedientes Personales, caja 24/17.

70. Gascón de Torquemada, *Gaçeta y nuevas*, 105, 93, 224. This notice of Malpica's death refers to him only as mayordomo of Fernando, suggesting that by that time the infante was not perceived as having an ayo.

71. Guzmán, "Memorias," RAH, Colección Salazar y Castro, MS 9/476, fols. 78v, 86v.

72. Cabrera de Córdoba, *Relaciones*, 299, 520.

73. Guzmán, "Memorias," RAH, Colección Salazar y Castro, MS 9/476, fol. 105v.

74. Gascón de Torquemada, *Gaçeta y nuevas*, 41–42.

75. Accounts of Francisco Guillamas Velazquez, 1610–11, AGS, Tesoro, Inv. 24, leg. 578; memorial of the Count of Castelmellor, mayordomo of the queen, for expenses incurred in 1610, 8 January 1619, APR, Sección Histórica, caja 81; Cabrera de Córdoba, *Relaciones*, 406, 413–14, 416.

76. Accounts of Francisco Guillamas Velazquez, 1610–11, AGS, Tesoro, Inv. 24, leg. 578.

77. *Jornada del Rey nuestro señor Don Felipe, tercero*.

78. Cabrera de Córdoba, *Relaciones*, 336.

79. Guzmán, "Memorias," RAH, Colección Salazar y Castro, MS 9/476, fol. 31.

80. Cabrera de Córdoba, *Relaciones*, 440, 502; Simón Díaz, *Relaciones breves*, 89–92.

81. On the tradition of raising the children of nobility at court, see Nader, *Mendoza Family in the Spanish Renaissance*, 77–79; and Motley, *Becoming a French Aristocrat*.

82. "Instrucciones para el servicio de los Príncipes de Savoya . . . 1604–1624," BPR, MS II-2096; "Representa[ció]n del Conde-Duque de Olivares, hecha al Rey dn Felipe 40 sobre la educa[ció]n de los cabelleros Pages de S. M.," 5 March 1637, BN, MS 10994.

83. "Etiquetas y cuentas de las casas reales," APR, Sección Histórica, caja 113. Diego de Guzmán, writing years later, identified his nephew as a menino rather than a page and later gentleman de la boca; 20 December 1629, AGS, Estado, leg. 2756. "Gentileshombres de la boca," APR, Sección Histórica, leg. 2923.

84. "Orden e instruccion que dio Don Antonio de Toledo al ayo de los paxes, 2 Enero 1609," BPR, MS II-2096; "Instruccion para el que fuera ayo de los pajes de su Magd.," BN, MS 17772, fols. 168–77.

85. Hurtado de Mendoza, Discursos, 151–59.

86. Cabrera de Córdoba, Filipe Segundo, 3:206.

87. Pedro Mantuano dedicated his Casamientos de España y Francia (1618) to Francisco Calderón, Count de la Oliva, menino of the prince.

88. "Precedentes para el recibimiento de huéspedes," 13 August 1647, APR, Sección Histórica, caja 81; Almansa y Mendoza, Cartas y novedades, 163; "Damas de la Reina," APR, Sección Histórica, leg. 2914; Gascón de Torquemada, Gaçeta y nuevas, 135, 138.

89. APR, Expedientes Personales, caja 113; "Damas de la Reina," APR, Sección Histórica, leg. 2914.

90. Novoa, Historia de Felipe III, 61:127; Gascón de Torquemada, Gaçeta y nuevas, 65, 105, 142.

91. Gascón de Torquemada, Gaçeta y nuevas, 113, 319, 382; "Gentileshombres de la boca," APR, Sección Histórica, leg. 2923.

92. Gascón de Torquemada, Gaçeta y nuevas, 399, 404; "Gentileshombres de la boca," APR, Sección Histórica, leg. 2923.

93. Philip III, Cartas de Felipe III a su hija Ana, 44, 47; Constable of Castile to Philip III, 9 August 1600, AGS, Estado, leg. 1288; "Damas de la Reina," APR, Sección Histórica, leg. 2914. Sophia is probably the "dama enana" called Doña Cufia in palace records and the same Doña Sufia of whom José Moreno Villa found traces in household accounts from 1601–17. Locos, enanos, negros, y niños palaciegos, 145.

94. Concerning the discourse on favorites in the early seventeenth century and the career of Philip III's favorite, see Feros, Kingship and Favoritism, esp. 40–47.

95. Duke of Lerma to Philip IV, 13 April 1621, and memorial of the Cardinal-Duke, BN, MS 1390, fols. 12v–13, 13v–20.

CHAPTER 3

1. Torre, "Maestros de los hijos"; Liss, Isabel the Queen, esp. 251–53, 256; Vives, De institutione feminae christianae, liber primus, xxiv. Allessandro Geraldini's treatise, De eruditione nobilium puellarum, is not extant.

2. Mendez Silva, Breve, curiosa, y ajustada noticia, fols. 93–94; Brandi, Emperor Charles V, 55–60; Fichtner, Ferdinand I of Austria, 13–14, 102.

3. March, Niñez y juventud.

4. March, Niñez y juventud, 1:130, 221n10, 296, 2:97; Philip II to Honorato Juan, 3 July 1554, in Colección de documentos inéditos, 26:395–96; Gachard, Don Carlos et Philippe II, 11; Herrero Mediavilla and Aguayo Nayle, Archivo biográfico, fiche 643, nos. 341–45.

5. Aldea Vaquero, Marin Martínez, and Vives Gatell, *Diccionario de historia eclesiástica de España*, supplement, 432–38; Cabrera de Córdoba, *Filipe Segundo*, 4:61–63.

6. Liss, *Isabel the Queen*, esp. 251–53, 256; Mattingly, *Catherine of Aragon*, 9, 21; Nader, *Mendoza Family in the Spanish Renaissance*, 6.

7. Juan Martínez Siliceo to Charles V, 26 November 1535 and 2 May 1536, in March, *Niñez y juventud*, 1:68, 71.

8. Amezúa y Mayo, "El hermano mayor," 37.

9. Count of Cifuentes to Charles V, 17 January 1541, in March, *Niñez y juventud*, 1:132.

10. Claremont, *Catherine of Aragon*, 65–66, 70; March, *Niñez y juventud*, 1:226, 215; Sepúlveda, *Historia de varios sucesos*, 76n1.

11. "Instruccion para el que fuera ayo de los pajes de su Magd.," BN, MS 17772, fols. 168–77.

12. Guzmán, "Memorias," RAH, Colección Salazar y Castro, MS 9/477, fol. 75.

13. Guzmán, *Reyna católica*, fol. 134v; Sánchez, *Empress, the Queen, and the Nun*, 162.

14. Guzmán, *Reyna católica*, fol. 197v; Guzmán, "Memorias," RAH, Colección Salazar y Castro, MS 9/477, fol. 35.

15. "Cédulas reales," BN, MS 1007.

16. "Reglas por el gobierno de la casa de la Reina Doña Ana," 1575, BPR, MS II-836.

17. Guzmán, "Memorias," RAH, Colección Salazar y Castro, MS 9/476, fol. 124–124v.

18. Guzmán, "Memorias," RAH, Colección Salazar y Castro, MS 9/476, fol. 124–124v; Antonio de Jesús María, *D. Baltasar de Moscoso i Sandoval*, para. 148. Antonio de Jesús María refers specifically to the communication between Altamira and Simón de Rojas but generalizes this type of contact between tutor and aya.

19. Guzmán, *Reyna católica*, fol. 197.

20. Guzmán, "Memorias," RAH, Colección Salazar y Castro, MS 9/476, fol. 124v.

21. Guzmán, "Memorias," RAH, Colección Salazar y Castro, MS 9/477, fols. 64v, 119, 142, 149v.

22. Guzmán, "Memorias," RAH, Colección Salazar y Castro, MS 9/477, fols. 39–50v.

23. Cabrera de Córdoba, *Relaciones*, 464.

24. Lazaro Diaz del Valle y de la Puerta, "Epilogo y nomenclatura de los s[eño]res Ynquisidores Generales," BN, MS 17495, no. 4.

25. Cabrera de Córdoba, *Relaciones*, 469; "Casa de los pajes," APR, Sección Administrativa, leg. 1049.

26. APR, Expedientes Personales, caja 19/31.

27. Cabrera de Córdoba, *Relaciones*, 469; Novoa, *Historia de Felipe III*, 61:34.

28. Catalina de Zúñiga to Fernando de Castro, 30 June 1612, Archivo de la Casa de Alba, C-58, no. 178.

29. Torres Amat, *Memorias para ayudar*, 9–10.

30. APR, Sección Histórica, caja 113.

31. BN, MS 6043, fols. 144–45. The catalog of the Biblioteca Nacional identifies Albanell as the author of these epigrams, but the document itself—clearly the original, given its folds and seal—indicates that the lines were sent to him as a letter, although of course that does not entirely preclude the possibility that he wrote them.

32. Catalina de Zúñiga to Fernando de Castro, 30 June 1612, Archivo de la Casa de Alba, C-58, no. 178.

33. Gaspar Piquero de Menes to Philip IV, 25 May 1622, and to "Ill[ustrissi]mo S[eñ]or," 28 May 1622, AGS, Patronato Eclesiástico, leg. 105, no. 157.

34. Archbishop of Granada to Philip IV, 23 August 1622, AGS, Patronato Eclesiástico, leg. 106.

35. See, e.g., Barker, *Brother to the Sun King*, esp. 17–40; and Spielman, *Leopold I of Austria*, esp. 32–35. Although he eventually inherited his father's title, Leopold was born and raised a second son.

36. Vega y Toraya, *Vida del venerable siervo de Dios*, 259–67; Gascón de Torquemada, *Gaçeta y nuevas*, 202. On Rojas's written works, see below, chapter 4.

37. Count-Duke of Olivares to Philip IV, [1632?], in Marañón, *El Conde-Duque de Olivares*, 443, 444.

38. Anonymous description of the deathbed of Philip III, BN, MS 2352, fols. 7–10.

39. Juan Diaz, on behalf of the dean and *cabildo* of the Holy Church of Toledo, to Philip IV, 2 June 1621, AGS, Patronato Eclesiástico, leg. 103, no. 145.

40. APR, Sección Histórica, caja 81; Gascón de Torquemada, *Gaçeta y nuevas*, 210.

41. Guzmán y Santoyo, *Sermón*. John Elliott discusses the use of "planet king" as applied to Philip IV in *Count-Duke of Olivares*, 177.

42. Guzmán, "Memorias," RAH, Colección Salazar y Castro, MS 9/477, fol. 266; Aldea Vaquero, Marin Martínez, and Vives Gatell, *Diccionario de historia eclesiástica de España*, 3:1870.

43. Mendez Silva, *Breve, curiosa, y ajustada noticia*, fols. 102–3; nominations for the office of sumiller de cortina, APR, Capilla Real, caja 65/8. A Bernardino Manrique is also mentioned among the gentlemen de la boca in 1626. APR, Sección Histórica, leg. 2923. Although Manrique clearly served in the ecclesiastical household of the infante Fernando, it is possible that Mendez Silva exaggerated his role in the infante's education in honor of the house of Villar Don Pardo, to which he was somewhat attached through patronage.

44. Camón Aznar, *Summa artis*, 66–73; Harris, "Aportaciones"; Garcia Figar, "Fray Juan Bautista Maino."

45. Gallego, "Felipe IV, pintor."

46. Memorial of Susana Castellon, September 1626, AGS, Estado, leg. 2753; Simón Díaz, *Relaciones breves*, 217; Francisco de Jesús, *El hecho de los tratados*, 58; Stoye, *English Travellers Abroad*, 242; Howell, *Epistolae-Ho-Elianae*, 1:77.

47. Philip IV, *Testamento de Felipe IV*, iii; Cesar Firrufino, *Platica manual* and *El perfeto artillero*. Richard L. Kagan mentions a J. C. Ferrugino who may have taught math and artillery to nobles in the house of the Marquis of Leganés in Madrid. "Olivares," 237.

48. Van der Essen, *Le Cardinal-Infant*, 46; Simón Díaz, *Relaciones breves*, 436. A "maestro Roales" is listed among the royal chaplains in 1632. AGS, CMC, Época 3, leg. 3068.

49. González Dávila, *Teatro de las grandezas*, 330.

50. Cortesão, *Cartografía e cartógrafos portugueses*, 2:294–361; Sousa Viterbo, *Trabalhas nauticos dos portuguezes*, 1:171–83. Cortesão and Sousa Viterbo disagree concerning whether Lavaña went to Italy.

51. Philip II, decree appointing Juan Bautista de Labaña, 25 December 1582, in Cortesão, *Cartografía e cartógrafos portugueses*, 2:295–96; see also 2:294–360.

52. Cortesão, *Cartografía e cartógrafos portugueses*, 2:317.

53. The cartographic career of Lavaña is discussed, and several maps from his works are reproduced, in Cortesão and Teixeira da Mota, *Portugaliae monumenta cartographica*, 4:63–72. González Dávila, *Teatro de la grandezas*, 330–31. Lavaña's requests for additional funds to publish the genealogy continued for several years. See, e.g., AGS, CJH, leg. 485, pt. 16, no. 45, 26 February 1608; leg. 489, 17 October 1609; and leg. 529, pt. 14, no. 4, 15 September 1614. He was also given funds for

"a certain secret matter in the king's service" for which he was required to give no account. AGS, Tesoro, Inv. 24, leg. 580c, [1618?].

54. Cortesão, *Cartografía e cartógrafos portugueses*, 2:324; "Noticias de algunos lugares de Andalucía de Relaciones de Gabriel de Santeans, sacados por comision de su Magd.," BN, MS 6043, fols. 104–132v. These reports on various parts of Andalucía are described as collected for the use of Lavaña in his "decripción de España," 1624. Arboles genealógicos, BN, MS 11499.

55. AHN, Cámara de Castilla, leg. 4425, no. 171, listing Thomas de Lavaña among the *ayudas de cámara* on 14 November 1633; memorial of Tomás de Alabaña, APR, Expedientes Personales, caja 1334/7; appointment of Tomás de Alabaña as royal secretary, 31 March 1647, AGS, Quitaciones de la Corte, leg. 40, 484–89; Gascón de Torquemada, *Gaçeta y nuevas*, 140.

56. One famous example of his influence was in the expansion of purity-of-blood statutes for holders of religious offices. See the discussion of this role in Kamen, *Inquisition and Society*, 118–20.

57. Cabrera de Córdoba, *Relaciones*, 10.

58. Galcerán Albanell, "Parecer sobre la residencia de los obispos," in Valladares de Sotomayor, *Semanario erudito*, 14:205–17. The editor identifies this text as written on 4 April 1635. Since Albanell died in 1626, the correct date is probably 1625. A manuscript copy of this letter, BN, MS 10436, also contains this mistake, although it clearly identifies Albanell as the author. The mistake must be that of the original transcriber.

59. "Resoluçion que tomó el Rey Nuestro Señor cerca de algunas cosas que importavan aesta monarquía de su Magd. por setiembre de 1618," BN, MS 2348, fols. 401–4.

60. "Papel dado al Rey," BN, MS 2352, fols. 411–14; Gascón de Torquemada, *Gaçeta y nuevas*, 222.

61. Guzmán, *Reyna católica*, fol. 132.

62. Gascón de Torquemada, *Gaçeta y nuevas*, 256.

63. Archbishop of Granada to the Count of Olivares, 28 August 1621, BN, MS 1390, fols. 4–5, and numerous other locations.

64. Archbishop of Granada to Philip III, 3 March 1621, and to Philip IV, 21 December 1621, 18 January 1622, February 1624, 11 March 1624, AGS, Patronato Eclesiástico, legs. 103, no. 68; 105, no. 13 and unnumbered; 108, nos. 36 and 61. City of Granada to Philip III, protesting Albanell's attempts to naturalize his servants in order to grant them benefices within Granada, 20 January 1622, AGS, Patronato Eclesiástico, leg. 105, no. 49. Albanell also wrote letters of condolence to members of the royal family after the death of Philip III and to Philip IV concerning the oath taking of the viceroy of Catalonia, cited in Torres Amat, *Memorias para ayudar*, 9–10.

65. Guzmán, *El Santo Rey Fernando III*.

66. The instruction is excerpted in Fernández Montaña, *Nueva luz y juicio verdadero*, 278–82.

67. García de Toledo to Charles V, 27 August 1557, quoted in Amezúa y Mayo, "El hermano mayor," 38.

68. Juan Martínez Siliceo to Charles V, 19 March 1540, in March, *Niñez y juventud*, 1:72.

69. Juan de Zúñiga to Charles V, 6 August 1543, in March, *Niñez y juventud*, 1:257.

70. Watson, *Vives*, lxx; Simón Díaz, *Bibliografía de la Literatura Hispánica*, 7:295.

71. Brantôme, *Vies des dames illustres*, 137–38, 141; Freer, *Elizabeth de Valois*, 2:134.

72. Lhermite, *Le passetemps*, 1:198, 275; 2:352–53. Various memorials and responses, 14 August, 26 July 1606, 31 January 1607, summer 1618, AGS, CJH, legs. 466, no. 22; 468, no. 23; 475, no. 22; 555, pt. 19, no. 36.

73. March, *Niñez y juventud*, 1:68–69, 2:357.

74. See Yates, *Art of Memory*, 173–98, or the more detailed essays on Lull reprinted in Yates's *Lull and Bruno*, chaps. 1–2.

75. Philip II to the infantas, 1 October 1582, in Philip II, *Cartas de Felipe II a sus hijas*, 76, 190n145.

76. García de Toledo to Charles V, 27 August 1557, in Amezúa y Mayo, "El hermano mayor," 38.

77. Sepúlveda, *Historia de varios sucesos*, 76n1. Prizes for such occasions included sword blades, colored plumes, inkwells, and perfumed gloves.

78. Cabrera de Córdoba, *Filipe Segundo*, 3:204.

79. "Todo este Quaderno es de letra de el sr Phelipe III siendo príncipe," BN, MS 1451.

80. The edition of Julius Caesar is noted in the Biblioteca Nacional catalog as having been transferred to printed materials, with no indication of its new call number, Catálogo Antiguo Aa 49. The translations of Cicero are mentioned in El Escorial MS L.I.15, "Relación de papeles de Felipe III," described in Zarco Cuevas, *Catálogo de los manuscritos castellanos*, 2:173.

81. Philip IV, "Epílogo breve," xvi.

82. Philip IV, "Epílogo breve," xviii.

83. Philip IV, "Epílogo breve," x–xi.

84. BN, MSS 9251 and 18646, no. 11.

85. Guzmán, "Memorias," RAH, Colección Salazar y Castro, MSS 9/476, fols. 74–75v, and 9/477, fol. 170–170v.

86. Vega y Toraya, *Vida del venerable siervo de Dios*, 268–69.

87. APR, Sección Administrativa, leg. 902, fols. 119–31, 182–86. One problem in the use of this list is that the books were being inventoried in order to be sold, so they were not necessarily available after her death. However, the list provides a sense of what a queen's personal collection might contain.

88. Soons, *Juan de Mariana*, 43–44, notes that Mariana's use of history differed in his *Historia de España* and his mirror-of-princes treatise, *Del rey y de la institución real*. This suggests an understanding of the distinction between writing history and teaching through historical example that few of Mariana's contemporaries appear to have shared.

89. Philip IV, "Epílogo breve," x.

90. "Puntos que pareçen dignos de consideraçión," BN, MS 8719, fol. 57; "Consejo sobre las cartas de Cárdenas de 6 y 7 de Mayo," 22 May 1615, AGS, Estado K, leg. 1429, no. 17; "Instrucción que el rey Don Felipe III dió escrita de su mano á su hija la infanta Doña Ana, cuando fué á ser reina de Francia," in Philip III, "Cartas autógrafas," 16.

CHAPTER 4

1. Cabrera de Córdoba, *Filipe Segundo*, 2:447.

2. Sepúlveda, *Historia de varios sucessos*, 4, 34–35, 73, 135.

3. Diego de Guzmán described this ritual in 1609 and 1610, including details of the persons having confessed and communed and, in one case, having been examined by a court doctor prior to entering the king's presence. Guzmán, "Memorias," RAH, Colección Salazar y Castro, MS 9/476, fols. 29 and 144; Fernández Alvarez, *Politica mundial*, 69. A similar ritual was observed elsewhere in Europe with varying degrees of devotion.

4. Novoa, *Historia de Felipe III*, 61:248.

5. Martínez Millán, "Familia real y grupos políticos," 94.

6. Sepúlveda, *Historia de varios sucesos*, 319.

7. Guzmán, "Memorias," RAH, Colección Salazar y Castro, MS 9/477, fols. 1v, 53; L. Muñoz, *Vida y virtudes*, 215–16, 226–29.

8. Alvaro de Carvajal, "Memória de las cédulas que estan por pagar a la limosna," 21 February 1608, and García de Paredes, "Memoria de las cédulas," 2 May 1609, AGS, CJH, legs. 482, pt. 25, no. 46, fols. 1–2, and 492, pt. 18, no. 35; Diego de Guzmán, "Memoria de los monesterios, 1598–1611," in Guzmán, "Memorias," RAH, Colección Salazar y Castro, MS 9/477, fols. 163–67.

9. Guzmán, "Memorias," RAH, Colección Salazar y Castro, MSS 9/476, esp. fol. 35, and 9/477.

10. Guzmán, *Reyna católica*, fol. 197v; Guzmán, "Memorias," RAH, Colección Salazar y Castro, MS 9/476, fol. 22. Smith, *Preaching in the Spanish Golden Age*, describes the standard length of a sermon as between an hour and an hour and a half (42) but notes that a homily of five to ten minutes might be given instead (31).

11. Guzmán, "Memorias," RAH, Colección Salazar y Castro, MSS 9/476, fols. 20, 59–75, and 9/477, fols. 118v–119.

12. Guzmán, "Memorias," RAH, Colección Salazar y Castro, MSS 9/476, fols. 22, 78v, 84v, 86, and 9/477, fol. 151.

13. Guzmán, "Memorias," RAH, Colección Salazar y Castro, MSS 9/476, fols. 29, 113v, and 9/477, fol. 60. The number of the queen's own children includes the child who died in 1603.

14. Guzmán, "Memorias," RAH, Colección Salazar y Castro, MS 9/476, fols. 20, 139–139v. Ana was also present the following year. Guzmán, "Memorias," RAH, Colección Salazar y Castro, MS 9/477, fol. 85v.

15. Cabrera de Córdoba, *Relaciones*, 468; Palafox, "Diario de la jornada," 460.

16. Guzmán, "Memorias," RAH, Colección Salazar y Castro, MS 9/476, fols. 236, 266, 268.

17. Honras reales, APR, Sección Histórica, caja 76.

18. "Copia de la carta que Dn Joan de Ribera arc[i]p[rest]e de Valencia escrivio al Rey Dn Felipe tercero nuestro señor acerca del ministerio de confesor de su Magd.," 29 September 1610, BN, MS 5788, fols. 1–3.

19. Letter addressed to "Ill[ustrissi]mo y R[everendissi]mo Señor," BN, MS 5758, fols. 4–20.

20. Francisco de Jesús was not a royal confessor but a court preacher. Although he was not unique in questioning the English marriage, he published an account of the entire process of negotiations, which lent his voice added weight. Francisco de Jesús, *El hecho de los tratados*.

21. Letter addressed to "Ill[ustrissi]mo y R[everendissi]mo Señor," BN, MS 5758, fol. 18.

22. Pizarro Llorente, "El control de la conciencia regia." Manuel de Castro, OFM, presents evidence of several Franciscan confessors of Spanish kings in "Confesores franciscanos en la corte de los Reyes Católicos" and "Confesores franciscanos en la corte de Carlos I."

23. *Un caballero de la Corte de Madrid*.

24. Pérez Bustamante, "Los cardenalatos."

25. "Sobre las partes de Frai Luis de Aliaga," BN, MS 2348, fols. 59–66; "Avisos hecho al Rey Felipe IV," BN, MS 2352, fols. 404–8; "Papel dado al Rey," BN, MS 2352, fols. 411–14; García García, "Fray Luis de Aliaga."

26. See, e.g., Sánchez, "Confession and Complicity," 136–37.

27. O'Malley, *First Jesuits*, 71, 123, 273, 275; Fichtner, *Emperor Maximilian II*, 116-17.

28. Guzmán, *Reyna católica*, fol. 130; Bireley, *Religion and Politics*, 7-8.

29. Sepúlveda, *Historia de varios sucesos*, 226. See also Sánchez, "Confession and Complicity," 134n3.

30. "Cédulas reales," BN, MS 1007, fol. 19.

31. Francisco de Arriva to the Duke of Lerma, 25 June 1616, AGS, Estado K, leg. 1471, no. 156; Guzmán, "Memorias," RAH, Colección Salazar y Castro, MS 9/477, fols. 10, 154-57.

32. Vázquez, "Fray Francisco de Arriba." Arriba's only published work, *Operis conciliatorii gratiae et liberi arbitrii*, grew out of the debate concerning grace. He also left several unpublished letters addressing this issue.

33. Orders of payment, 14 December 1611, last third of 1612, 1 May 1614, 26 August 1614, AGS, CJH, legs. 512, 522, and 529, pt. 14, no. 9.

34. Juan de Queros (Jean de Quercy) to Padre Rivas, 30 January 1614; Juan de Queros to Philip III, 31 January 1614; and Juan de Queros to Juan de Ciriça, 11 April 1614, all in AGS, Estado K, leg. 1468.

35. "Instrucción que el rey Don Felipe III dió escrita de su mano á su hija la infanta Doña Ana, cuando fué á ser reina de Francia," in Philip III, "Cartas autógrafas de Felipe III," 15-16.

36. "Consejo sobre las cartas de Cárdenas de 6 y 7 de Mayo," 22 May 1615, AGS, Estado K, leg. 1429, no. 17.

37. Vázquez, "Fray Francisco de Arriba," 474. The *compañero* was Francisco Fernández de S. Gabriel, who became Ana's confessor after Arriba returned to Spain.

38. Duke of Monteleon to Philip III, 14 January 1616; "Consejo sobre la carta del Duque de Monteleon de 16 Enero," 30 January 1616; and Monteleon to Juan de Cirica, 11 April 1616, AGS, Estado K, legs. 1471, no. 16, 1430, no. 12, and 1471, no. 88.

39. Francisco de Arriba to the Duke of Lerma, 6 June and 25 June 1616, AGS, Estado K, leg. 1471, nos. 123 and 156.

40. Philip III to Ana de Austria, 18 August 1618, in Philip III, *Cartas de Felipe III a su hija Ana*, 52-53.

41. Gascón de Torquemada, *Gaçeta y nuevas*, 116. Arriba may have been named bishop or promised a bishopric prior to his departure from Spain, for the Duke of Monteleon calls him "obispo" in his letter of 11 April 1616, AGS, Estado K, leg. 1471, no. 88.

42. Appointment of Padre Joseph González, 6 May 1612, AGS, CJH, leg. 512; Cabrera de Córdoba, *Relaciones*, 374, 522; Guzmán, "Memorias," RAH, Colección Salazar y Castro, MS 9/477, fol. 175.

43. Cabrera de Córdoba, *Relaciones*, 506.

44. Espinosa Rodríguez, *Fray Antonio de Sotomayor*, 11-15. Sotomayor refers to his appointment as confessor on 3 July 1616 in a memorial of 25 June 1619, AGS, CJH, leg. 564, pt. 18, no. 5.

45. Espinosa Rodríguez, *Fray Antonio de Sotomayor*, 16-22.

46. "Jornada del Católico Rey Felipe Tercero á Portugal," BN, MS 2350, fols. 1-6; Simón-Diaz, *Bibliografía de la literature hispánica*, 12:501. Juan de Santa María also wrote *Chronica de la provincia de San Ioseph*.

47. Novoa, *Historia de Felipe III*, 61:102-3.

48. Almansa y Mendoza, *Cartas y novedades*, 165, 169; Vázquez, "Fray Francisco de Arriba," 465; González Dávila, *Teatro de las grandezas*, 327.

49. Francisco de Jesús, *El hecho de los tratados*, 48, 75, 88; Guzmán, "Memorias," RAH, Colección Salazar y Castro, MS 9/477, fol. 276.

50. Report of the Count of Frankenburg summarizing the imperial position concerning the marriage, 23 October 1626, AGS, Estado, leg. 2993.

51. Report of the Count of Frankenburg, 23 October 1626, AGS, Estado, leg. 2993.

52. Carrocera, "El Padre Diego de Quiroga." Carrocera places Quiroga's appointment as beginning with the death of Juan de Santa María, which he dates to 18 November 1627, but that, most likely, was the date of Venido's death.

53. Summary of the opinions of members of the junta, 31 July 1628, AGS, Estado, leg. 2993.

54. Philip IV's note on the summary of the junta, AGS, Estado, leg. 2993.

55. Elliott, *Count Duke of Olivares*, 394. Numerous letters of Olivares to Quiroga, dated 1629 to 1646, are contained in BL, Add. MSS 24,909.

56. Carrocera, "El Padre Diego de Quiroga," 87–88; Bireley, *Religion and Politics*, 161–62, 194, 216–18.

57. Philip IV to Sor Luisa, 9 June 1648, in Pérez Villanueva, *Felipe IV y Luisa Enriquez Manrique de Lara*, 76.

58. "Relación de los criados de la princessa," RAH, Colección Salazar y Castro, MS 9/475, fol. 68; "Conferencias de las dos casas," AGS, Estado K, leg. 1617, no. 45; payment to Francisco Majistraldo, 12 May 1618, AGS, CJH, leg. 556, pt. 11, no. 5; "Jornada del Católico Rey Felipe Tercero á Portugal," BN, MS 2350, fols. 1–6; Gascón de Torquemada, *Gaçeta y nuevas*, 116.

59. Vega y Toraya, *Vida del venerable siervo de Dios*, 218–19.

60. Guzmán, "Memorias," RAH, Colección Salazar y Castro, MS 9/477, fols. 154–57.

61. Vega y Toraya, *Vida del venerable siervo de Dios*, 219–23.

62. *Ave María*; Arcos, *Vida del venerable y reverendissimo Padre Maestro Fr. Simón de Rojas*.

63. Catalina de Zúñiga to Francisco de Castro, 30 June 1612, Archivo de la Casa de Alba, C-58, no. 178.

64. Vega y Toraya, *Vida del venerable siervo de Dios*, 362, 366.

65. Rojas, *Tratado de la oración*, esp. 70–74, 77–93, 145–49.

66. Vega y Toraya, *Vida del venerable siervo de Dios*, 366.

67. Rojas was beatified in 1715 and canonized in 1988. For accounts of Rojas's miracles, see esp. Vega y Toraya, *Vida del venerable siervo de Dios*.

68. Guzmán, "Memorias," RAH, Colección Salazar y Castro, MS 9/476, fol. 284v.

69. Espinosa Rodríguez, *Fray Antonio de Sotomayor*.

70. Guzmán, "Memorias," RAH, Colección Salazar y Castro, MS 9/476, fol. 15.

71. Céspedes y Meneses, *Primera parte de la historia*, 14.

72. BN, MS 2352, fols. 7–10.

73. Florencia, *Marial que contiene varios sermones*.

74. Smith, *Preaching in the Spanish Golden Age*, 146.

75. Gerónimo de Florencia to the Duke of San Lucar, 11 February 1625, APR, Sección Histórica, caja 81.

76. Guzmán, "Memorias," RAH, Colección Salazar y Castro, MS 9/476, fols. 174–97, 219, 270.

77. APR, Expedientes Personales, caja 7943/6; Gascón de Torquemada, *Gaçeta y nuevas*, 348.

78. Report of the Council of State, 10 December 1630, AGS, Estado, leg. 2649; Francisco de Jesús, *El hecho de los tratados*, 74, 88; Simón Díaz, *Relaciones breves*, 368.

79. Fernando to Philip IV, 6 September 1632, AGS, Estado, leg. 2961; Juan de San Agustín to the Count-Duke of Olivares, 24 January 1633, AGS, Estado, leg. 2960.

80. "Instrucción de lo que fr. Juan de S. Agustín ha de hazer en los neg[oci]os a que va a Madrid," 11 December 1632, AGS, Estado, leg. 2961.

81. Philip IV to Juan de San Agustín and the Count of Oñate, 17 March 1633, AGS, Estado, leg. 2960.

82. Gascón de Torquemada, *Gaçeta y nuevas,* 348.

83. Gascón de Torquemada, *Gaçeta y nuevas,* 92, 194; Espinosa Rodríguez, *Fray Antonio de Sotomayor,* 15, 31.

84. Agreda and Philip IV, *Cartas.*

CHAPTER 5

1. "Instrucción que el rey Don Felipe III dió escrita de su mano á su hija la infanta Doña Ana, cuando fué á ser reina de Francia," in Philip III, "Cartas autógrafas," 9–18.

2. Iñigo de Cárdenas to Philip III, 16 July 1611, AGS, Estado K, leg. 1465, no. 16.

3. Count of Ladossa to Philip III, 12 August and 6 October 1599, AGS, Estado, leg. 1287, nos. 184 and 210; see also Philip III, instructions to Iñigo de Cárdenas, 3 September 1611, AGS, Estado K, leg. 1465, no. 36.

4. Iñigo de Cárdenas to Philip III, 20 August 1611, AGS, Estado K, leg. 1465, no. 26.

5. Reports of Iñigo de Cárdenas, early 1611, AGS, Estado K, leg. 1464; consulta, 22 December 1611, AGS, Estado, leg. 1939, no. 104; Iñigo de Cárdenas to Philip III, 7 and 14 December 1611, AGS, Estado K, leg. 1465.

6. Iñigo de Cárdenas to Philip III, 6 and 7 October 1611; Cárdenas to Philip III and Cárdenas to Alonso de Velasco, both 26 September 1611, all in AGS, Estado K, leg. 1465.

7. Iñigo de Cárdenas to Philip III, 20 July 1611; Marqués de Campilla (i.e., Campiglia) to the Duke of Lerma, 23 September 1611; and Campilla to Rodrigo Calderón, 23 September 1611, AGS, Estado K, leg. 1465, nos. 19, 49, 50.

8. Duke of Lerma to Secretary Aroztegui, 15 October 1611, and Iñigo de Cárdenas to Philip III, 6 October 1611, AGS, Estado K, leg. 1465.

9. Philip III to Francisco de Castro, 24 November 1613, Archivio de la Casa de Alba, C-90, no. 54-4a.

10. Marqués de Campilla to Rodrigo Calderón, 23 September 1611, AGS, Estado K, leg. 1465, no. 50.

11. Guzmán, "Memorias," RAH, Colección Salazar y Castro, MS 9/477, fol. 170–170v; "Consejo sobre las cartas de Cárdenas de 6 y 7 de Mayo," 22 May 1615, AGS, Estado K, leg. 142, no. 17. Concerning Ana's knowledge of French, Philip III indicated in 1617 that Ana had written in French to Isabel. Philip III to Ana de Austria, 7 May 1617, in Philip III, *Cartas de Felipe III a su hija Ana,* 30. As late as 1627 she had an interpreter, although this may have been considered appropriate for certain formal occasions.

12. Iñigo de Cárdenas to Philip III, 16 May and 12 July 1611, AGS, Estado K, legs. 1465 and 1464.

13. Consejo, 28 August 1615, AGS, Estado K, leg. 1429, no. 35.

14. Iñigo de Cárdenas to Secretary Aroztegui, 12 June 1612, AGS, Estado K, leg. 1467.

15. Cabrera de Córdoba, *Relaciones,* 467–68, 484–85; Simón Díaz, *Relaciones breves,* 82–84.

16. Iñigo de Cárdenas, letters of 28 and 30 August 1612, AGS, Estado K, leg. 1467; BN, MS 2348, fols. 48–57.

17. Iñigo de Cárdenas to Philip III, 3 August 1613, and Cárdenas to the Duke of Lerma, 4, 9, and 10 August 1613, AGS, Estado K, leg. 1468.

18. Iñigo de Cárdenas to Philip III, 17 January 1614, AGS, Estado K, leg. 1465.

19. Cabrera de Córdoba, *Relaciones,* 515.

20. Iñigo de Cárdenas to the Duke of Lerma, 4 August 1613 and 2 January 1614, AGS, Estado K,

legs. 1468 and 1465; Cárdenas to Philip III, 16 January 1614 and two letters of 17 January 1614, AGS, Estado K, leg. 1465.

21. Consejo, 28 August 1615, and Philip III to Iñigo de Cárdenas, August 1615, AGS, Estado K, leg. 1429, nos. 35 and 36.

22. Three documents concerning the income of Estefanía Romero de Villaquirán, June 1607, AGS, CJH, leg. 481, pt. 22; "Relación de los criados y criadas españoles que servian a la sra Ynfanta Doña Catalina," 2 February 1600, AGS, CJH, leg. 473, pt. 13; "Relación de los criados de la princesa," RAH, Colección Salazar y Castro, MS 9/475, fols. 66v–68; memorial of Ysabel de Castro Villaquirán, [1622], AGS, Patronato Ecclesiástico, leg. 105, no. 48; Monteleon to the Duke of Lerma, 9 July 1616, AGS, Estado K, leg. 1471, no. 177.

23. "Instrucción que el rey Don Felipe III dió escrita de su mano á su hija la infanta Doña Ana, cuando fué á ser reina de Francia," in Philip III, "Cartas autógrafas,".

24. "Consejo sobre las cartas de Cárdenas de 6 y 7 de Mayo," 22 May 1615, AGS, Estado K, leg. 1429, no. 17.

25. "Instrucción que el rey Don Felipe III dió escrita de su mano á su hija la infanta Doña Ana, cuando fué á ser reina de Francia," in Philip III, "Cartas autógrafas," 15.

26. Philip III to Ana de Austria, 21 August 1617, 23 October 1617, and 6 June 1618, in Philip III, *Cartas de Felipe III a su hija Ana,* 33, 37, 47.

27. "Instrucción que el rey Don Felipe III dió escrita de su mano á su hija la infanta Doña Ana, cuando fué á ser reina de Francia," in Philip III, "Cartas autógrafas," 17.

28. Philip III to Ana de Austria, 16 November 1616, in Philip III, *Cartas de Felipe III a su hija Ana,* 15.

29. Rojas's biographer claims that the king had Rojas look over his instruction and discuss it with him. Similarities may thus reflect their conversation as well as common attitudes. Vega y Toraya, *Vida del venerable siervo de Dios,* 259–67.

30. O'Connell, *Teachings of Saint Louis.* Louis also wrote an instruction for his daughter, but Philip was referring to his better-known instruction to his son.

31. "Consejo sobre las cartas de Cárdenas de 6 y 7 Maio," 22 May 1615, AGS, Estado K, leg. 1429, no. 17.

32. Guzmán, *Reyna católica.*

33. Sánchez Cantón, "Noventa y siete retratos," 148.

34. Simón Díaz, *Relaciones breves,* 99–100; "Verdadura Relacion en la qual se da cuenta de los Real Desposorios que se celebraron en Burgos, dia del Evangelista San Lucas, que fue a 18 de Otubre deste present año 1615"; *Verdadara relacion.*

35. Francisco de Arriba to the Duke of Lerma, 6 June 1616, AGS, Estado K, leg. 1471, no. 123.

36. Kleinman, *Anne of Austria,* 27. Marvick, *Louis XIII,* 171, points out that Ana and Louis were understood by many to have been simply put into bed together, while intercourse was postponed. Louis' doctor's journal, however, maintained that the young couple actually had sexual relations that night.

37. Philip III to Ana, 1 July 1616, in Philip III, *Cartas de Felipe III a su hija Ana,* 9–10; draft, Duke of Lerma to the Countess de la Torre, 4 July 1616, AGS, Estado K, leg. 1471, no. 165; Monteleon to the Duke of Lerma, 7 and 9 July 1616, AGS, Estado K, leg. 1471, nos. 170 and 177.

38. Consejo, 30 January 1616, AGS, Estado K, leg. 1430, no. 12.

39. Iñigo de Cárdenas, notes on Monteleon correspondence, 31 May, 30 June, July 1616, and

Monteleon to the Duke of Lerma, 9 July 1616, AGS, Estado K, leg. 1471, nos. 159, 162, 164b, 177; Philip III to Ana, 4 February 1617, in Philip III, "Cartas autógrafas," 13.

40. Philip III to Ana de Austria, 3 October 1618, in Philip III, *Cartas de Felipe III a su hija Ana*, 55; Fernando Girón to Philip III, 21 October 1618, AGS, Estado K, leg. 1475, no. 94; Dulong, *Anne d'Autriche*, 18, 62.

41. Philip III to Fernando Girón, 2 September 1620, AGS, Estado K, leg. 1455, no. 180; Kleinman, *Anne of Austria*, 43–52, 57.

42. Monteleon to Philip III, 1 July 1617, AGS, Estado K, leg. 1473, no. 35; Kleinman, *Anne of Austria*, 53.

43. Gascón de Torquemada, *Gaçeta y nuevas*, 47, 72, 84; "Damas de la Reina," APR, Sección Histórica, leg. 2914.

44. Gascón de Torquemada, *Gaçeta y nuevas*, 81.

45. Instructions to Pedro de Toledo y Osorio, ambassador to France, 25 April 1608, AGS, Estado K, leg. 1617, nos. 1 and 2; Iñigo de Cárdenas to Philip III, 4 November 1613 and 18 April 1616, AGS, Estado K, legs. 1468, no. 116b, and 1471, no. 89.

46. Francisco de Jesús, *El hecho de los tratados*, 1–32; Gardiner, *History of England*.

47. Philip III to Monteleon, 2 January 1618, and Philip III to the Count of Gondomar, 18 August 1618, AGS, Estado K, leg. 1455, nos. 7 and 55.

48. Count of Frankenburg to Philip III, 6 April 1619 and 1620, AGS, Estado, leg. 2327, fols. 183 and 184.

49. Novoa, *Historia de Felipe III*, 61:308; Gardiner, *History of England*, 4:189–90; Count of Oñate to Philip IV, 8 September 1621, AGS, Estado, leg. 2327, fol. 179; Redworth, "Of Pimps and Princes."

50. "Capitulaciones q[ue] ofrece el rey de la Gran Bretaña . . . ymbiadas al sumo pontifice juntam[ent]e con las replicas de su Santidad," BN, MS 2354, fols. 229–231v. Although this document is undated, it probably dates from the fall of 1622, since a set of points for discussion dated 13 December 1622 is clearly based on this exchange. BN, MS 8719, fols. 70v–74.

51. Report of Fray Diego de la Fuente, 24 February 1623, concerning Alburquerque's audiences with the pope, and second report of Diego de la Fuente, 22 March 1623, BN, MS 8719, fols. 74–77v, 82v–87v.

52. Gardiner, *History of England*, 3:37–71, 370–87; 4:364–411.

53. Elliott, *Count-Duke of Olivares*, 147.

54. "Principio y prosecucion de la Junta grande, desde 7 de Abril hasta 31 de mayo de 1623," and "Pareceres de la Junta," BN, MS 8719, fols. 90v–93v, 121–22; Francisco de Jesús, *El hecho de los tratados*, 58–59, 72–76. Various opinions written by members of this junta were published separately later, including Montemayor, *Parecer que dió en la junta*.

55. "Principio y prosecucion de la Junta grande, desde 7 de Abril hasta 31 de mayo de 1623," BN, MS 8719, fol. 93v.

56. "Parecer de los casamientos," 18 July 1623, BN, MS 2354, fol. 224.

57. Gardiner, *History of England*, 5:17, 49; opinions of Gerónimo de Florencia, Luys de Torres, Pedro Gonçalez de Mendoza, and Hernando Salazar, BN, MS 8719, fols. 133–75.

58. Anonymous opinion on the marriages, BN, MS 8719, fols. 56–60.

59. "Proposiciones del rey de España y respuesta del rey de Bretaña," BN, MS 2354, fol. 232; "Las condiciones deste matrimonio en materia de relijion," BN, MS 8719, fols. 70v–74.

60. Francisco de Jesús, *El hecho de los tratados*, 88. The bishop of Segovia, Fray Iñigo de Brizu-

ela, a member of the Council of State and president of the Council of Flanders, had been Archduke Albert's confessor, so his expertise was both religious and political. The preachers were Francisco de Jesús, the author of the history, and Juan de San Agustín, later confessor of the cardinal-infante.

61. Peña, *Relación de las fiestas reales;* Forcex, *Fiesta eclesiastica.*

62. Simón Díaz, *Relaciones breves,* 217; Francisco de Jesús, *El hecho de los tratados,* 58; Howell, *Epistolae-Ho-Elianae,* 1:77. See p. 65, above.

63. See, e.g., Peña, *Relación de las fiestas reales;* Ruiz de Alarcón y Mendoza, *Elogio descriptivo de las fiestas;* Reynolds, "Mira de Amescua's 'Octavas al príncipe de Gales'"; *Vox Coeli;* and *Ave María,* fol. 9. See also Alenda y Mira, *Relaciones de solemnidades,* 214–31; and Redondo, "Fiesta y literatura."

64. Howell, *Epistolae-Ho-Elianae,* 1:60–61; Francisco de Jesús, *El hecho de los tratados,* 56.

65. Bowle, *Charles I,* 69–70; Gardiner, *History of England,* 5:29–30, 94.

66. This story is told in a number of sources, including Howell, *Epistolae-Ho-Elianae,* 1:63–64, and Gascón de Torquemada, *Gaçeta y nuevas,* 156.

67. Howell, *Epistolae-Ho-Elianae,* 1:64. See also Bowle, *Charles I,* 69; and Carlton, *Charles I,* 43.

68. Gascón de Torquemada, *Gaçeta y nuevas,* 156.

69. "Relacion de lo sucedido a Don Pedro de Granada, Mayo 1623," BN, MS 2354, fols. 238–241v.

70. Kleinman, *Anne of Austria,* 65; Lockyer, *Buckingham,* 240. See also Motteville, *Mémoires,* 36:343–44; and La Porte, *Mémoires,* 59:296–97.

71. Gardiner, *History of England,* 4:388–89; 5:52, 92. If this were in fact the case, María would already have been favorable to the marriage before the arrival of the prince. Her previous confessor had died in early 1623.

72. Francisco de Jesús, *El hecho de los tratados,* 48–49. Castro Egas, *Eternidad del Rey,* fol. 8. Gardiner, *History of England,* 5:27; see also 4:377 and 5:96, 121–22. Carlton, *Charles I,* 45.

73. For example, R. A. Stradling, in *Philip IV and the Government of Spain,* 336, refers to María as "ice-cold . . . a strong willed and imperious lady," while F. C. Montague, in *History of England from the Accession of James I to the Restoration,* 110, calls her "a good simple girl of narrow understanding and irreproachable piety."

74. Almansa y Mendoza, *Relacion de la partida.*

75. Cogswell, *Blessed Revolution,* 61, quoted in Redworth, "Of Pimps and Princes," 407.

76. Redworth, "Of Pimps and Princes."

77. Consulta of the junta, 8 October 1626; consulta of the Council of State, 29 May 1626, and the king's reply, n.d., all in AGS, Estado, leg. 2328.

78. Simón Díaz, *Relaciones breves,* 352; Simón Díaz, "La estancia."

79. "El papel del Conde Duque que va aqui," 28 June 1626, AGS, Estado, leg. 2328; Report of the Count of Frankenburg, 23 October 1626, AGS, Estado, leg. 2993.

80. "El papel del Conde Duque que va aqui," 28 June 1626, AGS, Estado, leg. 2328.

81. Matilla Tascon, *Catálogo de documentos notariales,* 455.

82. Report of the junta, 18 July 1628, AGS, Estado, leg. 2993; Gascón de Torquemada, *Gaçeta y nuevas,* 309; consulta, 20 December 1629, AGS, Estado, leg. 2756.

83. "Memoria de la casa," [July 1628?], AGS, Estado, leg. 2993.

84. "Relaçión de los criados que pareçe fueron sirviendo a la Sra. Emperatriz María, Infanta de España en el viaje a Alemania el año de 1629," AGS, Estado, leg. 2993.

85. "Relaçion de los criados que pareçe fueron sirviendo a la Sra. Emperatriz María, Infanta de España en el viaje a Alemania el año de 1629," AGS, Estado, leg. 2993; Palafox, "Diaro de la jornada," 476.

86. "Azafatas de los Se[ño]res Infantes," APR, Sección Histórica, leg. 2923; memorial of Ana María de Soto on behalf of her father, Baltasar Coronel, boticario, n.d., acknowledged by the Duke of Lerma, 10 July 1612, AGS, Casas y Sitios Reales, Obras y Bosques, leg. 302, fols. 236–37.

87. "Instrucciones para el Marqués de Cadreyta para la embajada de Alemaña," 23 February 1630, BN, MS 10818, no. 11.

88. Draft, Philip IV to María, queen of Hungary, n.d., BL, Add. MSS 14,004, no. 101, fols. 442–51.

89. "Desposorio de la Reyna de Ungría," 25 April 1629, BN, MS 2361, fol. 26.

90. Palafox, "Diaro de la jornada," 429–82; Harris and Elliott, "Velázquez and the Queen of Hungary."

91. Palafox, "Diaro de la jornada," 443, 456, 459–60.

92. Draft, Duke of Alba to V[uestra] E[xcelencia], September 1630, Archivo de la Casa de Alba, Caja 82, no. 37; "Escrito del príncipe de Bisignano San Severino en las diferencias de precedencias sucedidas en la entrada de S. M. della Reyna de Ungría en Naples," BN, MS 1390, fols. 20v–31; Palafox, "Diaro de la jornada," 441, 453, 466–67.

93. Palafox, "Diaro de la jornada," 453, 458, 463.

94. Palafox, "Diaro de la jornada," 442–43, 466–67.

95. Palafox, "Diaro de la jornada," 449–50, 460, 471.

96. Palafox, "Diaro de la jornada," 437–38, 461, 465, 473, 475–76, 481.

CHAPTER 6

1. Fichtner, *Ferdinand I of Austria; Rodríguez-Salgado, *Changing Face of Empire,* 33–40.

2. Fichtner, *Emperor Maximilian II,* 5.

3. Instructions and Secret instructions to Pedro de Toledo, 25 April 1608, AGS, Estado K, leg. 1617, nos. 1 and 2.

4. Secret instructions to Pedro de Toledo, 25 April 1608, AGS, Estado K, leg. 1617, no. 2; Pedro de Toledo to Archduke Albert, 12 October 1608, AGS, Estado K, leg. 1461, nos. 92 and 91.

5. Pedro de Toledo to Philip III, 11 October 1608, AGS, Estado K, leg. 1461, no. 88.

6. Secret instructions to the Duke of Feria, 9 August 1610, AGS, Estado K, leg. 1617, no. 3.

7. Iñigo de Cárdenas to Philip III, 12 July 1611, AGS, Estado K, leg. 1465.

8. Iñigo de Cárdenas to Philip III, 22 November 1611 and 4 November 1613, AGS, Estado K, leg. 1468, no. 116b, and leg. 1465.

9. Baltasar de Zuñiga, 10 February 1611, AGS, Estado, leg. 709, fol. 152.

10. Rodrigo Calderón to Philip III, 3 June and 10 June 1612, and Calderón to Baltasar de Zúñiga, n.d., AGS, Estado K, leg. 1467.

11. Magdalena Sánchez argues that Zúñiga suggested the election of one of the infantes only as a bargaining tool. "Dynasty, State, and Diplomacy."

12. A satirical poem in circulation after the fall of the duke began, "El mayor ladrón del mundo / por no morir ahorcado / se vistió de colorado" (The greatest thief in the world / in order not to die by the noose / dressed himself in [cardinal's] colors). Philip II, *Cartas de Felipe II a sus hijas,* 187n117.

13. Pérez Bustamante, "Los cardenalatos"; P. Williams, "Lerma, 1618."

14. "Las Razones que se pueden representar para que su Sant[ida]d haga gracia de el arcobispado de Toledo al Ser[enissi]mo Infante dn Fernando," Biblioteca del Monasterio Real de San Lorenzo de El Escorial, I.III.31.

15. Account book of Antonio Ximenez, AGS, Tesoro, Inv. 24, leg. 580c.

16. Nominations of persons for parochial offices, AGS, Patronato Eclesiástico, leg. 103, nos. 99 and 101, both dated 22 May 1621, and leg. 105, nos. 55 and 56, both dated 22 February 1622. Quintín Aldea Vaquero sees Navarrete as a teacher of the infante and posits that his *Siete libros de Seneca* (1627) and *De beneficiis* (1629) were used as teaching texts. Aldea Vaquero, *El Cardenal Infante*, 64n95.

17. See chapter 1, above. Early in his reign, Philip IV inquired how he should address his brother when writing to him and was told that he should address him as had his father, as "Most Illustrious Cardinal-Infante," and close with, "I entreat and charge you affectionately." Consulta, 28 April 1621, AGS, Patronato Eclesiástico, leg. 103, no. 73.

18. "Relación del baptismo de la princesa," BN, MS 2354, fols. 304–10.

19. Guzmán, "Memorias," RAH, Colección Salazar y Castro, MS 9/476, fols. 158–325, esp. 266, 271, 245v; Peña, *Relación de las fiestas reales*.

20. "Sucesos del año 1624," BN, MS 2355, fols. 502–3; "Sucesos del año 1626," BN, MS 2358, fol. 341v; Simón Díaz, "La estancia"; Guzmán, "Memorias," RAH, Colección Salazar y Castro, MS 9/476, fols. 251v, 274, 259.

21. Almansa y Mendoza, *Cartas y novedades*, 342.

22. Gonçalez de Salcedo y Butrón, *Panegyrico*, fol. 5.

23. "Discursos admirables en razon de la educacion de los princips e ynfantes; de cuya practica resultaran felicidados y glorias a la nacion," addressed to VPR, BN, MS 18757, no. 17, quotations from fol. 5–5v.

24. "Discursos admirables en razon de la educacion de los princips e ynfantes; de cuya practica resultaran felicidados y glorias a la nacion," addressed to VPR, BN, MS 18757, no. 17, fols. 5v–6, 6v.

25. Elliott and Peña, *Memoriales y cartas*, 1:52–53.

26. BL, Egerton MS 2081, fols. 269–73; Elliott and Peña, *Memoriales y cartas*, 1:165–70.

27. Elliott and Peña, *Memoriales y cartas*, 1:169.

28. Marañón, *El Conde-Duque de Olivares*, 443–46.

29. Antonio de Jesús María, *D. Baltasar de Moscoso i Sandoval*, para. 63.

30. Marañón, *El Conde-Duque de Olivares*, 445. Novoa, *Historia de Felipe IV*, 69:129, also presents Olivares as having asked Isabel, or having suggested that the king ask Isabel, to make this point.

31. Castro Egas, *Eternidad del Rey*, fols. 9–10.

32. Gonçalez de Salcedo y Butrón, *Panegyrico*, fols. 6, 30.

33. Castro Egas, *Eternidad del Rey*, fol. 2.

34. Novoa, *Historia de Felipe III*, 60:1, 170, and *Historia de Felipe IV*, 69:88, 97, 113, 140, 179.

35. APR, Sección Histórica, caja 81.

36. List of goods removed from the king's oratory by Juan Gomez de Mora, APR, Sección Administrativa, leg. 902. This document is undated, but all other inventories in this legajo were made directly after the deaths of royal persons, so it can be assumed that the removal of objects from Philip III's oratory for the stated purpose of clearing the room for Carlos's use took place soon after the king's death.

37. Guzmán, "Memorias," RAH, Colección Salazar y Castro, MS 9/476; Novoa, *Historia de Felipe IV,* 69:193.

38. APR, Sección Histórica, caja 81.

39. Cortesão, *Cartografia e cartógrafos portugueses,* 2:317; consulta of the Council of State, 24 November 1627, AGS, Estado, leg. 2754.

40. This was not the same Fernández de Córdoba who served as ayo. Summary of the memorial of Doña Luisa Mexia de Abendaño on behalf of her son, Francisco Fernández de Córdoba, to the Council of State, 25 November 1629, AGS, Estado, leg. 2756.

41. Gascón de Torquemada, *Gaçeta y nuevas,* 337, 342.

42. Gascón de Torquemada, *Gaçeta y nuevas,* 303, 78; APR, Sección Histórica, caja 81.

43. Gascón de Torquemada, *Gaçeta y nuevas,* 125, 127, 128, 134, 141.

44. APR, Sección Histórica, caja 81. The junta was made up of the inquisitor general; the bishop of Segovia, Iñigo de Briçuela; the confessor Florencia; the administrator of the archdiocese of Toledo, Alvaro de Villegas; and the Marquis of Montesclaros.

45. Guzmán, "Memorias," RAH, Colección Salazar y Castro, MS 9/476, fols. 158–270, esp. 160–162v, 174v, 215v, 207, 224, 222–222v, 164, and 270.

46. Guzmán, "Memorias," RAH, Colección Salazar y Castro, MS 9/476, fols. 199–211, esp. 199 and 206.

47. Guzmán, "Memorias," RAH, Colección Salazar y Castro, MS 9/476, fols. 243, 238v, 286, 255.

48. Two orders for 3,000 gold escudos each, 29 November 1623, AGS, CJH, leg. 594, pt. 14, nos. 44 and 45.

49. Novoa, *Historia de Felipe IV,* 69:42, 56, 192; Gardiner, *History of England,* 5:27.

50. Marañón, *El Conde-Duque de Olivares,* 446–49.

51. Novoa, *Historia de Felipe IV,* 69:192; Cabrera de Córdoba, *Filipe Segundo,* 4:200–202.

52. Marañón, *El Conde-Duque de Olivares,* 443, 444.

53. Novoa, *Historia de Felipe IV,* 69:56, 169–70, quotation from 192. Two poems attributed to Carlos are printed in *Poetas líricos de los siglos XVI y XVII,* 153.

54. "Apuntamientos del licenziado Don Fer[nan]do de Contreras presidente del Consejo Real de Castilla al Rey D. Phelipe 4'o n[uest]ro S[eñ]or sobre la educaçion del Infante d. Fer[nan]do Card[ena]l y Arzobispo de Toledo," 22 April 1623, Hispanic Society, MS HC 411/209, fols. 171v–179v.

55. "Apuntamientos del licenziado Don Fer[nan]do de Contreras . . . ," 22 April 1623, Hispanic Society, MS HC 411/209, fol. 178v.

56. "Memorial de algunas advertencias dirigido al serenissimo señor Don Fernando Cardenal Infante de España administrador perpetuo del Arçobispado de Toledo en nombre de su mayor obligaçion," BN, MS 5994.

57. "Memorial de algunas advertencias . . . ," BN, MS 5994, fol. 29–29v.

58. "Memorial de algunas advertencias . . . ," BN, MS 5994, fol. 38v.

59. "Memorial de algunas advertencias . . . ," BN, MS 5994, fol. 15v.

60. Memorials of Melchor de Moscoso, 25 September 1619, 3 February 1620, 1624, 2 September 1625, AGS, Patronato Eclesiástico, legs. 101, 102, 108, no. 31, and 109, no. 74.

61. Almanza y Mendoza, *Cartas y novedades,* 32; Novoa, *Historia de Felipe IV,* 69:64; Elliott and Peña, *Memoriales y cartas,* 212; Gascón de Torquemada, *Gaçeta y nuevas,* 337, 369; Castejón y Fonseca, *Primacia de la Santa Iglesia de Toledo,* 2:1212–16.

62. "De mi aposento, 4 Setiembre 1626," BN, MS 2358, fol. 302.

63. Junta of 13 September 1626, Archivo de la Casa del Infantado, MSS Montesclaros, libro 130, no. 3.

64. Junta of 19 April 1627, Archivo de la Casa del Infantado, MSS Montesclaros, libro 130, no. 4.

65. Novoa, *Historia de Felipe IV,* 69:55–67. Novoa presents the count-duke as overreacting to the palace activities, an assessment not contradicted by the paranoid tone of the account that Olivares prepared for the king, Valladares de Sotomayor, *Semanario erudito,* 29:255–65.

66. Gascón de Torquemada, *Gaçeta y nuevas,* 295; Hurtado de Mendoza, *Discursos,* 17–21.

67. Instruction of Philip IV to María, queen of Hungary, BL, Add. MSS 14,004, no. 101, fols. 442–51.

68. "Decreto de Su Magestad, 7 Abril 1631," BN, MS 2363, fol. 35.

69. Council of 3 September 1631, AGS, Estado, leg. 2649.

70. Gascón de Torquemada, *Gaçeta y nuevas,* 336; Novoa, *Historia de Felipe IV,* 69:196; "Sucesos del año 1631," BN, MS 2363, fols. 125–32.

71. Gascón de Torquemada, *Gaçeta y nuevas,* 341–42. On the public response to the infante's death, see A. Muñoz, *Tres romances.*

72. On specific issues of Fernando's government in Barcelona, see van der Essen, *Le Cardinal-Infant,* 61–82.

73. "Papel de puntos sobre le instru[cci]on de su Al[tez]a," 18 May 1632, and "Resp[ues]ta al papel de puntos," AGS, Estado, leg. 2961.

74. "Puntos q[ue] tocan a las instrucciones q[ue] se han de dexar al sr Infante," [May?] 1632, AGS, Estado, leg. 2961. A separate instruction, directed to the infante through Oñate and probably written at the same time, dealt with the specific issues to be addressed in the Corts.

75. These documents call him Watevila and Batevilla. Van der Essen, *Le Cardinal-Infant,* 64 and 478, identifies him as Louis, Baron de Watteville, captain of the guards and counselor of Fernando.

76. Appointment of Irarrázabal, 23 May 1632, AGS, Estado, leg. 2961; Elliott and Peña, *Memoriales y cartas,* 2:117n13. He was apparently the Count of Santa Clara mentioned in Appointment of Irarrázabal, 23 May 1632, though his actual title was viscount.

77. Much of AGS, Estado, legs. 2960 and 2961, concerns Fernando's government in Catalonia.

78. Marquis of Villafranca to Count-Duke of Olivares, 16 January 1632; response of the Council of State, January 1632; and appointment of Villafranca, 14 January 1633, all in AGS, Estado, leg. 2960.

79. Count of Oñate to Philip IV, 13 March 1633, and opinions of a council or junta, 19 March 1633, AGS, Estado, leg. 2961. On Oñate's key place in Spanish diplomacy in the second decade of the seventeenth century, see Brightwell, "Spain and Bohemia" and "Spain, Bohemia, and the Empire."

80. Juan de San Agustín to the Count-Duke of Olivares, 24 January 1633, AGS, Estado, leg. 2960.

81. Fernando to the Count-Duke of Olivares, 22 January 1633, AGS, Estado, leg. 2960. Aldea Vaquero cites a secret letter, to be opened only if necessary, that would give the Duke of Feria the right to overrule decisions of Fernando. *El Cardenal Infante,* 114.

82. "Instrucción de lo que fr. Juan de S. Agustín ha de hacer en los neg[oci]os a que va a Madrid," 11 December 1632, and "Minuta de las respuestas y resoluciones de su M[agesta]d," AGS, Estado, leg. 2961.

83. Marquis of Villafranca to an unknown recipient, 14 December 1632, and to Count-Duke of Olivares, 22 January 1633, AGS, Estado, leg. 2960; Fernando to Philip IV, 15 March 1633, AGS, Estado, leg. 2961.

84. Philip IV to Fernando, 4 March 1633, and Fernando to Philip IV, 13 March 1633, AGS, Estado, leg. 2961.

85. Cardinal-infante to the Count-Duke of Olivares, 25 January 1633, AGS, Estado, leg. 2960. Although the infante speaks in a friendly manner toward the count-duke and refers to him as having always been his friend, he refers to him only as count, rather than acknowledging his higher rank of duke, and addresses him as "tu," an intimate yet diminishing treatment very seldom used between adults of high status. I base my identification of the intended recipient of this letter on the infante's postscript, in which he notes that he has told his confessor to write to the recipient regarding Alonso Carrillo. The count-duke received such a letter dated 24 January 1633 from Juan de San Agustín. AGS, Estado, leg. 2960.

86. Advice of the Council of State, 16 March 1633, and three documents of 17 March 1633—Philip IV to the Count of Oñate and Juan de San Agustín, Philip IV to the Marquis of Villafranca, and instruction to the cardinal-infante—all in AGS, Estado, leg. 2960. Two other undated lists of points, probably meant to address the same issues, advised the king to write "paternal y amorossam[ent] e" to his brother and allowed Antonio de Moscoso access to Fernando in hopes of using him as another source of information concerning the infante's thoughts. Aldea Vaquero, *El Cardenal Infante,* 95–117, presents this exchange in a much more dramatic light, characterizing Fernando as immature, violent, and threatening disobedience.

87. Gascón de Torquemada, *Gaçeta y nuevas,* 349.

88. Consultas concerning the archbishopric of Toledo, 16 September 1632, AGS, Estado, leg. 2961.

89. APR, Sección Histórica, caja 81; Gascón de Torquemada, *Gaçeta y nuevas,* 367.

90. Gascón de Torquemada, *Gaçeta y nuevas,* 349, 366.

91. Aedo y Gallart, *Viage del Infante Cardenal.* For a modern analysis of Fernando's career until his arrival in Brussels, see van der Essen, *Le Cardinal-Infant.*

92. Stradling, *Philip IV and the Government of Spain,* 69, 336; Elliott, *Count-Duke of Olivares,* 5.

CHAPTER 7

1. Philip IV, "Epílogo breve," vii.

2. *Menosprecio de corte y alabanza de aldea* and *Aviso de privados y doctrina de cortesanos,* both published in Valladolid, 1539.

3. Bouza Alvarez, "La majestad de Felipe II"; Elliott, "Philip IV of Spain"; Feros, *Kingship and Favoritism,* 71–86.

4. Feros, "Vicedioses, pero Humanos," 103–4.

5. Rivadeneira, *Tratado.* On the anti-Machiavellians, see Bireley, *Counter-Reformation Prince,* esp. chap. 5 on Rivadeneira (Ribadeneira).

6. Rivadeneira, *Tratado,* 518–24, 546–47, 536, 539–40, 552–57, 559.

7. I have used a contemporary English translation of Santa María's work: *Christian Policie, or The Christian Commonwealth;* see esp. 374–427.

8. Elliott, *Count-Duke of Olivares,* 101. Philiberto's opposition to Uceda is the subject of uncredited letters in BN, MS 17858, fols. 139–46, 155–57. By 1621 Juan de Santa María appears to have aligned himself with Olivares; see below.

9. "Tratado del príncipe instruido," BPR, MS II-587. My thanks to Fernando Bouza for bring-

ing this manuscript to my attention. Still in manuscript form in the library of the royal palace in Madrid, its author is not identified, but Professor Bouza has since identified a manuscript by "the duke of Villahermosa" in the archives of the dukes of Alba as a rough draft of this piece. Francisco de Aragon, who called himself Duke of Villahermosa (though a lawsuit had resolved that the title belonged to his niece), published a treatise titled *Discursos políticos, así de razón de Estado como de la buena educación de un príncipe* (Zaragoza, 1620). Ferrer Valls, *Nobleza y espectaculo teatral*, 88.

10. "Tratado del príncipe instruido," BPR, MS II-587, fol. 3v.

11. "Tratado del príncipe instruido," BPR, MS II-587, fol. 6v.

12. Clearly, this advice was not followed in the case of Philip IV, who was described wearing a sword at ceremonial occasions from a very early age.

13. "Tratado del príncipe instruido," BPR, MS II-587, fol. 24v.

14. "Tratado del príncipe instruido," BPR, MS II-587, fol. 29.

15. "Tratado del príncipe instruido," BPR, MS II-587, fol. 37v.

16. Boyden, *Courtier and the King,* chaps. 5–6, presents the denouement of the privanza as a kind of mutual withdrawal by both the king and the favorite, the former to avoid criticism of the favor he had shown his friend and the latter to decrease the enmity directed toward him by Castilian nobles because of his success.

17. Mateo Renzi, "Tratado de el Privado Perfecto," BN, MS 5873, fols. 136–92, dedicated to Olivares.

18. See Bouza Alvarez, "La majestad de Felipe II," 59–61. Bouza provides another anecdote depicting the king joking with Don Diego in Philip II, *Cartas de Felipe II a sus hijas,* 190n146. Moura came closer than others to being a true favorite. Not only did he have the authority to answer consultas by 1591 and to transmit royal orders by 1596 (see Feros, *Kingship and Favoritism,* 43–44), he even massaged the king's feet. Escudero, *Los secretarios de estado,* 1:192.

19. "Tratado del príncipe instruido," BPR, MS II-587, fol. 43; Boyden, *Courtier and the King,* 12–14.

20. Castro Egas, *Eternidad del Rey,* fols. 4–5; Novoa, *Historia de Felipe IV,* 69:6.

21. Cabrera de Córdoba, *Relaciones,* 506, 288, 317.

22. Jerónimo Zapata to Sarmiento de Acuña, 18 September 1598, BPR, MS II-2153, reported that the king had indicated that he would no longer wear children's clothes and "wanted to dress like other men." My thanks to Antonio Feros for this citation.

23. Cabrera de Córdoba, *Relaciones,* 317, 336.

24. Philip III, *Cartas de Felipe III a su hija Ana,* 35–36.

25. Paz y Meliá, "Correspondencia del conde de Lemos con don Francisco de Castro," 350.

26. Gascón de Torquemada, *Gaçeta y nuevas,* 81; Céspedes y Meneses, *Primera parte de la historia,* 58.

27. Cabrera de Córdoba, *Relaciones,* 442; Novoa, *Historia de Felipe III,* 61:131, 141.

28. Novoa, *Historia de Felipe III,* 61:129, 141–53; Conde de la Roca, "Fragmentos históricos de la vida de D. Gaspar de Guzmán," in Valladares de Sotomayor, *Semanario erúdito,* 2:156.

29. "Resolución que tomó el Rey Nuestro Señor cerca de algunas cosas que importavan aesta Monarquía de su Magd. por setiembre de 1618," BN, MS 2348, fol. 403.

30. Novoa, *Historia de Felipe III,* 61:160.

31. The king, Lerma, and the Duke of Uceda all wrote letters dated 28 October 1618 from Velada; Uceda also wrote to Fernando Girón, ambassador in Paris, on 27 October 1618. AGS, Estado K, leg. 1455, nos. 78, 79, 80, 81; Gascón de Torquemada, *Gaçeta y nuevas,* 56.

32. Novoa, *Historia de Felipe III,* 61:244–45, 259.

33. Feros, *Kingship and Favoritism*, 128-29; Cabrera de Córdoba, *Filipe Segundo*, 3:142, 204, 4:92-93; Sepúlveda, *Historia de varios sucesos*, 4, 9-10, 24-25, 27, 34-35, 73, 135, 183.

34. Cabrera de Córdoba, *Relaciones*, 111, 208, 442, 443. Trevor J. Dadson argues that the Spanish crown's policy for Portugal aimed at tying its administration closer to that of Castile. "Duke of Lerma and the Count of Salinas," esp. 15-17.

35. Simón Díaz, *Relaciones breves*, 108.

36. Lavaña, *Viage de la Catholica Real Magestad*. Other accounts include Mouzinho de Quevedo, *Triumpho del monarcha Phillipp 3*, which presents the verses used as part of the entry decorations; and Aguilar y Prado, *Certissima relacion de la entrada*.

37. Novoa, *Historia de Felipe III*, 61:195-242, esp. 204 and 230.

38. Peter Brightwell provides a summary of Zúniga's previous career and a lively sense of his opinions on policy and his activities on the Council of State in three articles in *European Studies Review*: "The Spanish Origins of the Thirty Years War"; "Spain and Bohemia: The Decision to Intervene, 1619"; and "Spain, Bohemia, and the Empire, 1619-1621."

39. Philip IV, "Epílogo breve," viii.

40. "Discursos admirables en razon de la educacion de los príncipes e ynfantes; de cuya practica resultaran felicidados y glorias a la nacion," addressed to VPR, BN, MS 18757, no. 17, fol. 6.

41. *Platica que tuvo su Magestad*.

42. The instruction of Saint Louis, originally written in French, was soon translated into the Latin in which it was more generally known. It was the Latin version that Philip III transcribed as a child (BN, MS 1451). Philip II had a Spanish version prepared for his son, which is most likely the version Philip III passed on to his children. Parker, *Philip II*, 196. On Charles V's reference to this instruction, see Fernández Alvarez, *Politica mundial*, 208.

43. Stradling, *Philip IV and the Government of Spain*, 13.

44. "Apuntamientos de cosas que van sucediendo en Madrid hasta oy Savado 3 de Abril," BN, MS 7377, fol. 294v.

45. "Papel dado el Rey, BN," MS 2352, fols. 411-14.

46. Philip IV, "Epílogo breve," viii.

47. Philip IV, "Epílogo breve," ix, xi.

48. Quevedo Villegas, "Grandes anales de quince dias." Many of these changes are also reported, in a less apocalyptic tone, by Almansa y Mendoza, *Cartas y novedades*.

49. Pérez Martín, *Margarita de Austria*, 198.

50. These changes, mostly in the queen's household, are reported by Almansa y Mendoza, *Cartas y novedades*, 16. He calls Juana Zapata by the name Ana.

51. "Gentilhombres de la boca de su Mag[esta]d q[ue] lo fueron del Rey n[uest]ro Señor que aya gloria y volvieron a jurar en sus mismos assientos," APR, Sección Histórica, leg. 2923; Gascón de Torquemada, *Gaçeta y nuevas*, 91-108. The pattern of service in lesser positions at court is apparent in AGS, CJH.

52. "Relación de la Enfermedad y Muerte del Rey," BN, MS 7377, fols. 298-299v; Almansa y Mendoza, *Cartas y novedades*, 342.

53. "Relación de la suntuosa entrada debaxo de palio en la villa de Madrid, del Rey nuestro Señor don Felipe quarto que Dios guarde," in Simón Díaz, *Relaciones breves*, 124-25, 130-31.

54. Elliott, *Count-Duke of Olivares*, 7-15, 45.

55. Boyden, *Courtier and the King*, 17, 98. On Carlos II and his half-brother, see Kamen, *Spain in the Later Seventeenth Century*, 328–56; Bingham, *Making of a King*, 121–42; and Marvick, *Louis XIII*, 134–38, 220–21, 223.

56. Elliott, *Count-Duke of Olivares*, 30, 112–13; and above in this chapter as well as in chapter 6.

57. Elliott, *Count-Duke of Olivares*, 171.

58. Elliott and Peña, *Memoriales y cartas*, 1:7–11.

59. On the "Gran Memorial," see Elliott, *Count-Duke of Olivares*, 179–202; and Elliott and Peña, *Memoriales y cartas*, 1:37–47, with the document itself reproduced on 49–100. The project of unifying all the Iberian kingdoms of the Spanish monarchy under Castilian law suggests continuity between Lerma's policy toward Portugal, as described by Dadson in "Duke of Lerma and the Count of Salinas," and the regularization policies of Olivares.

60. Schroth, "Private Collection of the Duke of Lerma"; Brown, "Felipe IV, Carlos I."

61. Elliott, *Count-Duke of Olivares*, 171–78, quotation on 178.

62. Elliott, *Count-Duke of Olivares*, 318, 385–86.

63. Carlton, *Charles I*, 36–38, 43; Elliott, *Count-Duke of Olivares*, 171. For a general overview of events during the Prince of Wales's visit, see Gascón de Torquemada, *Gaçeta y nuevas*, 146–78.

64. Elliott, *Count-Duke of Olivares*, 171; Brown, "Felipe IV, Carlos I"; Sharpe, *Personal Rule of Charles I*, chap. 5, esp. 216–18; Andrés, "La despedida de Carlos Estuardo," 116.

65. Peña, *Relación de las fiestas reales*; Gascón de Torquemada, *Gaçeta y nuevas*, 320; Portugal, *Arte de galanteria*.

66. Gabriel de Santiago, "Relación verdadera de las fiestas reales," in Simón Díaz, *Relaciones breves*, 385.

67. Pellicer de Tovar, *Anfiteatro de Felipe el Grande*. The event described, which took place in honor of Baltasar Carlos's birthday on 13 October 1631, was not a typical bullfight but the culmination of a display of exotic animals and conflicts between various of these animals and the bull. The king did not fight the bull, but dispatched the animal with a single perfectly placed gunshot, not, it was noted, losing his serenity or composure while doing so (fol. 7v).

68. Molina Campuzano, "Contribuciones," 83–94.

69. McKendrick, *Theatre in Spain*, 213–18; Phillips, "Divisions and Sonatas of Henry Butler." One play that has been attributed to the king (with some dispute) is *El triunfo del Ave María*, published in *Teatro Español* 13, no. 12. Poems attributed to him are published in *Poetas líricos de los siglos XVI y XVII*, 151–52.

70. Gallego, "Felipe IV, pintor." See also Brown, *Velázquez* and "Felipe IV, Carlos I," 96.

71. Alpers, *Decoration of the Torre de la Parada*.

72. Simón Díaz, *Historia del Colegio Imperial*, 1:47; Fernández Navarrete, *Colección de opúsculos*, 2:101.

73. *Colección de documentos inéditos*, 3:548.

74. Moncada, "Nueva e importante universidad," esp. 233.

75. Motley, *Becoming a French Aristocrat*; Nader, *Mendoza Family in the Spanish Renaissance*, 78. Richard L. Kagan argues that Olivares's dire descriptions of the state of Spanish noble education were based on a misunderstanding of its structure; see Kagan, "Olivares."

76. Elliott, *Count-Duke of Olivares*, 187; Gascón de Torquemada, *Gaçeta y nuevas*, 268. See also Kagan, "Clio and the Crown," esp. 81–82.

77. Santiago Páez, "Las bibliotecas del alcázar," 320, 325–27.

78. Simón Díaz, *Relaciones breves*, 163–78, 367–69, 414–34.

79. Almansa y Mendoza, *Cartas y novedades*, 144. See also Portús Pérez, "El retrato vivos."

80. Gascón de Torquemada, *Gaçeta y nuevas*, 151; "Sucesos del año 1626," BN, MS 2358, fols. 147–48; Simón Díaz, *Relaciones breves*, 438.

81. Guzmán, Memorias, RAH, Colección Salazar y Castro, MS 9/476, fol. 284v. The play *Querer por sólo querer*, by Antonio Hurtado de Mendoza, was produced by order of the queen for the king's birthday in 1623.

82. Guzmán, Memorias, RAH, Colección Salazar y Castro, MS 9/476, fol. 272; order for funds to send jewels, 31 July 1622, AGS, CJH, leg. 586, no. 93; order for funds to transport a "una silla de manos y otros cosas," 21 July 1623, Archivo de la Casa del Infantado, MSS Montesclaros, libro 56, no. 40.

83. Gascón de Torquemada, *Gaçeta y nuevas*, 97–98. If others persuaded Philip not to allow his cousin to enter Madrid, it may reflect concerns that Philiberto was in position to become a favorite, as Juan de Santa María had apparently advocated in 1620.

84. Gardiner, *History of England*, 4:189–90; Novoa, *Historia de Felipe III*, 61:308.

85. Pedro de Robles, "Relación verdadera," in Simón Díaz, *Relaciones breves*, 393–95.

86. Philip IV to María de Agreda, 17 June 1646, in Agreda and Philip IV, *Cartas*, 108:64–65.

87. Galcerán Albanell to the Count-Duke of Olivares, 28 August 1621, BN, MS 1390, fols. 4–5.

88. Wolf, *Louis XIV*, 5.

89. Galcerán Albanell to Philip IV, 10 October 1622, BN, MS 18175, fol. 3; Simón Díaz, *Relaciones breves*, 161–63.

90. Guzmán, Memorias, RAH, Colección Salazar y Castro, MS 9/476, fols. 167–97.

91. Novoa, *Historia de Felipe IV*, 69:16–17, 28, 30–32, 39–41.

92. Novoa, *Historia de Felipe III*, 61:462–66, and *Historia de Felipe IV*, 69:4, 91, 130, 177. Novoa also blamed the Junta de Reformación, perhaps unaware that it had been initially established during the rule of Philip III.

93. Philip IV, "Epilogo breve," xiii–xiv.

94. "Si por castigo de nuestros pecados nos quita dios al Rey," 1627, Archivo de la Casa del Infantado, MSS Montesclaros, libro 130, no. 1. This paper provided for a government under Olivares in the case of the king's death and the education of the child the queen was expecting under the supervision of Olivares and the infantes.

95. Novoa, *Historia de Felipe IV*, 69:57–74.

96. Feros, *Kingship and Favoritism*, 58–60.

CHAPTER 8

1. Erasmus, *Institutio principis christiani*, 258.

2. Feros, *Kingship and Favoritism*, 70, 128.

3. Documents concerning the servants of Empress María are found throughout the records of the Council of Finance during the reign of Philip III. See, e.g., letters of Archduke Albert and Archduchess Infanta Margarita on behalf of their mother's former servants, 1614 and 29 April 1614, AGS, CJH, legs. 529, pt. 15, no. 3, fol. 3, and 530, pt. 14; "Memorial de la casa del Príncipe Filiberto," 1626, APR, Sección Histórica, caja 81; and Philip IV, orders concerning servants of Fernando, 21 July 1643, 8 June and 20 May 1644, APR, Sección Histórica, caja 81.

4. Consulta, 17 July 1633, AGS, Estado, leg. 2652.

5. Kleinman, *Anne of Austria;* Freer, *Elizabeth de Valois;* Carlton, *Charles I.*

6. Wormald, *Mary Queen of Scots.*

7. Barker, *Brother to the Sun King;* Moote, *Louis XIII, the Just,* 190–94.

8. Novoa, *Historia de Felipe IV,* 69:67.

9. Barker, *Brother to the Sun King,* 49–53.

10. Spielman, *Leopold I of Austria,* 35–37.

11. Elizabeth Marvick discusses these common dynamics of the relationship between king and favorite in "Favorites in Early Modern Europe." She characterizes both Lerma and Olivares as "father figure" favorites, whereas I see Lerma as an "older brother" favorite.

12. See Bingham, *Making of a King;* and Wolf, *Louis XIV.*

13. Wormald, *Mary Queen of Scots,* esp. 121–28.

14. Strong, *Henry, Prince of Wales.* Although many books express a sense of the loss to Spain resulting from the death of Baltasar Carlos, few approach the elegiac tone of an odd little book by Clare Benedict, *The Little Lost Prince,* which reflects on the image of the prince in a series of portraits by Velázquez.

15. In *Spain in the Later Seventeenth Century* Henry Kamen lays the groundwork for the study of this reign, although he pointedly focuses on general conditions and alternate sources of power rather than on the king.

16. Gaibrois de Ballesteros, *Las jornadas de María de Hungría.*

17. See, e.g., Rovner, *Lope de Vega on Kingship;* Kennedy, "La estrella de Sevilla"; Crapotta, *Kingship and Tyranny;* and Feros, "Vicedioses, pero Humanos."

Bibliography

MANUSCRIPT SOURCES

Archivo de la Casa de Alba, Palacio de Liria, Madrid
  C-82, no. 37.
  C-58, nos. 154, 160, 168, 177, 178.
  C-90, nos. 10, 54.
Archivo de la Casa del Infantado, Madrid
  MSS Montesclaros, libros 56, 130.
Archivo del Palacio Real, Madrid (APR)
  Capilla Real, caja 65/8.
  Expedientes Personales, cajas 19/31, 24/17, 36/19, 113, 759/6, 1113/32, 1334/7, 7943/6.
  Sección Administrativa, legajos 902, 1049.
  Sección Histórica, legajos 2914, 2923; cajas 56, 76, 81, 113.
Archivo General de Simancas (AGS)
  Casas y Sitios Reales (CySR), legajo 247.
  Casas y Sitios Reales, Obras y Bosques, legajo 302.
  Consejo y Juntas de Hacienda (CJH), legajos 432, 445, 458, 466, 467, 468, 473, 475,
    481, 482, 483, 485, 489, 492, 512, 522, 529, 530, 531, 554, 555, 556, 559, 564, 586, 594.
  Contaduria Mayor de Cuentas (CMC), Época 3, legajos 3068, 21761-1.
  Dirección General del Tesoro (Tesoro), Inventario 24, legajos 577, 578, 580c.
  Estado, legajos 198, 251, 265, 705, 709, 1099, 1287, 1288, 1289, 1939, 2324, 2327, 2328,
    2645, 2649, 2652, 2753, 2754, 2756, 2960, 2961, 2993.
  Estado K, legajos 1429, 1430, 1435, 1455, 1456, 1461, 1464, 1465, 1467, 1468, 1469, 1471,
    1473, 1475, 1617, 1636.
  Patronato Eclesiástico, legajos 103, 105, 106, 107, 108, 109.
  Patronato Real, legajo 31-20.
  Quitaciones de la Corte, legajo 40.
Archivo Histórico Nacional (AHN)
  Cámara de Castilla, legajos 4418, 4420, 4425.
Biblioteca del Monasterio Real de San Lorenzo de El Escorial
  MSS J.I.6, I.III.31, I.III.30.
Biblioteca del Palacio Real, Madrid (BPR)
  MSS II-587, II-836, II-2096, II-2153.
Biblioteca Nacional, Madrid (BN)
  MSS 915, 1007, 1390, 1451, 2347, 2348, 2352, 2354, 2355, 2358, 2361, 2363, 2577, 2751,

5758, 5788, 5873, 5994, 6043, 7377, 7444, 8719, 9251, 10436, 10623, 10818, 10857, 10994,
11499, 17495, 17772, 17858, 18175, 18191, 18646, 18656, 18757.
Biblioteca Zabálburu, Madrid
    Carpeta 85, nos. 27–71.
British Library, London (BL)
    Add. MSS 14,004, 24,909.
    Egerton MS 2081, fols. 269–73.
Hispanic Society of America, New York
    MS HC 411/209.
Real Academia de la Historia, Madrid (RAH)
    Colección Salazar y Castro, MSS 9/475, 9/476, 9/477.

PRINTED PRIMARY SOURCES

Aedo y Gallart, Diego. *Viage del Infante Cardenal D. Fernando de Austria.* Antwerp, 1635.
Agreda, María de, and Philip IV. *Cartas de Sor María de Jesús de Agreda y de Felipe IV.*
    Edited by Carlos Seco Serrano. Vols. 108 and 109 of *Biblioteca de autores españoles.*
    Madrid: Atlas, 1958.
Aguilar y Prado, Jacinto de. *Certissima relacion de la entrada que hizo su Magd y sus
    altezas en Lisboa.* Lisbon, 1619.
Almansa y Mendoza, Andrés de. *Cartas y novedades de esta corte y avisos recibidos (1621–1626).*
    Vol. 17 of *Colección de libros españoles raros ó curiosos.* Madrid: Miguel Ginesta, 1886.
———. *Relacion de la partida del serenissimo príncipe de Vvalia que fue a nueve de
    setiembre deste año de 1623.* Madrid: Diego Flamenco, 1623.
Altadonna, Giovanna. "Cartas de Felipe II a Carlos Manuel II, Duque de Saboya
    (1583–1596)." *Cuadernos de Investigación Histórica* 9 (1986): 137–90.
Antonio de Jesús María. *D. Baltasar de Moscoso i Sandoval.* Madrid: Bernardo de Villa-
    Diego, 1680.
Arcos, Francisco de. *Vida del venerable y reverendissimo Padre Maestro Fr. Simón de
    Rojas.* 2 vols. Madrid, 1670–78.
Arriba, Francisco de. *Operis conciliatorii gratiae et liberi arbitrii.* Paris, 1622.
*Ave María: Interrogatorio por donde se han de examinar los testigos que huvieron de
    dezir y deponer, a cerca de la santidad, excelencia de vida, virtudes, fama, y milagros
    que le Divina Majestad ha obrado, y obra cada dia por la intercession del Venerable
    Siervo de Dios el Reverendissimo Padre Maestro Fray Simón de Rojas.* N.p., n.d. BN
    Madrid, Impresos 3/14126.
Brantôme, Pierre de Bourdeille, seigneur de. *Vies des dames illustres.* Vol. 5 of *Oeuvres
    complètes du seigneur de Brantôme.* Paris: Foucault, 1823.
Cabrera de Córdoba, Luis. *De historia, para entenderla y escribirla.* 1611. Edited by
    Santiago Montero Diaz. Madrid: Instituto de Estudios Politicos, 1948.
———. *Filipe Segundo, rey de España.* 4 vols. Madrid: Aribau, 1876–77.

————. *Relaciones de las cosas sucedidas en la corte de España, desde 1599 hasta 1614.* Madrid: J. Martín Alegría, 1857.

Cartas de algunos padres de la Compañía de Jesús sobre los sucesos de la monarquía entre los años de 1634 y 1648. 7 vols. Madrid: Imprenta Nacional, 1861–65.

Castejón y Fonseca, Diego de. *Primacia de la Santa Iglesia de Toledo.* 2 vols. Madrid, 1645.

Castro Egas, Ana de. *Eternidad del Rey Don Felipe Tercero Nuestro Señor, el Piadoso.* Madrid: Viuda de Alonso Martín, 1629.

Céspedes y Meneses, Gonzalo de. *Primera parte de la historia de D. Felipe el IIII: Rey de las Españas.* Lisbon: Pedro Craesbeeck, 1631.

Colección de documentos inéditos para la historia de España. 113 vols. Madrid: Miguel Ginesta, 1842–95.

Contareni, Simon. "Relación que hizo á la república de Venecia Simón Contareni, 1605." In Cabrera de Córdoba, *Relaciones de las cosas sucedidas.*

Córdoba, Martín de. *Jardín de nobles doncellas.* Edited by Félix García. Madrid: Juan de Espinosa, 1953.

Elliott, John H., and José F. de la Peña, eds. *Memoriales y cartas del Conde Duque de Olivares.* 2 vols. Madrid: Ediciones Alfaguara, 1978.

Erasmus, Desiderius. *Institutio principis christiani.* Vol. 27 of *The Collected Works of Erasmus,* edited by A. H. T. Levi, translated by Neil M. Chesire and Michael J. Heath. Toronto: University of Toronto Press, 1986.

Espinosa Rodríguez, José, ed. *Fray Antonio de Sotomayor y su correspondencia con Felipe IV.* Vigo, 1944.

Fernández Navarrete, Martín. *Colección de opúsculos del Exmo. Sr. D. Martín Fernández Navarrete.* Edited by Eustaquio Fernández Navarrete and Francisco Fernández Navarrete. 2 vols. Madrid, 1848.

Firrufino, Julio Cesar. *El perfeto artillero, theorica y practica.* Madrid, 1642.

————. *Platica manual y breve compendio de artilleria.* Madrid, 1626.

Florencia, Gerónimo de. *Marial que contiene varios sermones de todos las fiestas de Nra Señora predicados a las Magestades de Philippo III. y Philippo IIII. Nuestro Señor.* Madrid, 1624.

————. *Sermón en las honras de la serenissima Reyna Doña Margarita, 19 diciembre 1611.* Madrid: Luis Sánchez, 1612.

Forcex, Francisco. *Fiesta eclesiastica que en el Seminario Ingles de Madrid mandó hazer el dia de nuestra Señora de Agosto desde año de 1623 su alteza de la serenissima Infanta María de Austria.* Seville: Francisco de Lyra, 1623.

Francisco de Jesús. *El hecho de los tratados del matrimonio pretendido por el príncipe de Gales con la serenissima infante de España María.* 1624. Translated and edited by S. R. Gardiner. London, 1869.

Furió Ceriol, Fadrique. *El consejo y consejeros del príncipe y otras obras.* Edited by Diego Sevilla Andrés. Valencia: Institucion Alfonso el Magnanimo, 1952.

Gascón de Torquemada, Gerónimo. *Gaçeta y nuevas de la corte de España.* Edited

by Alfonso de Ceballos-Escalera y Gila. Madrid: Real Academia Matritense de
Heráldica y Genealogía, 1991.

Gonçalez de Salcedo y Butron, Pedro. *Panegyrico, o oracion laudatoria, de los hechos, y vi-*
toriosos progressos de su alteza el Señor Infante Don Fernando de Austria. Madrid, 1636.

González Davila, Gil. *Teatro de la grandezas de la villa de Madrid.* Madrid, 1623.

González Palencia, Angel. *Noticias de Madrid, 1621–1627.* Madrid: Ayuntamiento, 1942.

Guevara, Pedro de. *Arte general y breve, en dos instrumentos, para todas las sciencias:*
Recopilada del arte magna y arbor scientiae, del Doctor Raimundo Lulio. Madrid, 1584.

———. *Nueva y sutil invención, en seys instrumentos, intitulado juego y exercicio de*
letras de las serenissimas Infantas Doña Ysabel y Doña Catalina. Madrid, 1581.

Guzmán, Diego de. *El Santo Rey Fernando III.* 1627. Facsimile ed. Seville: Caja de
Ahorros provincial de San Fernando, n.d.

———. *Reyna católica: Vida y muerte de Doña Margarita de Austria.* Madrid, 1617.

Guzmán y Santoyo, Christoval de. *Sermón que predicó el doctor Christoval de Guzmán*
y Santoyo, canónigo de la Santa Iglesia de Salamanca, en las honras que la dicha
ciudad hizo á la muy católica Magestad de Filipo III: Jueves quinze de Mayo deste
año de MDCXXI. Salamanca, 1621.

Howell, James. *Epistolae-Ho-Elianae: Familiar Letters.* 2nd ed. 3 vols. London, 1650.

Hurtado de Mendoza, Antonio. *Discursos de Don Antonio de Mendoza, secretario de*
cámara de Don Felipe IV. Edited by Fernando Quiñones de Leon, Marqués de
Alcedo. Madrid: José Blas, 1911.

Imago militiae auspiciis Ambrosii Spinolae / Imagen de la milicia y de un ejército firme
con el favor del marqués Spinola. Brussels, 1614.

Isabel Clara Eugenia. *Correspondencia de la Infanta Archiduquesa Doña Isabel Clara*
Eugenia. Edited by Antonio Rodríguez Villa. Madrid: Fortanet, 1906.

Jornada del Rey nuestro señor Don Felipe, tercero de este nombre, al reino de Portugal a
coronar al Príncipe Don Felipe, su hijo. Seville: Geronymo de Contreras, 1619.

La Porte, Pierre de. *Mémoires.* Edited by A. Petitot et L.-J.-N. de Monmerqué. Vol. 59 of
Collection des mémoires relatifs á l'histoire de France. 2nd ser. Paris: Foucault, 1827.

Lavaña, Juan Bautista. *Viage de la Catholica Real Magestad del Rei D. Filipe III N. S. al*
reino de Portugal. Madrid: Thomas Iunti, 1622.

Lhermite, Jehan. *Le passetemps.* Edited by C. Ruelens. Vols. 17 and 20 of *Antwerpsche*
Bibliophilen. Antwerp: Buschmann, 1890 and 1896.

March, José María, ed. *Niñez y juventud de Felipe Segundo: Documentos inéditos.* 2 vols.
Madrid, 1941.

Mendez Silva, Rodrigo. *Breve, curiosa, y ajustada noticia, de los ayos, y maestros que*
hasta oy han tenido los príncipes, infantes, y otras personas reales de Castilla. Madrid: Viuda del lic. Iuan Martin del Barrio, 1654.

Moncada, Sancho de. "Nueva e importante universidad en la corte de España."

Discourse 8 of *Restauración política de España*, edited by J. Vilar Berrogain. N.p.: Instituto de Estudios Fiscales, 1974.

Montemayor, Juan de. *Parecer que dió en la junta, el Padre Juan Montemayor, jesuita, acerca del casamiento de sus altezas*. Madrid, 1623.

Motteville, Françoise Bertaut de. *Mémoires pour servir á l'histoire d'Anne d'Austriche*. Edited by. C. B. Petitot. Vols. 36–40 of *Collection des mémoires relatifs á l'histoire de France*. 2nd ser. Paris: Foucault, 1824.

Mouzinho de Quevedo, Vasco. *Triumpho del monarcha Phillipp 3 las felicissima entrada de Lisboa*. 1619.

Muñoz, Antonio. *Tres romances en que se declara el sentimento general que ha causado la muerte de sereníssmo Infante D. Carlos*. 1632.

Muñoz, Luis. *Vida y virtudes de la venerable M. Mariana de S. Joseph*. Madrid: Imprenta Real, 1645.

Novoa, Matías de. *Historia de Felipe III, rey de España*. Vols. 60 and 61 of *Colección de documentos inéditos para la historia de España*. Madrid: Miguel Ginesta, 1875.

———. *Historia de Felipe IV, rey de España*. Vols. 69, 77, 80, and 86 of *Colección de documentos inéditos para la historia de España*. Madrid: Miguel Ginesta, 1878–86.

Ortiz, Alonso. *Diálogo sobre la educación del Príncipe Don Juan, hijo de los Reyes Católicos*. Translated and edited by Giovanni Maria Bertini. Madrid: José Porrúa Turanzas, 1983.

Palafox, Juan de. "Diaro de la jornada que hizo la seateríssima señora reina de Hungría." In *España y Europea en el siglo XVII*, edited by Quintín Aldea Vaquero. Madrid, 1986.

Palma, Juan de. *Vida de la serenissima Infanta Sor Margarita de la Cruz*. Madrid: Imprenta Real, 1636.

Passano de Haro, Andres. *Exemplar eterno de prelados impresso en el Corazon y executado en la vida y acciones del Don Baltasar de Moscoso y Sandoval*. Toledo: Francisco Calvo, 1670.

Paz y Meliá, Antonio, ed. "Correspondencia del conde de Lemos con Don Francisco de Castro, su hermano, y con el príncipe de Esquilache (1613–1620)." *Bulletin Hispanique* 5 (1903): 249–58, 349–58.

Pellicer de Tovar, Joseph. *Anfiteatro de Felipe el Grande*. 1631. Facsimile with a foreword by Antonio Pérez Gómez. Cieza: Ediciones Conmemorativas, 1974.

Peña, Juan Antonio de la. *Discurso de la jornada que hizo a los reynos de España el illustríssimo y reverendíssimo señor Don Francisco Barberino Cardenal . . . con relación . . . entrada que hizo en esta corte; bautismo de la señora infante; y fiestas de Corpus*. Madrid: Luis Sánchez, 1626.

———. *Relación de las fiestas reales de toros y cañas, que le Magestad Católica de el rey nuestro señor jugó en la villa de Madrid en 21 de Agosto*. Madrid: Juan Gonçalez, 1623.

Pérez Minguez, Fidel. "La Condesa de Castellar, fundadora del convento de las Carboneras." *Revista de la Biblioteca, Archivo, y Museo de Madrid* 8, no. 29 (1931): 41–52, no. 30 (1931): 152–70, no. 31 (1931): 253–73, no. 32 (1931): 392–419, and 9, no. 34 (1932): 150–80, no. 36 (1932): 409–27.

Pérez Villanueva, Joaquín, ed. *Felipe IV y Luisa Enriquez Manrique de Lara, Condesa de Paredes de Nava: Un epistolario inédito.* Salamanca: Caja de Ahorros, 1986.

Philip II. *Cartas de Felipe II a sus hijas.* Edited by Fernando J. Bouza Alvarez. Madrid: Turner, 1988.

Philip III. "Cartas autógrafas de Felipe III." Edited by Antonio Rodríguez Villa. *Revista de Archivos, Bibliotecas y Museos* 1 (1897): 9–18.

——. *Cartas de Felipe III a su hija Ana, reina de Francia (1616–1618).* Edited by Ricardo Martorell Téllez-Girón. Madrid: Imprenta Helénica, 1929.

Philip IV. "Epílogo breve." In *La historia de Italia,* by Francesco Guicciardini, translated by Philip IV, vol. 1. Madrid: Viuda de Hernando, 1889.

——. *Testamento de Felipe IV.* Introduction by Antonio Dominguez Ortiz. Madrid: Editora Nacional, 1982.

Pinheiro da Veiga, Tomé. *Fastiginia: Vida cotidiana en la corte de Valladolid.* Translated by Narciso Alonso Cortés. Valladolid: Ambito, 1989.

Platica que tuvo su Magestad con el Padre Florencia, y sus hijos, y otras personas de su corte a la hora de su muerte. Valladolid, 1621.

Portugal, Francisco de. *Arte de galanteria.* Lisbon: Iuan de la Costa, 1670.

Quevedo Villegas, Francisco de. "Grandes anales de quince dias." In *Obras de Quevedo,* vol. 23 of *Biblioteca de autores españoles,* 193–220. Madrid: Rivadeneyra, 1859.

Relación de los casamientos de la Reina Doña Margarita de Austria e Infanta Doña Isabel Clara Eugenia y recibimientos que se hicieron en Ferrara y de todo lo demás que allí pasó: Enviada por el duque de Sesa, embajador de Roma. Granada, 1599.

Rivadeneira, Pedro de. *Tratado de la religión y virtudes que debe tener el príncipe cristiano.* In *Obras de Rivadeneira.* Vol. 60 of *Biblioteca de autores españoles.* Madrid: Rivadeneyra, 1868.

Rojas, Simón de. *Tratado de la oración y sus grandezas.* Buenos Aires: Cursos de Cultura Católica, 1939.

Ruiz de Alarcón y Mendoza, Juan. *Elogio descriptivo de las fiestas. . . .* Madrid: Viuda de Alonso Martín, n.d.

Sánchez Cantón, F. J., ed. "Noventa y siete retratos de la familia de Felipe III por Bartolomé González." Transcribed by J. Moreno Villa, with preliminary notes by Sánchez Cantón. *Archivo Español de Arte y Arqueolgía* 13 (1937): 127–57.

Santa María, Juan de. *Christian Policie, or The Christian Commonwealth.* Translated by Edward Blount. London: Thomas Harper, 1632.

——. *Chronica de la provincia de San Ioseph de los decalços de la orden de los menores de nuestro seriphico padre S. Francisco.* 2 vols. Madrid, 1615–18.

Sepúlveda, Jerónimo de. *Historia de varios sucesos y de las cosas notables que han acaecido en España y otras naciones desde el año de 1584 hasta el de 1603.* Vol. 4 of *Documentos para la história del monasterio de San Lorenzo el Real de El Escorial,* edited by Julián Zarco Cuevas. Madrid: Imprenta Helénica, 1924.

Simón Díaz, José. "La estancia del Cardenal Legado Francesco Barberini en Madrid el año 1626." *Anales del Instituto de Estudios Madrileños* 17 (1966): 159–213.

———, ed. *Relaciones breves de actos públicos celebrados en Madrid de 1541 a 1650.* Madrid: Instituto de Estudios Madrileños, 1982.

Soto, Juan de. *Margaritas preciosas de la Iglesia.* Alcalá: Andres Sánchez, 1617.

Uhagón, Francisco R. de, ed. *Relaciones historicas de los siglos XVI y XVII.* Madrid: Sociedad de Bibliófilos Españoles, 1896.

Un caballero de la corte de Madrid escrive a un religioso dominico sobre la novedad que se rezcla de que el Rey nuesto Señor Don Phelipe V no confiesse con religiosos de dicha religion. Madrid, 1700.

Valladares de Sotomayor, Antonio, ed. *Semanario erudito.* 34 vols. Madrid: Blas Roman, 1787–91.

Vega y Toraya, Francisco de la. *Vida del venerable siervo de Dios y finísimo capellán de María Santíssima Padre Maestro Fray Simón de Rojas.* Madrid: Imprenta Real, 1715.

Vélez de Guevara, Luys. *Elogio del iuramento del serenissimo Príncipe Don Felipe Domingo.* Madrid, 1608.

Vera y Zúñiga, Juan Antonio de. *Epitome de la vida i hechos del Invicto Emperador Carlos V.* Madrid, 1622.

Verdadara relacion, en la qual se da cuenta del despedimiento del rey nuestro Señor y su hija la reyna de Francia, y de las entregas que se hizieron en Yrum, a 9 de noviembre deste año 1615. Valencia: Felipe Mey, 1615.

Vives, Juan Luis. *De institutione feminae christianae, liber primus.* Vol. 6 of *Selected Works of J. L. Vives,* edited by C. Fantazzi and C. Matheeussen, translated by C. Fantazzi. Leiden: Brill, 1996.

Vox Coeli, or Newes from Heaven. N.p., 1624.

SECONDARY SOURCES

Aldea Vaquero, Quintín. *El Cardenal Infante Don Fernando o la formación de un príncipe de España.* Madrid: Real Academia de la Historia, 1997.

Aldea Vaquero, Quintín, Tomás Marín Martínez, and José Vives Gatell, eds. *Diccionario de historia eclesiástica de España.* 4 vols. Madrid: CSIC, 1972–75.

———. *Diccionario de historia eclesiástica de España.* Supplement. Madrid: CSIC, 1987.

Alenda y Mira, Jenaro, ed. *Relaciones de solemnidades y fiestas públicas de España.* Madrid: Sucesores de Rivedeneyra, 1903.

Allen, Paul C. *Philip III and the Pax Hispanica, 1598–1621: The Failure of Grand Strategy.* New Haven, CT: Yale University Press, 2000.

Alpers, Svetlana. *Decoration of the Torre de la Parada.* Pt. 9 of *Corpus Rubenianum Ludwig Burchard.* Oxford: Harvey Miller, 1982.

Amezúa y Mayo, Agustín G. de. "El hermano mayor: Príncipe Don Carlos." *Boletín de la Real Academia de la Historia* 114 (1944): 33–67.

———. *Isabel de Valois.* 3 vols. Madrid: Ministerio de Asuntos Exteriores, 1949.

Andrés, Gregorio de. "La despedida de Carlos Estuardo, príncipe de Gales, en el Escorial (1623) y la columna trofeo que se levanto para perpetua memoria." *Anales del Instituto de Estudios Madrileños* 10 (1974): 113–32.

Aram, Bethany. *La reina Juana: Gobierno, piedad y dinastía.* Translated by Susana Jákfalvi. Madrid: Marcial Pons, 2001.

Ariès, Philippe. *Centuries of Childhood: A Social History of Family Life.* Translated by Robert Baldick. New York: Vintage Books, 1962.

Atarés, Conde de. "Consejos de Felipe II a Felipe III." *Boletín de la Real Academia de la Historia* 141 (1957): 659–719.

———. "Consejos instructivos de Felipe II a su hijo Felipe III." *Boletín de la Real Academia de la Historia* 139 (1956): 159–93.

Barker, Nancy Nichols. *Brother to the Sun King: Philippe, Duke of Orléans.* Baltimore: Johns Hopkins University Press, 1989.

Benedict, Clare. *The Little Lost Prince.* Edinburgh: Andrew Elliot, n.d.

Bingham, Caroline. *The Making of a King: The Early Years of James VI and I.* Garden City, NY: Doubleday, 1969.

Bireley, Robert. *The Counter-Reformation Prince: Anti-Machiavellianism or Catholic Statecraft in Early Modern Europe.* Chapel Hill: University of North Carolina Press, 1990.

———. *Religion and Politics in the Age of the Counterreformation.* Chapel Hill: University of North Carolina Press, 1981.

Bouza Alvarez, Fernando J. "Corte es decepción: Don Juan de Silva, Conde de Portalegre." In Martínez Millán, *La corte de Felipe II.*

———. "La majestad de Felipe II: Construcción del mito real." In Martínez Millán, *La corte de Felipe II.*

———. *Locos, enanos y hombres de placer en la corte de los Austrias.* Madrid: Temas de Hoy, 1991.

Bowle, John. *Charles I, a Biography.* Boston: Little, Brown, 1975.

Boyden, James M. *The Courtier and the King: Ruy Gómez de Silva, Philip II, and the Court of Spain.* Berkeley and Los Angeles: University of California Press, 1995.

Brandi, Karl. *The Emperor Charles V: The Growth and Destiny of a Man and of a World-Empire.* Translated by C. V. Wedgwood. London: Jonathan Cape, 1963.

Brightwell, Peter. "Spain and Bohemia: The Decision to Intervene, 1619." *European Studies Review* 12 (1982): 117–41.

———. "Spain, Bohemia, and the Empire, 1619–1621." *European Studies Review* 12 (1982): 371–99.

———. "The Spanish Origins of the Thirty Years War." *European Studies Review* 9 (1979): 409–31.

Brooks, Mary Elizabeth. *A King for Portugal: The Madrigal Conspiracy, 1594–95.* Madison: University of Wisconsin Press, 1964.

Brown, Jonathan. "Felipe IV, Carlos I, y la cultura del coleccionismo en dos cortes del siglo diecisiete." In *La España del Conde-Duque de Olivares,* edited by John H. Elliott and Ángel García Sanz, 83–97. Valladolid: Universidad de Valladolid, 1990.

———. *Velázquez: Painter and Courtier.* New Haven, CT: Yale University Press, 1986.

Caeiro, Francisco. *O Archiduque Alberto de Austria, vice-rei e inquisidor-mor de Portugal.* Lisbon, 1961.

Camón Aznar, José. *Summa artis: Historia general del arte.* Vol. 25, *La pintura española del siglo XVII.* Madrid: Espasa Calpe, 1977.

Cánovas del Castillo, Antonio. *Estudios del reinado de Felipe IV.* 2 vols. Madrid, 1888–89.

Carlton, Charles. *Charles I: The Personal Monarch.* London: Routledge & Kegan Paul, 1983.

Carrocera, Buenaventura de. "El Padre Diego de Quiroga, diplomático y confesor de reyes (1574–1649)." *Estudios Franciscanos* 150 (1949): 71–100.

Castro, Manuel de. "Confesores franciscanos en la corte de Carlos I." *Archivo Ibero-Americano* 35 (1975): 253–312.

———. "Confesores franciscanos en la corte de los Reyes Católicos." *Archivo Ibero-Americano* 34 (1974): 55–125.

Claremont, Francesca. *Catherine of Aragon.* London: Robert Hale, 1939.

Cogswell, Thomas. *The Blessed Revolution: English Politics and the Coming of War, 1621–1624.* Cambridge: Cambridge University Press, 1989.

Cortesão, Armando. *Cartografia e cartógrafos portugueses dos séculos XV e XVI.* 2 vols. Lisbon: Seara Nova, 1935.

Cortesão, Armando, and Avelino Teixeira da Mota. *Portugaliae monumenta cartographica.* 5 vols. Lisbon, 1960.

Cortés Echánove, Luis. *Nacimiento y crianza de personas reales en la corte de España, 1566–1886.* Madrid: CSIC, 1958.

Crapotta, James. *Kingship and Tyranny in the Theater of Guillen de Castro.* London: Tamesis Books, 1984.

Dadson, Trevor J. "The Duke of Lerma and the Count of Salinas: Politics and Friendship in Early Seventeenth-Century Spain." *European History Quarterly* 25 (1995): 5–38.

Dulong, Claude. *Anne d'Autriche, mère de Louis XIV.* Paris: Hachette, 1980.

Echevarría Bacigalupe, Miguel Angel. *Alberto Struzzi, un precursor barroco del capitalismo liberal.* Leuven, Belgium: Leuven University Press, 1995.

Elliott, John H. *The Count-Duke of Olivares: The Statesman in an Age of Decline.* New Haven, CT: Yale University Press, 1986.

———. "Philip IV of Spain: Prisoner of Ceremony." In *The Courts of Europe: Politics, Patronage, and Royalty, 1400–1800,* edited by A. G. Dickens. London: Thames & Hudson, 1977.

Escudero, José Antonio. *Los secretarios de estado y del despacho.* 4 vols. Madrid, 1976.

Ettinghausen, Henry. "The News in Spain: *Relaciones de Sucesos* in the Reigns of Philip III and Philip IV." *European History Quarterly* 14 (1984): 1–20.

Fernández Alvarez, Manuel. *Politica mundial de Carlos V y Felipe II.* Madrid: CSIC, 1966.

Fernández Martín, L. "La Marquesa del Valle." *Hispania* 39 (1980): 550–638.

Fernández Montaña, José. *Nueva luz y juicio verdadero sobre Felipe II.* Madrid: Maroto é hijos, 1882.

Feros, Antonio. *Kingship and Favoritism in the Spain of Philip III, 1598–1621.* Cambridge: Cambridge University Press, 2000.

———. "'Vicedioses, pero humanos': El drama del rey." *Cuadernos de Historia Moderna,* no. 14 (1993): 103–31.

Ferrer Valls, Teresa. *La práctica escénica cortesana: De la época del emperador a la de Felipe III.* London: Tamesis Books, 1991.

———. *Nobleza y espectaculo teatral (1535–1622): Estudio y documentos.* Valencia: Universitat de Valencia, 1993.

Fichtner, Paula Sutter. *Emperor Maximilian II.* New Haven, CT: Yale University Press, 2001.

———. *Ferdinand I of Austria: The Politics of Dynasticism in the Age of the Reformation.* Boulder, CO: East European Monographs, 1982.

———. "Habsburg Household or Habsburg Government? A Sixteenth-Century Administrative Dilemma." *Austrian History Yearbook* 26 (1995): 45–60.

———. "Of Christian Virtue and a Practicing Prince: Emperor Ferdinand I and His Son Maximilian." *Catholic History Review* 61 (1975): 409–16.

Franzl, Johann. *Ferdinand II: Kaiser im Zwiespalt der Zeit.* Graz, Austria: Verlag Styria, 1978.

Freer, Martha Walker. *Elizabeth de Valois, Queen of Spain, and the Court of Philip II.* 2 vols. London: Hurst & Blackett, 1857.

———. *The Married Life of Anne of Austria, Queen of France, Mother of Louis XIV.* 2 vols. London: Tinsley Brothers, 1865.

Gachard, L. P. *Don Carlos et Philippe II.* Brussels, 1863.

Gaibrois de Ballesteros, Mercedes. *Las jornadas de María de Hungría (1606–1646).* Madrid: Centro de Intercambio Intelectual Germano-Español, 1926.

Galino Carrillo, María Angeles. *Los tratados sobre educación de príncipes (siglos XVI y XVII).* Madrid: CSIC, 1948.

Gallego, Julián. "Felipe IV, pintor." In *Estudios en literatura y las bellas artes dedicados al Professor Emilo Orozco Díaz*, by A. Gallego-Morell et al., 1:533–40. Granada: University of Granada, 1979.

García Figar, Antonio. "Fray Juan Bautista Maino, pintor español." *Goya* 25 (1958): 6–12.

García García, Bernardo José. "Fray Luis de Aliaga y la conciencia del rey." In *I religiosi a corte: Teologia, politica e diplomazia in Antico Regime*, edited by Flavio Rurale. Rome: Bulzoni Editore, 1998.

———. *La Pax Hispanica: Política exterior del duque de Lerma*. Leuven, Belgium: Leuven University Press, 1996.

Gardiner, Samuel R. *History of England from the Accession of James I to the Outbreak of the Civil War, 1603–1642*. 10 vols. 1883–84. Reprint, New York: AMS Press, 1965.

Hamann, Brigitte. *Die Habsburger: Ein biographisches Lexikon*. Vienna: Ueberreuter, 1988.

Harris, Enriqueta. "Aportaciones para el studio de Juan Bautista Maino." *Revista Española de Arte* 4 (1935): 333–39.

Harris, Enriqueta, and J. H. Elliott. "Velázquez and the Queen of Hungary." *Burlington Magazine* 118 (1976): 24–26.

Herrero Mediavilla, Victor, and L. Rosa Aguayo Nayle, eds. *Archivo biográfico de España, Portugal, e Iberoamérica*. New York: K. G. Saur, 1990. Microfiche.

Hofmann, Christina. *Das spanische Hofzeremoniell von 1500–1700*. Frankfurt: Peter Lang, 1985.

Kagan, Richard L. "Clio and the Crown: Writing History in Habsburg Spain." In *Spain, Europe and the Atlantic World: Essays in Honour of John H. Elliott*, edited by Richard Kagan and Geoffrey Parker, 73–99. Cambridge: Cambridge University Press, 1995.

———. "Olivares y la educación de la nobleza española." In *La España del Conde-Duque de Olivares*, edited by John H. Elliott and Ángel García Sanz. Valladolid: University of Valladolid, 1990.

Kamen, Henry. *Inquisition and Society in Spain in the Sixteenth and Seventeenth Centuries*. Bloomington: Indiana University Press, 1985.

———. *Spain in the Later Seventeenth Century, 1665–1700*. New York: Longman, 1980.

Kennedy, Ruth Lee. "La estrella de Sevilla." *Revista de Archivos, Bibliotecas, y Museos* 78 (1975).

Kleinman, Ruth. *Anne of Austria: Queen of France*. Columbus: Ohio State University Press, 1985.

Kusche, Maria. *Juan Pantoja de la Cruz*. Madrid: Editorial Castalia, 1964.

Liss, Peggy. *Isabel the Queen: Life and Times*. New York: Oxford University Press, 1992.

Lockyer, Roger. *Buckingham: The Life and Political Career of George Villiers*. London: Longman, 1981.

Lumsden-Kouvel, Audrey. "Schism in England, Representations in Spain: Interpretations of Henry VIII's Divorce in Spanish History and Drama." Paper presented at the annual meeting of the Society for Spanish and Portuguese Historical Studies, Chicago, 7–10 April 1994.

Marañón, Gregorio. *El Conde-Duque de Olivares: La pasión de mandar.* Rev. ed. Madrid: Espasa Calpe, 1945.

March, José María. "El aya del Rey D. Felipe II y del Príncipe D. Carlos, Doña Leonor Mascareñas." *Boletín de la Sociedad Española de Escursiones* 46 (1942): 201–19.

Martínez Hernández, Santiago. "Pedagogía en palacio: El Marqués de Velada y la educación del Príncipe Felipe (III), 1587–1598." *Reales Sitios* 36, no. 3 (1999): 34–49.

Martínez Millán, José. "Familia real y grupos políticos: La Princesa Doña Juana de Austria (1535–1573)." In Martínez Millán, *La corte de Felipe II.*

———, ed. *La corte de Felipe II.* Madrid: Alianza, 1994.

Marvick, Elizabeth Wirth. "Favorites in Early Modern Europe: A Recurring Psycho-Political Role." *Journal of Psychohistory* 10 (1983): 463–89.

———. *Louis XIII: The Making of a King.* New Haven, CT: Yale University Press, 1986.

Matilla Tascon, Antonio. *Catalogo de documentos notariales de nobles.* Madrid: CSIC, 1987.

Mattingly, Garrett. *Catherine of Aragon.* Boston: Little, Brown, 1941.

McKendrick, Malveena. *Theatre in Spain, 1490–1700.* Cambridge: Cambridge University Press, 1989.

Molina Campuzano, Miguel. "Contribuciones a la reconstitución de imagenes del pasado material madrileño." *Revista de la Biblioteca, Archivo, y Museo del Ayuntamiento de Madrid,* 3rd ser., 1 (1977): 69–110.

Montague, F. C. *The History of England from the Accession of James I to the Restoration.* London: Longmans, Green, 1907.

Moote, A. Lloyd. *Louis XIII, the Just.* Berkeley and Los Angeles: University of California Press, 1989.

Moreno Villa, José. *Locos, enanos, negros, y niños palaciegos: Gente de placer que tuvieron los Austrias en la corte española desde 1563 a 1700.* Mexico City: Casa de España, 1939.

Motley, Mark. *Becoming a French Aristocrat: The Education of the Court Nobility, 1580–1715.* Princeton, NJ: Princeton University Press, 1990.

Nader, Helen. *The Mendoza Family in the Spanish Renaissance, 1350–1550.* New Brunswick, NJ: Rutgers University Press, 1979.

Nalle, Sara T. "Absolutism and Absolution: The Royal Confessor in the Habsburg Monarchy." Paper presented at the Simposio Hispano-Luso-Norteamericano de Historia, Madrid, June 1985.

O'Connell, David. *The Teachings of Saint Louis: A Critical Text.* Chapel Hill: University of North Carolina Press, 1972.

O'Malley, John W. *The First Jesuits*. Cambridge, MA: Harvard University Press, 1993.

Parker, Geoffrey. *Philip II*. 3rd ed. Chicago: Open Court, 1995.

Pérez Bustamante, Ciriaco. *La España de Felipe III*. Vol. 24 of *Historia de España*, edited by Ramón Menéndez Pidal. Madrid: Espasa Calpe, 1979.

———. "Los cardenalatos del Duque de Lerma y del Infante Don Fernando de Austria." *Boletín de la Universidad de Santiago* 7 (1935).

Pérez Martín, María Jesús. *Margarita de Austria, reina de España*. Madrid: Espasa Calpe, 1961.

Phillips, E. VanVorst. "The Divisions and Sonatas of Henry Butler." PhD diss., University of Washington, 1982.

Pizarro Llorente, Henar. "El control de la conciencia regia: El confesor real Fray Bernardo de Fresneda." In Martínez Millán, *La corte de Felipe II*.

Poetas líricos de los siglos XVI y XVII. Vol. 42 of *Biblioteca de autores españoles*. Madrid: Rivadeneyra, 1857.

Portús Pérez, Javier. "El retrato vivos: Fiestas y ceremonias alrededor de un rey y su palacio." In *El Real Alcázar de Madrid: Dos siglos de arquitectura y coleccionism en la corte de los reyes de España*, edited by Fernando Checa, 318–43. Madrid: Comunidad de Madrid, 1994.

Redondo, A. "Fiesta y literatura en Madrid durante la estancia del príncipe de Gales, en 1623." *Edad de Oro* 17 (1998): 119–36.

Redworth, Glyn. "Of Pimps and Princes: Three Unpublished Letters from James I and the Prince of Wales Relating to the Spanish Match." *Historical Journal* 37 (June 1994): 401–9.

———. *The Prince and the Infanta: The Cultural Politics of the Spanish Match*. New Haven: Yale University Press, 2003.

Reynolds, John J. "Mira de Amescua's 'Octavas al príncipe de Gales.'" *Renaissance Quarterly* 22, no. 2 (1969): 128–39.

Rodríguez-Salgado, M. J. *The Changing Face of Empire: Charles V, Philip II, and Habsburg Authority, 1551–1559*. Cambridge: Cambridge University Press, 1988.

Rovner, Philip. *Lope de Vega on Kingship*. Ann Arbor, MI: University Microfilms, 1958.

Ruiz Alcon, María Teresa. "Armaduras infantiles en el Palacio de Oriente." *Reales Sitios* 3, no. 10 (1966): 40–48.

Saltillo, Marqués del. "El Real Monasterio de la Encarnación y artistas que allí trabajaron, 1614–1624." *Revista de la Biblioteca, Archivo y Museo de Madrid* 13, no. 50 (1944): 267–92.

Sánchez, Magdalena S. "Confession and Complicity: Margarita de Austria, Richard Haller, S.J., and the Court of Philip III," *Cuadernos de Historia Moderna*, no. 14 (1993): 133–49.

———. "Dynasty, State, and Diplomacy in the Spain of Philip III." PhD diss., Johns Hopkins University, 1988.

——. *The Empress, the Queen, and the Nun: Women and Power at the Court of Philip III of Spain.* Baltimore: Johns Hopkins University Press, 1998.

Sánchez Cantón, F. J. *Inventarios reales.* Vols. 10 and 11 of *Archivo Documental Español.* Madrid: RAH, 1956–59.

Santiago Páez, Elena. "Las bibliotecas del alcázar en tiempos de los Austrias." In *El Real Alcázar de Madrid: Dos siglos de arquitectura y coleccionism en la corte de los reyes de España,* edited by Fernando Checa. Madrid: Comunidad de Madrid, 1994.

Schroth, Sarah. "The Private Collection of the Duke of Lerma." PhD diss., New York University, 1990.

Sharpe, Kevin. *The Personal Rule of Charles I.* New Haven, CT: Yale University Press, 1992.

Simón Diaz, José. *Bibliografía de la literatura hispánica.* 14 vols. Madrid: CSIC, 1960–94.

——. *Historia del Colegio Imperial.* 2 vols. Madrid, 1952.

Smith, Hilary Dansey. *Preaching in the Spanish Golden Age: A Study of Some Preachers of the Reign of Philip III.* Oxford: Oxford University Press, 1978.

Soons, Alan. *Juan de Mariana.* Boston: Twayne, 1982.

Sousa Viterbo, Francisco Marqués de. *Trabalhas nauticos dos portuguezes nos seculos XV e XVI.* 2 vols. Lisbon, 1898.

Spielman, John P. *Leopold I of Austria.* London: Thames & Hudson, 1977.

Stoye, John. *English Travellers Abroad, 1604–1667.* New Haven, CT: Yale University Press, 1989.

Stradling, R. A. *Philip IV and the Government of Spain, 1621–1665.* Cambridge: Cambridge University Press, 1988.

Strong, Roy. *Henry, Prince of Wales, and England's Lost Renaissance.* London: Thames & Hudson, 1986.

Torre, Antonio de la. "Maestros de los hijos de los Reyes Católicos." *Hispania* 16 (1956): 256–66.

Torres Amat, Felix. *Memorias para ayudar a formar un diccionario crítico de los escritores catalanes.* Barcelona: J. Verdaguer, 1836.

van der Essen, Alfred. *Le Cardinal-Infant et la politique européenne de l'Espagne, 1609–1641.* Vol. 1, *1609–1634.* Louvain, Belgium: Bibliothèque de L'Université, 1944.

Vañes, Carlos Alonso. *Doña Ana de Austria: Abadesa del Real Monasterio de Las Huelgas, sus primeros años de gobierno (1611–1614).* Madrid: Patrimonio Nacional, 1990.

Vázquez, Isaac. "Fray Francisco de Arriba O.F.M. en las controversias 'de auxiliis.'" *Verdad y Vida* 23 (1965): 464–508.

Vilar, Jean. *Literatura y economía: La figura satírica del arbitrista en el Siglo de Oro.* Translated by Francisco Bustelo G. del Real. Madrid: Revista de Occidente, 1973.

von Ranke, Leopold. *The Ottoman and the Spanish Empires.* Translated by W. Kelly. London: Whittaker, 1843.

Watson, Foster. *Vives: On Education.* Cambridge, 1913.

Willard, Charity Cannon. "Isabel of Portugal, Patroness of Humanism?" In *Miscellanea di studi e ricerche sul quattrocento Francese.* Turin: Giappichelli Editore, 1967.

Williams, Ethel Carleton. *Anne of Denmark, Wife of James VI of Scotland, James I of England.* London: Longman, 1970.

Williams, Patrick. *The Great Favourite: The Duke of Lerma and the Court and Government of Philip III of Spain, 1598–1621.* Manchester: Manchester University Press, 2007.

———. "Lerma, Old Castile, and the Travels of Philip III of Spain." *History* 73 (October 1988): 379–97.

———. "Lerma, 1618: Dismissal or Retirement?" *European History Quarterly* 19 (1989): 307–32.

Wolf, John B. *Louis XIV.* New York: Norton, 1968.

Wormald, Jenny. *Mary Queen of Scots: A Study in Failure.* London: George Philip, 1988.

Yates, Frances A. *The Art of Memory.* London: Routledge & Kegan Paul, 1966.

———. *Lull and Bruno: Collected Essays, Volume One.* London: Routledge & Kegan Paul, 1982.

Zarco Cuevas, Julian. *Catálogo de los manuscritos castellanos de la Real Biblioteca de El Escorial.* 3 vols. Madrid: Imprenta Helénica, 1926.

Index